MW00895553

## The Invention of the Western Film

A Cultural History of the Genre's First Half-Century

*The Invention of the Western Film* ranges across literature, visual arts, social history, ideology, and legend to provide, for the first time, an in-depth exploration of the early Western, from short kinetoscopes of the 1890s through the "classic" features of the 1940s. By examining the American Indian's rise and demise during the silent era, the interplay between A- and B-Westerns of the 1930s, and film noir–influenced Westerns of the 1940s, Scott Simmon's pioneering study silhouettes the genre's evolution against a myriad of cultural forces. This lively, encyclopedic book revitalizes familiar Western icons John Wayne and John Ford, and recovers forgotten masterworks from the Western film's formative years.

Scott Simmon is Professor of English and Codirector of the Film Studies program at the University of California, Davis. He curated the DVD sets *Treasures from American Film Archives* and the forthcoming *Saving the Silents* for the National Film Preservation Foundation, and reconstructed the landmark early features *Within Our Gates* and *Where Are My Children?* for the Library of Congress. His writings include books on film preservation and on directors King Vidor and D. W. Griffith.

# The Invention of the Western Film

## A CULTURAL HISTORY OF THE GENRE'S FIRST HALF-CENTURY

SCOTT SIMMON
University of California, Davis

CAMBRIDGE
UNIVERSITY PRESS

32 Avenue of the Americas, New York NY 10013-2473, USA

Cambridge University Press is part of the University of Cambridge.

It furthers the University's mission by disseminating knowledge in the pursuit of education, learning and research at the highest international levels of excellence.

www.cambridge.org
Information on this title: www.cambridge.org/9780521554732



First published 2003
Reprinted 2007

*A catalogue record for this publication is available from the British Library*

*Library of Congress Cataloguing in Publication data*

Simmon, Scott.
The invention of the western film : a cultural history of the genre's first
half-century / Scott Simmon
p. cm.
Includes bibliographical references and index.
ISBN 0 521 55473 X – ISBN 0 521 55581 7 (pbk.)
1. Western films – United States – History and criticism. I. Title.
PN1995.9.W4 S53 2002
791.43′6278–dc21

2002035117

ISBN 978-0-521-55473-2 Hardback

*Once again,*

*for Annette.*

# Contents

# Illustration Credits

The film illustrations are a mix of production publicity stills (labeled "stills" below) and frame enlargements (reproducing the on-screen image, and labeled "frames"). Figures marked AMPAS are photographs courtesy of the Academy of Motion Picture Arts and Sciences; those marked GEH are courtesy of the George Eastman House; and those marked LC are courtesy of the Library of Congress, Motion Picture, Broadcasting, and Recorded Sound Division.

# Preface: The Western and the West

I am genuine white . . . and I am willing to own that my people have many ways, of which, as an honest man, I can't approve. It is one of their customs to write in books what they have done and seen, instead of telling them in their villages, where the lie can be given to the face of a cowardly boaster. . . .

Natty Bumppo ("Hawk-eye") in James Fenimore Cooper's
*The Last of the Mohicans* (1826)[1]

Before the Western came the West, although their relationship has its chronological twists. Consider a couple of incidents, from near the start and end of the brief historical era that most inspires the Western film.

In 1849 Kit Carson was searching through New Mexico for a white woman taken captive by the Jicarilla Apaches, a certain Mrs. J. M. White. Locating their camp, he noticed among the debris an abandoned book, which turned out to be a novel about the scouting exploits of Kit Carson, probably one published the same year titled *Kit Carson: Prince of the Gold Hunters.* As it happened, the real Carson could not match the skills of his fictional double, and Mrs. White was found dead. He long remained troubled by the thought that she must have been given hope in her captivity by reading this Western "in which I was made a great hero, slaying Indians by the hundred."[2]

In 1890 the Teton Sioux leader Sitting Bull was shot by deputized native police as he was escorted from his cabin on the Standing Rock Reservation in South Dakota. (His killing during the "Ghost Dance" spiritual revival further roiled the atmosphere that led the U.S. Cavalry toward the Wounded Knee massacre of two hundred Sioux in South Dakota two weeks later.) Witnesses to Sitting Bull's death reported that during the melee his favorite horse, apparently confused by the smoke and gunfire, sat back on its haunches, proffered a front hoof to "shake," and then performed a routine of tricks learned during Sitting Bull's season with Buffalo Bill Cody's Wild West show.[3]

Sitting Bull's horse and "Death Cabin" reappear in history three years later, on display in Buffalo Bill's new show, which was set up just outside the grounds of Chicago's World's Columbian Exposition. A celebration of the four hundredth anniversary of America's "discovery," this 1893 exposition is also remembered now as the venue for the American Historical Association conference where Frederick Jackson Turner gave his influential talk on "The Significance of the Frontier in American History," which lamented the "closing" of the frontier West.[4] The Western film might be said to open the following year with such Edison Company titles as *Sioux Ghost Dance* (1894). If there is a strict chronology here, it is not without ironies.

You can't spend much time even in the contemporary West without encountering such grimly absurdist moments where the history of the West and the invented Western conjoin to bite back. I'm reminded of being jostled from predawn sleep while traveling cross-country by Greyhound bus in the 1980s as we pulled into a breakfast stop on an Osage reservation in Oklahoma. "HOME OF F-TROOP" read the unpromising sign over the restaurant and souvenir shop, in reference to the even-then long-canceled ABC television sitcom about cavalry-and-Indian shenanigans. Through groggy half-consciousness we ordered our ham and eggs from sullen Native American teenagers outfitted in nineteenth-century U.S. Cavalry uniforms. Though this wasn't like finding Jews in SS uniforms staffing some Auschwitz McDonald's, it had just enough echoes to jolt us awake.

This book has been written on the far edge of the West – in San Francisco, four blocks from the eighteenth-century Franciscan Catholic outpost, Mission Dolores. For film fans like myself, this is where Jimmy Stewart tracks Kim Novak to "Carlotta Valdez's" grave in Hitchcock's *Vertigo;* but as the bronze plaque on the adobe wall of the mission graveyard reminds tourists, the spot also memorializes "CALIFORNIA'S APOSTLE, PADRE JUNÍPERO SERRA," who initiated the mission system that brought forced labor, intractable laws, and fatal diseases to the region's natives. California is, after all, where recent historians of the West feel the least compunction in labeling the treatment of Native Americans "genocide."[5]

At the outset then, writing a history of the Western film in the twenty-first century means acknowledging the competing appeals of Hollywood entertainment, historical evidence, and evolving ethics, as well as balancing the mortal seriousness against the crazy comedy inherent in both the West and the Western. There are a number of ways to write about the relationship between the Western film and the West, each full of compromises, and it's worth quickly laying out the options and the choices upon which I've settled.

It has been tempting for books about the Western to scold films for their evident failure to reproduce history with any accuracy. The very titles of *There Must Be a Lone Ranger: The American West in Film and Reality* and *God Bless You, Buffalo Bill: A Layman's Guide to History and the Western Film* suggest that this can be accomplished with some wit, although other writers about the Western film – Ward Churchill and Jon Tuska, for instance – go straight to outrage over Hollywood's distortions of history.[6] The opposite tactic is the one that Jane Tompkins announces in her pithy *West of Everything* when she says that "The Western doesn't have anything to do with the West as such," or that Peter French implies in his *Cowboy Metaphysics* when he says in frustration about the accuracy of Western films, "Did it really happen that way? Who cares? . . . I don't." While this certainly simplifies the problems of writing about Westerns, it may make things a bit too easy on us all. My feeling is that Janet Walker in her anthology *Westerns: Films through History* has it about right when she points out that Western films also include historical interpretation among their other traits.[7] The films, that is, offer up arguments through narrative about America and its history, and if we must judge them, it would be less for accuracy than coherency. My sense too is that we need to *start* from acknowledgment of the genre's racism, rather than arriving at it as if it were a discovery.

I've found that admitting that I'm writing about Western movies can be an excellent conversation stopper. After the pause, responses are usually along the lines of, "Do you *like* Westerns?" – asked in a tone conveying that the questioner quite sensibly hates them. I've inadvertently become something of an expert on the range of reasons why people – OK, why women especially – have come to avoid Westerns, but the reasons might be said to fall broadly into two categories: (1) dislike of the retrograde cultural attitudes carried by Western films, not only their treatment of non-European races but also their ways of representing gender; and (2) dislike of the tedious repetitiousness of the tales told over and over again. Admittedly, these are two formidable reasons, and yet these very traits of Westerns may turn out to provide opportunities for thinking about the genre and for structuring a study of it – or so I have tried to redeploy them here.

First, all of that cultural baggage carried by Western films should allow them to be unpacked through a cultural history, by which I mean examining film aesthetics within a wide context of literature and visual arts, of social histories of the eras depicted and of the years when the films were produced, and of the ideologies propounded by the films. Westerns have always felt free to express their belief in America and have been permitted to speak about religion and politics in ways generally forbidden Hollywood genres set in the contemporary world. Second, the repetitiousness of the stories told within Westerns means that it should be possible to place a limited number of films and filmmakers at the center of our investigations and, by spinning short connections to related films and figures, still arrive at a relatively full genre history within a reasonable length. The compromise is that there will be gaps in the history, but I've opted for this structure over any complete chronology, which in any case soon gets defeated by the sheer number of Western films. (Jon Tuska reports that he's seen eight thousand.)[8] The Western's notoriously limited repertoire of character types, situations, locations, props, and actors can make the films appear "all the same," but it also allows the debates carried on through the films to be more transparent than within more flexible Hollywood genres. In a sense, each significant Western sums up the genre as it exists to that point, makes new arguments, and by its unconvincing and unresolved spots leaves questions for other films to answer. We'll try to tune into this cultural dialogue.

For reasons hinted above, it seems essential to begin with the "encounter" between Native and European worlds. I've gone back to uncover a new history of the rise and fall of the Indian in silent film, which, I'll argue, is a story more central to both film history and American culture than is the relatively familiar one about the origins of the movie cowboy. I've also tried to seek out places where the genre still surprises with its vitality, as within B-Westerns in the 1930s and film-noir-inflected Westerns in the 1940s. Beyond their loose chronology of moviemaking, the book's three parts survey the major narratives repeatedly told about the West, taking them up in the order they found prominence in Western history: the "encounter" in Part One, overland pioneering in Part Two, and the creation of community in Part Three. *The Invention of the Western Film* ends around the years when many histories of the genre begin. It has, however, seemed worth carrying certain topics beyond any strict chronological cutoff, and especially at the end of Part Three we'll trace the fate of "classic" Western principles through more recent decades.

If the West essentially preceded the Western, it now looks as if the West has also outlived the Western. The many premature obituaries for the Western film – the first few published in 1911 – might warn us off such a pronouncement, but the genre is beginning to feel clinically dead, especially if a living genre requires a critical mass of productions. One can still film a Western, just as one can still paint a fresco, but there's no denying that the active tradition, the community of artisans, and the receptive audience are gone. No Westerns were released theatrically in 2002, and the distinction of the most recent theatrical Western at the time I write – *Texas Rangers* (2001) – is to have the lowest per-screen box-office take in industry memory.[9] If Westerns aren't dead, it is strange also that so many characters in the few recent ones prove to be dead men returning from beyond the grave (as in *Purgatory* [1999] and *South of Heaven, West of Hell* [2000]). One of the pleasures for me in returning to the earliest years of the Western film's invention – a word I choose for its implication that the genre grew from conscious choices more than collective myths – is immersion in an era when filmmakers were finding the force of visual language. And, yes, since you ask, I *do* like Westerns – for their love of the land, for their feeling for physicality, for their taut verbal wit, and for their unapologetic contentions.

I have been mulling over this book for longer than I'm willing to admit – long enough, I'm afraid, to have forgotten many of the acknowledgments due (but thanks to Clark Evans for companionship on that westbound Greyhound). Initial promptings and inspiration came from the late Raymond Durgnat, the only genius I've known and one of the handful of distinctive writers about film. His ideas about Westerns, from our collaborations, remain everywhere throughout this book. I'm grateful to the Library of Congress and the Pacific Film Archive for allowing me to host retrospectives on the Western and to archivists at those institutions and at the Museum of Modern Art and the UCLA Film and Television Archive who arranged viewings of preserved films. Students at the University of California, Berkeley, and the University of California, Davis, who groaned theatrically on hearing that their genre courses would be about Westerns, gave unexpected fun and encouragement. For finding space for drafts of my thoughts about Westerns, thanks to editors at *Film Comment, Films,* and *Literature/Film Quarterly,* and to Jim Kitses and Gregg Rickman, editors of *The Western Reader.* For help with the photographic illustrations, I'm indebted to Patrick Loughney at the Library of Congress, Matt Severson at the Academy of Motion Picture Arts and Sciences, Caroline Yeager at the George Eastman House, and David Wells at the National Film Preservation Foundation. At Cambridge University Press, Senior Editor Beatrice Rehl kept long faith, and the remarkable Michael Gnat again made the production process a pleasure.

This book is for Annette Melville, who, amazingly, is always ready to watch one more Western.

**The Invention of the Western Film**

A Cultural History of the Genre's First Half-Century

*The Last of the Mohicans* (1920). (Courtesy of the George Eastman House.)

PART ONE

# "My Friend, the Indian"

## LANDSCAPE AND THE EXTERMINATION OF THE NATIVE AMERICAN IN THE SILENT WESTERN

"These Indians are my friends, but I must send them to their death."

Intertitle in the 1925 film *The Vanishing American*

The early "moving picture" could revel in the mere discovery of landscape. *Arrival of Train, Cheyenne* (1903), *Coaching Party, Yosemite Valley* (1901), *Panoramic View, Lower Kicking Horse Canyon* (1901) – such glimpses of the West in motion had dotted turn-of-the-century peep-show parlors and punctuated vaudeville acts. The Western fully arrived as a genre, however, when the movie industry learned that its survival depended upon more systematic production of films with story lines, and by 1910 the Western had come to account for at least a fifth of all U.S. releases.[1] If it is worth taking up our exploration of the Western film with these early narratives, it is not only because of their numbers. What we find in the first one-reel Westerns, however stylistically simple they may be, are some of the wider possibilities that the Hollywood-studio era would come to forget – or suppress.

The initial surprise now in looking back at the Westerns that began to explode in popularity around 1908 is how often their stories center on Native Americans (and not always merely white impersonations of them), at a time when American Indians were not particularly prominent in popular culture, beyond misty or silhouetted nostalgia for photographic images of their "vanishing."[2] "Indian and Western subjects" was the industry trade-paper category for *The Red Girl* (1908), *The Aborigine's Devotion* (1909), *Her Indian Mother* (1910), *A Redskin's Bravery* (1911), *For the Papoose* (1912), *Hiawatha* (1913), and the like – to cite surviving examples.[3] Indians may well have entered American film for the reason that they came into the European tradition as a whole: Searching for stories to set in the landscape, pioneer filmmakers stumbled upon "Indians," the presumed men of nature.[4]

When we go back and watch surviving silent Westerns chronologically, there are a pair of subsequent surprises, because of how different the genre looks and because of what different things it has to say in its earliest guises, especially from around 1908–10. In landscape, Westerns from this era are lush, woodsy, and wet: filled with lakes, streams, and canoes, of chases through the underbrush, of hand-to-hand fights through forest clearings. In narrative, many of these Westerns are set entirely within tribal communities or feature a "noble redskin" as guide or savior to the white hero. Only later, around 1911, do we begin to find the wide vistas, rolling grasslands, arid deserts, and those savage Great Plains Indian wars that now appear so fundamental to the genre. The earlier styles and stories seem bound up with the industrial origins of U.S. moviemaking: The first American Westerns were shot in New Jersey, New York, and Connecticut. When the industrywide move to production on the West Coast came, more changed than the landscape, and I would argue that the new stories that began to be told were not necessarily advances. It is customary to condescend to the "primitive" style and "ersatz" landscapes of the earlier eastern-filmed Westerns, but for a variety of reasons, it may be worth taking their arguments seriously.

Through the first half of this Part One, we'll follow a large number of one- and two-reel Westerns directed by D. W. Griffith for the Biograph Company between 1908 and 1913. As individual creations, his Westerns are generally less engaging than those of Thomas Ince, whose three-reel *The Invaders* (1912) will be our focus toward the end of this part. But Griffith now has one great advantage over every other director of this era: Virtually all of his work survives, and thus in his fifty or so currently viewable Westerns we can follow the transition from eastern Westerns to far-Westerns – an abrupt shift both of landscape and narrative, as it turns out – that has parallels in the lost films of other directors, to judge from trade-paper descriptions.[5] It has been traditional to begin surveys of Western-film history around the time of Griffith's best-known Western, 1913's *The Battle at Elderbush Gulch,* with glances back at Edwin S. Porter's *The Great Train Robbery* (1903) and at the first cowboy hero, "Broncho Billy" Anderson. And yet a different sort of Western was so widely produced before 1911 that the first "Death of the Western" pronouncements came from trade journals that year, as elegies (*The Nickelodeon*'s "The Passing of the Western Subject") or plaints (*Moving Picture World*'s "The Overproduction of 'Western Pictures'").[6] Films such as *The Battle at Elderbush Gulch* and *The Invaders* actually arrive near the end of another history of nearly forgotten Western-film possibilities – one we'll explore before moving on to the more confining Hollywood tradition.

# 1. Indians to the Rescue

Much has been said and written the last twelve months on the desirability of providing American film subjects for American moving picture audiences. . . . There seems to be amongst exhibitors, among whom we have made the inquiry, a strong and increasing demand for Indian and Western subjects, and here probably we get the most satisfactory answer to our own question. Indian and Western subjects may fairly be considered American, because they deal with the aboriginal or original life of the pioneers of the country.

"What Is an American Subject?" *The Moving Picture World,* January 22, 1910[1]

The continuity of the film Western with the West is nowhere more startling than in the Edison Company's *Sioux Ghost Dance,* filmed in September 1894. This was less than half a year after Edison's first kinetoscope parlor had opened and fewer than four years after the last major Plains Wars cavalry battle: the Wounded Knee massacre of Sioux (Lakota) on the Pine Ridge Reservation, following the spiritual revival named for its circular "Ghost Dance" ceremony, which included calling upon ancestors to help clear the land of white invaders. This brief (about twenty seconds long) kinetoscope film of beaded and barechested men and boys is made even more otherworldly and death-haunted by the stark black backdrop common to all early films shot in Edison's one-room studio in West Orange, New Jersey. The Oglala and Brulé Sioux had stopped into the studio for a couple of hours one Monday morning while touring in Brooklyn with Buffalo Bill's Wild West show. The link to recent cavalry battles against the Sioux was not lost in the arch *New York Herald* report of the filming, headlined "Red Men Again Conquered":

A party of Indians in full war paint invaded the Edison laboratory at West Orange yesterday and faced unflinchingly the unerring rapid fire of the kinetograph. It was indeed a memorable engagement, no less so than the battle of Wounded Knee, still fresh in the minds of the warriors. It was probably more effective in demonstrating to the red men the power and supremacy of the white man, for savagery and the most advanced science stood face to face, and there was an absolute triumph for one without the spilling of a single drop of blood.[2]

Over the next few years the Edison Company ventured to distant locations to bring back similar ethnography-as-entertainment, such as *Carrying Out the Snakes* (1901), part of a series on the Hopi snake and antelope ceremony in New Mexico.[3] More startling in a different way is Edison's early welfare item, *Serving Rations to the Indians* (1898), probably shot in Utah. In this casually revealing thirty-second document, one Ute woman among a group exiting a log house on the tribe's reservation seems to spoil the group composition by walking toward the camera after she pointedly shakes off a shove from a white man. In the second of the film's two shots, native children leave the same house, by which time a white child in the background has learned to push an uncooperative native kid to walk in the proper direction.[4]

Notwithstanding a few other such disturbing oddities, the first decade and a half of desultory "Western" filmmaking had been dominated by the figures of the cowboy and the gun-toting "highwayman," before Indians made their mass entrance in 1908. Annie Oakley too had stopped by Edison's studio in 1894 to demonstrate some skillful, if humanly imperfect, shooting of tossed plates. Plentiful in the last years of the nineteenth century had been such nonfiction actualities as *Cattle Fording Stream* (1898) and *Lassoing Steer* (1898), single-shot films running a minute or two that are fully described by their titles. The cowboy as gunman dominates the earliest Western fictional anecdotes, such as the twenty-second *A Bluff from a Tenderfoot* (1899), where the strawhatted tenderfoot proves a quicker two-gun draw than knife-wielding cowboys angry at their poker-table loss – the "bluff" revealed when the tenderfoot's "guns" turn out to be a pair of fans, useful in a visual punch line to cool his sweaty brow. Similarly Billy Bitzer's two-minute *Cowboy Justice* (1904) finds a barroom gambler gunning down a cowboy and then dragged by other cowboys, in the second of the film's two shots, out to a (painted) lake and hanged from a (painted) tree; "When he is well hanged they shoot him full of holes," in the words of the film's deadpan publicity. Stylistically more convincing were outdoor location films, such as another 1904 two-minute film, *Western Stage Coach Hold Up*, filmed in Oklahoma in such long shot as to imply a hidden-camera documentary. The continuity of the Western with the West is suggested again even in such theatrically staged knockabouts as *Cripple Creek Bar-Room Scene* (1899), purporting to represent the contemporary Colorado gold-strike town through a thirty-second single shot in which poker-playing cowboys look on as a drunk is handily ejected by the woman barkeep, who first squirts him with seltzer. Occasionally glimpsed at the margins of these rudimentary narratives is the figure of the Indian, notably in two relative epics of 1903 directed by Wallace McCutcheon for the American Mutoscope and Biograph Company: the roughly nine-minute *The Pioneers* and twenty-minute *Kit Carson*.[5] Later in 1903, Edwin S. Porter's approximately nine-minute *The Great Train Robbery* was much more dynamically composed and edited, even if its main surprise in retrospect is how it led nowhere, either for its creator or the genre, beyond serving loosely as a narrative model for gun-wielding crime and horse-chase retribution.

In the first years of the twentieth century, especially in 1902 and 1903, it was beginning to look as if the motion-picture craze had had its day, and vaudeville houses began to drop what seemed yesterday's novelty. The problems were partly technical ones of uncertain standards but mainly commercial ones of competition and copyright piracy.[6] A less easily resolved problem remained even when movie-only nickelodeons became the primary exhibition venue after 1905: Simple, shorter actualities were becoming boring to audiences – who presumably would pay to see only so many herds of cattle – while longer story films were too frequently incomprehensible without some live explanation or lecture. In this regard, Porter's other significant surviving Western, the approximately twelve-minute *Life of a Cowboy* (1906), only brought to a head the narrative incoherence that had been barely finessed in the ambiguous temporal relationships of the shots in *The Great Train Robbery*.[7] The obscure story line of *Life of a Cowboy* found compensation in its spectacle (as in the opening shot's huge saloon, where cowboys beat a man who offers an Indian a drink) and its Wild West–show rope and horse tricks. Eventually, *Life of a Cowboy* settles into a rudimentary story about a highwayman who, with his band of Indians, is thwarted from robbing a stagecoach by a heroic cowboy. Much more than this is impossible to say without recourse to Edison's publicity description. Journalists, and presumably audiences, were regularly grumbling about the incoherence of multishot films: "It is not sufficient that the makers understand the plot – the pictures are made for the public."[8] By 1907, a stock-market crash and resulting recession coincided with the increasingly unresolved problem of how to make longer film stories comprehensible, especially to the nickelodeon's growing immigrant audience.[9]

Into this moment of economic crisis and narrative confusion strode the Indian, providing a solution, it seems to me, simultaneously industrial, cultural, and narratological. (And if the figure of the Indian got little thanks from the industry it helped rescue, there was a tradition for that too.)[10] The year 1908 saw the great growth in Indian films, both in the numbers produced and the centrality of natives to the narratives. During D. W. Griffith's first three months as a director in 1908, he made such Indian subjects as *The Redman and the Child, The Girl and the Outlaw, The Red Girl,* and *The Call of the Wild.* The U.S. industry at this time was in a losing war with French and Italian producers, who were widely – and rightly, in retrospect – regarded as making superior films that were flooding the American market. A January 1910 tally by *Moving Picture World* found "exactly one half" of the films released in New York "made abroad."[11] In economic terms, the solution for the U.S. filmmakers had to be in what we would now call "product differentiation," creating films if not obviously superior, then at least wholly distinctive from Europe's. As several scholars have discussed, the American landscape provided something unmatchable in Europe, a backdrop that branded a distinctive U.S. product and claimed authenticity for certain home-inspired film types, notably the Western.[12] The birth of the American film Western was due not merely to some vague inner need in American culture for frontier stories but also to the way that the American landscape lent itself commercially to the creation of an inimitable international product. What is also revealing, however, is that this international battle between European and American manufacturers begins well before the visually distinctive American landscape of the far West is put to any significant use and while U.S. film production remained almost entirely on the East Coast. The figure of the Indian, even more than the landscape, seems to have provided the initial terms for this international industrial dispute.

The explanation for this use of the Indian in the first Westerns probably needs to be found back in the imagery through which cultural and economic battles between Europe and the United States have historically been fought. Native Americans and their representation in art have generally been of interest to European Americans only at moments in U.S. history when some sort of resistance to Europe comes to feel culturally important.[13] At the start of the nineteenth century, for instance, when American novelists and dramatists were not much more confident than early filmmakers would be about the cultural value of their creations and were the butt of the British scoff that no one bothered to read an American book, U.S. commentators countered by proposing Indian subjects as "the chief hope for an original literature."[14] Again at the end of the nineteenth century, the new photographs of Anasazi ruins in the Southwest were being widely interpreted within the United States as evidence that the nation could now claim a civilization more ancient than Europe's, one that was architecturally complex and for which Native Americans could be admired (and, conveniently enough, just when tribes were ceasing to be seen as any threat).[15] The mid-nineteenth-century sculpture atop the U.S. Capitol building, titled "Freedom Triumphant in Peace and War," tops its ironies by crowning its female figure with a feather headdress huge enough to signify her Indian status to ground-level viewers.[16] That Europe understood – indeed, invented – the semiotics of this battle is evident back in the sixteenth-century allegorical tradition that signified the New World as an Indian queen.[17]

Thus, even as narrative filmmaking began, the "Indian" was already poised as cultural currency for this transatlantic economic battle. However, European filmmakers, the French in particular, were unwilling to concede anything to the Americans. The Pathé-Frères Company, which alone supplied about a third of the American releases in 1907, had produced such films as *Indiens et cow-boys* back in 1904, set in an all-purpose Indian village complete with Plains tipis and Northwestern coastal totem poles.[18] Pathé's (now lost) *A Western Hero* (1909) caused U.S. trade papers to fume over cowboys on English saddles and Indians in gingham shirts.[19] The answering thrust by Pathé was to open its own American studio, initially in Jersey City in 1910, and then to hire a Native American – James Young Deer, of Winnebago ancestry – to run its West Coast branch. Pathé's greatest in-joke of cultural co-option must be the way its familiar copyright logo, a "red rooster" silhouette, is put forward as a Native American icon and painted on the sides of tipis in its Indian films (as in *For the Papoose* [1912], among surviving films). Still, American filmmakers were starting from a home-field advantage, and after 1908 "Indian and cowboy pictures" were more than just a way of fighting off foreign invasions: They became the major export of American films to "the European market."[20]

Unresolved was the problem of narrative incoherence in longer story films that was still plaguing audiences in 1908. The answers would, in a sense, come only with gradual refinements of editing and intertitling. But here again the Indian proved uniquely helpful. If the problem was that films had to find simple ways to communicate a story visually, the image of the Indian was ideal because it came complete with a story in tow. As Brian Dippie has neatly encapsulated the history of Indian images in painting, "Show an Indian and you tell a story, and in the end it is always the same tale. That is the allegorical imperative of the Vanishing American."[21] The actor playing an Indian on the early silent screen might run though a wide range of presentational gestures – of anger, threat, stoicism, self-sacrifice, heroism – but the image always also came trailing that more elaborate and purportedly inevitable story about the progress of civilization and native decline. The challenge for filmmakers after 1908 would be to find ways to use this image with its established narrative and yet still play unexpected variations within individual stories.

# 2. The Eastern Western

Rusty, I don't like the West. All the people do is kill each other. I'd like the West better if it were in the East.

Chico Marx in *Go West* (1940)

The early Westerns shot in eastern landscapes still seem astonishingly unclichéd – although that may simply be another way of noticing that their look and argument were not endlessly repeated by Hollywood. D. W. Griffith's first Western (and probably his third film as sole director), *The Redman and the Child*, filmed in New Jersey in July 1908 and released the same month, is already emblematic. An older white man and a Sioux Indian are camped together in a tent alongside a forested lake.[1] We're on some Colorado frontier but near settlements, to judge from a well-dressed woman who leaves her five-year-old son for a visit with the Indian and the older man, who is his grandfather. The Indian amuses the boy by tossing him playfully into the air and by hiking with him to another lakeside clearing, where he gives the boy a sample of the gold nuggets he has hidden in a hollow tree trunk. While the Indian is off guiding surveyors to the top of a hill, a pair of white men destroy this idyll: They murder the grandfather and haul the boy roughly through the tall grasses until he reveals the hiding place of the Indian's gold. After the Indian discovers his friend's body, he reacts in a way oft-repeated in these first Westerns: He strips off his civilized clothing and, in loincloth, gestures with his fists to the sky. (The publicity material for the film suggests how such gestures came with established narrative when performed by an Indian character: "It is but a moment he stands thus, yet the pose speaks volumes.")[2] After a chase by canoe, the Indian rescues the child and enacts a just

**Figure 1.** D. W. Griffith and G. W. "Billy" Bitzer (at camera) on location, probably in New York State circa 1910.

but unforgiving vengeance by strangling one man underwater and stabbing the other onshore. In the film's last shot, the Indian gently caresses the head of the exhausted boy, who falls asleep in the canoe as they paddle slowly across the placid lake.

*The Redman and the Child* was the first Griffith film to receive any trade-paper notice, and the high praise would have prompted him and other companies to return to the film's spirit and style. For the *New York Dramatic Mirror*, it was "The best Indian film we have yet seen. . . . In many respects it is one of the best handled subjects ever produced by any company. The scenery is superb, the photography perfect, and the acting, especially of the Indian character, is of the highest class." *Variety* implied too the film's ability to represent the U.S. industry in that trade battle with Europe: It "compares very favorably with the best material in either the American or European market and makes a decided step forward in the artistic merit and photographic excellence of American films."[3] Throughout Griffith's first years as a filmmaker on the East Coast (Fig. 1), his most consistently ambitious works are his Westerns, virtually all of them centered around the figure of the Indian. Those set entirely within native communities, such as *The Mended Lute* (1909) and *The Song of the Wildwood Flute* (1910), compose their landscapes most elaborately, with love rivalries alongside lakes, chases down rivers, and schemings within darker woodlands. White characters, in other of his eastern-filmed Westerns, tend to be placed less lovingly within harsher landscapes and to arrive as villainous disruptions to forest idylls, as with the land-grabbing pioneers of *The Redman's View* (1909), the Black Hills gold seekers of *The Indian Runner's Romance* (1909), or the doctor in *A Mohawk's Way* (1910) who, as an intertitle narrates, "REFUSES TO WASTE HIS TIME ON AN INDIAN." The few positive white characters tend to be already half-linked to nature, such as the buckskin-clad "trapper" of *Rose o' Salem-Town* (1910).

The lush forest landscape and prominence of Indians in these films bring to mind one often-stated claim about the origins of the genre: "The Western was created in the early nineteenth century by James Fenimore Cooper."[4] The reference, of course, is primarily to Cooper's five "Leatherstocking" novels of the 1820s and 1840s, united loosely by the life history of Natty Bumppo (variously tagged "Deerslayer," "Hawk-eye," "Pathfinder," and "the trapper," as well as "Leatherstocking"), who is a half-reluctant intermediary between civilized and native peoples. It usually feels as if Cooper gets enlisted as originator of the Western genre for lack of any better-suited nineteenth-century candidate. His talkative Indians and long-winded Natty himself seem far from Hollywood's taciturn cowboys. More surprisingly, if Cooper is to be seen as Hollywood's precursor, his portraits of the pioneer traveling westward turn out to be extraordinarily sour and angry (most bitterly in the early Oregon Trail pioneers of *The Prairie*). Cooper's Native Americans and his forest hero Leatherstocking are equally doomed to extinction without heirs. The combination of fatalism about the natives, pathos about his hero, and pessimism about pioneering leaves Cooper bereft of any real optimism about America's future, and thus deeply opposed to the overt claims of the Hollywood Western.

For all that, Cooper may well be the key originator of the genre, if not in any simple way. The "classic" Western itself may be closer to his darkness and pessimism than we tend to think, but that's an issue for Part Three. Where Cooper seems more immediately an originator of the genre is in elaborating a shift in the way Americans portrayed the wilderness landscape. With Cooper, it became the one place open to freedom from civilization and its absurd laws, for perceptions of something genuine, even for rare bonds among the races – as opposed to a place for gothic nightmares and for acting out unconscious fears (as in Cooper's significant predecessor as an American novelist, Charles Brockden Brown) or, before that, as a place merely abstractly symbolic of God's ways.[5] Cooper made convincing to a wide readership the post-Puritan space of the frontier as a place of fragile harmonies, all the more valuable for its susceptibility to ecological ruin. This relatively modern place had been glimpsed tentatively in American writing through the many fictionalized lives of Daniel Boone, following John Filson's half-narrative *Kentucke* (1784), where the wilderness regularly freed Boone from civilization's melancholy.[6]

For Cooper, it requires a quite particular type of landscape to foster these harmonies, and his spatial arrangement of nature is the one we also find governing the early film Western. He might thus be credited as the inspiration of the Western genre on film, but only with the qualifying irony that he originates a visual style abandoned by Hollywood. This is a forest world, surrounded everywhere with water. Cooper increasingly idealized the lush woods (most completely in *The Deerslayer*), so that whatever the hardships of this wet world, it seldom rains (though a massacre is likely to coincide with "a frightful change . . . in the season").[7] Filmmakers no doubt had practical considerations for also setting their eastern-filmed tales in late spring or summer, when Griffith and the Biograph players, for instance, would make their location trips up the Hudson River into New York State.

Early filmmakers typically sought in the forest landscape small clearings, natural theatrical spaces open to the light and usually framed on the sides by overhanging trees, a Claude Lorraine convention that had been widely adopted into American landscape painting and is also employed in Cooper's fiction: "The whole scene formed a striking picture, whose frame was composed of the dark and tall border of pines," as an Indian encampment is introduced in *The Last of the Mohicans*.[8] Virtually every set-up in Griffith's *The Girl and the Outlaw* (1908), for example, adopts this visual model, sometimes adding dark branches overhanging the top of the frame. The overall stylistic conventions of filmmaking in these first years reinforce the landscape's theatricality: The camera is generally fixed in place, actors' bodies are filmed full length, and each shot is held for a relatively long duration. Thus, say, the sixth shot of *The Girl and the Outlaw* is a static minute-and-a-half image of a light-bathed forest opening framed on the sides and top by trees: Indians and a brutal white man ride in and hide in the dark edges of the frame; into the clearing rides a woman who is captured and led away; after a brief view of empty landscape another woman enters, finding evidence of the abduction. (This captivity narrative also has the typical unconventionality of the era: part female-bonding picture, part sadomasochistic passion tale, part forbidden Indian–white love story.) Cooper imagined such forest glades, bowers, and "Oak Openings" (the title of his last frontier novel) as theatrical spaces fostering spiritual freedom, as when one of the Deerslayer's companions "broke out of the tangled labyrinth of a small swamp, emerging into an opening. . . .This little area, which afforded a good view of the sky, although it was pretty well filled with dead trees, lay on the side of one of the high hills. . . . 'Here is room to breathe in!' exclaimed the liberated forester."[9]

The most honored geographical space in Cooper is the lake, notably *The Pioneers*' Lake Otsego or *The Deerslayer*'s Lake Glimmerglass, whose "mirror-like surface . . . seems made to let us get an insight into the noble forests," as Natty observes while pushing off from shore, "and by leisurely but steady strokes of the paddles, the canoe glided across the placid sheet. . . ."[10] The eastern Western filmic shorthand for harmony would likewise be this image of leisurely canoeing across a smooth lake that mirrors the forest, as in that final shot of *The Redman and the Child*, or of Indian couples in the last shots of *The Mended Lute* and *The Squaw's Love* (1911) contentedly floating into close-up after surviving riverside tortures and attempted murders. Lakes are too central to both Cooper and the first film Westerns to be merely idyllic. The Indian's strangulation of the first murderer in *The Redman and the Child* is made more effectively grim by a trick cut that sinks the body forever into the depths. And the greatest moment of satisfaction for Natty and his Mohican companion Chingachgook in *The Pioneers* follows their canoe chase of a swimming deer across the lake and the slitting of its throat, blood dyeing the waters.[11]

"I would not be understood that these lakes are always tranquil; but that tranquility is their great characteristic. There are times when they take a far different expression; but in scenes like these the richest chords are those struck by the gentler hand of nature."[12] This aesthetic argument by the painter Thomas Cole in his 1836 "Essay on American Scenery" is central to his friend James Fenimore Cooper and, more surprisingly, to the first film Westerns, a genre that would not subsequently place much weight on water imagery or, for that matter, on tranquillity. We tend to think of the Western finding its prephotographic visual origins in the vast, half-imaginary mountainscapes of Cole's pupil Frederic Church or those of Albert Bierstadt, but the first films built from a quieter "luminist" tradition centered around lakes of the Hudson River valley. Griffith's regular cinematographer, Billy Bitzer, perhaps most strikingly captured at Fishkill, New York, in *The Song of the Wildwood Flute,* what Cole vaunts as "a most expressive feature: the unrippled lake, which mirrors all surrounding objects": a sun-backlit shot toward rising campfire smoke that creates a shimmering mirrored lake, where a chief's daughter is wooed by her suitor (played by Native American actor Elijah Tahamont [Algonquian ancestry] under his stage name "Dark Cloud").[13]

Cole's aesthetic goal was to capture through a realistic style certain "sublime" ineffables, "tranquility and peace" above all.[14] This goal would seem far from that of the early film, which was still exulting in capturing movement through landscape. And yet such transcendent calm is, curiously enough, the positive value at the core of the earliest Western films. The strangest moments in Griffith's first Westerns, for viewers looking back at them now, are the regular "tableau shots" in which the actors clearly have been directed to freeze their postures and expressions. Only the wind through their hair and the trees reveals that we are not watching still images. Generally though not always, these tableaux come within the films' first or last shots, as briefly at the opening and closing of *The Redman's View* or strikingly at the opening of *The Broken Doll: A Tragedy of the Indian Reservation* (1910), where members of the tribe hold their poses quite artificially across a stark hillside. The stasis here is extremely theatrical and yet is clearly a conscious choice. It is not immediately clear what sort of narrative goal would demand these oddly static moments, although Cooper's precedent is again suggestive. He too adopts a convention, generally annoying to readers now, of bringing his action self-consciously to a halt so that he can meditate upon the landscape (". . . on reaching the margin of the lake, he beheld the view that unexpectedly met his gaze. It was, in truth, sufficiently striking to merit a brief description"); such static moments are also often cast by Cooper in explicitly theatrical metaphors ("The sun was already approaching the western limits of a wooded view, when the actors in its opening scene must appear on a stage that is more worthy of a particular description"). At such moments, Natty, "leaning on his rifle," is "unconsciously, like a poet also," and experiences through the smooth lake "that soothing of the spirit which is a common attendant of a scene so thoroughly pervaded by the holy calm of nature."[15] From here, we haven't far to travel to reach the placidity of Walden Pond and the spiritual cleansing Thoreau would find there: "Walden is a perfect forest mirror . . . in which all impurity presented to it sinks, swept and dusted by the sun's hazy brush, . . ."[16]

Notwithstanding all of the chases, melodramatic outrages, and murders in the first eastern-filmed Westerns, a surprising narrative project unites them, and that project looks back to something like a transcendent ideal. Put simply, the narratives seek to reestablish the tableau idyll of the first shot by the time they arrive at their last shot. If the final tableaux carry a further aura of loss and melancholy, that is primarily due to that automatic narrative noted earlier – the "allegorical imperative" of native decline that comes with the image of the Indian himself. A characteristic introductory shot of the Indian in these films finds him on a hillside or lakeshore staring off in three-quarter profile into space unseen by us, as in the tableau second shot introducing the title character of *Comata, the Sioux* (1909) or the introduction of the Uncas character in *Leather Stocking* (1909), Griffith's adaptation of *The Last of the Mohicans.* The iconography evoked here had evolved in American painting until this simple image of the Indian staring off into the middle distance was alone enough to imply an entire narrative of civilization's advance and the native's demise. Mid-nineteenth-century paintings and drawings of Indians had typically featured the Indian on a hillside, gazing down ruefully on valleys newly filled with pioneers, farms, perhaps trains. By 1908, Frederic Remington could evoke this allegory in a painting he titled *The Last of His Race* merely by showing the Indian alone on a hillside, gazing past the empty edge of the canvas.[17] In the eastern-filmed Western of this era too, a whole narrative of progress can be implied by the single gazing figure. But the figure of the Indian in these films would be asked to carry even greater narrative burden.

# 3. Our Friends, the Indians

I hold to nothing more firmly, am proud of nothing so much as of the fact that my red friends of the West have given me the title of friend.

James McLaughlin, *My Friend the Indian* (1910)[1]

The Pale Faces are our friends. Go to the Fort yonder and tell them of the danger that threatens.

Chingachgook to Uncas; an intertitle in the 1920 film of *The Last of the Mohicans*

As the title *The Redman and the Child* hints, many early eastern Westerns link the Indian with children. On one hand, this is a way of equating Native Americans and children as similarly innocent, premoral, a bit simple.[2] The linkage may also involve more a complex matrix of half-analyzed assumptions about both race and family. Considering Griffith's lingering Victorian obsession with the threats to children's innocence, their number in his eastern-filmed Indian dramas for the Biograph Company is no surprise. But the pattern plays out widely and is taken to further extremes among other surviving films, such as Pathé's *The Red Girl and the Child* (1910) or the World Film Company's *The Aborigine's Devotion* (1909), another tale of an Indian's vengeance after the murder of his white friend, which ends with his apparent adoption of the orphaned son.

These films may have been playing to their audience – an audience for the Western that seems already to have been weighted toward boys. Certainly it became clear by the time of the 1930s B-Western that boys made up enough of the audience to encourage low-budget production geared to matinees. For these first filmmaking years, reliable audience demographics are few, but anecdotal evidence suggests Westerns were already finding a "niche" audience – young and male. A January 1911 *Views and Film Index* article, "Pictures that Children Like," cited a 1910 survey that found young boys favoring "Indian and Cowboy" pictures above all.[3] That this survey was conducted for a New York Child Welfare society suggests social worries about this combination of audience and film content. (A larger survey at the end of the silent era found that, among girls, only "delinquent girls" favored Westerns; Girl Scouts disliked them.)[4] There are hints already in 1911 that the audience for Indian and Western films was objectionable to the film industry's higher-class aspirations. A *Moving Picture World* article that year grumbles about "unwashed boys in the front seats" at Westerns and claims that "the small boy alone continues to yearn for the moving picture Indians and cowboys."[5] There are also a couple of unusual non-Western films from the beginning and end of this era that play on such worries, clustered around violence and class, about the appeal to boys of Westerns. Biograph's *Terrible Ted,* filmed in 1907 before Griffith's arrival at the company, is a clever tale about a boy who is chastened by his mother for reading Wild West pulps; he goes into the New York City streets and pulls his gun on a cop to free another boy, then foils a stagecoach robbery, shoots a card cheat, saves a woman from a bear, and kills Indians who tie him to a tree – until he is awakened by his mother from this fantasy. Edison's *The Land beyond the Sunset* (1912) casts the boys' fantasy as a grim social problem: A New York newsboy, his grandmother drunk in the tenements, is treated to an "OUTING FOR POOR CHILDREN" by reformist women and ministers of the Fresh Air Fund; the boy's "FIRST SIGHT OF THE WORLD BEYOND THE SLUMS" leads him to hide in the woods from the rest of the group when they return to the city; he climbs into a rowboat without oars and pushes off into a vast body of water where, in the darkly idyllic final shot, he loses himself in the western sunset.[6]

The probable audience demographics and the children within the story lines no doubt both argue that there is something childish about Westerns that the genre will never outgrow. The only real surprise may be that the genre settles into its childishness so early. And yet these first eastern-filmed Westerns also hold something more deeply and admirably child*like* in their visuals and narratives. There is, after all, a reputable genre label for this impulse to return to a simpler, more childlike, green and watery woodland: the "pastoral." As a Renaissance poetic mode with origins before Virgil, the pastoral employed the figure of the shepherd to honor rural life, a space beyond civilization but also nearer to us than the harsher wilderness. The structural pattern of the pastoral was to reestablish the harmony of the first line by its final lines, if arriving at it through a deeper melancholy, as in Virgil's first *Eclogue,* which ends with the shepherd who has been exiled from his lands invited for at least temporary shelter on the fertile fields of his contented shepherd friend: "Still, you could take your rest with me tonight/ Couched on green leaves. . . ." It was only in America, however, that the literary convention of the pastoral transmuted into a seriously proposed political ideology – as Leo Marx definitively argued – especially as promoted by Thomas Jefferson and earlier though the portrait of faithful, generous Indians in Robert Beverley's *History and Present State of Virginia* (1805).[7]

James Fenimore Cooper had spent his own rather idyllic and indulged boyhood in the 1790s on what was then the edge of frontier civilization, in the central New York village his father had pioneered, Cooperstown. When he was nine, his eldest sister wrote of James and another brother, "They are very wild and show plainly they have been bred in the woods."[8] His first Leatherstocking novel, *The Pioneers* (1823), is in surface details an evocation of those boyhood years and in its opening as nearly a pastoral as anywhere in Cooper: "Beautiful and thriving villages are found interspersed along the margins of small lakes. . . . [E]very man feels a direct interest in the prosperity of a commonwealth, of which he knows himself to form a part."[9] And yet, as Alan Taylor has explored in slightly different historical terms, *The Pioneers* does not long remain a pastoral and becomes a complex assessment of the legacy of Cooper's father, part defense and part critique.[10] Clumsy locutions and unconvincing dialogue have made Cooper an annoyance to many readers – famously Mark Twain – but Cooper is a complex novelist particularly in being unable in the end to maintain pastoralism's political ideology in the face of his pessimism about American pioneering. In *The Pioneers,* "the wasteful extravagance of man" litters the village land with slaughtered passenger pigeons, strips forests of hardwood maple, and sweeps the lake of fish with nets.[11]

What has remained in popular memory from Cooper might be labeled a literary pastoral, in the sense that central to Virgil are the debates and friendship between his two shepherds, one at home on the land, the other dispossessed. For Cooper, of course, the friendship is between Natty Bumppo and his dispossessed Mohican companion, Chingachgook. This white–Indian friendship is likewise the key to the eastern-filmed Westerns, which continue the efforts of the pastoral to reconcile certain irreconcilable claims about possession of the land.

Such friendship is neatly represented, for instance, in the closing image of Griffith's *Rose o' Salem-Town,* filmed in Delaware and New Jersey in August 1910. It's an image that merits some scrutiny (Fig. 2a). Shaking hands are a "trapper" (Henry B. Walthall) and his Mohawk companion. With the help of other Mohawks, they have just restored the natural harmony of the film's first shots. Resting easily between the two men is a young woman, and her inclusion in this harmony is a revealing oddity to which we will want to return shortly.

*Rose o' Salem-Town* varies the usual iconography of natural harmony by substituting the Atlantic Ocean for a lake, and the intrusive white villains this time are Puritan elders who in the middle of the film contrive a witchcraft trial of the young woman and her mother. (This is an eastern Western in more than one sense, set as well as filmed in the East. If the Western genre is not merely regional but national, that is partly because all of the United States can claim their time as a frontier. Most early eastern-filmed Westerns are set in the far West, but a larger number than later have prerevolutionary story lines that justify their landscapes, as again in Griffith's *A Mohawk's Way,* whose publicity identifies it as having "a Cooper atmosphere." For Cooper's Indians the oceanside frontier is evoked nostalgically by lakes: "My race has gone from the shores of the salt lake," as Chingachgook laments the Atlantic.)[12] *Rose o' Salem-Town* opens with shots of the young woman flitting rather wildly around the shore. Called "THE SEA CHILD" and the "MAID OF THE SEA" in the intertitles, her skittish vibrancy echoes the ocean waves toward which she gestures in apparent explanation of herself when she first meets the trapper. Indeed, her very vitality seems one incriminating trait at the witchcraft trial, instigated by a black-garbed, Bible-carrying "PURITAN HYPOCRITE" angered at her rejection of him. The trapper, witnessing her imprisonment, rushes off into the forest. Among the many surprisingly subtle moments in the film is its depiction of a dispute *within* the Mohawk band about whether to assist the trapper in trying to free her. An older Mohawk shakes his head over the pleas, and the trapper's particular Mohawk friend seems to abide by that decision until after the old man has been assisted into his pelt-covered shelter.

**Figure 2.** White–Indian threesomes in (2a) *Rose o' Salem-Town* (1910) and (2b) *A Redskin's Bravery* (1911).

One reason that it only confuses things to talk of "the myth of the West" in relation to film is that so many contradictory myths fight for supremacy within individual story lines, even individual images. Ignoring for a moment more the claim implied by the woman between them, the handshake of the white trapper and his Indian friend at the end of *Rose o' Salem-Town* evokes an image more or less solidified into myth by Cooper. Its homosocial implications were famously expanded into an entire theory of American literature by Leslie Fiedler in *Love and Death in the American Novel* (1960), which took the image as central to *Adventures of Huckleberry Finn* and *Moby-Dick* as well as to Cooper, so that what we were said to witness is "an archetypal relationship which also haunts the American psyche: two lonely men, one dark-skinned, one white, bend together over a carefully guarded fire in the virgin heart of the American wilderness; they have forsaken all others for the sake of the austere, almost inarticulate, but unquestioned love which binds them to each other and to the world of nature which they have preferred to civilization."[13] Earlier, D. H. Lawrence had pushed Cooper's implications furthest in his unsurpassed 1924 *Studies in Classic American Literature:*

> What did Cooper dream beyond democracy? Why, in his immortal friendship of Chingachgook and Natty Bumppo he dreamed the nucleus of a new society. . . . A stark, stripped human relationship of two men, deeper than the deeps of sex. Deeper than property, deeper than fatherhood, deeper than marriage, deeper than love. So deep that it is loveless. The stark, loveless, wordless unison of two men who have come to the bottom of themselves.[14]

A friendship between Indian and white is at the core of Griffith's eastern-filmed Westerns, especially in *The Broken Doll, The Red Girl, A Mohawk's Way, The Girl and the Outlaw,* and *Leather Stocking,* and is hinted elsewhere, as in that shared tent of *The Redman and the Child.* The dispute among the Mohawks in *Rose o' Salem-Town* reinforces that this friendship is deeper than the bonds of either man to his own race. Just as the white trapper fights the Puritans, the Mohawk must disobey his tribal elder to arrive at that final handclasp. Cooper's own clearest gloss on our film image comes over the grave of Chingachgook's son Uncas, the "last" Mohican: "Chingachgook grasped the hand that, in the warmth of feeling, the scout had stretched across the fresh earth, and in that attitude of friendship, these two sturdy and intrepid woodsmen bowed their heads together."[15]

Of course, the ironies of European Americans defining themselves through "friendship" with Native Americans are not hard to find. *My Friend, the Indian* is the title of a lost 1909 one-reel film from the Lubin Company, as well as the title of the 1910 autobiography by Indian Bureau agent James McLaughlin – quoted as an epigraph to this chapter – who will be remembered primarily for his indirect responsibility for the death of Sitting Bull during the Ghost Dance revival.[16] Such "friendship" regularly expands into the origin myth of America, as through the homosexual dance of Indian chief and white man in Hart Crane's poem *The Bridge.*[17] The friendship is given literary honesty along with an irony that seems half intentional when Thoreau seeks futilely in the three canoe trips of *The Maine Woods* a Native American guide who will be open and knowledgeable about his race.[18]

The entire point of all these handshakes and dances and canoe trips is exactly that they take place between men, outside the world of women, as the commentaries by Fiedler and Lawrence are keen to stress. In that light, our closing image from *Rose o' Salem-Town* seems a violation of America's very heritage by inserting a woman between the dusky male bonding in the wilderness. It is hard to know quite what to make of this film image, unless it – and perhaps the eastern-filmed Western more widely – may be putting forth a more elaborate argument than the one within the American literary tradition – or at least within mid-twentieth-century interpretations of that tradition.

Another, just slightly different image may help to clarify the film argument. Figure 2b is from the New York Motion Picture Company's *A Redskin's Bravery* (1911). Although the film is, for its year, staged rather primitively, this closing image is in some ways an even more surprising violation of the expected norms, especially for the way that the white woman rests her hand on the Indian's arms as she stands on the riverbank between the two men. Again in this film the Indian has lent "A HELPING HAND," as an intertitle mildly refers to the way he has saved the woman from two white attackers, strangling them underwater after a canoe chase, and then swimming with her back to shore. Briefly he had also assisted the white man after the attackers had knocked him from his horse. This final image then is not of two male friends separated by a woman but of a woman who knows the two men separately and brings the races together at the riverside calm after the struggle.

What these early films seem interested in doing is not really replaying Cooper's male myth as expanded by Fiedler and Lawrence but of somehow *using* that familiar myth to bolster another one – a myth that has something to do with creating an ideal community, an achievement that the Western genre will argue is possible only away from urban civilization, on the land.[19] We'll return to this subject especially in Part Three, but if later Hollywood Westerns are, surprisingly, less complex than the "primitive" eastern Western as to the creation of the ideal community, that is partially because they will come to regard Native Americans more simply, as essentially one more roadblock thrown by nature against the advance of pioneers.[20] The earliest eastern-filmed Westerns, whatever their simplicities of story lines, primitive stylistics, and obvious racisms, look to be making unclichéd attempts to reconcile two versions of the Western myth – call them the "male" and "female" versions – and to do so through the agency of the Indian. For just how such a relatively complex argument might be possible in such a primitive form, it's helpful to go back into a few of the details that lead up to that final image of *Rose o' Salem-Town.*

In this film, as in many of the greatest one-reelers – seldom running over fifteen minutes – the constraints of time force certain arguments out of the strict story line and into small parallelisms of imagery and analogies of expressive objects. *Rose o' Salem-Town* holds a wealth of such links. To put the film's four key terms simply: "witchcraft" is linked to the two "women," who are linked to "nature," which is linked to "Indians." Evidence of the mother's witchcraft, for instance, is noted by two Puritan deacons when they observe her walking through tall grasses gathering medicinal herbs (for ailing settlers whom we have twice seen consult her). Her daughter, already associated with the sea's vitality, is further condemned at her trial by a string of beads given to her by the trapper – perhaps shell wampum – at which the Puritan jurors point fearfully and that are likewise worn by the Mohawks, from whom presumably the trapper originally received them. Of course, the Indians in the film are themselves conventionally linked with nature: The Mohawks are most often framed darkly within their hillside camp in one of those static forest-clearing shots described earlier. Through such a series of images, the film makes a simple but telling equation of its key terms: women = witchcraft = nature = Indians. Among the curious things about this linkage is that as a result of it the Indian in that final handshake image is something other and something more than the dark half of a pure bond of masculinity.

If the ubiquitous figure of the Indian in these early eastern Westerns is not merely a blood brother of the white hero, what other role is he playing? An apparently perverse remark by D. H. Lawrence, when he veers off from analyzing Cooper, is suggestive: "The Indians, with their curious female quality, their archaic figures, with high shoulders and deep, archaic waists, like a sort of woman! And their natural devilishness. . . ."[21] The devil = nature = women = Indians: The equation varies only slightly in Lawrence. Griffith's *Rose o' Salem-Town,* however, makes Lawrence's argument imagistically. The qualities Griffith ascribes to Indians generally include most of the qualities he ascribes to women: "constancy" combined with emotional passion – stereotypical but not unadmirable traits. The title character of *Comata, the Sioux* can wait patiently through the years while the Indian woman he loves bears a child by a white man but finally also only just refrains from strangling the husband for his faithlessness. The *Biograph Bulletins* for Griffith's Westerns make a point of disabusing us of stereotypes of Indian "stoicism" and label those in both *A Mohawk's Way* and *The Mended Lute* "highly emotional." Placed within a European history of ideas, these Indians would be less the rationalist "noble savage" of (male) reason and logic as in Jean-Jacques Rousseau's *Discourse on the Origins of Inequality* (1755) than the "romantic savage" of (female) emotion such as the Oneida chief of Thomas Campbell's *Gertrude of Wyoming* (1809), who saves a white orphan by staying "true to nature's fervid feelings."[22]

If Indians are "lesser" than white men in Griffith, then, it's because they are so like women. But even this is not entirely simple in that Griffith is most consistent, and most Victorian, in assigning the highest ethics to women. For that reason, it is unsurprising that many of the white–Indian friendships in his eastern Westerns turn out to be among women themselves, as in the final images of the two women walking off arm in arm in *The Red Girl* and of their kiss in *A Mohawk's Way*. Indeed, that male myth figured through the interracial handshake is undercut by Griffith to genuinely comic effect in *The Broken Doll* when the Indian girl, having learned the gestures of white male friendship, returns to give pumping handshakes and hearty shoulder slaps to "HER FIRST AND ONLY FRIENDS," a pioneer mother and daughter.[23]

By the time that we arrive at the end of *Rose o' Salem-Town*, the young woman's mother has been condemned as a witch and burnt at the stake (or so it is implied when the Puritans attempt to get the daughter to confess her own witchcraft by forcing her to watch "HER MOTHER'S FATE" through the prison bars – a scene much criticized in contemporary reviews for its cruelty and anticlericalism).[24] So what we see in that final handshake image is an orphan, in need of a new family. Perhaps she is just old enough to need a husband. Of course, by the racial assumptions Griffith held to even more strongly than did Cooper, only one of these two men is racially qualified for that role, despite her open gaze of admiration at the Mohawk.[25] The handshake thus becomes some sort of certification of value for which the woman is not intrusive but the essential witness. The film thus makes one last equation of its various terms by linking "white man" with "Indian" in one specific sense: The trapper has been certified to have an Indian level of natural vitality. Some similar transference seems to be taking place in that final image from *A Redskin's Bravery* when the Indian links hands with the man who had earlier failed to protect his woman. (Should those racial and sexual assumptions seem merely archaic, it's worth recalling how in *Dances with Wolves* [1990] Kevin Costner's character needs authorization by the Sioux as a worthy husband for the white woman who has lived among them long enough to become their "daughter.")[26]

The white–Indian friendships that are so central to the first Westerns – and that then vanish to the edges of Westerns for fifty years – are playing with images more complex than male bonding. Put simply, the films' arguments would be that the figure of the Indian is less our brother than our parent, with everything necessary for both parental genders in one figure – thus the ideal family harmony of those closing shots of the orphan and his savior in *The Aborigine's Devotion* and *The Redman and the Child* (whose publicity calls "the Sioux Indian . . . as kind-hearted as a woman and as brave as a lion"). The boys in the films

– and the film audience of boys – travel deep into a prelapsarian Edenic garden, "deeper than the deeps of sex," as Lawrence would say. If Freud's "family romance" scenario is to be believed, those films act out the psychic need of children to deny their biological parents in order to imagine themselves descended from nobler ones.[27]

Although the Hollywood studio Western will regularly nod to a friendship between the hero and Indians, it will tend to do so in simpler and more conventional ways. "Tonto" (Spanish for "fool") will be the governing model.[28] When the fuller white–Indian friendship tales begin to return in the 1960s, prompted both by a counterculture admiration for the "primitive" alongside the collapse of the studio system, they will be led by extreme "eastern Westerns" shot in Eastern Europe beginning in 1962 in the rugged mountains and lakes of Yugoslavia, Bulgaria, and Czechoslovakia, based upon nineteenth-century German novelist Karl May's pairing of his Apache "Winnetou" with his Teutonic pioneer "Old Shatterhand," as well as upon Cooper. "Chingachgook ist mein Freund," announces an East German Natty Bumppo in the astonishing *Chingachgook, die große Schlange* [*Chingachgook: The Great Snake*] (1967).[29] After his rancher parents are murdered by a renegade cavalry officer in the West German *Old Shatterhand* (1963), the orphaned boy is next seen living idyllically with an Apache couple.

Of course, the Indian-as-parent is in many ways the most arrogant of expropriated images. When in, say, Willa Cather's novel *The Professor's House* (1925), the physically and morally perfect Tom Outland claims the ancient Southwestern Anasazi as his "ancestors" and ownership of their artifacts as "the pots and pans that belonged to my poor grandmothers a thousand years ago," he's assuming an Indian parenthood that, as an orphaned son of white pioneers, isn't his biologically. The Native American past becomes "ours" too.[30] This is more complex but hardly less presumptuous than when Longfellow ended *The Song of Hiawatha* (1855) with the dying Indian passing on his land and traditions to the white man for safekeeping. Such a claim combined with such a level of sentiment as Longfellow's was possible only following Indian "removal" west of the Mississippi in the 1830s.[31] Film industry trade papers found a similar explanation for the "vogue" in Indian stories. "Our Indians are no longer dangerous," noted *Moving Picture World* in 1911, and proposed a primitivist explanation: "We are almost tempted to envy the Indian for his lack of civilization. We feel that he is so much closer to nature and a suspicion steals over us that after all

**Figure 3.** The reunited white–Indian couple at the end of James Young Deer's *White Fawn's Devotion* (1910).

he is happier than we are."[32] The surviving four-reel *Hiawatha: The Indian Passion Play*, filmed independently and primarily in New York State with a Native American cast, is true to Longfellow in ending with Hiawatha calming his superstitious tribe and warmly welcoming the first Catholic missionary.

The artistic and ethical limitations of early eastern-filmed Westerns are evident enough; and yet they made efforts that Hollywood never even attempted. They toyed with genuinely pastoral fables that conclude in ways not exclusively exterminationist for the Native American characters. The great era for these films was very brief, between 1908 and 1911, and the vast majority are now lost. But seldom after these early films produced in the East do we find such moments as, for instance, at the end of *White Fawn's Devotion* (1910), where a Dakota pioneer reunites happily with his Indian wife and their daughter (Fig. 3). (He had been tempted by wealth in the East, causing the near-suicidal despair of his wife, misapprehensions about her death, and a chase by her tribe over cliffs and down rivers.)

This particular iconoclastic violation of taboos must owe something to the film's now-forgotten director, James Young Deer, of Winnebago ancestry and born on or near the tribe's Omaha Reservation in Nebraska. After work in Wild West shows and circuses, Young Deer appeared in small roles in several of Griffith's eastern Westerns. His presence, along with his Winnebago wife, Lillian St. Cyr (whose stage name was "Princess Redwing"), may account for Biograph's claim that Griffith's *The Mended Lute* (1909) is "more than reasonably accurate, these details having been supervised by an expert in the matter." *White Fawn's Devotion* had been filmed by Young Deer for Pathé-Frères near its Jersey City studio, and he would move permanently west later in 1910 for promotion to "Director and General Manager" of the company's new Los Angeles studio, after appearing in a few films by Lubin, Bison, and other companies. Young Deer seems only a competent director of actors, although he uses landscape locations to great advantage in action sequences, as at the close of *The Red Girl and the Child* (1910) where "Princess Redwing," playing the heroic Indian of the title and disguised in men's clothes, saves the white child by tempting kidnappers to chase her and the child over a rope she has strung across a sheer-walled river gorge. With satisfying pitilessness, she sends the pursuers plummeting to their deaths.

Whatever James Young Deer's limitations as a film stylist, his career hints at the wider opportunities, both in employment and narrative, that existed in the first Westerns, briefly. Young Deer prospered for a time in the West also, where he probably produced and directed at least sixty films (virtually all of them now lost).[33] He was almost certainly director of Pathé's surviving *For the Papoose* (1912), fascinating for its interracial custody plot about a half-Indian child and for the fact that the white father, who has fomented a battle as diversion, thoroughly deserves his death at the hands of his Indian brother-in-law, who wipes the bloody blade of his knife in satisfaction. It is also evident that Young Deer was pushing interracial "friendship" into areas unacceptable to critics, as in this revealing *Moving Picture World* review of his sadly lost *Red Deer's Devotion* (1911):

> Another feature of this film will not please a good many. It represents a white girl and an Indian falling in love with each other. While such a thing is possible, and undoubtedly has been done many times, still there is a feeling of disgust which cannot be overcome when this sort of thing is depicted as plainly as it is here, even to the point where the girl decides to run away and join her Indian lover.[34]

More acceptable was a focus on picturesque and passive traditions, as in another of Young Deer's lost one-reelers, *Old Indian Days* (1911), about which *Moving Picture World* condescended to note that "The showing of Indian customs, the Indian manner of living, cooking, feasting, traveling, wooing, etc., is very prettily done."[35] James Young Deer's name essentially vanishes from the movie business after 1913, the victim of changing tastes, or of the Hollywood production system, or of a complex vendetta from the Los Angeles sheriff's office, probably extending what Young Deer himself claimed with some bitterness was "the vengeance the white man meted out to Indians."[36]

# 4. The Death of the Western, 1911

There seems to be prevalent a sentiment that the Western photoplay has outrun its course of usefulness and is slated for an early demise. The old thrills are exhausted and people want something new. It is just simply the case of a gold mine that has been worked to the limit and can give no more desirable ore. Apparently all the old Western expedients are frayed to a frazzle and audiences have become familiar with them to the point of contempt. . . . Is there any hope for the survival of Western subjects? There is a little, but not much. The Western subject might gain a renewed lease of life if it made a change of base. . . . What the makers need is a change of background.

"The Passing of the Western Subject," *The Nickelodeon,* February 18, 1911

Death-of-the-Western pronouncements arrived only three years after the genre had first exploded in popularity. Even more confident about the Western's imminent demise than the 1911 *Nickelodeon* editorial excerpted above was the leading trade journal *Moving Picture World,* which later in 1911 summarized with apparent objectivity what it saw as an industrywide problem:

The Western pictures, as a distinct specialty, have now been parts of regular releases for years and have lost their popularity. If the makers of these pictures have any doubt on that subject, it would be a boon to the industry to have them make an impartial investigation among the patrons of moving picture houses in any part of the country. These lines are based, not upon theory or speculation but strictly upon the facts, ascertained in personal research of the writer and others in various parts of the country. Women especially, always the friends of the moving picture, are utterly tired of them. Always the same plot, the same scenery, the same impossible Indians, the wicked halfbreeds, the beautiful red maidens, the fierce warriors, the heroic cowboys, the flight from the Indian village at night.[1]

This commentator, W. Stephen Bush, had focused his ire the previous month on unauthentic screen Indians: "We have Indians à la Français, 'red' men recruited from the Bowery and upper West End Avenue. . . . You cannot escape the moving picture Indian. Recently I visited five moving picture houses in a Southern tour and five in a city in New England. The Indian was everywhere."[2]

These first film critics, looking back on a medium with a fifteen-year history, were finding the Western to be less a genre than what we would now call a cycle – a group of films that briefly achieved an odd burst of unexpected popularity – something like 1950s biker films or 1970s slasher movies. Still, there are reasons beyond mere hindsight to look skeptically on the tone of objectivity in their death-of-the-Western pronouncements, which hold several assumptions about what audiences and exhibitors want, or ought to want. One such assumption is that if audiences grow restless, they must desire different genres, rather than genre cross-breedings or evolutions in genre components. "Progressive and intelligent exhibitors," Stephen Bush also assumes, will want to "outgrow . . . entertainment on the dime-novel order."[3] Bush in particular had class aspirations for the art of the movies – he was the critic complaining of "unwashed boys" in front seats at Westerns – and his dismay at the numbers of Westerns encountered in his tours of nickelodeons outside Manhattan hints at the beginnings of distinct genre markets, both regional and gender-based. Westerns already may have been growing particularly popular not only with boys (as opposed to those "friends of the moving picture," women) but in rural towns as well. At the beginning of 1911 *Moving Picture World* had surveyed exhibitors to ask which films "had been specially recalled by request of the spectators" and found "the highest encomium" for Griffith's Indian Western *The Mended Lute* coming from the Dakotas.[4]

Nevertheless, as strange as such death-of-the-Western pronouncements seem now – made back when the longest Western still ran about fifteen minutes – the numbers of such pronouncements suggest that they must have been voicing a widespread sense. In retrospect, these 1911 verdicts *are* accurate about the death of the Western of a certain kind: the death of what we've been labeling the "eastern Western."

Every major motion picture company then active in producing Westerns participated in a move of locations and studios from the East to the West Coast, although there were as many variations as companies. Eventually, of course, all settled around Los Angeles, although that destination was not obvious in the first tentative explorations of the West. Arguably, the four key early explorers of filmmaking in the West were the Selig Polyscope Company, the Essanay Film Manufacturing Company, the New York Motion Picture Company's Bison subsidiary (under Thomas Ince's management by 1911), and the Biograph Company (under Griffith's direction). Selig and Essanay, based in Chicago, began already halfway west. As early as 1907, Selig claimed the "genuine novelty" of a Rocky Mountain setting.[5] Surviving Selig Westerns, however, suggest that the company toured through some spectacular western locations without ever quite finding a director or acting ensemble to merit them, notwithstanding early stunt work by Tom Mix. Essanay's Indian-head logo was curiously inappropriate for a company that relied less than the others on tales of Native Americans and instead founded the cowboy hero on film in "Broncho Billy" Anderson – the name given the engagingly oafish character played by Essanay's cofounder, Gilbert M. Anderson (born Max Aronson), after 1910, when the company's Westerns had come to be produced in Niles Canyon in Northern California. Anderson originated essentially the same character in temporary locations throughout the West, as in the rare surviving *A Ranchman's Rival* (1909), where Anderson walks Colorado plateaux to foil a fake-minister seduction scheme that owes more to theatrical melodrama than to any inspiration from the Rocky Mountain background.[6] Other employees of Essanay split away in 1910 to form the Chicago-based American Film Company, with units briefly in Arizona and New Mexico and then, under director Allan Dwan, near Los Angeles, where their Westerns show an off-the-cuff charm unmatched by any other company, to judge again from the few surviving examples.

Among the more distinctive variations on the shift away from production in the Northeast was the peripatetic Kalem Company's use of its Jacksonville, Florida, studios to make wildly melodramatic films about the nineteenth-century Seminole ("ONE DOES NOT LIVE LONG IN THE SWAMPS," an intertitle informs us in *Tangled Lives: A Strange Culmination of the Seminole War* [1911]). Lubin, a major company based in Philadelphia, also opened a Jacksonville studio, but its great venture west was the unit under Romaine Fielding, who from 1912 through 1915 made throughout the desert Southwest more than a hundred thoroughly unconventional and uncompromisingly dark films, to judge from the two-reel *The Rattlesnake: A Psychical Species* (1913) and from Linda and Michael Woal's research into a body of work otherwise almost entirely lost.[7]

French companies carried the economic battle with U.S. filmmakers into the West itself. Although the scorned "Indians à la Français" continued to ride across Europe, as in the Éclipse Company's "Arizona Bill" series, filmed in France from 1911 to 1913, other French companies moved physically west.[8] In 1910, the Méliès Company sent a unit from New Jersey to San Antonio, Texas, under Georges Méliès's renegade older brother, Gaston. By the time Gaston and the company moved on to California and then, in 1912, even further west into the South Pacific islands, the Méliès films had developed the lowest possible reputation in the industry; but their surviving San Antonio Westerns have a sophistication of gestural acting matched among the often rough-hewn productions of the West only by Griffith's Biographs.[9] Pathé-Frères, as we have seen, trumped the Americans in 1910 by installing James Young Deer as manager of its new West Coast studio.

Why this universal production move? The winter weather of the Southwest was one obvious attraction, and for a few independent companies the remote locations may have delayed the arrival of lawyers for the monopolistic Motion Picture Patents Company, as filmmakers such as Allan Dwan and Fred Balshofer later enjoyed relating with suitable gunfight embellishment.[10] There was also the opening up of new landscapes – what that *Nickelodeon* editorial calls a "change of base" and "change of background." And, although that same editorial warns filmmakers that "Nature makes a poor villain," there were new ways of using the landscape itself as antagonist, as in films about desert thirst, such as D. W. Griffith's *The Last Drop of Water* (1911) or Thomas Ince's *The Empty Water Keg* (1912). One constant remained the presence of Indians, one of whom dies of desert thirst in Gilbert M. ("Broncho Billy") Anderson's *The Dead Man's Claim* (1912). However, the shift to West Coast production brought to Indians abrupt changes – and troubling ones.

## 5. The Far-Western

Eastward I go only by force; but westward I go free.
Henry David Thoreau, "Walking" (1862)[1]

In production terms, the only unusual variation by the Biograph Company and D. W. Griffith was in each year moving west and back east again, wintering in Southern California and returning to New York each April or May. The pattern continued for four years, from January 1910 until Griffith left Biograph in 1913. As I've noted, the other unusual fact about these films in retrospect is that virtually all of them still survive. Thus they provide us now with the opportunity for seeing the changes brought into films themselves by the production move west.

With shocking immediacy, Griffith's first Westerns actually shot in the West find a new use for American Indians – and that use is essentially as an expendable plot device. In his first western-filmed Western, *In Old California* (1910), Indians are servile, cringing figures who tote messages for the colonial California governor when they are not bowing to him. It's the sort of role that would have been played in blackface in Griffith's non-Westerns, even if, arguably, there is regional truth in that depiction of the treatment of California's mission Indians. In his second western-filmed Western, *The Twisted Trail* (1910), the Indians enter without a hint of motivation to attack Mary Pickford on a mountain road, an act for which they are later perfunctorily beaten by a posse. Looking back now, such an unmotivated attack seems unremarkably ordinary – this is how "Indians" behave in "Westerns" – until we recall that absolutely nothing like it occurs in any of Griffith's eastern-filmed Westerns.

The changeover in representations of Native Americans is not in-

**Figure 4.** Murdering an infant (4a) to the horror of a settler (Lillian Gish, 4b) in *The Battle at Elderbush Gulch* (1913).

stantly complete: Griffith's first films in the West notably include his elaborate one-reel adaptation of Helen Hunt Jackson's novel about mission Indians, *Ramona* (1910), subtitled on film *A Story of the White Man's Injustice to the Indian.* Still, Westerns will soon enough find little need to motivate a massacre committed by Indians. The stereotype fills in for motivation – Injuns attack whites – and speeds up the story,[2] but that narrative requirement for one-reelers was ongoing and doesn't explain the abrupt shift in Indian images. American Indians as marginally characterized instigators of massacres are so familiar from the Hollywood era that they might need little exploration, except that it is this pattern – not that of the eastern Western – that won the Western. In addition, there is the way that this image of Indians arrives alongside film's first exploration of the landscape of the West. The new landscape and the new film image for Native Americans appear linked in ways that seem more than a little sinister.

By the time Griffith arrived at *The Battle at Elderbush Gulch,* his last major Biograph Western, filmed in Southern California in 1913, he had come as close as he ever would to mastering filming in the West. As with his first Western filmed in the East, "the red man" and "the child" are again the two poles around which *The Battle at Elderbush Gulch* revolves. But the reversal is now complete. No longer allies, the red man and the (white) child are now opposing sides of a war on the plains and are deployed against each other in ways astonishingly violent for pre–World War I filmmaking, as in Fig. 4a, where an Indian swings an infant over his head the better to crush its skull. The story line focuses on other children – a pair of "waifs" (Mae Marsh and Leslie Loveridge) and a young couple (played by two nineteen-year-olds, Lillian Gish and Bobby Harron) with their infant – who all arrive West in the same stagecoach. Soon after the waifs settle into the ranch where their uncle works, trouble begins with a neighboring tribe. The battle erupts via a plot point of stunning ludicrousness even if one accepts its melodramatization of conflicting white–native "thoughtworlds": "THE CHIEF'S SON" arrives back at camp too late for what an intertitle narrates as "THE DOG FEAST. SUNKA ALAWAN. 'WAYATAMIN SUNKA E YA E-E-YO' ('MAY YOU EAT DOG AND LIVE LONG')." The Indians' effort to restock the depleted stew pot with Mae Marsh's puppies results in her uncle shooting the chief's son, an event that "FANS THE EVER READY SPARK OF HATRED TO REVENGE." The ranch house is besieged until a Mexican ranch hand (previously a slumping figure needing discipline from the foreman) rides heroically for cavalry troops who arrive just in time to rout the Indians and avert the need for a ranchman to shoot a sacrificial last bullet into Lillian Gish's head. A storage chest in the ranch house opens to reveal children and puppies safe.

If this narrative line is vastly altered from anything filmed in the East, so too is the look of *Elderbush Gulch.* Here the action spreads across wider and whiter spaces, often observed from a great prospect, as with the battle in the town (Fig. 5a), the citizens fleeing across the plains (Fig. 5b), and the troops attacking the Indians at the ranch house (Fig. 5c). The tribe, no longer framed idyllically by trees, is spread rather awkwardly across the scrub-grass flatlands, as for the dog-feast dancing (Fig. 5d). During the battle especially, the dust and smoke flatten and whiten the landscape.

Griffith was only the most recent American artist to find in the apparent blankness of the West confusing aesthetic choices that came with unacknowledged complications. Back as far as Coronado's sixteenth-century expedition north from Mexico, Europeans and then Americans were regularly bewildered and horrified by what seemed the Southwest's desert emptiness.[3] As we have seen, Griffith was accustomed to working in a European tradition, inherited via Thomas Cole and the Hudson River painters, in which transcendent beauty was evoked by forested lakes and rivers. And in fairness to Griffith, he and other pioneer filmmakers were faced with bringing desert landscape

**Figure 5.** High-angle shots (5a–c) and "dog-feast" dancing (5d) in *The Battle at Elderbush Gulch.*

into popular art a decade or so before writers and painters like Willa Cather or Georgia O'Keefe began to teach intellectuals how to see it.[4] The Southwest remained relatively unphotographed until the 1890s with the exception of government survey photographers, and it wasn't until that decade that inexpensive gravure allowed for wide distribution of photo images.[5] Among turn-of-the-century popular artists, Frederic Remington's aesthetic problems are revealing. For all his fascination with the cavalry and Indians, he never discovered how to depict western landscape, which even in his finished paintings tends to be featureless washes of color or vegetationless sketches behind figures grouped into the foreground. If Remington now seems most artistically satisfying as a sculptor, that's partly because the medium allowed him to remove completely horses and riders from the land.[6]

Temperamentally unsuited to solve these problems, Griffith showed unease with empty space long before his attempts to film in the Southwest. In his earliest, slow-cut Biographs, if a shot is unbalanced or framed to include blank space, we can be sure that some action will fill it before the next cut. A character will enter to sit in the empty chair (e.g., *Betrayed by a Handprint,* 1908) or, outdoors, a character will enter to fill the empty clearing (e.g., *The Bandit's Waterloo,* 1908). The rare exceptions to this pattern invariably use empty space unfilled at the next cut to signify something gone terribly wrong in the world, an emotional loss otherwise inexpressible by the characters. A loved one may walk out of the frame, leaving another to face a betrayal represented by blank space (e.g., *Her Awakening,* 1911).[7] The most haunting such moment surely comes as the last shot of *The Country Doctor* (1909), after the death of the doctor's daughter while he is off tending another child: The camera pans away from his closed front door and slowly takes in 180 degrees of the unpeopled landscape.

Considering the sensitivity to space of D. W. Griffith and his cinematographer, Billy Bitzer, it is surprising just how clumsy their first films in the desert West are about deploying figures in the landscape. In *The Chief's Daughter* (1911), shot among the cholla and prickly pear cacti of Southern California's deserts, the actors stand front and center, blocking as much scrubland as possible. The film's newly extreme close-ups (as when the Chief's daughter comes to a "REALIZATION" of "BETRAYAL" by her white lover) seem experiments also to evade the land.

Griffith's third Western shot in the West (after *In Old California* and *The Twisted Trail*) reveals another uncomfortable outsider's take on western space. *A Romance of the Western Hills* (1910), shot primarily in the California Sierra foothills, is a curious contemporary tale of "THE INDIAN GIRL ADOPTED BY TOURISTS," as an intertitle bluntly puts it. Bowler-hatted white men and their flower-hatted wives wander among tipis, haggling over the price of beads. The adoption is complete after an old Indian trades his daughter (Mary Pickford) for a few dollars and a pocket watch. Although one shouldn't assume that Griffith directs no satire at the ways that the whites act toward the natives, the film reinforces how both the Southwest landscape and native cultures were being reinvented as "tourist attractions." Whatever else this implies about ethnography's evolution into entertainment, it's also a way of taming a landscape previously seen by European eyes only as horrifyingly blank. The trick of this reinvention means that the land can be possessed without being inhabited, and owned without being occupied. Griffith's western-filmed Westerns never quite lose this sense of the land as a tourist space, to be passed through rather than lived in, and observed from an emotional distance.[8] His two-reel *A Pueblo Legend* (1913), shot at Isleta Pueblo just north of Albuquerque, relies furthest on the tourist eye and a vacant exoticism, placing Mary Pickford again as an Indian maiden in front of authentic Pueblo dancers.[9]

Through their four yearly seasons in the West, Griffith and Bitzer slowly refined ways of seeing the West. Some of their initial responses were evasive – simple iris lens effects to limit the surrounding white space, or denying difference altogether by searching out woodsy landscapes that could be molded into eastern framing (as with most of the shots in *The Twisted Trail*). Mid-nineteenth-century painters had initially adopted similar solutions, as in most of Albert Bierstadt's grand panels of the Rockies, seen as lush and watery, or in Thomas Moran's twisting western trees, borrowed from studies he had made in Rome's Borghese Gardens.[10] Even John Mix Stanley's very early Southwest desert painting *Chain of Spires along the Gila River* (1855) tames the arid southern Arizona landscape within a curious Claudian frame, draping saguaro over one riverbank and fantastically enlarged cholla cacti over the other, and then hauling in antlered stags from some distant realm. For all Stanley's experience of the West with the U.S. Army in the 1846–8 Mexican War, his painting is as surreal as a Henri Rousseau dreamscape. Perhaps it was not possible to *see* the West in painting until the dissemination of photographs, if believing precedes seeing (as E. H. Gombrich and John Berger famously demonstrated).[11]

It took until *The Battle at Elderbush Gulch* and other late Biograph Westerns for the landscape solutions arrived at forty years earlier by still photographers and artists to be incorporated into Griffith's moviemaking in the West. Post–Civil War government survey photographers had shown easterners how to see the West. William Henry Jackson's favored solution, adopted too by Thomas Moran in his first sketches of the far West, was to organize images around a rock outcropping, a principle with romantic heritage to familiarize it (and often further anthropomorphized by the names – "Giant's Club," "Teapot Rock," "Toll Gate Rock," and so on – that pioneers bestowed on landmarks Jackson photographed and Moran painted).[12] More challenging were the flatter deserts on which Griffith often worked, closer in landscape to the uninviting sinks and mineral flats of Nevada photographed by Timothy O'Sullivan just after the Civil War. Although O'Sullivan sometimes fell back on a few traditional aesthetic principles, such as centering images around small lakes (which looked more idyllic without their smell of sulfur) or adding humans in semiclassical poses for scale, he also invented others, such as raising his camera high enough to make foreground of flatlands.[13] This little trick, obvious enough in retrospect, was increasingly adopted by Griffith and Bitzer when in desert shots they would raise the camera well above the actors' eye levels, the slight downward angle eliminating most of the blank sky that had made such dull compositions in their first desert Westerns.

A related solution was the prospect shot from high atop a hill, a shot that Griffith put to immediate use in the West, notably in *Ramona,* which experiments with extreme depth of field between a burning Indian village far in the background and the foreground anguish of "Alessandro the Indian" (Henry B. Walthall). The prospect shot was one Griffith had grown comfortable with in the East (in *The Redman's View* and *Comata, the Sioux,* notably), and it came West trailing eastern literary and painterly pedigrees. James Fenimore Cooper would regularly have characters ascend a hill to give us our bearings and anticipate action (especially in *The Last of the Mohicans* and *The Pathfinder*). Although eighteenth-century European theorists of the picturesque scorned such perspective in painting – for its lack of foreground objects and murky distant detail[14] – American painters of the West had found the shot useful ever since George Catlin's many long-distance Indian villages seen from nearby hillsides in the 1830s. The prospect shot grows increasingly central to Griffith's visualization of the West, as in Figs. 5a–c from *The Battle at Elderbush Gulch.* Whatever else the prospect shot achieves however, it's yet another way to keep the land distant.

There was one other solution to the problem of filming in the desert West, in retrospect the most obvious and simple. That was to allow the desert to remain horrifying, to remain blank, to be distinctly itself – the Timothy O'Sullivan solution essentially. There's a case to be made that Griffith's best, or at least most modern, far-Westerns finally arrived here, in such films as *The Female of the Species* (1912), *Just Gold* (1913), *Over Silent Paths* (1910), or *The Last Drop of Water* (1911), where "THE GREAT DESERT" intertitle announces a shot dominated by white sands, a wagon train rolling slowly across the top of the frame (not unworthy of O'Sullivan's images of wagons lost in sand dunes). However, these are all grim tales of the dead West: death by thirst and murder, with humans at their ethical worst, if usually redeemed in the reels' last minutes. Such a solution – to let the West be the West – brought implications from which Griffith shied.

Aesthetic choices, as always, imply something more, and we'll want to come back to the unacknowledged political claims within the visual styles chosen for filming in the West. But first we need to look further into the strangely altered narratives that suddenly appeared within this new western landscape. These stories would win the Hollywood Western.

# 6. Wars on the Plains

I don't go so far as to think that the only good Indians are the dead Indians, but I believe that nine out of ten are, and I shouldn't inquire too closely into the case of the tenth.

Theodore Roosevelt[1]

The Westerns first shot in the West were clearly taking off from a new model rather than looking back to anything remotely resembling Cooper's Leatherstocking tales. The films tended to feature wagon trains (in larger budgets) or stagecoaches (in limited ones), isolated pioneer towns, and quite often cavalry troops. Indians, if named by tribe or implied by style, were usually Sioux, Comanche, Cheyenne, or Apache (in descending order of popularity). Tribes remained; but as individual characters, Indians were vanishing.

The new story type was evidently modeled on what we would call the Plains Wars, that relatively brief period from the 1850s through the 1880s during which tribes of the middle- and far-West were massacred or (more commonly and less dramatically) decimated by disease and starvation, as buffalo herds were slaughtered and reservation confinement became the only real survival option for Native Americans. The cowboy begins in these films to make his reappearance (usually without cows), as with the three horseback cowboys who first come across the hostile tribe in *The Battle at Elderbush Gulch.* A hero on horseback was alien to Cooper, in whose novels only women and foppish men ride horses, which must in any case be slaughtered before they give away one's position in a forest fight; "I am little skilled in horses," Natty Bumppo readily admits.[2] Cooper's real heroes – both natives and whites – run on foot through the landscape, as they do in the eastern-shot Western film.[3] The horseback heroes in these first western-filmed Westerns are often initially the massed troops of the U.S. Cavalry, and the cowboy remains surprisingly marginal, with the exception of the much simpler series after 1911 with Tom Mix. Even "Broncho Billy" Anderson seldom rode a horse, notwithstanding his reputation as an early cowboy.[4] The most striking shift in the western-filmed Western is in the level of violence: both the intensity of individual episodes (as with that infant murder in Fig. 4 from *Elderbush Gulch*) and the scale of mass death (as in the prospect shots of bodies surrounding the cabin in the same film).

With the production move west, most of the major film companies drew on the Plains Wars model – wagon-train pioneers, savage Indian attacks, cavalries to the rescue – as in (to mention again only surviving examples) Kalem's *On the War Path* (1911), Bison's *The Indian Massacre* (1912), Vitagraph's *The Fatherhood of Buck McGee* (1912), and Selig's *Captain Brand's Wife* (1911). In this Selig version, for instance, the cavalry captain writes for his wife to join him in Fort Apache, Arizona, with a letter whose postscript ought to have caused second thoughts: "P.S.: The Apaches are giving us trouble." Her infant survives being thrown from a picturesque cliff by the Apaches. Her husband is not so lucky.

Griffith's variations, beginning with *Fighting Blood* (1911) and *The Last Drop of Water* (1911), seem characteristic of the genre's wider turn to starker violence. In *The Battle at Elderbush Gulch,* the grim climactic heroism comes when little Mae Marsh crawls over battlefield corpses to pry a screaming infant from the death grip of a ranch hand whose mouth hangs open slackly. More astonishing for its year is the ending image of Griffith's impressive and complex two-reeler *The Massacre* (1912), whose title turns out to be a double-edged reference to two slaughters, first of Indians then of whites, both pointedly including women and children among the dead. This time, the cavalry rides in too late to save the wagon train and finds a mass of pioneer bodies. Only one small hand struggling through the tangle of bodies reveals that Blanche Sweet has survived with her infant by hiding beneath the corpses.[5]

It is often noted that the Western in these years begins to discover the courtly grace of cowboys, but what film most evidently learns in the wide, bright, harsh, "empty" landscape of the West is how to narrate killing. This, more than anything about horses or ranching, seems to have been the discovery that saved the genre itself from the death so widely predicted for it in 1911. It is impossible now to experience how new these films were, since their gunfight violence and Plains Wars narratives were the pattern Hollywood adopted. Less obvious is where this new story pattern might have originated.

One of several problems with locating "the" origin of the Western in James Fenimore Cooper is how extremely elliptical he is about the bloodletting that becomes central to the film genre. At moments of violence Cooper's diction becomes even more frustratingly roundabout. It is difficult to decipher even what is being described when he evades, for instance, "the disgusting signs of mortality" after a man is scalped in *The Deerslayer.* Larger scenes of slaughter are typically omitted altogether between chapters, as with the massacre of Hurons in the same novel between the end of Chapter 30 ("The scene that followed is not easily described") and the opening of Chapter 31 ("The picture next presented . . . need scarcely be laid before the eyes of the reader").[6]

Searching among writers of Westerns closer in time to the first films doesn't provide much more in the way of a model for the Plains Wars slaughter story. Owen Wister's *The Virginian* (1902), so widely influential for its knightly cowboy and reconciliation of U.S. regions (with its eastern narrator, western setting, southern hero, and northern heroine), places surprisingly little emphasis on violence except as brief ritual, and has not the slightest interest in Native Americans. Zane Grey had broken into popularity in 1911, but his early villains are less likely to be Indians than businessmen, Mormons, and Germans. Among scholars who have read widely in nineteenth-century popular fiction of the West, Christine Bold, Daryl Jones, Richard Slotkin, and David Reynolds have located bloody tales of Plains Wars Indian fighting but without finding any writer to correspond remotely to the influence or power of Cooper's eastern-style Westerns. Because of the sheer numbers of pulp dime-novel Westerns – accurately named for their price when they began in the 1860s – one can find some evidence of almost any story pattern. Curiously, however, the Plains Wars slaughter story seems never to have been particularly popular. In the earlier dime novels of the 1860s and early 1870s, backwoods hand-to-hand Indian fighting stories are still influenced by Cooper and the Daniel Boone tales. From the mid-1870s, the dime-novel Indian grows perhaps more cunning, but the story focus shifts to settled frontier communities as a space for the testing of lone heroes, where Indians are not one of the major plagues.[7]

We might fall back on Cooper as an originator of the far-Western through his uncharacteristic 1827 Leatherstocking novel *The Prairie,* set in what he took to be the "hard and unyielding" lands west of the Alleghenies but east of the Rockies. Writing without having seen the prairies, Cooper imagined "a comparative desert," something more like what the far Southwest turned out to be. For his wagon-train pioneers, "these naked plains" are a confusing, alienating space. Natty Bumppo, remembering the sound of trees felled by the pioneers, comments bleakly, "I often think the Lord has placed this barren belt of Prairie, behind the states, to warn men to what their folly may yet bring to the land!" Searching for a way to structure narrative on flat land, Cooper anticipates W. H. Jackson's photographic solution: "Amid the monotonous rolling of the Prairies, a single, naked, and ragged rock arose . . ." – around which most of the novel takes place. But *The Prairie* also turns out to be no model for the philosophy of far-Western film. Its wagon-train pioneers are small-minded, criminal despoilers of the land, deserving their demise. And, although the Sioux warriors are invariably "crafty," Cooper can't resist giving old Natty one last, loyal Indian "friend," a Pawnee known as Hard-Heart.[8]

It would give our look into the pre-feature-era Western a symmetry could we find a writer to provide the far-Western film with the sort of narrative model that Cooper gave the eastern Western. However, the Plains Wars story type is not back in Wister or Zane Grey, nor to any significant degree in the dime novel, nor in Cooper's own anomalous far-Western. If we were forced to come up with one writer who regularly employed the Plains Wars narrative, it might be an ex-cavalryman named Charles King, but in novels not published until after 1883, and even these tend to use Indian wars as background to heavy romantic melodramas at the forts.[9] It becomes evident that the movie Western, as it developed production in the West, drew inspiration outside of literature, even of the pulp variety. It is hard to avoid the conclusion that the far-Western began to dramatize something more widely public, a cultural conversation put forward this time more as historical truth.

The most fully imagined alternative to Cooper – the one that disputes his characterization of Indians and then sets up large-scale racial battles as key to the American story – comes not in fiction but from nineteenth-century historians, first in Francis Parkman's career-long history of prerevolutionary conflicts among English, French, and Indians (published 1851–92), "the history of the American forest," as he called the works collected as *France and England in North America.*[10] Parkman retained his youthful love of Cooper's fiction but took issue with the novelist's Indians: "Cooper is responsible for the fathering of those aboriginal heroes, lovers, and sages, who have long formed a petty nuisance in our literature. . . . The long conversations which he puts into their mouths are as truthless as they are tiresome."[11] Unlike Cooper, Parkman had personally explored the prairies, emerging with *The Oregon Trail* (published 1849), a travel memoir whose first-person unreliability about Native Americans is unintentionally revealing. That Indian "children would scream in terror at the sight of me" is offered as evidence that "they knew nothing of the power and true character of the white men . . ." – this in a chapter following one entitled "Hunting Indians."[12] However much it is now clear that Parkman in his subsequent histories distorted his sources to downplay the skills and rationales of Native Americans, he is consistent for admiring them to the extent that they live up to what he takes to be the uncompromising brutality of the world. When Parkman says about the Sioux, "War is the breath of their nostrils," he is not unadmiring.[13] It is this vision of frontier space as a large-scale and violent battle to the death that the far-Western film adopts in place of Cooper's more genteel adventures.[14]

The first steps in converting this Plains Wars narrative into visuals were taken by late-nineteenth-century painters, notably Frederic Remington, and by Wild West shows, especially those produced by William F. "Buffalo Bill" Cody. Both promoted as the essential Western story an action melodrama of the U.S. Cavalry against horse-mounted tribes of whooping Indians. For both, of course, the central defining image came in Custer's "Last Stand," which Remington first painted at age fourteen, a few months after the June 1876 Little Bighorn battle, and which Buffalo Bill first produced as a live pageant in 1887 and revived through 1905.[15] When George Armstrong Custer himself went west with his brother Tom, he saw the land in the essentially pastoral terms taught by the lush landscape painters: "Tom and I sat on our horses as the view spread out before us, worthy of the brush of a Church, a Bierstadt. . . ."[16] But Custer's own story would be encapsulated through a distinctly different visual image of the West as a violent instant of irreconcilable races and heroic death. Remington painted his most elaborate *Last Stand* in 1890 (which evaded landscape this time by massing Custer's men over a hilltop), but Remington's version was surpassed in popularity by even larger-scale paintings that crowded every inch of canvases with desperate hand-to-hand fighting and scalped corpses.[17]

Rather than anything in Cooper on the one hand or ranching on the other, this seems to have been the narrative imagery behind the most distinctive films initially shot in the West. It's revealing that the Western, of the type that would win in Hollywood, found its origin more completely than any other film genre in something taken for public history. It may be for this reason that the Western has managed to be simultaneously the most retrograde and most contemporary of genres, in that it has found it easier than any other film genre to speak socially, to use civic debate within story formula. As a result the Hollywood Western could incorporate ideas – about politics, religion, philosophy – increasingly forbidden elsewhere in twentieth-century popular American entertainment (a subject we'll take up in Part Two).

The earliest Westerns shot in the West by D. W. Griffith seem finally to capitulate to the public terms of their time. To judge from those trade-paper pronouncements, the eastern Western had had its day, but the requested "change of background" was only the first and most obvious shift. Beyond their Plains Wars narratives, Griffith's far-Westerns also began to speak a more contemporary political discourse, illustrating a "strenuous life" logic propounded most loudly by Theodore Roosevelt. *Fighting Blood* (1911), for instance, shot in the grassy hills of Southern California's San Fernando Valley near Lookout Mountain, hints its tone in its title. A Civil War veteran commands his Dakota frontier cabin like a military compound, marshaling his nine children each morning for a rifle-shouldered marching drill and flag-raising ceremony (Figs. 6a, b). Chafing under the regulations, his eldest son is exiled and rides off, wiping a tear from his eye. Soon he comes across an (unexplained and unmotivated) "INDIAN OUTBREAK" – an attack by horse-mounted Sioux on another isolated log cabin – and is able to prove himself his father's son by shooting Indians with his six-gun during a covered-wagon chase and then by bringing back the cavalry in time to save his family's home (Figs. 6c, d). The relatively large-scale one-reeler is a little lesson in paternalism and patriotism. Father does know best about military preparedness, and the U.S. flag achieves an iconic status never previously seen in Griffith. This is a Teddy Roosevelt lesson, titled with two of TR's favorite words: "fighting" (the force that pushed the frontier westward) and "blood" (the Anglo-Saxon racial heritage that won the West).[18] Similarly, Griffith's *The Last Drop of Water* (1911), shot in nearby locations a month further into summer and emphasizing drier cactus flatlands, is a tale of wagon trains uniting "TO REPEL INDIAN ONSLAUGHTS" and ultimately saved by the flag-

**Figure 6.** *Fighting Blood* (1911): The regimented family (6a) raises the colors (6b). When Sioux attack, the cavalry rides to the rescue (6c), and the family salutes its heroic son (Bobby Harron, 6d).

waving cavalry. The human drama within this relative epic ends with the self-sacrificial atonement of an alcoholic known in the intertitles as "THE WEAKLING" – the word Roosevelt used as his universal damnation, from "weaklings" who failed in their "national duties" in the Philippines to a "weakling" reviewer who had the presumption to dismiss Roosevelt as a serious historian.[19]

Indeed, Theodore Roosevelt's major historical work, *The Winning of the West* (four volumes, published 1889–96), self-consciously picks up the West as a narrative of racial fighting where Francis Parkman left off the story in the 1760s. Like Parkman (to whom he dedicated this work), TR first explored the West to recover from a weak body and wounded spirit, also emerging with a travel memoir, *Hunting Trips of a Ranchman* (1885), before beginning those historical volumes, which take as their major theme "the eternal border warfare between the white men and the red" and where "The most ultimately righteous of all wars is a war with savages."[20]

# 7. The Politics of Landscape

I don't intend to blend with any landscape! I intend to fill it!
Errol Flynn in *Silver River* (1948)

If the first Western films drew from James Fenimore Cooper, then the next group, filmed in the West itself, drew its martial spirit from something offered up more ominously as historical truth, telling stories in which Native Americans were relegated to an undercharacterized horde. Still, both story patterns were available when filmmaking began. Why should Cooper have been a model from 1908 through 1910, only to lose out completely to the Plains Wars model from 1911 onward? It might be possible to fall back on some shift in "the spirit of America," perhaps relating filming in the Southwest to rumbles from the 1910 Mexican border revolution. But that's both evasive and unconvincing.

It is worth remembering that this was not the first such shift downward in sympathy for Native Americans within the histories of American popular arts. On stage, the "Indian play" had achieved popularity with Edwin Forrest's 1829 success as "King Philip" in *Metamora; or, The Last of the Wampanoags,* and "noble savages" remained the rule through the Civil War. Playwrights generally shifted to ennobling the white fighter against Indians in the 1870s, after Frank Mayo's 1872 success in *Davy Crockett* and of Buffalo Bill Cody's first onstage appearances the same year.[1] The dime novel too evolved in the decade after the Civil War away from characterizing Indian haters as "ugly" or "deranged" and toward representing Indian fighting as more heroic, less pathological.[2] In the changeover from eastern Westerns to far-Westerns, film history recapitulated more abruptly those shifts in the images of

Indians. For film, the additional issue is this: Why did that shift in Indian imagery accompany the shift in filming locations? It's worth trying to tease out an explanation.

Industry economics led filmmakers into new landscapes, partly for mundane reasons of weather, for variations in "background" unavailable to European competitors, and even in a few cases as escape from Patents Company investigators. But the new landscape itself brought complications. Recall that the first problem filmmakers faced in the West – and in Griffith's case never solved – was the old problem for Europeans that the land appeared too "empty": too bright and too white, too flat and too featureless. The eastern land itself had been able to provide an enveloping focus under the aesthetics of eastern painters. In Thomas Cole's two paintings of *The Last of the Mohicans* – titled *Cora Kneeling at the Feet of Tamenund* and *The Death of Cora* – tiny human figures are virtually lost within lush forests and towering rocks.[3] This was not an aesthetic solution available for the West, whose spaces traditionally brought a disquiet alleviated only when its landscape was filled. For a painter such as Remington, the western landscape is finally effaced entirely by foregrounded humans. For D. W. Griffith, the production move west seems to have accelerated his experiments in closer views of actors, both facial close-ups and full-body shots newly cut off at the knees, thus not incidentally allowing actors to fill more of the frame than they had in eastern Westerns. When Errol Flynn shouts the line used as the epigraph above – "I don't intend to blend with any landscape! I intend to fill it!" – he only exaggerates the key visual principle of the Western as it comes to be invented in the West: To fill the land is the heroic role. That logic reaches its unintentionally gruesome culmination in the choral hosannas over a montage of L.A. freeways, already car-clogged, at the end of *How the West Was Won* (1962).

American pioneers had always had a stake in seeing the land as empty, even in the East. James Fenimore Cooper's father, William Cooper, in his 1807 memoir *A Guide in the Wilderness* offers an evocative account of his first view in 1785 of the wild land in New York that he would eventually tame into the city of Cooperstown: "I was alone three hundred miles from home, without bread, meat, or food of any kind; fire and fishing tackle were my only means of subsistence. . . . I laid me down to sleep in my watch-coat, nothing but the melancholy Wilderness around me."[4] But, as Alan Taylor documents, this Adamic vision of the empty land cannily erases evidence of several prior communities and a tangle of legal claimants, including the cabins of hunters, a Lutheran utopian settlement, and a school run by a Christianized Mohawk.[5] (It's part of *The Pioneers'* complexity to bring back these claimants to the same land: Natty speaking for the hunters, Chingachgook for the Indians.) As late as the 1870s, the survey team for which William Henry Jackson took photographs regularly encountered free Native Americans and was once attacked by a Ute tribe; but his photographs presented to eastern viewers a space in which the only evidence of habitation are ancient Anasazi ruins, and even those framed as tiny curiosities in the vast lands.[6]

This is the politics of space: Empty land is there for the taking. That argument had, of course, been made about the West for centuries. William Cooper's guidebook and W. H. Jackson's photographs are only two of the more revealing moments between, say, Thomas Jefferson's late-eighteenth-century view of the West as the place available to relieve the pressure of urban problems and John C. Van Dyke's early-twentieth-century paean to the "immense wilderness of space" in the "barren" desert.[7] But what was new in the twentieth century is that this old argument could finally be fleshed out through the invention of the movies, which brought the technology to visualize the "blankness" of the land *and* to dramatize the human action needed to fill it.

When early filmmakers arrived in the desert West, the disquietingly empty space seems itself to have suggested a plot line new to the movies but with a historical heritage: a plot line that sets two races, Indian and white, both depicted as equally nomadic, on horses or in wagons, contending for the open space. Political discourse by this time made it evident to all but "weaklings" that even empty space was not strictly there for the taking but would require "fighting."

The pre-feature-length Westerns of 1908–13 were set in two quite different landscapes of the East and the West, and those landscapes brought two starkly different narratives, even to the same filmmaker, D. W. Griffith. It is logical enough to imagine a filmmaker, then as now, writing a story and then searching out locations on which to shoot it – and in individual cases this was no doubt the way things worked. However, everything about the overall history of the first years of the Western film argues something like the reverse: The land preceded the story. Eastern landscape asked for one sort of story while western landscape demanded quite another.

There is no doubt something heartening in this about the enduring power of the land itself. And yet in this early evolution of the film Western – especially in the way that Native Americans vanish as distinct individual characters – it's hard not to see the first step in the genre's long history of ethical retreats.

# 8. Pocahontas Meets Custer: *The Invaders*

IF MY DAUGHTER IS HERE, LET HER SPEAK.
Chief of the Sioux in *The Invaders* (1912)

We have thus far looked broadly at the shifts of landscape and narrative in the early history of the Western. In practice, a number of eastern-shot films anticipate traits of the far-Western, just as a few eastern-Western styles and attitudes linger for a time in the productions of the West. In many ways, these holdovers and exceptions are the most complex and compelling films of the era.

Griffith's *The Redman's View* (1909), for instance, shot in New York State, is a grimly unrelenting tale that anticipates certain Plains Wars styles, especially in its rocky, windswept landscapes. The trick involved shooting high on Mount Beacon, above the Hudson River valley, in November, achieving a bleakness of location that Griffith and Bitzer wouldn't duplicate until moving into the desert West. As in films shot in the West, land possession is played as a racial dispute, here schematically dramatized with broad gestures and settled by the threat of unfired guns (Fig. 7a). The film reveals its eastern origins in its relatively individualized Indians – who have their romances and family conflicts – set against white men identified only as "THE CONQUERORS." At gunpoint, the Indians (Southern Plains Kiowas, according to the film's publicity) are set on "THE EXODUS – THE LONG TREK," walking or riding in travois across wide, treeless lands and wrapped in blankets against the evident chill. "IS THERE NO LAND WHERE WE MAY REST OUR HEADS," asks an intertitle (Fig. 7b), answered in the negative by another group of armed pioneers. The film's title works out to mean "The Red Man's Point of View," and for all the film's difficulty in making drama from a long, passive march, there's nothing like *The Redman's View* in Hollywood until John Ford's *Cheyenne Autumn* more than fifty years later.

From the reverse angle, several of the very early California films shot by Fred Balshofer for Bison beginning in late 1909 retain eastern styles, particularly after the company evaded Patents Company lawyers by moving location work from L.A.'s Griffith Park into then-remote San Bernardino mountains around Big Bear Lake, a wooded enclave that lent itself to canoe chases and adventure stories like *Little Dove's Romance* (1911), in which Indians and whites unite when an Indian guide turns murderously jealous.[1]

Throughout the history of the Western, the most fascinating films find their dynamism by balancing between cultural moments, by transforming their era's conflicts into apparently assured narrative. (In Part Three, we'll look into the resulting fragile optimism of even the classic Western.) One fascination of *The Invaders,* a three-reel Western from 1912, is that although it was filmed on the West Coast and relies on the shift into the Plains Wars narrative, it complicates its argument by retaining certain older and eastern patterns. Even with its straightforward visual style, it manages to dramatize quite complexly the conflicts and guilts of American history. The result is arguably the first great Western, with qualities D. W. Griffith never approached in the genre on either coast. Especially because *The Invaders* is also one of the few early non-Griffith Westerns available on DVD, it makes a useful point to pause in more detail over the traits of the early Western.

*The Invaders* is quite the epic for its era. At three reels, or about forty minutes, its length was matched among Westerns at its release in November 1912 only by *Custer's Last Fight* of the month before and by a *Life of Buffalo Bill* in June of that year. Both *Custer's Last Fight* and *The Invaders* were produced by Thomas Ince and probably directed by Francis Ford (who plays Custer in the earlier film and commandant of the cavalry fort in *The Invaders*), although Ince was credited publicly with direction as well.[2]

Thomas Ince had arrived west in late 1911, hired by the New York Motion Picture Company to take over production of their Bison Westerns, which, notwithstanding the woodsy locations, had been staged

**Figure 7.** The forced "exodus" in *The Redman's View* (1909).

by Fred Balshofer unimaginatively, to judge from surviving examples. Ince's own earlier films from 1911 also look relatively crude, and their production with Mary Pickford in Cuba, to escape the Patents Company, could hardly have been smooth. In the West, he seems immediately to have chosen harsher, more obviously western locales than Balshofer: flatlands, sand dunes, and cactus vegetation. Only one of Ince's twenty Bison films – *The Empty Water Keg* (1912) – is known to survive from before someone hit upon the idea of hiring a large contingent from "The Miller Brothers 101 Ranch Real Wild West Show," based in Oklahoma but on tour in California. The New York Motion Picture Company already leased twenty-eight square miles above Santa Monica, and its small canyons and rolling grasslands made for a location – soon known familiarly as "Inceville" – that could pass for the Dakotas when the camera was pointed away from the surf.[3] Ince's first narrative film with the 101 Ranch, the two-reel *War on the Plains* (1912), so naïvely relishes access to the new crew and equipment that his camera cannot resist clumsily panning back and forth across the wagon train into town, returning to the seven oxen wagons and forty horse-mounted pioneers herding longhorn cattle. By the film's midpoint, the 101 Ranch's other key asset has been put on display: Oglala Sioux who encircle and attack the wagons.[4] (Ince had to sign a separate contract with the Commissioner of Indian Affairs to hire these fifty-or-so Sioux, from the Pine Ridge Reservation in South Dakota, who were wards of the government before the 1924 Indian Citizenship Act.)[5]

By the time of *The Invaders,* ten months and about forty Westerns later, Ince had promoted his regular lead actor, Francis Ford, to director on many of the films. Ford had greater experience than Ince with West-

And in consideration
of the above lands being
ceded to the United States,
the said Government
will forbid the settle-
ment of the remaining
tribal lands of the
Sioux nation.

**Figure 8.** A treaty between the Sioux nation and the United States at the opening of *The Invaders* (1912).

erns, having acted and directed for the Méliès Company in Texas.[6] If Ince notoriously claimed personal credit for films directed by Francis Ford and others among his growing staff of directors, it is nevertheless true that Ince deserves as much credit as anyone for inventing Hollywood's producer-centered system that organized filmmaking around preproduction scripts, which soon came from his office with the following ominously polite caution: "It is earnestly requested by Mr. Ince that no change of any nature be made in the scenario either by elimination of any scenes or the addition of any scenes or changing any of the action as described, or titles, without first consulting him."[7] The irony is that to the extent that Ince regimented filmmaking, he proved that no individual was essential to the process, a logic that came to include producers as well. The intimate, single-producer studio would itself barely survive within Hollywood, which may help explain why Ince's own distinctive productions came early, beginning with these 1912 Westerns and arguably peaking in 1914, a decade before his early death, with such gritty, unconventional features as *The Bargain* and *The Italian.*

*The Invaders* is deceptively complex right from its title, which seems evidently to refer to the tribes of Indians who will attack and torture the whites. As the film progresses, however, the title begins more to refer to the whites themselves, after surveyors for the transcontinental railroad break the settled peace of a treaty. Similarly, the title of Ince's (and Francis Ford's) earlier *The Indian Massacre* (1912) had relied for its double edge on English syntactic ambiguity: Assumptions that "Indian" must be an adjective (massacre *by* Indians) are undercut halfway through the film by recognition that the word can be an object as well

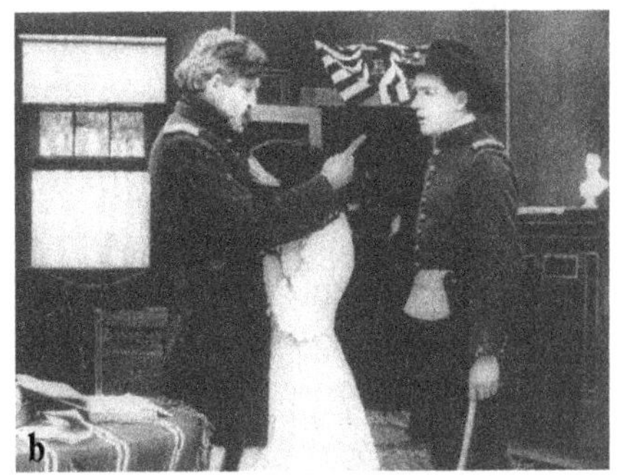

**Figure 9.** *The Invaders:* Fathers, daughters, and suitors within the Sioux band (9a) and the cavalry outpost (9b).

(massacre *of* Indians). (Native American novelist Sherman Alexie slyly reverses this trick for his 1996 novel *The Indian Killer.*) "The invaders," as we might have guessed had we thought about it, would not necessarily be those already living on the land.

In outline, the plot of *The Invaders* looks like a draft for Francis Ford's younger brother John Ford's *Fort Apache* (1948). (John was still in high school at the time of *The Invaders;* in *Fort Apache,* Francis can be glimpsed playing a grizzled bartender.) The Plains Wars adversaries in *The Invaders* are the U.S. Cavalry, based at fictional "Fort Reid" in the Dakotas' Platte River country, set against the Sioux and eventually the Cheyenne. The treaty signed with formal handshakes and apparent mutual trust in the first scene grants "the Sioux nation" exclusive sovereignty to a limited territory in exchange for ceding other lands to the U.S. government (Fig. 8). A year later the commandant has a troubled conference with his subordinates after receiving an order to provide "military escort" to the railroad surveyors through this land. The Sioux chiefs return to the fort to lodge a complaint and leave shaking fists at the commandant's overelaborate explanation. They ride to the Cheyenne's valley to make an alliance against the white invaders of their lands.

Interwoven into this broad historical conflict are a pair of parental stories. Both the cavalry commandant and the main Sioux chief have a daughter, and each father must reluctantly approve her suitor (Fig. 9). One link between the historical and parental tales is the action of a surveyor (who has laughed off cavalry protection), who spies the chief's daughter, Sky Star, through his theodolite and strikes up a brief romance with her – to the jealous anger of her Sioux suitor.

In the ensuing battle, the surveyors will be flayed over boulders and a large contingent of the Seventh Cavalry will be surrounded and massacred, but those within "THE DEPLETED POST" will survive because of warning provided them by the chief's daughter. Injured in a fall while riding to give the warning, she is nursed by the commandant's daughter. Sky Star's presence in the fort allows the commandant to conduct through its walls diversionary negotiation with the chief over this apparent hostage from his family, although she dies of her wounds while they negotiate. The delay allows time for Lieutenant White, the fiancé of the commandant's daughter, to ride back with reinforcements who rout the Indians.

As a tale, this is ordinary enough. If it plays out in compelling ways, it's partly because the little romantic and family dramas never overtake the sweep of historical forces and the prominence of the land. The film seems powered paradoxically by an old-fashioned style, even for 1912.

The trade-paper response to Ince's first Western with the 101 Ranch outfit, *War on the Plains,* had been enthusiastic. *Moving Picture World* rhapsodized "that here we have looked upon a presentation of western life that is real and that is true to the life, and that we would like to see again and again. . . ."[8] They got their wish. *The Invaders* is an elaboration on the same Plains Wars motifs on the same locations from most of the same cast and crew, and it received equally strong reviews: "an intense photodrama that is artistically satisfying from the beginning," with "exceptionally fine ensembles" of actors.[9] What was new in the praise for Ince – over, say, that trade-paper enthusiasm about Griffith's first eastern Western, *The Redman and the Child* – was the sense that Ince had hit upon something "real": "We have had plenty even of the Fenimore Cooper style of Western drama, based on fact, no doubt, but lurid, highly colored and imaginative to a degree. It marks a distinct step in advance when a manufacturer sees his mistakes and now sets forth to present to the public the great West as it really was and is."[10]

It is tempting to write off this enduring critical impression that Ince's Westerns remain "authentic" under the same terms that Brian Dippie has used to explain how various "Custer's Last Stand" paintings were praised as authentic in the late nineteenth century: "since another tenet of western art holds that truth depends on getting the details right, however preposterous the basic conception."[11] Unlike any other film genre, the Western would regularly be judged under such standards of the authenticity of details, and before long Westerns took to making explicit claims like that in the opening titles of John Ford's transcontinental railroad epic *The Iron Horse* (1924) to be "accurate and faithful in every particular of fact and atmosphere. . . ." One way of looking into *The Invaders* is to explore what sort of "authenticity" initial audiences could have seen in it, and what sort of validity, if any, it might still claim.

What first led audiences and critics to see "authenticity" in *The Invaders* and other Ince Westerns seems to have been their reliance on the formula of the Wild West show, best known then and now through "Buffalo Bill's Wild West." Buffalo Bill Cody himself refused to diminish his productions by adding "Show" to his title; what he claimed to offer was a sample of the genuine old West itself, contained safely within arenas, authenticated by his very presence and by occasional guest stars, such as Sitting Bull for a tour in 1885 and then by the Sioux survivors of the Wounded Knee massacre for a season in 1891–2. The Wild West shows brought together elements of the circus (P. T. Barnum had staged a "Grand Buffalo Hunt" in Hoboken, New Jersey, as early as 1843) with rudimentary bits of Western stageplay plotting, so that a Wild West show would typically feature horse races and roping tricks but also end with some narrativized "Hunt on the Plains" complete with a battle against Indians. It was apparently too much even for Buffalo Bill to have had Sitting Bull impersonate himself in "Custer's Last Fight," the popular climactic act Cody waited to introduce until two seasons after Sitting Bull left (although Robert Altman's *Buffalo Bill and the Indians* [1976] plausibly imagines Buffalo Bill trying to persuade Sitting Bull to inaugurate the reenactment). The outfit that appears as actors in *The Invaders,* "The Miller Brothers 101 Ranch Real Wild West Show," was among Buffalo Bill's competitors, and he performed with them for a season in 1916 near the end of his life.[12] The original Wild West shows were presumably not as kitschy as later Hollywood representations (see 1944's *Buffalo Bill,* especially for its "Cheyenne courting blanket"), but neither do they appear particularly authentic in kinetoscope actualities such as *Parade of Buffalo Bill's Wild West Show* (1898) nor in Cody's own later film documents, such as *Buffalo Bill's Wild West and Pawnee Bill's Far East* (1910), which underlines the circus atmosphere by placing horses and Indians alongside elephants and French Zouave marchers. Nothing still visible on film accounts for a reaction like Mark Twain's to Buffalo Bill's Wild West:

> It brought vividly back the breezy, wild life of the great plains and the Rocky Mountains, and stirred me like a war song. Down to its smallest details, the show is genuine – cowboys, vaqueros, Indians, stage coach, costumes, and all; . . . it is wholly free from sham and insincerity and the effects it produced upon me by its spectacles were identical with those wrought upon me a long time ago by the same spectacles on the frontier.[13]

Certainly Mark Twain would have known western authenticity when he saw it, but the euphoric tone of his comment bears comparison with his deflating comic sourness about the West in *Roughing It* (1872), based mainly on his 1861 stagecoach trip to Nevada and then on to California. Even for those with memory of the "Old" West, the Wild West shows offered a nostalgia-tinged "authenticity."

What Buffalo Bill was unable to do, despite several attempts between 1912 and 1914, was to carry this successful formula into film. In Cody's own production of a three-reel *The Life of Buffalo Bill* (1912), the camera keeps distant and characterization is absent. The large cast and Native American performers are undercut by such details as a tipi with "CHIEF" painted on it in English, suggesting how much of the production was imported directly from the props of Buffalo Bill's Wild West show. Cody rides in at the film's opening to "DREAM OF THE DAYS OF HIS YOUTH," after which he is impersonated by a younger actor in three episodes, ending with "THE FAMOUS DUEL BETWEEN CHIEF YELLOW HAND AND BUFFALO BILL WHICH PREVENTED THE CHEYENNE FROM JOINING THE SIOUX" at Little Bighorn. When Buffalo Bill takes "THE FIRST SCALP FOR CUSTER," the real Cody "AWAKENS FROM HIS DREAM," a clever cover for the film's large distortions of history.[14] It was left to Thomas Ince to transform the Plains Wars formula into convincing filmmaking. Ince openly borrowed from Buffalo Bill's Wild West pageant in the 1912 film of *Custer's Last Fight,* as well as in obvious impersonations of Buffalo Bill Cody himself in other Ince films: *Blazing the Trail* (1912, where the long-haired, goateed figure in tasseled buckskin shoots the buffalo that precipitates the battle with Indians), *War on the Plains,* and *The Indian Massacre* (where the Buffalo Bill figure leads wagon trains) – this impersonation despite Cody winning a 1911 lawsuit against the independent Yankee Film Company that led the

New York Supreme Court to rule that "Buffalo Bill has a sort of copyright on goatees of the peculiar form and color that adorn his chin."[15]

What all of this perhaps only reminds us is that the "real" owes everything to established convention, no less here than in those lush early paintings of the Southwest.[16] In at least one way, however, *The Invaders* is demonstrably more authentic than any surviving Western that I know of before it and almost all of them since. This comes from the way it uses its Oglala Sioux performers, who play all the Indian roles with the exception of the chief's daughter. Wild West shows had made a point of employing Native Americans as part of their appeal to authenticity. Such casting had become a film trade-paper issue too, especially as the camera began to move closer to actors. *Moving Picture World* in 1910 claimed that "The public is no longer satisfied with white men who attempt to represent Indian life. The actors must be real Indians and the acting thus becomes exceedingly realistic. This represents the change in the ideas of the public and the methods of the producing companies."[17] Filmmakers complained that this was easier said than done. Later in 1910 future cowboy star Tom Mix wrote back to his boss William Selig in Chicago that all the Indians he could find in California didn't "look" like Indians and had short hair.[18] To a certain extent, *The Invaders* solved this problem by casting Sioux, who like other Plains tribes "looked like Indians" to white audiences – including, no doubt, Mark Twain, whose "nausea" over "Goshoot" Indians (Gosuite/Shoshone) in *Roughing It* seems to arise from their failure to match the image he finally found incarnated in Buffalo Bill's Wild West.[19] Such conventions came not only through the models for U.S. coins and the performers in Wild West shows themselves but also through the almost exclusive focus of public debate and government policy on relations with Plains tribes, at least since the 1864 Sand Creek massacre of Cheyenne.[20] By the 1910s, even the children of the far-Western American Indians so despised by Twain had themselves begun adopting Plains tribal clothing.[21] The result of this homogenization of "the Indian" image seems to have been that Native Americans actors from eastern tribes had film careers that ended early (such as Elijah Tahamont [Algonquian] or James Young Deer [Winnebago]) while others who "looked Indian" had long Hollywood employment (most famously the Italian-American "Iron Eyes Cody," born Oscar DeCorti).[22]

Beyond the curious issue of whether Native Americans look like Indians, one of the things that distinguishes *The Invaders* from *The Life of Buffalo Bill* and even from other Ince films is the time that it spends creating individual characterizations among the Sioux. There is the slightly pushy suitor (seen in close-up in Fig. 15a) who assumes too easily that his gift of four horses will win Sky Star's devotion and who inserts himself forward too insistently in meetings with the Cheyenne and the cavalry until he has to be elbowed back into the group by the chief. At the news that the surveyors have invaded Sioux lands, the chief himself displays a moment of initial disbelief, grasping his informant's vest, and then neatly underplays an inward-gazing despair before he gestures about the white-man's writing and then reenters his tipi to seek out the tattered treaty, looking it over again as if some clause had escaped him or been mistranslated by the Sioux in a felt hat who interprets English for him. None of the actors in *The Invaders* are credited onscreen, and those playing the key roles of the suitor and the chief remain unidentified. (The chief has sometimes been misidentified as William Eagleshirt, the Sioux lead in other Ince Westerns.) Among the group at consultations in the Sioux camp can be glimpsed Luther Standing Bear, playing one of the lesser chiefs. Standing Bear's later autobiographical histories – *My People the Sioux* (1928), *My Indian Boyhood* (1931), and *Land of the Spotted Eagle* (1933) – increasingly make the case that the landscape of the West was never "empty."[23] His life story reinforces how close in time is *The Invaders* to the history it interprets. Only thirty-six years, after all, had elapsed since the defeat of Custer's Seventh Cavalry by another alliance of Sioux and Cheyenne – that obsessively reimagined moment in 1876 that *The Invaders* clearly intends to evoke in the enactment of its Seventh Cavalry massacre. Luther Standing Bear – who was about eight when his father returned from the battle to tell him in subdued tones of victory over "Long Hair" Custer – had learned buffalo hunting from his father but was also in the first class to be indoctrinated into assimilation at the English-only Carlisle (Pennsylvania) Indian Industrial School, where he gave up his earliest name, Plenty-Kill, and chose "Luther" from a list on the blackboard.[24]

He and the other Sioux performers in *The Invaders* all rely on relatively restrained gestures carried through the full body. As silent-film actors, they tend to flow their signs of meaning cohesively into one another, whereas the white actors will tend to break their expressions of meaning into separate, more hieroglyphic gestures, conveyed primarily through the hands and face. The Sioux suitor will make, for instance, three swinging arm gestures, shoulder dips, and head nods to signify the importance of his gift of horses to both father and daughter; compare Francis Ford as the commandant, who points separately at his daughter and then at the lieutenant to signify his acceptance of their engagement. The tendency of the Indian actors to play gesturally smaller led Ince to complain that one of his challenges was to work them into sufficient anger against the whites for it to register onscreen,[25] and it is true that grander gestures, such as the one where the chief shakes his fist at the commandant, appear awkward, badly timed, and obviously "directed." But their restraint in expression makes the Sioux's acting style read now as quite modern, more "authentic" by later conventions. The apparently curious casting of Japanese actor Sessue Hayakawa as the Sioux son of William Eagleshirt in Ince's *The Last of the Line* (1914) makes certain sense in these terms, for Hayakawa's acting was notably more subtle and modern than those against whom he was cast (as evident especially in Cecil B. De Mille's 1915 *The Cheat*). It was probably Eagleshirt who evoked rare trade-paper praise for an unnamed Native American actor among Ince's ensemble:

> One of the Indians of the company – he enacts the part of the chief – is a star actor. His gestures and movements are a source of perpetual study. The directors have apparently let Lo play his own role and he does it to perfection. The chief is quite as good in comedy as tragedy – a delight in one and impressive in the other.

("Lo" was common journalistic shorthand for an Indian, from Pope's "Lo! The poor Indian. . . .")[26]

Any authenticity that can still be located in early Westerns tends to be merely visual, although that is not insignificant in silent film. It may come down to the costumes or the props, often enough left over from years before, but also to something even more impossible to verify now, something that can be seen in *The Invaders* in, say, the way a Sioux extra swings into an effortless bareback gallop when he rides to contest the treaty violations, or in the way another extra, playing a Cheyenne, does a little hunched run that is also a war dance after the pact between the tribes is concluded. Beyond such unverifiable gestural instants, a search for authenticity in the Western is doomed, if only because the pioneers' West was such a hodgepodge of objects hauled from everywhere else, just as the culture of the American West as a whole remains a patchwork of imported notions. What must then be

**Figure 10.** *The Invaders:* The chief's daughter, Sky Star, at home in the landscape (10a) and later witnessing the massacre of the surveyors (10b).

implied behind such paeans as Mark Twain's to the "genuine" reality of such blatantly theatrical pageants as the Wild West show is that it is the West *itself* that is authentic, versus existentially inauthentic life lived elsewhere. It's this sense of the West as the locale where authenticity innately resides that lingers even in more contemporary nature writers, as when Edward Abbey escapes the cities in order to locate "The shock of the real" through Utah's rock arches.[27]

Landscape is the reality that *The Invaders* has over Buffalo Bill's shows. By its use of the far-Western land, *The Invaders* generally argues another variation on the visual politics we traced in Griffith. Bright and wide landscapes are set up as empty spaces that must be filled by racial battles. For instance, in the first of a pair of prospect shots, the chief's daughter, Sky Star, is seen wandering high on a mountainside picking wildflowers, doing nothing more – and nothing less – than relishing the open space, most of the frame filled by the treeless hills below her (Fig. 10a). By the time we see her again in a similar shot, it is as witness to the massacre of the surveyors far below (Fig. 10b). But Ince and Francis Ford complicate this spatial argument by also cleverly deploying Inceville lands in "eastern" ways, especially by artificially creating a small lake and then carefully framing it to imply surrounding woodlands.[28] The shot seen in Figure 11 brings back the narrative philosophy of the eastern Western: Sky Star's tranquil canoeing introduces a pastoral world before the breaking of the treaty. *The Invaders* can visually allude to the pastoralism of the eastern Western, but it will not be able to reestablish this spirit at its end.

As early French film historian Jean Mitry was the first to argue, writing from memory of the films before most of them had been lost,

**Figure 11.** Sky Star (Anna Little) peacefully canoeing at the opening of *The Invaders.*

Ince's aesthetic was distinctly antitheatrical – based less on plot than in image and landscape – notwithstanding Ince's personal background, like Griffith's, as an actor in touring theatrical stock companies. When Mitry refers to Ince films as authentic – "a kind of 'dramatization' of the real" – he does so to stress their "concrete" and "understated" qualities.[29] The battle scenes of *The Invaders* are much more slowly cut than Griffith's far-Westerns and with none of his intercut close-ups to details of hand-to-hand fighting. The result is less coherent – it's often impossible to follow what's happening in the cavalry battle even in the excellent surviving print – but nevertheless more convincing in a documentary sense. The swirling dust gives the Custer-inspired images the immediacy of battle chaos, reinforced even by a camera operator who pans and back and forth seeking some center to the confused action.

The style of *The Invaders* is archaic even for 1912, but that may not be to its discredit, partly (as I've suggested) because of the way the Western film genre devolved ethically in its move west and partly (as

I'll discuss later in this chapter) because of the way the distanced style of *The Invaders* itself makes an argument about the determining role of environment and historical forces over the individual heroics that came to dominate Hollywood. The sequence where the surveyor first spies Sky Star (Fig. 12) relies on the obsessively repeated film grammar of turn-of-the-century Peeping Tom films, such as *As Seen through a Telescope* (1900). The slow cutting and lack of intercut close-ups in the action sequences bring back the long-distance documentary style of a film like *Western Stage Coach Hold Up* (1904).

*The Invaders* is in a primitive tradition too in the sense that Westerns can seem authentic to the extent they are without evident "art." In this, Ince's film is far from Griffith's and closer to a much more independent early-Western film-production practice represented especially in the fascinating films starring and produced by Al Jennings or Nell Shipman. For instance, Jennings's six-reel *The Lady of the Dugout* (1918) gets its authenticity not from its mere overt claim to be "based on absolute facts" of Jennings's curious career (a former outlaw and bank robber, he eventually ran for governor of Oklahoma, the state that had put a bounty on his head). Rather its thoroughly convincing archaic authenticity comes from the way the windswept lands and rough settings reinforce the film's story of a starving family who live in the half-underground sod house of the title, and the way the West becomes a place of failures and abandoned towns – both of which must owe something to director W. S. Van Dyke, nephew of *The Desert*'s author John C. Van Dyke. True, one can carry only so far the argument that film artlessness plays as authenticity. Inept staging and rudimentary editing in Nell Shipman's two-reel *Trail of the North Wind* (1923) undercut the conviction of a bear-trap sequence shot in a genuine blizzard. If Jennings and Shipman are the regional dead-ends in independent silent Westerns, it's also because the "real" was never an industry goal. "The Western picture seems a constant temptation to 'realism' of a most undesirable variety," warned *Moving Picture World* in 1911; the filmmakers "give us too close a view of 'hold-ups,' hangings, lynchings, massacres. . . ."[30]

As a story about the U.S. Cavalry, *The Invaders* makes a larger claim to historical authenticity than, say, a film about rambunctious ranch

**Figure 12.** *The Invaders:* The railroad surveyor spots Sky Star through his theodolite.

hands. The problem it faces is more familiar through John Ford's loose "cavalry trilogy": *Fort Apache* (1948), *She Wore a Yellow Ribbon* (1949), and *Rio Grande* (1950). In using the cavalry to allegorize an ideal of community in a hostile world, John Ford can't avoid implying that he is offering up historical truth. In asserting what the cavalry spirit should have been, that is, he can't help implying that that's how it was. On this level, Francis Ford was more authentic than his younger brother, despite the simplifications of *The Invaders* and to some extent because of them. Although the 1912 film doesn't include any historical head titles of the sort that would later become routine, it is evidently set just after the Civil War, around 1866, when the Union Pacific railroad was surveying through the Black Hills and other Sioux and Cheyenne territory. *The Invaders* omits the portrait of President Grant that decorates the commandants' offices in other Ince Westerns of 1912, such as *The Post Telegrapher,* and that sets those films somewhat later, in the 1870s. Various earlier treaties, notably one at Fort Laramie in 1851, had created the kind of agreement signed in the first scene of *The Invaders* that allowed for army posts and a few roads in exchange for forbidding further settlement in Sioux lands.[31] The isolated survey crews for the Union Pacific through the Platte Valley would probably not so easily have laughed off army protection, especially around the time of the "Fetterman massacre" (as it was known in newspapers) or the "Battle of the Hundred Slain" (as it was known among the Sioux). This most famous of cavalry disasters before Custer – in which Captain Fetterman and his troops died at the hands of Sioux and Cheyenne in December 1866 – comes closest to the representation in *The Invaders:* The death of a small party (woodcutters, in the Fetterman case) draws out cavalry troops who are themselves surrounded and killed, leaving the depleted fort and its commandant to be besieged.[32]

This historical conflict is represented starkly in *The Invaders* with fairly anonymous scenes of smoke signals and Indians burning telegraph poles. Compared to later Hollywood versions something seems missing, but it is something that makes the film more powerful. What is missing essentially are the scapegoats that later Westerns will use to individualize conflict between Native Americans and whites. The money-grubbing gun runner, the predatory Indian agent, the gold-mad Black Hills miner, the book-learned West Point officer untried in the ways of the West: Such figures represent historical truths, but Hollywood will use them to tell stories of the Plains Wars where we need only ferret out individual "troublemakers" to prevent the wars that *The Invaders,* by omitting these figures, sees as ruled by larger historical forces and governmental decisions. One might place the blame in *The Invaders* on eastern capitalists except that they are so abstracted by the single message about the "transcontinental railroad" as to be indistinguishable from American progress generally. The film tends to adopt the historical point of view of the post–Civil War cavalry officer who, in letters home and later memoirs, typically cast himself as blameless, placed by a corrupt federal government in an impossible middle position between put-upon Indians and western business interests who wanted them swept out of the way. Observing the 1867 Medicine Lodge treaty, close in time and place to the one represented in *The Invaders,* Captain Albert Barnitz complained that the Cheyenne had little idea of what they were signing, and he predicted a war "in consequence of misunderstanding of the terms of the present and previous treaties."[33] The cavalry was, after all, also charged with *protecting* Indians from often abusive civilians, as melodramatized in another Ince Western, *Past Redemption* (1913), about illegal liquor sales. General George Crook would have been in command of the Department of the Platte at the time of the events represented in *The Invaders,* and his justification in his *Autobiography* is essentially the one adopted by the film: "The trouble with the army was that the Indians would confide in us as friends, and we had to witness this unjust treatment of them without the power to help them. Then when they were pushed beyond endurance and would go on the war path we had to fight when our sympathies were with the Indians."[34]

Due to John Ford's well-known cavalry trilogy, one tends to think of the cavalry as a constant throughout the Western genre. However, in the thirty years between the corporate conglomeration of Hollywood in the late 1910s and John Ford's trilogy in the late 1940s one can count on both hands the Westerns that center on the cavalry, if we exclude formulaic cavalry-to-the-rescue endings.[35] (The exceptions tend to cluster at the opening of World War II, using Custer to discuss military glory.) If evasions too reveal a genre's history, it is worth wondering why the cavalry was missing during the era when Indian slaughter became most routine on film. One might look for an answer historically, as in the self-image of the cavalry from General Crook. Although the army high command included rabid Indian haters like Generals Sherman and Sheridan, midlevel career cavalry officers who had closer contact wrote often of their admiration of Indian military skills and of the wrongs committed by whites. The Indian killing in U.S. history that comes closest to genocide came not from the cavalry but from civilians in Northern California unrestrained by the army.[36] The film Western genre as a whole seems to borrow enough from history to discover that the cavalry film is not at all the right vehicle for the sort of pro forma Indian slaughter of the Hollywood studio era. In an apparent exception such as 1941's *Saddlemates,* the soft-hearted cavalry has to be taught the hard truth of Indian treachery by tougher cowboys.

However much the U.S. Cavalry of the Plains was historically an unglamorous force whose ugly primary job was to harry Native Americans, films accepted the point of view of cavalry officers themselves, who saw the cavalry as the army's elite. That point of view, however, necessarily brought with it a topic that much occupied the cavalryman himself: the relations between whites and the Plains Indians. Cavalry films thus end up being vehicles to debate explicitly how so many Indians did "vanish," an issue taken for granted throughout most of the history of the Hollywood Western. Although the cavalry doesn't really make its appearance in the history of the Western until production moves to the West Coast, its presence paradoxically brings back a certain eastern-Western spirit. The answer to why the cavalry is largely missing for thirty years of the Western seem to be this: The cavalry brings with it uncomfortable topics that that the studio-era Hollywood Western generally wants to leave undiscussed. In one of the rare cavalry films of the 1930s, for instance, a fascinating B-Western called *The*

*End of the Trail* (1932), Tim McCoy plays a midlevel officer framed for gun running because he has been "unduly friendly toward the Indians"; he quits the army to go live with the Arapahos until returning as a peacemaker.

When the cavalry film returns with John Ford in the late 1940s it may be because these issues seem again worth discussing, as post–World War II Hollywood began its cycle about discrimination against Jews and African Americans. When the next, and apparently final, cycle of cavalry Westerns came in the late 1960s and early 1970s, it was again to discuss race, this time in the context of the Vietnam War, in the simple if horrifying way that *Soldier Blue* (1970) restages the 1864 Sand Creek massacre to evoke the 1968 My Lai massacre, or the emotionally powerful way *Little Big Man* (1970) reenacts the 1868 Washita River massacre, or the complex way that Robert Aldrich uses the cavalry in *Ulzana's Raid* (1972) to explore the institutionalization of a mindset that John Ford had seen as a pathological anomaly. (John Wayne's obsessive racism in Ford's *The Searchers* separates him even from other Indian fighters. That obsession is what bonds the cavalry in Aldrich's film.)

Beyond the scapegoats, something else seems missing from *The Invaders,* something that again paradoxically increases its power. The film has no individual center of interest. The commandant, the chief, his daughter, and her Sioux suitor are each onscreen for roughly ten minutes within the film's forty minutes. The surveyor, the commandant's daughter, and her fiancé appear for about six minutes each. Certainly none of the film's actors can be called its lead. Another likely reason that cavalry films vanished for thirty years is that the Hollywood Western came to focus on the lone gunman. When the cavalry returned in Westerns of the 1950s, it was also as a way to worry over what that decade called "the organization man" and over the loss of individualism within a hierarchical power structure, military standing in for civilian.[37] In *The Invaders* the lack of individual heroism results in a story that almost lacks heroism altogether, with the significant exception of the chief's daughter. Its story is set in motion by two pieces of paper – the treaty and the order to protect the surveyors – and both the cavalry and Indians seem pawns of impersonal historical forces, and are never close to mastering their fates.[38] If there is a power anywhere on view, it is that of the land itself, with broad sweeps of canyon hills that overwhelm the fighters and the swirling dust that obliterates their images.

**Figure 13.** The fort commandant (Francis Ford) shouting negotiations during the siege in *The Invaders.*

The argument *The Invaders* makes about history is the argument that Ince was making about film production itself: Individual heroics are less important than group action. No single individual is essential to the processes of history, just as no one is essential to the process of filmmaking. Ultimately, of course, the Hollywood industry would buy neither side of this argument. In filmmaking it soon settled on the star system, which regarded certain individuals as unique and irreplaceable. In its view of history, it would promote individual heroes. You couldn't have one without the other. There's quite a lot to be said for Ince's attempt to do without both.

By its end, *The Invaders* is the story of a siege. "THE DEPLETED POST" is surrounded by massed Sioux and Cheyenne. Isolated after their telegraph line is cut, the soldiers fire cannons through the fort's log walls as the commandant barks orders and the Indians outside circle closer on horseback and foot (Fig. 13). This siege image is as fundamental in the far-Western (in "Custer's Last Stand" paintings but also in less historically specific ones such as Remington's *Fight for the Waterhole* [1903]) as it was in the East. James Fenimore Cooper had organized sieges around a "block-house" (*The Pathfinder*), a lake-surrounded "castle" (*The Deerslayer*), or "rock" (*The Prairie*). The commander of a besieged fort is typically the father of a daughter (played on film by such unlikely pioneers as Joan Crawford in *Winners of the Wilderness* [1927] and Shirley Temple in *Fort Apache*). "All that you see here, claim alike to be my children," explains Colonel Munro in Cooper's *The Last of the*

*Mohicans,* alluding to his two daughters while expanding his responsibility.[39]

This paternal role brings the commandant a further responsibility emphasized by the only close-up shot in *The Invaders:* Before the Indians breach the walls of the fort, he must prepare to put his last remaining bullet into his daughter's head (Fig. 14a). Far from being an unwilling victim, she kneels, pleads, and reaches up to nestle his gunbarrel to her temple (Fig. 14b). Although I know of no surviving Western films before 1912 that rely on this fate-worse-than-death tradition, it was a widely enough established convention through fiction and stageplays to be comprehensible without intertitles. Griffith could rely on it earlier in 1912 for the title of his contemporary pirate tale *The Lesser Evil,* in which a captain fights his drunken crew away from Blanche Sweet ("ONE BULLET LEFT – SHE WOULD CHOOSE THE LESSER EVIL," explains an intertitle), and again in 1913 in *The Battle at Elderbush Gulch* when an anonymous hand points its six-gun at Lillian Gish's head just before the cavalry arrives. The folk wisdom behind this choice goes back at least to "King Philip's War" in seventeenth-century New England,[40] but in the film Western it doesn't seem to have been dramatized until production moved west and into the tales of the Plains Wars. The tradition could be said to have some authenticity, if a history of fears can be so labeled. Besieged by Sioux and Crows on the Plains in 1867, an Army wife wrote in her diary that the women had "decided that if the Ft could not be held then we preferred to be shot by our own officers rather than to be taken captive."[41] The pattern becomes obsessive in Hollywood, as in the gentlemen's obliging guns that edge into close-up frames above praying female heads in *Stagecoach* and *Union Pacific* (both 1939). By 1950 James Stewart can give his troubled, clouded gaze at Shelley Winters during a siege in *Winchester '73* and have her take it from there: "I understand about the last one." As in *The Invaders,* these threats are all averted at the final instant (and only Shelley Winters has the chutzpah to demand a souvenir: "May I have it? You just never know when a girl might need a bullet"). It's another mark of *Ulzana's Raid*'s savage iconoclasm to have its Army officer follow through and shoot the woman. The apocalyptic end of the tradition must arrive in John Milius's post-Western *Red Dawn* (1984) when a teenaged girl begs for a bullet before the arrival of the "Reds" – Russian communists whose invasion has reached Arizona. Behind all but the last of these are fears less of unspeakable torture by savages

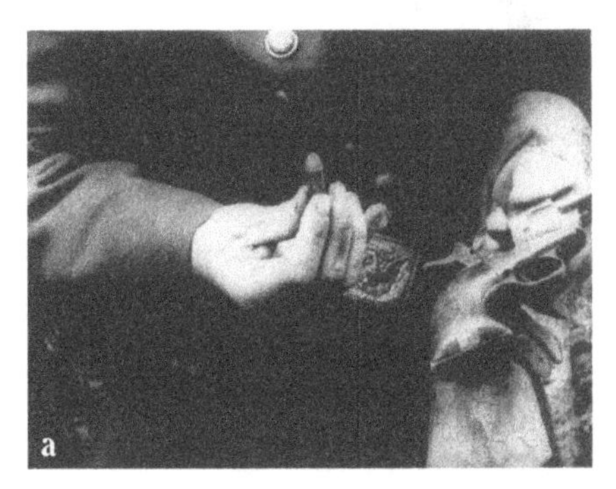

**Figure 14.** *The Invaders:* The commandant saving the last bullet for his daughter.

than of taboos about race mixing. Although legend has it that frontier men too saved bullets for themselves – including, if newspaper reports are to be believed, the last two soldiers in the Fetterman massacre[42] – the movie version almost exclusively concerned the white woman protected from the clutches of the red man.

When the sexes and races are reversed – the red woman and the white man – we arrive at a different fable, one also played out within the fort of *The Invaders*. The chief's daughter, Sky Star, turns out to be a Pocahontas: a young and beautiful Indian princess who through romance with a white man learns friendship with his community and acts to save it from the savagery of her people, even at the cost of her own life. As simple as the structure of *The Invaders* is, it gets some of its power by uniting the essential eastern-Western fable of self-sacrificial redemption with the essential far-Western fable of self-sacrificial redemption: Pocahontas meets Custer.

It took almost two hundred years for the idea of a romance with Captain John Smith to be added to the history of Pocahontas (ca. 1595–1617), the Powhatan chief's daughter whose 1614 marriage to Virginia planter John Rolfe was initially central to the retellings of her life, as the lost model for peaceful amalgamation of the races.[43] Movies followed the subsequent nineteenth-century versions of her life in which her romantic attraction, innocent and unconsummated, for Captain Smith leads Pocahontas to protect his community. Even the few exceptions in eastern-filmed Westerns in which the white man and chief's daughter do marry – such as James Young Deer's *White Fawn's Devotion* – prove tales of troubled unions. In *The Invaders* the couple is introduced through the film language of male voyeurism (see Fig. 12), but

**Figure 15.** *The Invaders:* Her Sioux suitor discovers Sky Star with the surveyor.

the chief's daughter strikes a balance between innocently refusing the surveyor's kiss and eagerly placing his ring onto her engagement finger (Fig. 15b). And although the surveyor has initially gone after the Indian maiden in a spirit of male bravado, showing off the telescoped sight of her to his coworkers, he returns more solemnly, repelling their joshing. Sky Star has rushed the surveyor away after his quick kiss of her hand before her Sioux suitor can run down the canyon to catch them together (Fig. 15a). However, she arrives too late to save the surveyor from the first attack, her father's plans for which she has overheard through their tipi walls. In riding to warn the surveyor, she has been fatally delayed by falling from her horse and down a mountainside, but after witnessing his death she struggles on to the fort until collapsing just outside its gates.

*The Invaders* ends with a relatively static tableau, a calm coda to its scenes of battle. In the film's only self-consciously artistic lighting effect, a shaft of late-afternoon sunlight falls through a doorway to illuminate Sky Star's deathbed, as the commandant's daughter kneels alongside in prayer and her father and fiancé stand solemnly (Fig. 16). For all her active heroism, Sky Star meets death in a soft bed under a white spread, not unlike the historical Pocahontas (who died in England at about age twenty-three, after having been received by the king and attending a new Ben Jonson play). Sky Star's death in bed is one expression of her choice to save the whites through an action that might be seen as traitorous to her tribe, a choice that earlier Pocahontas tales explain through her conversion into Christianity.[44] (Griffith goes some distance into that motivation earlier in 1912 with *Iola's Promise,* where the Pocahontas figure, played by Mary Pickford, refers to the

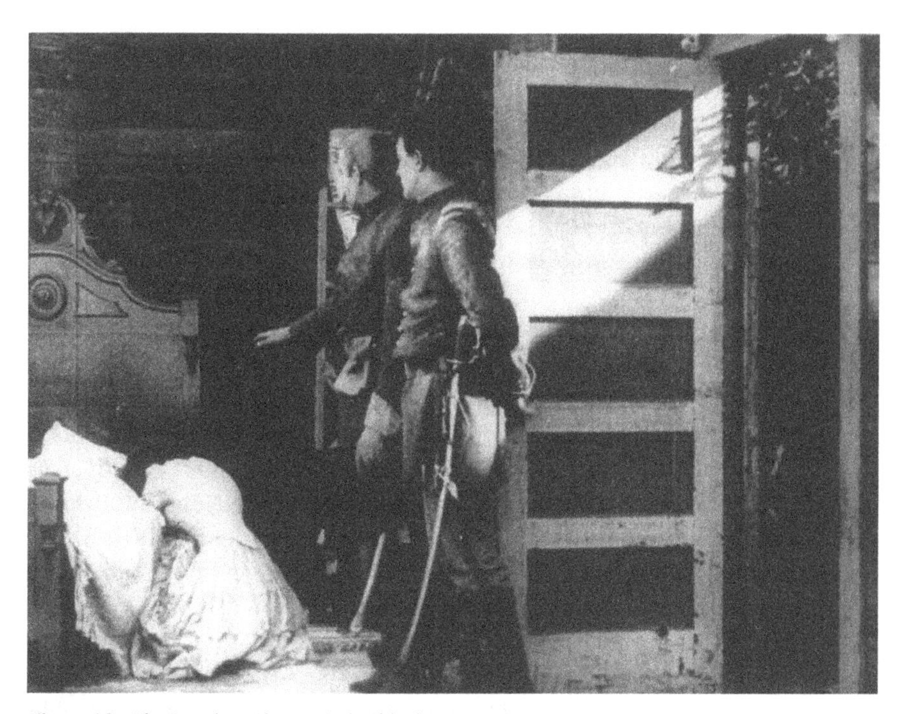

**Figure 16.** *The Invaders:* Sky Star's deathbed.

whites by their Christian symbol – the "cross-heart" people – before dying to save her white love interest from attack by her tribe.)

This death-in-bed image also can't avoid paraphrasing the undramatic historical way that Pocahontas and most Native Americans actually did "vanish" – through contact with European diseases.[45] And like the historical Pocahontas, who was kidnapped at about age fourteen and held in Jamestown to ensure that her father would not attack the colony, Sky Star functions in the fort as a hostage during negotiations with the Sioux. But this rare fact from Pocahontas's known history has never suited her fable.[46] She and Sky Star must be visually honored for their conscious disregard of themselves, modeled on the suspiciously self-serving tale of his salvation first recounted in print by John Smith himself in his *Generall Historie of Virginie* (1624). In paintings, Pocahontas is usually portrayed at the moment she throws herself over Smith's body to protect him from her father's upraised weapon and, even more invariably, she is painted as lighter skinned than the rest of her tribe, as if her conversion has already begun.[47] In this too, *The Invaders* follows a tradition in its apparently inconsistent casting as Sky Star of Anna Little, the one non-Sioux player among the film's Indians (although she claimed some Native American ancestry). By 1912, Pocahontas could be painted as a "Christy Girl" in Howard Chandler Christy's *Liberty Belles,* as the first historical stage toward the apotheosis of the "American Girl."[48] The sweet, well-dressed, pampered, and inactive commandant's daughter who never leaves the fort in *The Invaders* is contrasted with the riding and independence of Sky Star, but the Pocahontas tradition since the nineteenth century reinforces that Sky Star's self-sacrifice is a choice made so that America can become a unified nation, complete with its all-American girls. We can regret that both Sky Star and the surveyor have to die (paying the ultimate price for their interracial attraction, like Cora and Uncas in *The Last of the Mohicans*) before the transcontinental railroad can bring the (white) nation together. Indeed, regret is an essential element of the story, requiring bedside prayers.[49] Audiences for the film in 1912 might have recalled newspaper stories the year before about a Native American dubbed Ishi, "the last of the Yashi" or "the last wild Indian," who had wandered alone and starving into Oroville, California.[50] In its final deathbed image, *The Invaders* too finally succumbs to the inevitable narrative woven around the image of the Vanishing American.

# 9. "No Indians Wanted"

> The Red Indians who have been fortunate enough to secure permanent engagements with the several Western film companies are paid a salary that keeps them well provided with tobacco and their worshipped "firewater." It might be thought that this would civilize them completely, but it has had a quite reverse effect, for the work affords them an opportunity to live their savage days over again, and they are not slow to take advantage of it. They put their heart and soul in the work, especially in the battles with the whites, and it is necessary to have armed guards watch over their movements for the least sign of treachery. . . . With all the precautions that are taken, the Redskins occasionally manage to smuggle real bullets into action; but happily they have always been detected in the nick of time, though on one occasion some cowboys had a narrow escape during the production of a Bison film.
>
> Ernest Dench, "The Dangers of Employing Redskins as Movie Actors" (1915)[1]

Within a year after the release of *The Invaders,* trade journals were informing budding scriptwriters that film companies had begun hanging out "No Indians Wanted" signs: "none of the companies will state that they desire Indian dramas. They are played out."[2] The warning was intended to discourage unsolicited scenarios about Indians, but the implications for Native American actors must have been obvious too. Ernest Dench's chapter entitled "The Dangers of Employing Redskins as Movie Actors," excerpted above, in his early study of the Hollywood industry, *Making the Movies,* rather hysterically brought production practices themselves into the trade-paper complaints about positive Indian representations. A major *Moving Picture World* editorial back in the year of *The Invaders* had grumbled that "The noble redskin, who used to sell land that he never bought or paid for, drink the proceeds and then murder the purchaser in cold blood, is becoming immortalized."[3]

By the year of Dench's book, 1915, all of the major Western productions had shifted with surprising rapidity into "features" of five reels or more, while only the lowest budgeted Westerns retained shorter formats. Among the changes accompanying this shift seems to have been the "vanishing" of American Indians in several disturbing senses. Although it is natural to think of the figure of the Indian as essential to the Western, in fact we have had to search far back into an era usually ignored to unearth a time when they were key to American film. It is canny of Jane Tompkins, because of her concentration on the Hollywood sound era in *West of Everything,* to surprise herself with the "bizarre" discovery that she can locate "no Indian characters" at all beyond "props, bits of local color, textual effects."[4] A glance through the fifteen years of the silent feature-length Western may suggest how that situation came about.

Thomas Ince had lost his contract with the Pine Ridge Reservation Sioux in 1914 during a business struggle with the Miller Brothers, owners of the 101 Ranch. Though a few Native American actors remained, Ince's ability to continue filming histories of the clash of groups was further hindered when the U.S. Army began planning, with some innocence, for America's entry into World War I by requisitioning horses.[5] Ince's first feature-length Western, *The Bargain* (1914), which is also William S. Hart's first feature, remains a stunning film, with taut and ethically complex characterizations set within unusual desert Arizona landscapes near the Grand Canyon. But reviews pounced upon the film's archaic qualities: "a reckless attempt to revive a style of motion picture which we had hoped was a thing of the past, . . . nothing more than an old-fashioned 'Western.'"[6] More admired at the time, and still better known today, were the first Western features directed by Cecil B. De Mille (1914–15): *The Squaw Man, The Virginian,* and *The Girl of the Golden West.* The immediate origin of all three in well-established stageplays is evident in their theatrical staging and pudgy, unathletic stars. "Authenticity" was never an issue here.

De Mille's *The Squaw Man* – its title refers to a Briton who marries a Ute Indian woman – has the distinction of being the first feature to have been shot primarily in the town of Hollywood itself, and it anticipates in several ways the future of the Indian in the silent feature as it played out its sad history in Hollywood. We'll come back to this film in a moment. As American filmmaking conglomerated in Hollywood corporations and as feature length became standardized, there also came a narrowing of story options. The "Hollywood movie" became more and more synonymous with romantic tales of love intertwined with adventure, until the creation of the male–female couple became a story element so essential that it is difficult to recall a time when wider possibilities abounded.[7] This was not a promising development for the representation of Native Americans, except in the increasingly rare cases of films set primarily within tribal communities.

The subsequent history of Indian images in silent-era Hollywood becomes a story with two paths – one about war, the other about love – neither leading anywhere except to Indian death. Placing Indians on the Plains warpath becomes an increasingly perfunctory action device. John Ford's curious variation in *The Iron Horse* (1924), when transcontinental rail workers are surrounded by attacking Cheyennes, is to have the ride-to-the-rescue accomplished by Pawnees. More revealing of the spirit of the time are the intertitle additions made to Ince's and Francis Ford's *Custer's Last Fight* (1912) when it was rereleased in 1925: Although nothing in the film's images reinforces such an interpretation, the new 1925 titles now inform us that the federal government was overly generous in dealing with the irrational Sioux nation (". . . IN 1868 CONGRESS . . . GRANTED TO THE SIOUX FOR THEIR *EXCLUSIVE* USE A VAST TERRITORY – THUS FILLING THEM WITH PRIDE AND INSOLENCE" and "THESE HOSTILE INDIANS OVERLOOKED NO OPPORTUNITY TO DO THEIR DEADLY WORK").[8]

*The Squaw Man* turned out to be a harbinger of the spirit in which Indians would be incorporated as characters into silent features, as opposed to the increasing number of films that used Indians merely as masses of warriors. If the question for Hollywood came to be how to incorporate Indians into romance plots, the answer seemed to be interracial romance tragedies. The figure of the "squaw man" – the white man with an Indian wife – had appeared in many earlier films, by Griffith and Young Deer among others. Selig's *Buck's Romance* (1912) had treated such a union as a great joke among cowhands but one that also held the threat of nightmare – from which Buck awakens in the final shot to hug his white wife and child. De Mille's *The Squaw Man* is also not without a certain perverse wit, as in its reversed shotgun wedding where the Briton's pal in Montana must pull a gun on a Justice of the Peace to force him to perform a marriage with the Ute chief's pregnant daughter, but it's a film where every interracial bond is an expression of despair, heavily played, and the Indians are not so much threatening as merely gullible (as again in De Mille's *The Virginian*). Young Deer's wife, Lillian St. Cyr, credited as usual under her stage name "Princess Redwing," takes the thankless role of the Ute wife, one "Nat-U-Ritch," who twice saves her husband's life – from a gunman and a snowstorm – and then perfunctorily sets the world in order by committing suicide (Fig. 17).

Features about Indian men involved with white women found a single, strangely obsessive plot pattern in the silent era: The Indian is taken off the reservation and onto a college campus, where he mistakes a certain social friendliness among the men for racial equality – until he dates a white woman. Beginning, at least among surviving films, with Lubin's one-reel *Red Eagle's Love Affair* (1910), the story may have been revitalized by sidelong allusions to the 1912 Olympic games triumph (and tragedy, in the 1913 gold-medal revocations) of Jim Thorpe (Sauk and Fox ancestry). The features *Strongheart* (1914), *Braveheart* (1925), and *Redskin* (1929) play variations, and are modern in the way that they treat athletics as a trap for collegiate stars lulled into forgetting about racism off the field. The films themselves build on this irony but hedge their liberalism by creating noble Indian supermen who come around to learning the importance of keeping the races unamalgamated, notwithstanding pleas from their white lovers. In *Strongheart* ("supervised" by D. W. Griffith and filled with his former Biograph Company players), "THE STUDIOUS INDIAN" of the title (Henry B. Walthall) displays his athletic heroism among the tribe in the woods and then graduates from the Carlisle Indian Industrial School to Columbia University, where he becomes a football hero. Although "STRONGHEART BEGINS TO FEEL THE LAW OF RACE" when he is wrongly accused of selling play signals, Columbia coed Blanche Sweet accepts his marriage proposal. The argument that forces him to renounce her and return to the reservation comes from an Indian elder: "'YOUR POOR PEOPLE PAID FOR YOUR WISDOM – IT BELONGS TO THEM.'" In the 1925 version, football star "Braveheart" (Rod La Rocque, of Irish and French extraction) is also author of a book about Native American legal rights, *The Red Man*, whose royalties go back to his tribe. College men begin to worry at a party, "Braveheart is all right on the *team*... but...," and ultimately he agrees with their implication, sending his lover away: "You are white, I'm red.... Return to your

**Figure 17.** The tableau finale of Cecil B. De Mille's *The Squaw Man* (1914): Nat-U-Ritch (Lillian St. Cyr, "Princess Redwing") dying in the arms of her husband (Dustin Farnum), as her father, Chief Tabywana (Joseph Singleton), looks on and their son is cradled by Diana, Countess of Kerhill (Winifred Kingston).

people, with an Indian's blessing." In the complex *Redskin*, "Wing Foot" (Richard Dix) evokes enough evident lust from the college flappers to provoke warning to one of them from a chubby undergraduate boy ("Say, what's the idea, gettin' all steamed up over an Indian?") and a reminder from another student to Wing Foot that he is "tolerated" for his speed on the track (Fig. 18a). The standard moral for such films, acknowledging racism while simultaneously playing separatism as racial pride ("My mistake was in thinking I ever had a chance among you whites," as Wing Foot puts it. "I'm going back to my own people, where I belong"; Fig. 18b), is cleverly reconciled in *Redskin* with interracial understanding. The conflict shifts to one between Wing Foot's Navaho people and the Pueblo tribe of his grade-school girlfriend, so that a romance solution becomes possible alongside "the greatest gift of the heavens – tolerance" (and so that the film can employ its two-color Technicolor in spectacular and authentic tribal locations: He lives in Canyon de Chelly; she on Acoma Pueblo).

**Figure 18.** *Redskin* (1929): Navaho athlete Wing Foot (Richard Dix) is informed that he is "tolerated" in college for his speed on the track (18a); his father refuses to shake hands when he returns in white man's clothes to the reservation (18b).

In *Redskin,* Richard Dix – a white actor whose hard-jawed inexpressiveness registered as "Indian" – was returning to the impersonation of a Navaho he played four years earlier in the ambitious and astonishingly confused *The Vanishing American* (1925). "Nophaie" is the usual college star – football and baseball – in the Zane Grey novel on which the film is based, and he incites the usual sexual longings ("Marian felt the pound of her heart, the sudden shock of delight and pride in the Indian's sheer physical prowess"), although the film adaptation puts his heroism on the World War I battlefields.[9] More directly than any other silent feature, *The Vanishing American* investigates the assumptions of its title and arrives at a sympathetic melodrama of reservation abuses: a child cheated of his horses, a man driven to insane hallucinations, a woman dead under blankets after unpicturable sexual abuse at the hands of the Indian Bureau agent. Zane Grey had also included more direct reference to native decimation by the disease frontier, through Nophaie's slow death by influenza "plague." Although there is something to Richard Slotkin's contention that Grey was an opportunist without ideology, his novels nevertheless exploit, if they don't explore, historical wrongs committed against Native Americans.[10]

The problem for both the film and novel *The Vanishing American* is that such "sympathy" is conjoined to an unforgiving social-Darwinist explanation of the forces of history – beginning with what must be the American cinema's only epigraph from English social philosopher Herbert Spencer: "We have unmistakable proof that throughout all past time there has been a ceaseless devouring of the weak by the

**Figure 19.** *The Vanishing American* (1925): The opening intertitle (19a); and the reservation school teacher (Lois Wilson) giving Nophaie (Ricard Dix) the Bible that will, in the end, fail to stop a fatal bullet (19b).

strong . . . a survival of the fittest" (Fig. 19a). The gentle eastern-Western–style friendship between Navaho man and white woman (Fig. 19b) is buried under the philosophy of the film's first half hour: Opening shots of empty Monument Valley are filled by a thousand-year survey under the Francis Parkman–Theodore Roosevelt view of history as warfare among races. The Anasazi, sleeping in the shadows of their cliff houses, are "an indolent, harmless people drowsing in the dust of centuries," and thus all too ready for their conquest by a (historically imaginary) "fiercer, harder people."[11] The film ends up running on two irreconcilable tracks. One track believes in Hollywood's individual heroism, with Nophaie offered the timely recompense of U.S. citizenship while the narrative punishes a single troublemaker in the form of the mustachioed Indian agent. On the other track runs a grim social Darwinism in which "race after race has trod its way from darkness into dark." To set the world right again, Nophaie too must die, not quite as a suicide this time but by a bullet shot from a brother Navaho, penetrating the Bible over his heart. In his novel, Zane Grey explained, "For Nophaie saw clearly that nature was the great law. . . . The individual must perish that the species might survive."[12] Such an implied social-Darwinist vision of the world as unending group warfare better meshed with Thomas Ince's way of treating history in *The Invaders,* where the sweep of history and government policy overcame any merely benevolent individual efforts. In the film of *The Vanishing American,* Hollywood's individual heroism is contradicted by an astonishing vision of history under which an Anasazi holy man prays for the arrival of Spanish conquistadors ("a stronger race") to vanquish their vanquishers. This logic leads to the arrival of Coronado and, a few hundred years later in the film's capsule epic, to Kit Carson leading the cavalry: "These Indians are my friends, but I must send them to their death." This interesting definition of "friendship" is not quite what the eastern Western had in mind, although it will be incorporated into American film for at least the next thirty years.

Silent features do have a number of less confused, more satisfying moments, among which is the surprising plot device in such films as *Wagon Tracks* (1919) and *North of 36* (1924) where white men who have committed crimes against Indians are handed over to have their punishment meted out by unforgiving tribal law. In the unclichéd and spectacular *North of 36*, a story of the first cattle drive north from Texas (something like *Red River* with a visionary pioneer woman in John Wayne's role), the despoiler of "The Virgin Wilderness," who rapes a bathing Comanche girl, is apprehended by the U.S. Cavalry after the outfit's arrival in Abilene. To the pleas of the criminal, the cavalry make a remarkable response: "Don't argue with us, your punishment is in the hands of . . . the Indian nation." After a peace treaty signing, the cavalry troops watch Comanche warriors sharpening knives and leading their prisoner offscreen, vultures circling in the sky.

Where the silent Western remains most watchable, with or without Indians, is in features that retain the casual, anecdotal quality of the earliest movies, telling tales that have not yet had time to turn self-consciously "mythic," with cowboys as the jokers they are back in *Buck's Romance* (1912) or giving the apparently improvisational performances of the early "Flying A" Westerns that Allan Dwan turned out at the pace of three a week. The problem for the Western genre seems to be that when Indians are included, even early features begin to feel the need to justify the historical record. In surviving silent features about Indians, the closest we get to the apparently effortless, preconventionalized style are the Westerns staring Douglas Fairbanks. *The Half-Breed* (1916), also directed by Allan Dwan and written by Anita Loos, begins the way *The Squaw Man* ends, with an Indian woman's suicide after giving birth to a white man's son – who grows into Fairbanks's title character. Although the film runs through the standard white woman–Indian man plot points, it rewrites them with sharp satire. This time the woman's coy lust is played with awareness of the absurdities ("I hear you have a very nice wigwam") and with a casual sensuality so rare in the Western

**Figure 20.** Chetoga (Chauncey Yellow Robe) instructing his son in *The Silent Enemy* (1930).

and so typical of early Douglas Fairbanks. *The Half-Breed* touches deftly too on tolerance when Fairbanks's "Leaping Brook" instills "pride" in the previously buffoonish town Indians brought low by medicine-show liquor. However, *Wild and Woolly* (1917), written again by Loos, for all its amusing satire about an easterner played by Fairbanks who is such a "nut" about the West that he lives in a tipi within his father's New York mansion, leaves a sour taste by playing out a story that requires Fairbanks to go west and demonstrate his athletic heroism by killing off drunk reservation Indians when a town hoax involving a mock uprising goes wrong.[13]

The Western thrives by being evasive. Some issues that might be expected to trouble the genre are evaded for decades. The representation of women notably is so untroubling in most of the genre's history that it takes a subtle commentator indeed to find much of interest except as repression. For the next decades of the sound era, the same becomes true for the Indian, with notably few exceptions (among them would be *The End of the Trail* [1932], *Massacre* [1934], and *Devil's Door-*

*way* [1950]). Beyond evoking some generalized outrage or embarrassment, depending on your mood and your race, the representation of Native Americans becomes dully predictable for decades to come. If we have looked deeply into American Indians in the very earliest Westerns, it's also because their images in film become so dismal or merely scenic that we'll have little heart to return to them except in passing for the rest of this book. The silent era does end, however, with a powerful anomaly, the last silent eastern Western, entitled *The Silent Enemy* (1930). Filmed in Ontario with an all-native cast,[14] it reads on paper like the sort of project that should get credit only for honorable intentions but turns out to be a gripping drama of pre-Columbian Ojibwas (Anishinabes) fending off starvation (Fig. 20). The vogue for popularized ethnography in the 1920s had been taken up by Paramount Pictures (in *Grass, Stark Love, Chang,* and *Moana*), which also financed this surprising film. Notwithstanding commercial touches in the low-cut buckskin dresses and a love triangle that pits an honorable hunter against a slinking medicine man, *The Silent Enemy* allows the silent era to close off with a film about Native American life that – in its portrait of the struggle for life over a snowswept winter – finds something that remains genuine within the catchphrase "survival of the fittest."

# 10. The West of the Mohicans

Aren't they rude! These Indians certainly are a problem.
Shirley Temple in *Susannah of the Mounties* (1939)

Maybe we made a mistake in trying to maintain Indian cultures. Maybe we should not have humored them in that.
President Ronald Reagan, June 30, 1988.[1]

Although crude in production values, the earliest Westerns have qualities of substance and style that were forgotten by the genre and never recovered. When it abandoned the eastern landscape and the narrative patterns that followed from it, the film genre lost something that corresponds to what is admirable and enduring within James Fenimore Cooper's fiction. Just how all-encompassing was the change that resulted from the production move west can, perversely, be witnessed through the devolution on film of Cooper's own *The Last of the Mohicans.* This quintessential eastern Western was itself unable to withstand the pervasive force of the far-Western. The tale survived with its philosophy recognizable only through the silent era.

The first adaptation was one of D. W. Griffith's eastern Westerns called *Leather Stocking,* filmed in New York State in the summer of 1909 and promoted with rare modesty as to its fidelity to Cooper ("while we have made no attempt to follow his story closely, we present a vivid appreciation of his work"). Considering its one-reel format, however, it takes no greater liberties than later versions, if shifting everything around in the lush landscape, so that, for instance, Natty's disguise as a bear late in the novel becomes an opportunity for Griffith to shoot a canoe chase when the disguise is discovered by the Hurons. For an eastern Western it is relatively violent, including a scalping implied before a shot cut; but it still finds space for the circular narrative of pastoralism, beginning with a deftly played meeting of "Leather Stocking" (James Kirkwood) and "Uncas" (Owen Moore), who both hunch behind riverbank bushes until recognizing the other, and ending with the handshake of the two friends after the pastoral world is restored – though without the death of a "last" Mohican because this version combines Cooper's father and son into the single Indian friend.

The one enduring adaptation of the novel comes with the 1920 *Last of the Mohicans,* which manages to locate an unsuspected compelling core within that interracial-romance obsession of feature-length silents (Fig. 21). This version rebalances Cooper's plot to bring to the center the dark sister Cora Munro in the astonishing performance of Barbara Bedford, whose cross-race desire is so unflinching that it can be undercut only slightly by the unconvincing object of her desire in a heavyset Uncas and by intertitle language that tries desperately to soften the sexuality in her gaze. Although original director Maurice Tourneur was injured in a fall early in production, replacement Clarence Brown seems to have maintained Tourneur's usual mastery of shot framing, here finding an eastern style of dark and woodsy enclosures within spectacular California Sierra landscapes (as in the frame enlargement facing the opening of Part One).[2]

In Hollywood's sound era, however, Cooper's tale grows weirdly indistinguishable from a far-Western. The first sound version, a Mascot serial from 1932, is easy enough to mock for plot expansion that puts the sisters into peril twelve times, once each episode. Still, the evident cheapness of the production can pass for a rough frontier spirit, and some of the casting is convincing, notably Harry Carey (John Ford's regular silent lead) as a suitably middle-aged Hawkeye, the calm center of chaos, even if other casting seems mildly deranged (especially sixty-five-year-old silent star Hobart Bosworth as Chingachgook and great comic actor Mischa Auer as the Marquis de Montcalm). More surreal is evidence in action sequences that the story is becoming a far-Western, as in the covered wagon chase of Episode 4, "Riding with Death." The hints of a shift west in the serial are taken further in the crushingly high-toned 1936 version, full of ballroom dancing and British twits, which converts Hawkeye into a romantic lead suitable for pairing with one of the sisters. Handsome Randolph Scott brings the expectation of a traditional Western hero (after starring in nine Zane

**Figure 21.** The 1920 version of *The Last of the Mohicans:* Besieged in the cave are (*left to right, foreground*) Uncas (Albert Roscoe), Cora (Barbara Bedford), Hawkeye (Harry Lorraine), and Chingachgook (Theodore Lerch); in the background Major Haywood (Henry Woodward) and Alice (Lillian Hall) tend a wounded British soldier.

Grey Westerns for Paramount earlier in the thirties), reinforced by speeches perfectly antithetical to Cooper's character (who, recall, laments even the sounds of trees felled by wagon-train pioneers). Scott's Hawkeye is the cheerful advance guard for urbanization: "Why, out beyond the Ohio is a land where no white man has ever been. Every time I open a new trail I like to think that others will follow, maybe someday build a big city at its end." This is a Hawkeye of the sort that might have been dreamed by Cooperstown founder William Cooper but never by his son.

The full transformation of the novel into a far-Western arrives in Columbia's stupefying 1947 version, *Last of the Redmen,* directed by George Sherman but worthy of Edward D. Wood Jr. It's not just such *Sunset*-magazine style details as the Navaho rug on the table in the nicely furnished cave, with its skylight and hinged rock door, behind which the sisters are hidden from the Hurons, but the landscape itself that amuses – dust everywhere and dying pine trees from what must have been a particularly dry California summer. "All this wilderness! Just waiting for men to come and take it!" pants Cora, bodice heaving. Hawkeye spouts Irish blarney ("He's a sly one, that Magua . . .") until Major Haywood can take no more: "I'm a little tired of your 'wit,' Mr. Hawkeye." The far-Western chases and fun fistfights feature the sort of Indians that can be tripped, one after another, by a bewigged boy sticking his leg out from under a wagon. These are "Cooper's Indians" of the sort that Mark Twain found jumping mindlessly off a log one after another in *The Deerslayer* ("In the matter of intellect, the difference between a Cooper Indian and the Indian that stands in front of the cigar-shop is not spacious").[3] It shouldn't have been possible to carry Cooper's story more perversely into the far-Western mode, but that is achieved by *Der Letzte Mohikaner,* a 1965 German coproduction (known in English-language release as *The Last Tomahawk*), filmed in stunningly arid Spanish deserts whose only visible vegetation is a single prop saguaro cactus used as target practice in a scene where Cora Munro proves a six-gun quick draw. In one of the few lingering eastern touches, the war on the Plains is fought against Indians in "Mohawk" haircuts. The Magua character leads the daughters and Captain Haywood, now of the cavalry, and their wagon train through a false shortcut – as he does in the novel – this time through a canyon gorge. ("Are you sure this is the route? . . . When is this long stretch of desert over?") Colonel Munro's fort, populated with cowboys, is buried under tons of rock when the Hurons and their outlaw companions blow up a nearby butte.

It would be kindest to leave Cooper's abused novel buried peacefully under *Der Letzte Mohikaner*'s mountain of rubble had not Michael Mann in his 1992 version set out righteously to "counter some of the misconceptions" of both Cooper and Hollywood by creating something more historically accurate to the "history of the Northeastern Woodlands American Indians."[4] His casting of American Indian Movement (AIM) activists Dennis Banks (Anishinabe–"Chippewa" ancestry) in a small role and Russell Means (Oglala Sioux ancestry, born on the Pine Ridge Reservation) as Chingachgook was a step toward the sort of authenticity seldom seen since the era of *The Invaders.* However, the 1992 *Last of the Mohicans* ends up characteristic of Hollywood Westerns after the studio era: It sets out with the best of intentions to be revisionist, especially regarding race, but ends up strangely conformist, defeated by some timid choices and also by the power of the Western genre itself. Part of this film's Hollywood traditionalism comes from using the 1936 version as its immediate source. Updating Randolph Scott's romantic Natty, handsome Daniel Day-Lewis evidently "stirs" the "blood" of Cora before she says so. The key change is that Day-Lewis's Hawkeye has essentially turned Indian, adopted at the age of "one or two" by Chingachgook, whom he calls "my father."[5] We've returned here to that boys' fantasy so common in eastern Westerns of 1908–10, where Indians are "our" parents. The result for Cooper's story line, moreover, is that the biologically white Hawkeye displaces the native son Uncas – who is briefly paired with blond, shell-shocked Alice before they both die – and that Cora's sexual gaze, now directed not at Uncas but at Hawkeye, loses all of the interracial radicalism that it had way back in the 1920 version. Whereas the pathos of Cooper's Hawk-eye came from his being a loner at home in no realm – too savage for an eastern bride and yet, as he so often reminds us, too much the white man ever to feel quite at home with Indians – the 1992 Hawkeye is idealized in both worlds, a perfect match for the eastern girl while also completely an Indian. The result is that both Mohicans become quite marginalized, and Russell Means's character can eulogize his own vanishing with a departing speech ("I, Chingachgook, the last of the Mohicans") borrowed word for word from the complacent 1936 film.[6]

Michael Mann's version has an emotional force greater than any of the other adaptations, but it's force that comes only when the characters stop talking. His film, that is, reconnects the story with the power of silent film, especially in two ten-minute dialogueless sequences – the slaughter in the valley followed by a canoe chase, and the final cliffside fight against Magua – that draw emotion from the lush eastern landscape of North Carolina's Great Smoky Mountains.

# 11. Desert Places

I have it in me so much nearer home
To scare myself with my own desert places.
Robert Frost, "Desert Places" (1936)[1]

If the Western genre lost something when it abandoned eastern landscape, there's little denying that it gained something else, something less easy to quantify that involves using open vistas to evoke visionary possibilities or a testing solitude. D. W. Griffith was, for once, quite modern in seeing desert places less as spaces open for economic exploitation than for fearful alienation. His *The Female of the Species* (1912) characteristically uses the desert's wind, sand, and cacti to reinforce a grim tale: "THE WIFE AND HER SISTER HALF MAD WITH LONELY BROODING, OBSESSED WITH VENGEANCE," in an intertitle's language. Victor Seastrom's (i.e., Sjöström's) *The Wind* (1928) is the silent masterwork of such desert spaces, with Lillian Gish's easterner driven mad in the man's West.

The pastoralism of the eastern Western was also, we might as well admit, a way to cling to something a bit cozy, to the manicured greens of Jefferson's "little mountain" Monticello, to the lawns of suburbia. Pastoralism, both as a poetic mode (extolling middle ground between city and wilderness) and a visual style (cradling people under protective branches), probably also needs to be recognized as conservative and unadventurous – something that is as true for Virgil (praising the golden reign of Emperor Augustus) as it is for Griffith (idealizing the plantations of the Old South) and Cooper (reacting against American egalitarianism, after seven years in England, by praising "castes that are more or less rigidly maintained").[2] It was again D. H. Lawrence who saw through clearly to the terms of Cooper's failure with the landscape: "white men have probably never felt so bitter anywhere, as here in America, where the very landscape, in its very beauty, seems a bit devilish and grinning, opposed to us. Cooper, however, glosses over this resistance, which in actuality can never quite be glossed over."[3] The resistance of this landscape is what post–World War II Westerns, so much darker than their textbook reputations, learn to show us when they finally clear away the distractions of history and leave bitter men on desert places wiped blank for their testing.

In the American tradition, to move west is to free yourself of the cultural bonds to England, something neither Cooper nor Griffith had the slightest desire to do. To throw yourself into the blank spaces of America has always been to discover possibilities away from stale European culture, if at the price of the fear that comes from being lost in apparently limitless space. "My bareness! my bareness! seems America to say," wrote Emerson in his journal, speaking for a long American literary tradition that knows well the fears of blankness, as in Melville's oceans, but nevertheless seeks out bareness as the route to escape established eastern culture, as in William James or Wallace Stevens or Robert Frost.[4] There is regular amazement that certain writers, such as Zane Grey, had never actually seen the far West when they wrote their first Westerns or, like Owen Wister, seldom cared to visit it later. But such ignorance of the West is in some sense the very point. What you already know is not a field for the imagination. What you know, you can describe, but not envision as open to every possibility – which is why "the West" was an invention of Europe and why Cooper would place Natty on "the prairie" without having seen it. Arguably, it was best *not* to have experienced the real West at all, which could only limit imagination. Filmmakers, tied to photographic reality, had that imaginative luxury only in the first eastern-filmed Westerns.

There may only be one insurmountable problem with the liberating sense of the West as the ideal bare space, so privileged in American literature. "Empty" space cannot evade its political and historical components. Redefinitions were required to eliminate Native Americans, already inhabiting the land. Long before European Americans set eyes on the arid and open Southwest, "desert places" were political constructs, defining a dank wilderness worthless and frightening because presumed to be inhabited only nomadically by Indians. The "Squalid, horrid American Desart" was the Puritan minister and writer Cotton

Mather's damnation of the densely overgrown New England landscape, full of the Indians that Mather argued the "Devil decoyed . . . hither . . . in hopes that the gospel of the Lord Jesus Christ would never come here."[5] When in *The Last of the Mohicans* Colonel Munro laments the captivity of his daughters by Magua's Hurons, whom his party is tracking up the center of a mossy stream, overgrown with thickets on its banks, he expects to "find their fainting forms in this desert."[6] Clearest about the political implications of the lush eastern "desert" was Alexis de Tocqueville at the end of his first chapter of *Democracy in America* (1835): "Although the vast country that I have been describing was inhabited by many indigenous tribes, it may justly be said, at the time of its discovery by Europeans, to have formed one great desert. The Indians occupied without possessing it."[7]

Such writers were maintaining the established usage – Shakespeare evokes the "desert" of the "unfrequented woods" in *The Two Gentlemen of Verona* – but as the word "desert" itself moved west in the nineteenth century, it acquired that sense of openness and bareness that twentieth-century American film would finally be able to visualize imaginatively, following from the American literary tradition.[8] The price of the imaginative gain, however, was removal of living Native Americans from the open space now demanded by the word. In conformist poet William Cullen Bryant's genially visionary "The Prairies" – attempting to redeem what was long labeled the Great American Desert and published in 1833, only three years after President Jackson's Indian Removal Act pushed Native Americans west of the Mississippi – "the red man" can be lamented as "a race that long passed away" while we await Sabbath-worshiping pioneers, "that advancing multitude /Which soon shall fill these deserts."[9] Nathaniel Hawthorne underlines his modernity in *The Scarlet Letter* (1850) by recognizing that the Indian might remain in the "desert" to the extent that the race serves to represent for whites what is missing from the constrained Puritan imagination. The outcast Hester Prynne's "intellect and heart had their home, as it were, in desert places, where she roamed as freely as the wild Indian in his woods."[10] By the twentieth century, in "What the Desert Means to Me," Zane Grey seeks out the open spaces of the Grand Canyon and Death Valley because "nothing can grip men's souls and terrify women's hearts like the desert. . . . During these lonely hours I was mostly a civilized man, but the fleeting trances belonged to the savage past. I was a savage." If the American Indian vanishes in the West of the imagination, it's because the white man can now claim to have become his own Indian.[11]

The terminology of moviemaking itself made another such telling voyage west as the film industry consolidated its claim on the region. For the first narrative films before 1910, "Indian and Western subjects" or sometimes "Indian and cowboy pictures" are what trade papers call our genre. Soon, the priority gets reversed, and "Western and Indian films" becomes a trade label.[12] By the end of the silent era, the evolution is complete: The "Indian" has vanished and we are left with the "Western."

*The Big Trail* (1930). (Courtesy of the Academy of Motion Picture Arts and Sciences.)

PART TWO

# "It's Time for Your History Lesson, Dear"

## JOHN WAYNE AND THE PROBLEM OF HISTORY IN THE HOLLYWOOD WESTERN OF THE 1930S

With the coming of sound to the Western in 1929, the genre goes schizophrenic. In one sort of Western, high-budgeted and high-minded, a line of dialogue such as the one taken for the title above is in keeping with the overall spirit. "It's time for your history lesson, dear," are the opening words of instruction from a woman to her young sister before they embark on an arduous overland journey in the 1840s in *The Big Trail* (1930), a 70mm widescreen epic and John Wayne's first Western. (To her difficult question, "Who discovered the Columbia River?" she wants not the name of the first European – Bruno de Heçeta, of Spain – but the first American, Robert Gray, who arrived seventeen years later.) Vastly more numerous for close to twenty years beginning in the early 1930s was another sort of film, the "B-Western," where we are likely to forget history and hear such a line of dialogue as, "It don't seem natural that a radio big-shot would go around blowing up reservoirs." This particular little qualm of rational logic – in *The Man from Music Mountain* (1943) – is rare in a form that more often rests quite comfortably in some realm of uncertain time and unspecific place. With sound, the Western heads down two paths that seem to lead in very different directions.

The Hollywood studio A-Westerns of the 1930s – films such as *Billy the Kid* (1930), *Cimarron* (1931), *Annie Oakley* (1935), *The Plainsman* (1936), *Wells Fargo* (1937), *Dodge City* (1939), and the like – share an obsession with history, initially perhaps as a way to justify the worth of the genre at a time when it had come to be held in particularly low repute and not long after trade papers predicted that it would fall victim to the transition to sound and to films with modern heroes.[1] Most A-Westerns of the decade are biographies of legendary westerners or tales of landmark events in pioneering. The few exceptions tend to be remakes of successful silents.

During the 1930s there were at most fifty films that can be labeled A-Westerns, in contrast to more than one thousand B-Western features produced in those years in the United States.[2] Although a handful of films straddle the types, the boundary between them is not as hazy as it might seem, because the B-Western is not just a later critical category. For theater owners of the thirties, it identified a distinct place in exhibition programs. The B-Western was so labeled initially because it played second on double-bills, after the major "A" feature, and seldom ran more than seventy minutes, usually just under an hour. One of the responses that exhibitors had made to the Great Depression, especially after its full effects hit in 1932, was to offer audiences at least a three-hour show, complete with two features, a newsreel, cartoon, previews, and additional gimmicks, from dish-nights to bingo. B-films in the 1930s might occasionally have budgets as high as $150,000, but many B-Westerns, including a number of John Wayne's, were budgeted at closer to $15,000 and even less, with shooting schedules reckoned in days, not weeks. (By contrast, cost overruns on *The Big Trail* brought it to a reported $2 million.)[3] Thus the "B" in B-Westerns is also reasonably thought of as shorthand for "Budget," and in many rural and small-town theaters B-Westerns would show alone or be paired together.[4] The absurdities resulting from their slapdash production methods are many, from flubbed lines to failed stunts, alongside more intentional oddities. In *Pals of the Saddle* (1938), John Wayne rides up with three other cowboys, two of whom must share a horse because they are a ventriloquist and his cowboy-hatted dummy, with whom Wayne carries on a painful double-entendre dialogue about "giving you the bird." In *Gangsters of the Frontier* (1944), Tex Ritter fools the outlaw gang into thinking he is still in the ranch house by putting on a Tex Ritter gramophone cylinder. In *Ride Him, Cowboy* (1932), John Wayne's horse, Duke, is given a "fair trial," and in *The Golden Stallion* (1949), Roy Rogers's horse, Trigger, is sentenced to death. At such moments, one can savor in the Western something of the dream logic that French surrealists sought within the most apparently ordinary of movies.

It is the rare B-Western that shows much interest in the historical or even the legendary sweep of the American West – the "first" cattle drives or wagon trains – which tends to be glimpsed only in long-shot stock footage borrowed from higher-budgeted productions (as *Daniel Boone* [1936], for instance, uses shots from *The Big Trail*). When the B-Western does represent the pioneer past, it's often in odd ways, even by standards of the genre.

To take a quick set of examples: There happened to be three U.S. films released in the 1930s with the title *New Frontier*. The first *New Frontier*, from 1934, is a one-reel federal-government-produced documentary promoting back-to-the-land "farming co-operatives" in Texas for unemployed "white collar workers," but the other two are John Wayne Westerns from Republic Pictures. The 1935 *New Frontier* (directed by Carl Pierson) casts Wayne as a scout during the 1889 Oklahoma "land rush" of white settlement on former Indian territory.[5] The Oklahoma rushes were elaborately re-created both in silents (*Tumbleweeds* [1925], *3 Bad Men* [1926]) and sound-era A-Westerns (1931's Academy Award winner for best picture, *Cimarron*), but the rush in this *New Frontier* is tossed off with a few seconds of newspaper headlines and superimposed footage of racing wagons. Grabbing "free land" rings too easy to Wayne. "Not for me, Dad," he tells his soon-to-be-murdered father, "I'll take mine the hard way." Among the oddities of this film are outlaws who ride around shouting, "We gotta have food!" before they fall back on gold theft, and trail scouts moaning about unemployment: "With the new railroad reaching into the wastelands, there won't be work for us." Such hardships evidently have more to do with the 1930s than the 1880s, although when Wayne's girl suggests a solution in line with the earlier *New Frontier* documentary – "Why don't you wait until the government help arrives?" – he only hugs her for voicing such a cute notion. The 1939 *New Frontier* (directed by George Sherman)[6] opens with a stock-footage montage of the Civil War and covered wagons struggling west, followed by a pioneer family naming their apparently empty valley "New Hope"; then the film turns to scenes of John Wayne riding for the Pony Express, chased by a band of Indians. When Wayne beats the Indians into a town, we're let in on the film's first trick: The chase has been staged as part of the town's fiftieth "anniversary jubilee." We're six minutes into the fifty-five-minute film before it reveals itself as set in the contemporary world, in a new West that looks exactly like the Old West, if now with white townsfolk made up as Indians ("You fellas really look keen in those outfits!"), playing gently with that racial displacement in the "vanishing" of cinema's Native Americans that we noted at the end of Part One. Agricultural discontent arises when "Metropole City" steals the valley's water on a grand scale (paraphrasing the early-twentieth-century history of California's Owens Valley). Before these troubles develop, the community offers a conservative prayer to God: "if it's alright with You, we'd like keep on just as we have in the past." The other option voiced is, "Why not be sensible and start making plans for the future?" This *New Frontier* appears to be teasing out some relationship among the past, the present, and the future. All three eras are on display simultaneously, with the future represented by a model of the possible new town. So it's not that this B-Western lacks historical consciousness exactly, but it deploys it with the lightness of a joke that for its first minutes fools its audience.

These three 1930s *New Frontiers* are really linked only coincidentally by their name – a term popularized by Henry Wallace, President Franklin D. Roosevelt's secretary of agriculture and third-term vice-president.[7] But it seems characteristic of the era, and of the focus of the Western genre of this time, that all three films fret about historical change, about whether it should be welcomed or feared, and about whether it has been brought about by sinister antipopulist forces. In scenes of prayer in all three films, the citizens worry about whose side of history God may be on. The two B-Westerns turn out to have as much concern as does the federal "back-to-the-land" documentary about the relationship of the discontents of urban life to America's long valorization of farming. Thus, behind all three films appear to be certain persistent ideas, expressed fervently by Thomas Jefferson – and put into practice by him through the Louisiana Purchase – about the value of western lands to prevent America from succumbing to urban ills of unemployment and revolution, as evident to Jefferson from eighteenth-century France as they became again in the depression economics of the 1930s.

Among Hollywood genres, the Western is far and away the most comfortable propounding ideas about American historical and political life. And as the Western begins the sound era, it voices its political and social contentions as clearly as it ever will, with arguments that will be little changed until the collapse of the studio system in the 1960s. It is worth our trying to excavate those arguments here, because they turn out to be stated most directly in the early sound-era A-Westerns. Still, those other thousand Westerns of the thirties must have a certain claim also, if only by their sheer numbers, and it would be evasive to confine ourselves solely to the better-known titles and to ignore what may be going on in all the others, as far removed as they appear to be from any overt historical arguments. For all their laughable qualities, it is possible that the lowly B-Western made attempts at answering questions about America that left the A-Western baffled.

If we want to explore both the A- and B-Western of the 1930s, and whatever unacknowledged links might exist between them, we can hope for no better guide than John Wayne, who starred in about forty B-Westerns between his two A-Westerns at the beginning and end of the decade: Raoul Walsh's *The Big Trail* in 1930 (the film with the history quiz) and John Ford's *Stagecoach* in 1939 (the film that finally solved the problems that stumped this entire decade of Western filmmaking). As Garry Wills explored at book length, Wayne "embodied a politics,"[8] but it was a politics that the Western genre embodied first. Genre and star drew from each other beginning in the 1930s.

The 1930s A-Western – and John Wayne in *The Big Trail* in particular – will be useful to us for being so revealing about the philosophy of the Hollywood Western. But even within this single example, the genre's ideas turn out to be no coherent set of propositions but a shifting set of contradictions. That's not so surprising. After all, it is the very point of "myth" to hold irreconcilable ideas within apparently stable narratives. What is more surprising is that the ambitious A-Western sets up a dialogue about the nature of American history and the relationship of that history to contemporary life that it proved so completely ill-equipped to resolve. Perhaps something of the dissatisfying qualities of thirties A-Westerns – nobody's favorite films – results from their so often lecturing us with a history lesson that they never follow through to its implications. It's my sense that the B-Western, for all its slapdash productions and formulaic plot lines, found ways to resolve the historical debate that escaped the A-Western. As in that last *New Frontier* of 1939, the B-Western seems to have cut through the ponderous pedantries of history lessons by instead elbowing its audiences with the slyest of jokes about the relationships of America's troubled present to the dreams of its past.

But first, the A-Western calls. . . .

# 12. *The Big Trail* and the Weight of History

THERE IS NO ROAD, BUT THERE IS A WILL,
AND HISTORY CUTS THE WAY.
Intertitle in *The Big Trail*

With the use of dialogue a picture becomes either more intellectual or more stupid," wrote a critic for *The Nation* reviewing *The Big Trail* and two other A-Westerns released in October 1930. He left little doubt that "the present revival of the Western film" fell firmly into the "more stupid" category. *The Big Trail*'s popular and critical failure relegated what *Variety*'s review rightly called its "wholly inexperienced" star John Wayne to a decade in B-Westerns.[1] Still, if nobody would call *The Big Trail* "intellectual" exactly, it's full of revealing ideas if we want to look into the genre's philosophies.

The immediate appeal of *The Big Trail* lies in its visuals. Although its rough textures were taken as merely crude in New York reviews, it has a gritty splendor unmatched by any Western since, especially in the panoramas of ox- and horse-drawn "prairie schooners" and cattle herds spread across dusty flatlands, washed away in a river crossing, and lowered down sheer cliffs (see Fig. 24). The spectacle is most striking in the film's "Grandeur" version, the Fox Film Corporation's 70mm format, one of several widescreen experiments in Hollywood timed badly to coincide with depression contractions among studios and exhibitors still paying for the conversion to sound. *The Big Trail* was released a week after King Vidor's *Billy the Kid,* which used MGM's slightly simpler but equally doomed "Realife" widescreen process (filmed in 70mm but released in masked 35mm).[2] In its production *The Big Trail* can only have been a logistical nightmare (Fig. 22). Adding to the complexity of Fox's sophisticated sound-on-film equipment, every dialogue scene appears to have been shot with at least three cameras and sometimes more – regular-aperture 35mm cameras with cinematography credited to Lucien Andriot and 70mm widescreen cameras under Arthur Edeson – and then 35mm German, Italian, and Spanish-language versions were shot on the same sets and locations (with only El Brendel, who plays a henpecked pioneer, able to repeat his speaking role in the German version, and Charles Stevens, who plays the murderous Lopez, repeating his role in the Spanish version). The unwieldy production moved from Yuma, Arizona (for desert scenes), to Sacramento, California (for the opening Mississippi riverboat scenes), to St. George, Utah, and the Grand Tetons in Wyoming (for canyon scenes), and then back to the California Sierras (for snow scenes) and Sequoia National Park (for the concluding scenes among giant redwoods). The Grandeur version is also about thirteen minutes longer and superior in a number of small ways even beyond its spectacle.[3] Director Raoul Walsh found Fox prop boy and bit player Marion "Duke" Morrison, who first took the name John Wayne for this film, to be unwaveringly professional throughout the four-month shoot, while Walsh numbered among his difficulties the veteran stage actors hired to play two of Wayne's three motley antagonists: "With their appearance, the name of the picture should have become *The Big Drunk*. This part of the cast probably scattered more empty whiskey bottles over the western plains than all the pioneers."[4] John Wayne's inexperience shows particularly in the visionary speeches he is required to expound at several points, but his relatively understated delivery, bodily ease, and natural gestures already set him apart from the elocution or declamations of the actors playing against him.

Among directors subsequently known for styling themselves personally as wild westerners in Hollywood, Raoul Walsh had the fullest genuine experience of the region, from his boyhood in border-town Texas through his filming of Mexican revolution battles in Torréon for the 1914 fiction feature *The Life of General Villa*.[5] Landscape in Walsh's films is typically more powerful than the humans who pass through it – memorably the looming canyon walls of his postwar Westerns *Pursued* (1947) and *Colorado Territory* (1949), and the unforgiving desert of *Along the Great Divide* (1951), as well as in less expected places, such as in his gangster films *High Sierra* (1941) and the early *Regeneration* (1915), with its determinist feeling for Manhattan's Bowery.

**Figure 22.** Location shooting on *The Big Trail* (1930) with six cameras and sound-recording equipment. Director Raoul Walsh, in white shirt and hat, leans against the equipment stand.

As with many of Walsh's subsequent Westerns, *The Big Trail* is structured though a journey.[6] Pioneer families "from every state in the union" set out in the spring for six months of hard travel, seeking to settle remote lands "beyond Oregon" that only Wayne's character has seen. "'Cept for trappers, never a white man has left his tracks there," he tells them. The film's release was timed to coincide with the "Oregon Trail centennial" celebrated widely in 1930, notwithstanding that the trail west from Missouri to Oregon and California hadn't really begun as an emigrant wagon route until 1841.[7] Silent Westerns had previously exploited the scenic hardships of the route, so that *The Big Trail* arrived with a sense of overfamiliarity to critics – "only a noisy *Covered Wagon*," *Variety* groused, in reference to James Cruze's 1923 Oregon Trail epic, which had repopularized the genre after the fallow years of the late teens and early 1920s. Set in 1848–9, Cruze's film featured an even larger caravan of wagons, and included Tully Marshall in roughly the same role that he would play in *The Big Trail*, as a grizzled scout who sets the heroine straight about the worth of the young scout. Typical of silent films, *The Covered Wagon* relatively personalizes its Indians, who are introduced through a discussion among Pawnees about the worrisome significance of a plow abandoned by an earlier wagon train. The trail-west plot had also structured such surviving silent features as *Wagon Tracks* (1919) and the early epic ten-reel *Argonauts of California* (1916), and back into the first one- and two-reelers filmed in the West by D. W. Griffith (especially *The Last Drop of Water* [1911] and *The Massacre* [1912]) and Thomas Ince (especially *War on the Plains* [1912] and *Blazing the Trail* [1912]). But much more self-consciously than its precursors, *The Big Trail* celebrates history.

The film is organized under the optimistic principles common to Hollywood historical films, where history becomes the emotionalized story of uplifting individual effort, free from troubling alternatives.[8] By the 1930s, it's the rare A-Western that fails to make claims about its historical accuracy, usually in an opening crawl of written text, itself implying greater authenticity than mere ephemeral speech. In the cases when A-Westerns confess to altering the little facts of history – nudged too by lawyers for living descendants – it is in the service of a larger national truth. James Cruze's *Sutter's Gold* (1936) is rare in admitting that its story is "not taken from the pages of history. Rather, it is legend and fiction, inspired by fact." Cecil B. De Mille's *The Plainsman* (1936) manages to phrase its disclaimer as a boast: "The story that follows compresses many years, many lives, and widely separated events into one narrative – in an attempt to do justice to the courage of the plainsmen of our west." Should we ignore the weight of period detail – which is what the films substitute for historical evidence – some character may bluntly remind us, "That's a symbol of America's future" (as Colonel Dodge says when his railroad beats a stagecoach into Dodge City in the 1939 Technicolor film of that title).

*The Big Trail* celebrates an idea about a particular past that it shares with almost all of the A-Westerns of the 1930s: the mid-nineteenth-century "frontier," or what its opening text title calls "THE CONQUEST OF THE WEST." Eventually the film Western discovered that there was another way to think about the historical process through which western lands evolved, in which the concept of the "border" takes over from the "frontier." That discovery would revitalize the genre in the late 1960s – through both the Spanish/Italian stylistics of "spaghetti Westerns" and the Mexican stories of Sam Peckinpah – and incidentally anticipate the writing of "New Western History," which shared an understanding with those films that there were peoples "on the other side of the frontier" and that the history of the West didn't need to be narrated "entirely on an east-to-west track," as historian Patricia Nelson Limerick has put it. But the thirties A-Western rested comfortably with its earlier understanding of history, well before historians would begin to refer nervously to the frontier as "the f-word."[9]

"I want the empire, honey," a Texan explains gently to his girl, with disarming candor, in *Horizons West* (1952). The woman in a Western hears such ambitions often, and is likely to respond, "All the empire I really wanted was just a corner" with you – as a schoolmarm puts it in *The Outcasts of Poker Flat* (1937).

*The Big Trail* likewise domesticates its empire conquest though a twenty-five-hundred-mile misunderstanding between a young man, Breck Coleman (played by twenty-two-year-old John Wayne), and a woman, a southern belle named Ruth Cameron (played by twenty-one-year-old Marguerite Churchill, who was also subsequently relegated to B-films). Coleman agrees to become scout for the wagon train on which she will be heading west so that he can follow out his suspicions that the wagon boss, Red Flack (Tyrone Power Sr.), and a bullwhacker named Lopez (Charles Stevens) had murdered an old friend. That murder looks to have been the work of Indians – we see discovery of the body in a flashback – but Wayne's character has lived among Indians and knows better. In the domestic spaces of Independence, Missouri, he is less at home. The beamed ceilings of the cabins confine Wayne's body, and in one such space he meets Ruth Cameron by mistaking her from the back for an old friend, tipping her rocking chair and kissing her before catching his mistake.

It is Hollywood's method generally to set up some domestic insult or sexual misunderstanding and then to associate the woman and man with a wider set of conflicting values. When, in the final reel, the romance is consummated, the ideas that each represent are also reconciled. Each half of the couple will be seen to have what the other lacks, so that when they join they create the perfect union: The lower class meets the rich, the stuffy intellectual meets the free sprit, the city sophisticate meets the country innocent, the body meets the soul, and so on. As Rick Altman explored fully in *The American Film Musical*, the pattern, "built around stars of opposite sex and radically diverging values," structures fables of reconciliation between the sexes, the economic and social classes, and various subsidiary oppositions.[10] To apply Altman's binary pattern, if Wayne in *The Big Trail* might be labeled tenacious, avenging, a horse rider, a westerner, and a man, then the Ruth Cameron character is his structural opposite: easily offended, pacifistic, a wagon rider, a southerner, and a woman.

It is worth noting this pattern, but only because it turns out *not* to be followed in any significant way in the Western, despite a few efforts by critics to apply it.[11] There's little denying that the woman in the A-Western is so marginalized that the very ideas she embodies prove unworthy even of synthesis into the films' resolutions. Typically, the woman will simply abandon her philosophy – one memorable display comes when Quaker bride Grace Kelly in *High Noon* (1952) shoots her husband's nemesis in the back. While a Hollywood screwball comedy or musical will dramatize abstract ideas by dividing them between the sexes, in the Western conflicting ideas are more often parceled out among different men or internalized as conflicts within one lone, troubled man. *The Big Trail* is superb at presenting its conflicts physically through bodies and gestures: Wayne's graceful movements are emphasized by the swinging tassels of his tight buckskin as he circles around his enemies, who are stiffly dressed and speak with suspicious eloquence (in the case of Thorpe, an oily southerner), or two-thirds his size and muttering in Spanish (in the case of Lopez, the Mexican), or encased in a shaggy bearskin coat and growling half-articulate phrases (in the case of Flack, the wagon master).[12] Wayne also leaps and skips around the primly walking woman when he first attempts to explain his mistake in kissing her. While Westerns sometimes begin with the Hollywood romance plot, in the end they seldom know quite what to do with the woman, except to turn her into one of the boys or, as here, a nagging impediment.

*The Big Trail* misses more than its share of opportunities to free itself from the genre's limitations, because of how the overland trail historically tended to blur traditional sex roles and to mix the male and female spheres of polite nineteenth-century society.[13] Among *The Big Trail*'s nonspeaking extras, women wield axes and rifles alongside their menfolk, but the Ruth Cameron character, although she's now head of her family ("Colonel Cameron," her father, has apparently died re-

**Figure 23.** *The Big Trail:* Scout Breck Coleman (John Wayne) cannot deny to the Cheyenne "Black Elk, an old friend of mine," that he "wants" Ruth Cameron (Marguerite Churchill). "Oh, you've no better taste than to tell me that before all of these savages," she complains. "You've made me the joke of the Plains!"

cently), must attach herself to the southerner Thorpe, who lies about "my old plantation in Louisiana," and then she must wait to be rescued in her broken wagon by Wayne, all the while complaining, especially after he expresses desire for her in front of Indians (Fig. 23). Even *Variety* sympathized that "Miss Churchill" has "not a great deal to do."[14] The film reinforces sex roles among pioneers by cutting together biological-imperative shots: breast-feeding women, nursing horses, nursing dogs, nursing cats, and finally nursing hogs.[15] El Brendel's comic immigrant in *The Big Trail* (Swedish? Dutch? German?) is the horrible example of what happens when men are ruled by women, with his twenty-five-hundred miles of mother-in-law jokes and muddy scapegoat slapstick.

Philosophies are thus linked to women in *The Big Trail*, as in the genre as a whole, to the extent that those ideas will prove dismissible.

At some point in Hollywood Westerns, a woman will propose, with varying levels of sexual blackmail, the possibility of a pacifist solution. In *The Big Trail,* Ruth pleads to Wayne's character, "They say you're going to hunt down Flack and Lopez . . . but you can't do this awful thing, take two lives. . . . Don't go, Breck, don't go. . . . Don't you see, it doesn't matter about them, I'm afraid for you." Gary Cooper endured the two most famous variants on his characters' wedding days. In *The Virginian* (1929) the schoolmarm argues against his main-street showdown with Trampas: "Think of what it means, killing in cold blood. I've tried to forgive the other killings. . . . Think of me, you and I, our lives together. . . . If you do this, there'll be no tomorrow for you and me." A quarter-century later Coop is still grimly enduring the lecture in *High Noon:* "I'm begging you, please, let's go. Don't try to be a hero. . . . We've got our whole lives ahead of us. . . . If you won't go with me now, I'll be on that train when it leaves here." Men shift awkwardly through the speeches, then offer up a terse phrase about "things a man just can't run away from," as John Wayne puts it in response to the plea from Dallas (Claire Trevor) in *Stagecoach.* It is true that the more extreme dismissals of women's ideas by men in Westerns are also ways that the films themselves can joke a little about the isolation of their heroes, as when William S. Hart is given the dialogue intertitle in *Tumbleweeds* (1925), "Women ain't reliable, cows are." But the definitional antagonism of men and women in Westerns is never used as dynamically as it is routinely in Hollywood's other genres to explore conflicting ideas. When the man and woman come together at the end of a Western, it's without the satisfying reconciliations that end, say, a Katharine Hepburn–Cary Grant screwball comedy or an Astaire–Rogers musical. "Cowboys don't get married – unless they stop being cowboys," as Lee Marvin explains the mutual exclusivity in *Monte Walsh* (1970), and a coupled life for John Wayne beyond the final kiss is, if not completely unimaginable, at least never represented on film in the thirties. (Only in John Ford's *Rio Grande* of 1950 does Wayne join into a "Western of remarriage.") His B-Westerns were popularly known as "one-kiss movies": Fans were aware that the first time he kissed the heroine, they could head for the exits – that moment would invariably be within the film's last shot.[16] As a grander epic, *The Big Trail* allows itself a kiss and a peck, spread over the last three shots.

What one might say in defense of all this is that the Western has at least a point of view, rather than Hollywood's usual accommodation to everybody's harmony. But the stance comes at the price of missed chances, both in dramatizing the conflict of ideas and in using the dynamism of actresses. (For a particularly painful case, see Louise Brooks in her last film role, opposite John Wayne, in *Overland Stage Raiders* [1938].) Only when the Western settles into questions of what is required to build a community do women play somewhat more complex roles, as we'll explore in Part Three. The kiss of the man and woman at the end of *The Big Trail* comes not from a synthesis of philosophies that each represent but only after her capitulation, her admission that her arguments can now be forgotten: "Sorry I was so stupid."[17]

# 13. What's the Big Idea?

Who's the brains of your outfit?
Tim McCoy in *Ghost Patrol* (1936)

The A-Western is conscious, pompously conscious, of its responsibility to represent America's essence. Its falsifications of history's details claim to be at the service of a grander national truth. For several decades Hollywood rested content with a relatively static idea about this national essence, and yet the genre survived by responding to changing times and audience moods. The underlying trick seems to be that the Western "myth" has never been as monolithic as that word suggests but has been made up of unstable residues of American traditions of thought, a half-digested heritage from many individual authors. The myth is built from contradictions, and those contradictions inspire most of the Western's dramatic conflicts. Even Claude Lévi-Strauss, in *Myth and Meaning*, was "not far from believing that, in our own societies, history has replaced mythology and fulfils the same function."[1]

Although they would be the last to confess it, Westerns are less anti-intellectual than intellectually opportunistic. Ideas have value if they can be put into practice. The same, after all, can be said of many American expropriations of European philosophies, including Jefferson's use of the Enlightenment.[2] The Western will bolster its claims by grabbing what it needs from traditions of thought that are wildly incompatible on their own. Tensions come too from Hollywood's overall preference for kinder, gentler philosophies and the Western's secret lust for something darker. *The Big Trail* is only unusual – and useful for us – because of how openly it flaunts the contradictions, displaying both

**Figure 24.** The cliff claims a wagon as pioneers struggle westward in *The Big Trail* (1930).

the "hard" and "soft" sides of America's natural, religious, and political creeds.

## Nature's Nature: Philosophies of the Land

Even without dialogue, Westerns stake a claim about the natural world's relationship to American history. Is nature gentle and generous and thus in league with national advancement? Or leering and savage, opposed to us? Only the first option seems likely for commercial Hollywood. However, the Western always prefers something harsher.

Everything about the visual style of *The Big Trail* works to stress the toughness of nature – rough wagon wheels sink into sand, reluctant pack oxen are whipped onward, boulders weigh down gravesites along the trail. The most difficult way down a cliff seems chosen by the pioneers, so that even the longhorn cattle must be lowered in elaborate cantilevered slings (Fig. 24). (When this sequence is restaged, complete with one wagon crashing down the cliff, in the last and arguably the worst of Hollywood's Oregon Trail films, *The Way West* [1967], Richard Widmark is allowed the rational question, "Couldn't we go around it?") *The Big Trail* faces every elemental hardship: dust storms, flooding rain and impassable mud, raging winds and blizzards. There are river deaths in water and desert deaths from lack of water. The only missing element is fire; for that we must go to *The Texans* (1938), a Chisholm Trail epic where Comanches set "fire grass" ablaze in another futile attempt to halt the pioneers.

When the covered-wagon emigrants depart from the civilization of Missouri in *The Big Trail,* they head into a unknown state of nature where "continual fear, and danger of violent death" are the expectations and "men have a desire and will to hurt."[3] These are Thomas Hobbes's famous terms in *Leviathan* (1651) for the unregulated state of the world. That "the life of man" might be "solitary, poor, nasty, brutish, and short" – in Hobbes's best remembered phrase – doesn't match America's self-image, but even the U.S. Constitution, notwithstanding its schoolroom reputation as a testament to idealism, may be (as historian Richard Hofstadter argued in the 1940s) to some extent a Hobbesian document in its codification of our Founding Fathers' experience of man's depravity.[4] The Western's way of leavening this unforgiving philosophy is to mix it with social Darwinism, which at least allies brutal nature with something like progress. "You'll see how cruel nature is," instructs the wilderness hero of Zane Grey's novel *The Man of the Forest* (1920), but such cruelty is necessary for progress: "Trees fight to live – birds fight – animals fight – men fight. They all live off one another. An' it's fightin' that brings them all closer an' closer to bein' perfect."[5]

In the silent Western, social Darwinism had gingerly won its argument even within the frequent tales of religious conversions in new towns. A sermon in *Travelin' On* (1922) is interrupted by a parishioner wondering if we descended from "the same folks as Jocko" – an organgrinder monkey – whereupon the film cuts to William S. Hart out among the cacti, surviving by adopting a solitary, Hobbesian philosophy. As an intertitle puts it, Hart is "steeped in the creed that a man can trust himself but nothin' else that travels on lessin' four feet." Typically Hart will consent to take along one woman before abandoning civilization, although in *Travelin' On* he rides off alone, reading on horseback, still puzzled by this Bible in which so many others seem to believe. "Survival of the fittest" became implicit in the vocabulary of

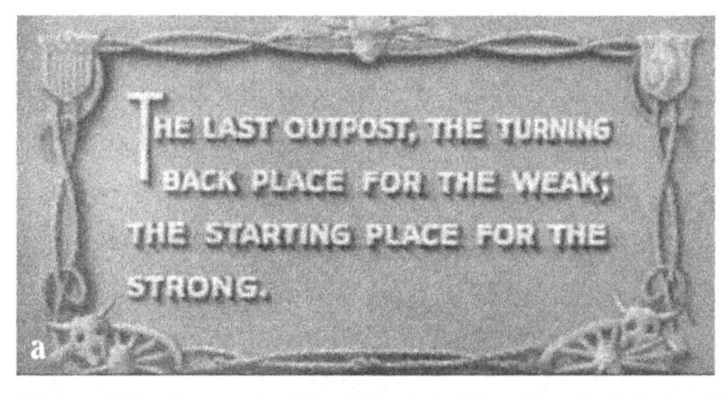

**Figure 25.** Survival of the fittest in *The Big Trail:* Intertitle from the "Grandeur" version (25a), and Coleman (John Wayne) standing over the frozen Lopez (Charles Stevens) (25b).

Westerns, which often speak biologically. In the wonderfully entertaining *Clash of the Wolves* (1925), even Rin-Tin-Tin knows "that the first sign of weakness means death" and hides evidence of the cactus thorn in his paw. When in *Buffalo Bill* (1944), Cody (Joel McCrea) comes across an old Indian left to die by her tribe, he must explain to an aghast Maureen O'Hara, "That's nature's way, Louisa." *The Big Trail*'s text intertitles – which come along between sequences in a transitional holdover from silent film – distinguish "THE WEAK" from "THE STRONG" (Fig. 25a), and the most obsessive spoken biological phrase in the film ranks "breeds" of men: "Indians have never stopped our breed of men from traveling into the setting sun"; Breck Coleman (Wayne) in particular is "the breed of man that would follow out a trail to the end." After the southerner Thorpe has been shot in the back, the two remaining villains are labeled in the intertitles (of the Grandeur version) as "TWO HUMAN WOLVES" who play out a survival-of-the-fittest endgame in the snow, with Flack finally stealing Lopez's blankets, telling him that in any case, "You'll be froze to death in an hour" (Fig. 25b).

British social philosopher Herbert Spencer's pre-Darwinian phrase "survival of the fittest" may have been quoted at the opening of *The Vanishing American* (1925), but the Western also generally adopts his less popularized argument that laws of evolution lead to a world of "the greatest perfection," toward peace ultimately, Spencer contended, not war.[6] *The Big Trail* is also characteristic of how the Western will eventually try to limit the pervasiveness of the brutalist world: It is outlaws who continue to live by Hobbes's "two cardinal virtues" in war – "force and fraud" – while our hero will be constrained by other rules.[7] The Western film evolves less by changing its vocabulary than by putting the more extreme social-Darwinist ideas into more suspicious mouths. In the post–World War II wagons-west film *California* (1946), it's a former slave-ship captain who will spout unqualified survival-of-the-fittest rationale during the gold rush. In Philip Kaufman's *The Great Northfield Minnesota Raid* (1972), outlaw Cole Younger has an easy time tricking a dishonest banker all too ready to swallow his own slick Gilded Age rhetoric: "After all, it's a game of wits, survival of the fittest." Lizards and scorpions, ancient survivors, herald our entry into the most unforgiving social-Darwinist worlds.[8]

In *The Big Trail,* John Wayne delivers a speech through a snowstorm to the discouraged and divided pioneers, some of whom are ready to turn back east (Fig. 26). A remarkably historically minded scout, Wayne is able to shout forth the central argument of the genre against the blinding wind:

> We can't turn back. We're blazing a trail that started in England! Not even the storms of the sea could turn back those first settlers. And they carried it on further. They blazed it on through the wilderness of Kentucky. Famine, hunger, not even massacres could stop them. And now we've picked up the trail again, and nothing can stop us. Not even the snows of winter, nor the peaks of the highest mountains. We're building a nation! But we've got to suffer. No great trail was ever blazed without hardship. And you've got to fight. That's life! And when you stop fighting, that's death.

The culminating idea of this speech – which turns the trick, the pioneers agree to continue – is that "life" is advanced by "fighting." The argument of course is not merely social Darwinist but in line with a whole range of intellectual and popular shifts in thinking at the turn of the twentieth century, toward seeing the essence of life in terms of relatively primitive struggle. Higher philosophical variations would include Nietzsche's "will to power," Henri Bergson's vitalist *élan vital,* even Freud's id.[9] Within popular variants, the shift has recently been discussed as a wide cultural battle to recover perceived masculine virtues – especially against domestic melodramas authored by women – that the Western both contributed to and mined.[10]

As we noticed earlier, it was Theodore Roosevelt who argued most stridently that "life" is "fighting." More than any other single figure, Roosevelt both expressed and enacted ideas that would be dramatized in the A-Western. He worried over the social implications of simple natural selection, and *The Big Trail* uses his vocabulary to argue biologi-

**Figure 26.** John Wayne's snowstorm exhortation to the pioneers in *The Big Trail:* "We can't turn back. . . . We're building a nation!"

cally for the Lamarckian genetic theory in which he believed – the inheritance of acquired traits – right from its dedication to "THE MEN AND WOMEN WHO PLANTED . . . COURAGE IN THE BLOOD OF THEIR CHILDREN," and a later intertitle (in the standard-aperture version only) tracks human phylogeny back through the vegetative to the inanimate land itself in "MEN AND WOMEN CROSSED WITH HICKORY AND BRED FROM GRANITE ROCKS."[11] "Strenuous life" was for Roosevelt the only one worth living. Although he employed that term to argue for expansionist foreign policy, he dramatized the necessity for such a life domestically by casting himself in his *Autobiography* as an eastern greenhorn who masters western ways. While on roundups of cattle, "I usually showed that kind of diplomacy which consists in not uttering one word that can be avoided." On a cold night in a Dakota barroom of the 1880s, a two-gun-waving cowboy chooses out bespectacled Teddy and shouts, "Four eyes is going to treat." He pretends to obey, but "As I rose, I struck quick and hard with my right just to one side of the point of his jaw. . . . He fired his guns." Roosevelt – a boxer at Harvard

– knocks him cold and "I took away his guns. . . ."[12] Small wonder that Owen Wister's *The Virginian,* into which this scene could be dropped, is dedicated to Roosevelt, "the greatest benefactor we people have known since Lincoln." After TR encountered a bear in Montana, he admitted to his sister than "doubtless my face was pretty white," but his nerves remained steely: "the blue barrel was as steady as a rock."[13] He neglects to mention that his spurs and pearl-handled revolver were made in New York by Tiffany's.[14]

In his *Big Trail* speech above, John Wayne still mirrors Teddy Roosevelt, down to the their tasseled buckskin. TR's beloved shirt – on view in the frontispiece to his *Hunting Trips of a Ranchman* (1885) – had cost him a hundred dollars (several months wages for working cowboys), but he justified it through a history of patriotic fashion:

> [The] hunting shirt made of buckskin was the most . . . distinctly national dress ever worn in America. It was the dress in which Daniel Boone was clad when he first passed through the trackless forests of the Alleghenies and penetrated into the heart of Kentucky . . . it was the dress worn by grim old Davy Crockett when he fell at the Alamo.[15]

Wayne's buckskin shirt in *The Big Trail* clings closer to his body; the looser fit and more flamboyant tassels favored by Roosevelt will be Wayne's fashion thirty years later when he casts himself as grim old Davy Crockett in his production of *The Alamo* (1960). Back in his *Big Trail* speech, Wayne is agreeing with Roosevelt that Daniel Boone – who blazed the trail "on through the wilderness of Kentucky" – would best exemplify the historical value of the life of fighting.

The Western film's sense of history grows partly from the historical novel, whose central feature, as György Lukács argued, is nationalist fighting and war.[16] It's here too that Cooper's Leatherstocking novels might again be thought of as one origin of the Western, for the way that they brought into the American landscape an allegory of nationalist fighting. By the time that moviemaking begins, the fighting within historical novels had added the biological justifications usually labeled "naturalist" in fiction (as in western-set novels by Frank Norris or Jack London). The Western hero is always the best fighter, a principle whose inviolability is impossible to overstate. It even shows up in the one-armed hero played by an aging Spencer Tracy in the post-Western *Bad Day at Black Rock* (1955), who can still lick town thug Ernest Borgnine in a fistfight.

Given the agreement that life is fighting, Hollywood could turn to a more precise debate in the early thirties: how to distinguish ethically among ways of fighting. John Wayne's (circular) argument in the *Big Trail* speech is that fighting is justified by looking back at the history of America. The wrong sort of fighting, then, must neglect history and be for merely economic gain. This fighting without a sense of history is demonstrated not only by Wayne's three antagonists in *The Big Trail* – two of whom have murdered his old hunter friend to steal his season's haul of wolf pelts – but also by the entire Hollywood genre that was proving the most popular in the initial years of sound, the gangster film, beginning with the first "all-talking" feature, *The Lights of New York* (1928), into *The Doorway to Hell* – released a week before *The Big Trail* – and on to the better remembered Edward G. Robinson and James Cagney films. King Vidor's *Billy the Kid,* another October 1930 release, was built around this debate over how to justify brutal fighting.[17]

Wayne's speech further justifies "hardship" by arguing that American history requires not merely fighting but also "suffering." This is a trickier idea to put over in the Western because it asks us to appreciate passivity – something done to us over time rather than something we accomplish – and because such suffering is central to the ostensibly antithetical "woman's film" and domestic novel. *The Big Trail*'s solution is to dramatize six months of suffering by pioneers – who fortunately endure their suffering across spectacular landscapes – while evading the wider agricultural suffering of new settlers, who in life often discovered that their crops failed in more arid western lands (a variety of suffering only given full dramatization after the studio era, as in the Swedish production *The New Land* [1972] and in independent films such as *Northern Lights* [1978] and *Heartland* [1980]).

Again, as the Western genre evolves after World War II, it retains its established vocabulary but puts the words into more questionable mouths. When in Richard Brooks's *The Last Hunt* (1956), Robert Taylor argues for the Hobbesian world of "Killing, fighting, war – that's the natural state of things," it's an early hint that he'll sink into a pathological exterminator of buffalo. More nuanced is John Wayne's return to his *Big Trail* words in *Rio Grande* (1950): "It's a life of suffering and of hardship," he tells his son about life in the western cavalry, and by that era the film can agree with him without entirely dismissing the counterargument from his wife.

It's worth noting that the ongoing appeal of all of this "suffering" is more than merely a holdover from discredited social Darwinism and grows also from the legitimate recognition that if "life" is worth anything, it must be about more than simple comfort.[18] A Western that precedes Cooper in this sense would be the autobiographical narrative published in 1819 by a certain Estwick Evans, who set out from his New Hampshire home to walk alone with his two dogs (soon eaten by wolves) through four thousand miles of what was then the West, setting out in "the season of snows . . . that I might experience the pleasure of suffering."[19]

Estwick Evans was another of those white men seeking to become something of an Indian ("I wished to acquire the simplicity, native feelings, and virtues of savage life") while also being a true romantic about nature: "How sublime is the silence of nature's ever active energies. There is something in the very name of wilderness, which charms the ear, and soothes the spirit of man. There is religion in it."[20] *The Big Trail,* like most Hollywood Westerns, makes an attempt to balance its appeal for suffering and fighting with a view of nature as healing, as soft and divine, a view that might be labeled after Jean-Jacques Rousseau (for passages in *Émile*) or British romantic poets (including Byron's evocation of a contemplative Daniel Boone in *Don Juan*), or even Thomas Jefferson (for his facts about the "sublime" Virginia lands).

Before John Wayne calls on the wagon-train emigrants to remember America's fight against unforgiving nature, he has lulled Ruth into this contradictory vision.[21] His campfire dance with her on the trail has been broken into by Thorpe, but that evening Wayne rides past her wagon before heading into open country to a Pawnee village. "Isn't that dangerous?" she worries, momentarily forgetting her pose of offense. His answer comes in another soliloquy of a length that few future directors would ask of Wayne:

> Lord, no. I love it. Especially now that it's Spring, and everything's so happy. Why, there's trees out there, big tall pines, just a'reachin' and a'reachin', as if they wanted to climb right through the gates of heaven. And there's brooks too, with water smiling all day long. But the part I like best is the night, lying out there beneath a blanket of stars, with that ol' moon smiling down on you.

And every time you look up, there she is, sort of guarding over you, like a mother minding her young. Sometimes it's so beautiful that I just lie there, listening. Birds singing, brooks lapping, and the wind sort of crooning through the forest like some great organ. Oh, I've always loved it. But I reckon I'm going to be lonely this time. You know, you can get sort of used to havin' somebody not like you.

This last allusion to their continent-long conflict puts a merciful end to a speech that Wayne delivers like a job of work, and the philosophy here is one that sound films learned to convey without words. *The Big Trail* is at its most idyllic putting this argument visually, as in shots of the tall trees that Wayne evokes, branches backlit through mist. There is no clash between the beauty of the trees and their falling under the emigrants' axes, in scenes shot with the same loving light. *The Big Trail* has nothing of Cooper's sense that fallen trees are the best symbol of man's hubris, evoked especially when Natty observes the "progress" of the wagon train in *The Prairie* with "a bitter smile" as "tree after tree came whistling down."[22] Rather the film takes up the dynamic pantheism of Whitman, for whom the axe was emblematic of America's energy (as in "Song of the Broad-Axe" and "Pioneers! O Pioneers!").

If nature in *The Big Trail* is far more convincing in its hard rather than its soft incarnation – which Wayne seems embarrassed evoking in words – that's in line with early-thirties Hollywood generally. There seems to have been a grittier "pre-Code" understanding of nature in the years before 1934 that came across in less forgiving landscapes and tougher tales of endurance: Compare William Wyler's harsh late-1929 *Hell's Heroes* to the 1936 Richard Boleslawski *Three Godfathers* and 1948 John Ford *3 Godfathers*, both remakes of the same story of desert survival. Wyler's alkali flats (shot on the edges of Death Valley), where sandstorms briefly bury the three outlaws, match the grimness of his resolution (in which all three die saving an infant) and the pitilessness of the dialogue (when they first come across the infant, Charles Bickford suggests, "See how far you can throw it"). By the 1936 version, the three still die, but the landscape (of California's Red Rock Canyon) has become less hellish, replaced by varied characterizations including what must be the genre's only outlaw Ph.D., who takes solace from reading Arthur Schopenhauer's vitalist pessimism ("Just jokes," as he characterizes Schopenhauer to Walter Brennan). By the time of Ford's sentimental Technicolor version, John Wayne survives into responsible adoptive fatherhood. In *The Big Trail,* only at the end does nature fully soften, through the reconciliation of our couple, free of words, as the camera tilts from their kiss to the tops of enveloping redwoods.

## Heaven's Gates: Philosophies of Faith

It's often said that the Western rejects Christianity to celebrate individualist heroism.[23] A defining moment would come in Owen Wister's novel *The Virginian* (1902) when the Virginian is at his least forgiving after sitting through a sinners-in-the-hands-of-an-angry-God sermon and contrives to send the sanctimonious minister packing by keeping him up all night, claiming to be wrestling with sin – a comic idea from this ideal figure.[24] Among the earliest film versions of this transference from pious Christianity would be D. W. Griffith's *The Spirit Awakened* (1912), where a "true Christian" ranch hand, who spends his off hours in the horse stable reading his Bible, finally abandons his ineffectual turn-the-other-cheek pacifism to race down and wield a knife against a thieving "renegade."

The genre as a whole, however, may be doing something more than simple rejection because of the ways that it incorporates both broad traditions of Christian faith in America. To outline the two traditions schematically: What one might label the "soft" or deist side, with its benevolent God, can be traced back in time through Emerson's transcendentalism, William Ellery Channing's Unitarianism and the early-eighteenth-century "liberal" theologians associated with Harvard College, and further back into such texts as Giles Firmin's Socinian *The Real Christian; or, A Treatise of Effectual Calling* (1670), whose merciful God approves of "self love." The "hard" tradition, with its wrathful God and emphasis on innate depravity and public conversions, would find nineteenth-century representatives in Lyman Beecher and Timothy Dwight and be traceable through Jonathan Edwards – who delivered his "Sinners in the Hands of an Angry God" sermon in 1741 – and back into the Puritan settlers.[25]

The soft side of American religious tradition – like the gentler hand of nature – might seem the only one congenial to Hollywood, especially after the Virginian ejects fundamentalism from the twentieth-century Western right at its start. And yet one of the Western's projects is to sneak back this harder, Puritan tradition in ways large and small. In the 1930s the critic and poet Yvor Winters, while lamenting Puritan influence on American literature, emphasized that "The Puritan view of life was allegorical. . . . [I]t separated man sharply and certainly into two groups, the saved and the damned, and, technically at least, was not concerned with any subtler shadings."[26] Such a Manichaean melodrama underlies the Hollywood Western, which in the 1930s arrives at its interest without significant moral ambiguity or subtler shadings between good and evil. Beyond that, the Western hero retains traits of the grimmest Puritanism and embodies a reclusive interiority that was only an ideal even for seventeenth-century Puritans. In *The Big Trail,* John Wayne's character has several old hunting friends among the travelers, but his watchful manner and confident gestures create a physical aura that separates him from everyone else and allows his young character to give off a curious impression of isolation – a necessity for the Puritan if his scrutiny of every act and private council with God was not to be broken. Wayne's Breck Coleman has both spring-loaded inner awareness – especially in his reactions with a knife – and an exterior calm, shunning emotionalism even when expressing emotion. "Inner-direction" (in the sense that sociologists used the term in the 1950s for a premodern ideal) becomes key to John Wayne's career, memorably evoked in what Wayne in interviews called the "lonely" clutch of his own elbow in the closing shot of *The Searchers* (an homage to Harry Carey, who can be seen using the gesture in John Ford's first feature, *Straight Shooting* [1917]).[27] In the few cases when this sort of characterization is underlined in dialogue, it comes out as in Anthony Mann's *The Man from Laramie* (1955) when James Stewart's fellow wagon driver confesses to him, "I'm a lonely man, Mr. Lockhart. So are you. I don't suppose we spoke ten words coming down here. But I feel I know you, and I like what I know."

John Wayne's dialogue in *The Big Trail* is generally in the "plain style" beloved by Puritans and taken up by movie cowboys, but it's worth recalling that Puritans condemned only eloquence that was obfuscatory. Wayne also delivers – in that snowstorm exhortation to the backsliding pioneers – a jeremiad: the rhetorical sermon formula that evoked the courage of the Puritan founders, called out for a return to their zeal, and directed an imperiled people toward their destiny. In his "political sermon" (another name that New England Puritans gave to the jeremiad), Wayne evokes the deprivations of the first Puritan settlers – whom "not even the storms of the sea could turn back" – both to shame by comparison his wavering followers and evoke for them the promise of ultimate success. As Sacvan Bercovitch argues about this rhetorical formula in *The American Jeremiad,* even the earliest seventeenth-century sermons on this continent looked back at the spiritual heroism of the Puritan founders not merely to castigate the present but to see continuity with the past and to demand progress for the future.[28] As Bercovitch notes in an earlier study, *The Puritan Origins of the American Self* – using Cotton Mather's life of John Winthrop as exemplar – the Puritan biographical method was to fuse faith together with an individual life, the geography of the land, and American history. The portentousness that can be so unsatisfying in *The Big Trail* and so many history-obsessed A-Westerns of the 1930s has as background this Puritan argument that an individual life history can prophetically reveal the exceptionalist future of "America" – the word that Cotton Mather seems to have been the first to use in its modern nationalist sense.[29]

Like most Western heroes, Wayne travels in *The Big Trail* through the Puritan world fraught with dangers that take forms both human and natural – a "pilgrim's" progress, to use a favorite Wayne appellation. He survives because he expects humans to be as evil and nature to be as unforgiving as they prove, without him, to be. Man's measure for a Puritan is how he copes with this world and, with evil so close, the Western hero must be rigid to withstand temptation. The obvious temptations – women, drink, dollars – are relatively easily resisted. Much more alluring is primitive violence. In John Wayne's career, we're never particularly worried about any but this last temptation, although he will be beset by such weaker allies as his longtime deputy, Dude (Dean Martin), in *Rio Bravo* (1959), who has a history of temptations by the other three. The stampede that crushes one of Thomas Dunson's (Wayne's) trail hands during the cattle drive north in *Red River* (1948) is started by a clatter of pans knocked over by a weak cowboy's impulse for a taste of sugar in the night, but the temptation into which Dunson will fall is to bullwhip the cowboy in a violent punishment beyond the call of justice. The rest of *Red River* builds itself around the question of whether Dunson will find the strength to resist an unnecessary gun battle against his adopted son.

The contradiction at the heart of the Puritan ethic is extended, rather than resolved, by the Western hero. The Puritan saw work as a moral yardstick and success in the world as a sign of spiritual salvation, of election (as opposed to the older and Catholic sense of work as post-paradise punishment). Thus the Puritan must be inner-directed while also driven to public demonstrations of his or her worth. One active response, the striving for success, runs from Benjamin Franklin's Poor Richard through Horatio Alger into the gangster film. As Robert Warshow suggested in the single most influential essay about the Western film, if its hero doesn't show the nervous frenzy of the gangster, it is because his work is almost indistinguishable from his self.[30] "Work" becomes a calm display of skill with a gun, or in the case of Wayne in *The Big Trail*, a knife. The Western may be at its most Puritanic in its merciless stance toward any faltering, because of how physical failure represents spiritual failure. There's a death sentence on weakness, or even nervousness. The standard scene of the shooting lesson is always a spiritual lesson in inner calm: Only gangsters jerk the trigger, son.

The Western hero's personal mission must coincide with public good. Wayne's character, Breck Coleman, explains to the murdering wagon master, Red Flack, why he's staying with the emigrants: "I've got two reasons. One is I told Welmore I'd scout the train through. The other is a little personal business I aim to transact at the end of the trail. See if you can figure out what that is, Flack." Although this principle of double duty is usually only implied, Wayne (as John Wyatt) states it baldly again in the protofascist *Westward Ho* (1935), "dedicated to the Vigilantes" who bring law to California in black uniforms. As he explains to sympathetic state officials, who apologize for being unable legally to fund vigilantes, "Since childhood, I've lived on the trail of bandits, hunting the men who murdered my parents, stole my brother. If it takes the rest of my life, I'll continue to hunt them down. At the same time, with the proper aid, I can do a good service to this country." Behind the genre's repeated connection of the merely personal with the patriotic is the Puritan concept of a twofold "calling": the need to listen simultaneously to the inner call for personal redemption and the outward call for a social vocation.[31]

None of this is too surprising, although it is worth remembering that the Western is the only Hollywood genre even permitted to discuss religions – Mormonism and Quakerism are favorites – and that the genre's religions can be hard and unforgiving to the extent that they facilitate progress. The founding syllogism from John Winthrop, first governor of the Puritan colony in Massachusetts Bay, went as follows: (1) "The whole earth is the Lord's garden," (2) He has said, "Increase and multiply," therefore (3) it is our duty to push westward.[32] In *Brigham Young – Frontiersman* (1940), the title character is forgiven by the film for faking a "revelation" because it motivates the Mormons to strike out in wagon trains west from Illinois in the 1840s, in contrast to those who go west for only economic reasons. (A shifty Mormon played by Brian Donlevy later says mockingly, "I just had a revelation – there's gold in California.") Early in the film, the Mormon prophet Joseph Smith (Vincent Price) is treated with suspicion by would-be adherents, but not by the film itself, because he acts less like a man of the cloth than a hands-on pioneer, carving out his own land, chopping his own trees. What Smith envisions is "not an easy religion" – and all the better for its acceptance into the genre.

This harsh strand of the Western, echoing angry-God fundamentalism and Old Testament fury, finds its purest evocation in *Hell's Hinges* (1916), returns with *Hellfire* (1949), and gets a rococo send-off with Clint Eastwood's *High Plains Drifter* (1972). John Wayne's modest entry in this tradition is the 1935 version of *New Frontier.* None of these Westerns flinches from the logical implications of the genre's embrace of archaic Puritanism. They drag their heroes through *imitatio Christi* and end with conflagrations of unredeemable towns. Blaze Tracy (William S. Hart) torches the wild town of "Hell's Hinges" after its boss exiles the few good citizens into the desert; *Hellfire* substitutes the Bible, called "the rulebook," for any looser code of the West and must be the only Western with "Amen" as an end title; Clint Eastwood's character may already have arisen from the dead before returning on his mission of fiery retribution in *High Plains Drifter.* In the 1935 John Wayne variation, an Old Testament sermon about the Lord coming with fire "to render his anger with fury" inspires a one-armed parishioner to torch the saloon in a blaze that consumes the town. The minister's prophecy that "the slain of the Lord shall be many" is fulfilled in a three-sided battle spectacularly silhouetted by the town's flames.

By the end of this 1935 *New Frontier,* Wayne and the film itself appear surprised by the harsh turn it has taken. The film apologizes with a soft closing sermon: "And it is with hope that our great nation will always remember the struggle and tragedy endured by you, the pioneers, who fought lawlessness to the end that there shall be peace and happiness in the years to follow." This rational, tolerant, optimistic, happy side of religion is familiar in Hollywood films but in Westerns often feels like a pro forma benediction for all that has come before.

It is true that categorizing Westerns as darkly "Puritanical" makes them sound perversely harsh, since Hollywood films, Westerns included, never finally forbid simple pleasures nor the love of a good woman. Westerns use the tension between Puritanism and the softer U.S. tradition – call it deist, or Unitarian, or Arminian – where progress westward comes from the fruitful collaboration between benevolent God and men who naturally know right from wrong. In the sense that deism posits God's purpose not as His glory but our happiness, it's the reigning religion of Hollywood cinema, where progress and democracy conjoin to ensure the survival of the decentest. That John Wayne will win all his shootouts is a principle so inviolable that suspense arises only when he mistakenly faces another decent man, as at the end of *Red River.* The motto of a sect of Arminians, "We can do it if we will," is in line with the positive-thinking emphasis on "will" in *The Big Trail:* "THERE IS NO ROAD, BUT THERE IS A WILL, AND HISTORY CUTS THE WAY."[33]

On story-line levels certainly the Western makes a point of shunning the sour, raised-on-prunes-and-proverbs representatives of Puritanism, of the sort that the Virginian sends running. Ministers are regularly figures of fun, too physically weak and usually too hypocritical to confront the depth of evil found in the Western. "Hard ridin' and soft religion don't mix, Mr. Parson," argues an intertitle in King Vidor's *The Sky Pilot* (1921). The Western's impulse is to follow Thomas Jefferson here, loving God but "revolted" by men who derive "pence and power" by claiming to represent Him on earth.[34] By the early 1930s, however, Hollywood's self-censorship Production Code artificially curtailed the genre's skepticism by discouraging the satire of ministers so common in silent Westerns. Even the repeated silent plot formula of having the evil town minister unmasked in the last reel as some sort of spiritual imposter was explicitly forbidden by the Code's rule 8.1: "Ministers of religion, or persons posing as such, shall not be portrayed as comic characters or as villains so as to cast disrespect on religion."[35] After the Production Code was well established, a hypocritical parson like the one in the interesting *The Outcasts of Poker Flat* (1937) must be redeemed by the last reel, winning the heroine against all narrative logic (including Bret Harte's, whose pair of stories on which the film is based kills off the major characters).[36]

Among *The Big Trail's* bows to softer religion is Wayne's speech linking tall trees to the gates of heaven, and illustrated in the light cast through the giant sequoias that throws a benediction on the couple in the film's last shot (Fig. 27). This metaphor of trees as a natural church reaffirms an American convention found, for instance, when Cooper's Natty Bumppo joins a gathering of Indians:

> The arches of the woods, even at high noon, cast their somber shadows. . . . It was probably from a similar scene that the mind of man first got its idea of the effects of gothic tracery and churchly hues, this temple of nature producing some such effect, so far as light and shadow were concerned, as the well known offspring of human invention.[37]

Likewise Washington Irving, when "overshadowed by lofty trees" in his *Tour of the Prairies* (1835), "was reminded of the effect of sunshine among the stained windows and clustering columns of a Gothic cathedral . . . and the sound of the wind sweeping through them, supplies occasionally the deep breathing of the organ."[38] This last natural-church metaphor is one that Wayne takes up in *The Big Trail:* ". . . the wind sort of crooning through the forest like some great organ." Leave it to Hollywood to be as ecumenical as possible about this happy metaphor, as in *California* (1946), which admires giant sequoia "trees so big you can carve yourself a Presbyterian church out of any one of them"; "Yeah, with enough wood left over for a synagogue and a Baptist mission."

*The Big Trail* also kneels to softer religion in two community prayer scenes, asking guidance at the start of the journey and thanks at trail's end. Still, it's probably significant that when Ruth instructs her young sister to include Wayne's character among her prayers ("Aren't you going to ask God to take care of Breck Coleman?"), she demurs: "Oh, Zeke says that Breck Coleman can take care of himself." We return here to that transference away from Christianity into purely secular heroism. And yet the Western hero retains the Puritan spiritual resistance through style. Increasingly in his career, Wayne will ride off alive but alone, clutching that elbow.

## Democracy's Discontents: Philosophies of Politics

By incorporating contradictory contentions about nature and religion, the Western strives to be dynamic and inoffensive, while also providing cover for its secret love of the darker philosophies. In its political philosophy, there is less obvious conflict: The Hollywood Western begins and apparently ends with praise for small-community democracy. Still,

**Figure 27.** Giant sequoias in the final scene of *The Big Trail* (with John Wayne and Marguerite Churchill almost lost at their base).

the Western finds dramatic tension and historical resonance by associating its stock characters with a range of American political traditions.

*The Big Trail* takes place within an actively democratic world, opening with a discussion among a three-generation family, as they make final preparations of their wagons, about how the decision will be made for the exact destination the emigrants should seek. "Ma" wonders why

"Dad" doesn't just decide for them, since "you're the leader," but he scrupulously makes clear that he's been "elected" only "leader of the Missourians" and that the larger national community is "thrashing that matter out now" in a "powwow" (a usage that unintentionally underlines parallels in the U.S. Constitution with Native American confederations, especially Iroquois).[39] However uncontentious the principle of small-scale participatory democracy seems in the genre, its characters get weight by carrying competing political echoes. For instance, if the wagon-train settlers extend key tenets of Jeffersonian democracy, John Wayne's scout is closer to extending those of Jacksonian democracy – a distinction we'll try to sort out below. Similarly, the film finds drama by associating Wayne's antagonists – Indians, a Mexican, a southerner, a mountain man – with the history of impediments to Anglo pioneering. "We're blazing a trail that started in England," Wayne reminds the pioneers in the snowstorm.

The wagon-train settlers are in search of an independent agrarian ideal most familiarized through Thomas Jefferson (and opposed, for instance, to the older Puritan suspicion of frontiersmen who "coveted the earth" and sought "elbow-room" outside of the settled community, in Increase Mather's disdainful terms).[40] Jefferson's most quoted words except for those in the Declaration of Independence are in praise of the farmer: "Those who labour in the earth are the chosen people of God, if ever he had a chosen people, whose breasts he has made his peculiar deposit for substantial and genuine virtue."[41] Jefferson opens this passage in *Notes on the State of Virginia* by differentiating these farmers from Europe's unenviable manufacturing workers in "the mobs of great cities." "The small land holders," he wrote privately, "are the most precious part of a state" precisely because they are the most free and thus, in Jefferson's eyes, the most ethical: "Corruption of morals in the mass of cultivators is a phænomenon of which no age nor nation has furnished an example."[42] Wherever else in the past one might find this agrarian ideal – and Jefferson admired Latin versions in Horace and Virgil – his point was that only in America could the ideal be realized in practice, because here city workers could never be permanently impoverished so long as they had the option "to quit their trades and go to laboring in the earth."[43] More than anything else, it was the availability of "free land" in the West that would thus continue to distinguish new America from old Europe. *The Big Trail* makes a point of discussing the ownership – or rather the lack of it – of land "north of Oregon" that the farm emigrants finally decide to seek, in looking for vacant land on which to found "a second Missouri."

One feature of Jefferson's agrarianism that has made it seem so "poetic" or pastoral, as distinct from the similarly land-centered economics of the French physiocrats of his day, is his insistence that the ideal democracy is made up of farms of family size.[44] In this, he was concerned less with any scale of efficient agricultural productivity than with "virtue" and the active citizenship presumed to be facilitated by the small farm. Through various Homestead Acts that deeded essentially free, 160-acre (and later 320-acre) western tracts to settlers, his ideal became enshrined in failed government policy, like so many ideas about the West better left in the imagination.[45] *The Big Trail* and most wagons-west films rest upon this idealization of family units. The trail west was usually known in the guidebooks that began to be published in the 1840s as "The Oregon and California Trail," and a choice between the two territories had to be made by the time travelers reached several undistinguished forks in the trail in western Wyoming known collectively as "The Parting of the Ways." In the 1840s California was the more typical destination for single men and miners, Oregon for families, who were encouraged also by congressional proposals for generous Oregon homestead grants. The joke in Oregon by the 1850s was that "a pile of gold-bearing quartz marked the road to California; the other road had a sign bearing the words 'To Oregon.' Those who could read took the road to Oregon."[46] The emigrants of *The Big Trail* first show their ethical seriousness by opting for a far-northwest destination, and later movie wagon trains to California often need to be explicitly justified as creating families in that wild, masculine state – as in William Wellman's *Westward the Women* (1951), with its wagons full of mail-order brides. A mark of the unredeemable financial scheming of the southerner Thorpe in *The Big Trail* is that he convinces Ruth Cameron to break off from the main group and travel with him "to the country they call California" – until his death saves her from that fate. It is by contrast with family farming that mining in Westerns is such a suspicious activity, as in Michael Curtiz's unusual early Technicolor *Gold Is Where You Find It* (1938), where California miners mock the Sacramento valley farms ("Oh, farming was alright in its day") that they flood with tailings stripped by their hydraulic operations. In its visual argument, *The Big Trail* again opts for illogical hardship by featuring parched desert travel of the sort endured historically less on the route to Oregon than on the trail to California through western Nevada. The film's widescreen format emphasizes not only the sweep of land but the large community of farmers on the move.

One of the enduring contradictions within the Hollywood Western is that it wants to idolize farmers but can't abide depicting farmwork. *The Big Trail* admires farmers working – but only on the trail, not when they reach their land, where cultivated fields and log-cabin homes appear with the magic ease of four overlapping dissolves. The contradiction is mirrored within the often contradictory writings of Jefferson. *Notes on the State of Virginia,* notwithstanding its famous paeans to farmers, never finds the space to describe any actual farms and saves its detailed descriptions for cascades, caverns, and wild mountains. That Jefferson himself never came close to independence on his Monticello estate in Virginia – he was an increasingly indebted, slave-based planter – no doubt made the ideal all the more appealing.[47] However much he conceived of "yeoman" farmers in abstract terms, as president he backed up the conceit with the very practical Louisiana Purchase, ready for their emigration. The Louisiana Purchase itself contradicted everything Jefferson professed to believe about limitations of executive power, a contradiction that Jefferson's keenest biographer, Joseph Ellis, argues can be attributed only to "the special, almost mystical place the West had in his thinking. . . . Jefferson like to think of the West in much the same way that some modern optimists like to think about technology, as almost endlessly renewable and boundlessly prolific."[48]

Andrew Jackson echoed Jefferson in telling his nephew, "I find . . . virtue to be found amongst the farmers of the country alone."[49] But through his image as a frontier fighter against Indians and British, Jackson's public leadership style diverged from Jeffersonian democracy's "gentle condescension" and came closer to that incarnated in *The Big Trail* by John Wayne's fighting trailblazer.[50] Jackson is the first U.S. president presumed to be cut from the same cloth as the people he leads, a leader known for his "intuition" rather than his "intellect" (as Nathaniel Hawthorne reported secondhand) and for having "never studied the niceties of language" (as Roger Taney, his chief justice, gently put it).[51] "To him knowledge seemed entirely unnecessary," the sometime Western novelist and playwright James Kirke Paulding said in justification, "He saw intuitively into everything."[52] In *The Big Trail*, Wayne's background is vague to the point of legend ("He comes from the plains, the mountains, he lived with the Indians, . . . he knows everything," a worried Lopez warns Flack), but he's the natural leader of the emigrants for the very reason that he knows, and can defeat when called upon, the Indians and the wilderness. This was the very claim to self-created leadership first discovered by Jackson's presidential campaigns, in which slogans and songs linked Jackson ("educated in Nature's school") to fellow middle-states pioneer Daniel Boone.[53] Legends aside, Jackson spent a number of lonely evenings in the White House cutting open his arm with his penknife, to prevent hemorrhaging from one of the bullets permanently lodged in his body after a wild town gunfight in Tennessee.[54] Wayne is physically tougher than the farmers he leads, and he differs moreover in not seeking property, a distinction that parallels Jacksonian democracy's moderation of the Jeffersonian obsession with the virtue of farmland ownership.[55]

The most celebrated Andrew Jackson text – now available on wall plaques and engraved under plastic busts – is picked up within John Wayne's character: "One man with courage makes a majority."[56] This interesting redefinition of democratic rule is propounded by Wayne to the emigrants out among the snowy Rockies, "I'm the law here, that's all" – even though we've seen no explanation, beyond his courage and toughness, why he should usurp legal authority from a democratic community explicitly willing, when faced with an attempted murder, to "call a settlers' meeting in the morning to try them." Wayne corrects the elected leader, "You can call a settlers' meeting to bury them." The Western is always threatening to redefine participatory democracy in terms of "natural aristocracy," to use Jefferson's term for the "best" leaders that Jackson has been said to fulfill.[57] In the early 1930s an amazingly diverse range of overtly political American films were agreeing, in ways that can't help but seem ominous in retrospect, that democratic communities were unable to solve problems without a single strong, even dictatorial leader – from Gregory La Cava's *Gabriel over the White House* (1933) to King Vidor's *Our Daily Bread* (1934) to the Columbia studio's idolatrous feature-length documentary *Mussolini Speaks* (1933).[58] A circuitous argument for this redefinition of democracy comes in Owen Wister's *The Virginian* after the narrator encounters the ideal cowboy leader in the person of the Virginian himself:

> It was through the Declaration of Independence that we Americans acknowledged the *eternal inequality* of men. . . . By this very decree we acknowledged and gave freedom to true aristocracy, saying "Let the best man win, whoever he is." Let the best man win! That is America's word. That is true democracy. And true democracy and true aristocracy are one and the same thing. If anybody cannot see that, so much the worse for his eyesight.[59]

Under this logic, we have to question our opening assumption about the Western's uncontentious praise of small-community democracy. The Western doesn't exactly dispute the value of "democracy" – the word itself is too sacred for that – but it redefines it in unrecognizable terms until it becomes a synonym for leadership by the superior man.

One way of writing a political history of the Western would be as a dispute over the definition of democracy. Whose rights are promoted? Whose are redefined out of existence? That would be a larger book. But if we stick to John Wayne as our guide through the forest of Western films, we can hazard a few hints about how the genre, for all its simple plotting, creates complex distinctions by associating characters with a history of contending American democratic traditions. *The Man Who Shot Liberty Valance* (1962), for instance, sets itself up as a Jeffersonian Western, while the earlier *Stagecoach* (1939), also directed by John Ford, looks more Jacksonian. *Liberty Valance,* that is, has many reservations about its conclusion, but ultimately something else wins out over the initially indispensable frontier individualism of Tom Doniphon (Wayne): a Jeffersonian democracy lugged from the East with his law books by Ransom Stoddard (James Stewart, whose Jeffersonian ancestry goes back to 1939 with his entrance as "Thomas Jefferson Destry" in *Destry Rides Again* and as "Jefferson Smith" in *Mr. Smith Goes to Washington*). When Stoddard convenes a schoolhouse discussion of liberty, the film is not unaware of the historical ironies of Doniphon's ranch "boy" (African-American actor Woody Strode) reciting what was "writ by Mister Thomas Jefferson." The film finds humor in Doniphon telling citizens assembled for a barroom vote that "one of the fundamental laws of democracy" is no drinking during elections, but only the serious Jeffersonian thrust of the film makes sense of the plot logic of having outlaw Liberty Valance (Lee Marvin) turn his sadism against the "free press" – Jefferson's "noble institution, equally the friend of science and of civil liberty"[60] – and of having cattlemen such as Wayne's Doniphon ultimately ousted for family farmers. *Stagecoach,* on the other hand, supports a democracy based more upon a Jacksonian fighting spirit. Within the stagecoach itself, the one irresolvable conflict is between the thieving banker, Henry Gatewood (Berton Churchill), and the rest of the passengers. "What this country needs is a businessman for president," Gatewood sanctimoniously tells them before badmouthing the cavalry – Jackson's military fighters – and Gatewood's eastern, citified villainy is of the sort that Jackson, living up to his image as "the wild man from the West," famously personalized in his showdown against the private Bank of the United States: "The bank, Mr. Van Buren, is trying to kill me, *but I will kill it!*"[61] *Stagecoach*'s businessman – a figure whose villainy was first conventionalized in Jacksonian-era stage melodrama – is contrasted to the self-sufficiency of the rest of the travelers, who pointedly take a vote and decide by majority, if not quite unanimously, to continue on and who pull together when the baby is born and Indians attack. An escaped prisoner, "the Ringo Kid" – John Wayne's character – has been apprehended near the start of the journey; but the sheriff turns his back when they arrive in Lordsburg long enough for Ringo to exterminate murderous brothers, and then allows him and his newfound love a final escape across the Mexican border. "Well, they're saved from the blessings of civilization," Doc Boone (Thomas Mitchell) comments archly. *Stagecoach* endorses an individual's fighting spirit even against civilization's reasonable laws. "One man with courage makes a majority," indeed.

*The Man Who Shot Liberty Valance* may use Jeffersonian democracy to cover John Ford's disillusion, or the later era's; but both it and *Stagecoach* agree that there is no place *within* the community for the individual vitality represented by Wayne, and that seems to be the Western's hidden and bitter final conclusion about egalitarian democracy. In its political philosophy, as with its philosophies of nature and religion, the Western is again darker than it lets on.

# 14. Manifestations of Destiny

Say! Looks like some new history goina be writ!
Kit Carson (Harry Carey) in *Sutter's Gold* (1936)

Shall we go, Mr. Terry? It seems Mr. Carson isn't interested in American history.
John C. Fremont (Dana Andrews) in *Kit Carson* (1940)

*Émile*, Jean-Jacques Rousseau's 1762 philosophical narrative about nature, history, and education, includes an arch parable. Adolescent and self-centered Émile is being raised out in the country by a tutor, "Jean-Jacques," who sets out apparently to teach him the principles of farming. Before Émile's beanstalks are ready for harvest, however, he finds them torn up, and weeps over the injustice. It turns out that the lesson he is being taught is not about farming at all but about private property: The plants had been uprooted by a gardener with previous claim to the plot, who is himself outraged that his rare melon seeds had been ruined by Émile's mere beans. In the social world, there is "hardly any" empty farmland.[1]

Westerns would agree that this is a cautionary parable – but about the problems of old Europe. *The Big Trail*'s purest argument for the existence of empty land on the American continent is made silently through camera angles and bodies. Pushing further the high-angle shots of *The Covered Wagon* (1923) and a century of landscape painting,[2] *The Big Trail* is punctuated with God's-eye widescreens of wagons snaking across valleys and deserts, with shimmering mountain vistas extending to the edge of the horizon. Still, *The Big Trail* is unusual among Westerns for investigating a little further, in dialogue at least, the assumption that empty land exists somewhere vaguely to the west. The film's would-be settlers have no particular destination in mind beyond their dream of "a likely stretch of country," an unoccupied "second Missouri anywheres out yonder." In the scene illustrated at the very beginning of Part Two, Wayne's Breck Coleman, the only one among them actually to have seen the far West, sits easy on his horse while he describes the bounteous natural wonders of a land "north of Oregon" even while he tries to discourage the pioneers: "But it's a long, tough pull from here, twenty-five hundred mile the way you'd have to go. No, it's too far off." What settles things, however, is Wayne's answer to their question, "How many people settled there now?" He tells them, "It's Indian country. 'Cept for trappers, never a white man has left his tracks there. Only one tradin' post in that whole country." The emigrants question Wayne further about "who owns" the post itself – "a Missouri trapper owns it."

The implication around all of this is that the wagon-train emigrants can expect to come to own the land themselves for several reasons with common-law traditions behind them. To a certain extent, the pioneers will be able to claim ownership by simply getting there first, through the principle of "first in time, first in right," which carried the most weight in American resource law, notwithstanding difficulties in distinguishing among legitimate acquisition, speculation, and theft.[3] As made explicit in Wayne's answer, Indians wouldn't be defined as "people" for purposes of legal ownership, just as Plymouth Colony governor William Bradford could write early in the seventeenth century of "the unpeopled countries of America."[4] *The Big Trail*'s farmers will be claiming ownership also by a second, subtler principle, because they will bring agriculture to the land. Through a labor theory of value, they would claim to pay for the land with their work to improve it – as opposed to the previous claimants that Wayne dismisses, the white trappers as well as the Indians. The principles here (via John Locke, Jefferson, and less well-remembered eighteenth-century legal thinkers) are that cultivation of the earth provides, in Benjamin Franklin's words, "the only *honest way*" to acquire wealth, and that labor expended upon land is the only validation of its legal possession – thus elevating farmers above not only trappers but also miners and cattlemen who, the presumption is, use the land in more transitory ways.[5] In practice, of course, such agricultural "improvement" in the ecology of the Great Plains often rapidly exhausted the thin topsoil, leading to only temporary occupancies or "settle and sell" farming. Still, permanent ownership by land improvement is held dear in Western films, undercut finally only by too-strident claims, as when Max von Sydow as a Swedish emigrant farmer in 1850s Minnesota in *The New Land* (1972) throws back his head to proclaim, like Rousseau's Émile, "I've earned a right to my ground!" after a kind-hearted trapper comes with tales about the genocide of the previous, Native American possessors of his land. The final small step to the claim of ownership by improvement in *The Big Trail* is putting up fences, which are being built in the background throughout the penultimate scene. This ownership-by-enclosure goes back in America to Massachusetts Bay governor John Winthrop, who in a convenient inversion allowed that Native Americans could keep what land *they* wanted to "inclose" – then "we may lawfully take the rest. . . ."[6] These principles combine to explain what de Tocqueville meant by his apparently contradictory characterization of America at the time of European discovery: "The Indians occupied without possessing it."[7]

The Western film makes a certain effort to disguise how obsessed it is over such disputes about possession. In his key early essay about the genre, Robert Warshow was led astray in saying of the Western that "Possessions too are irrelevant."[8] It was an easy error to make, and an influential one, but to say that is to fall for one of the genre's most fundamental sleights of hand. The Western distracts the eye first with unencumbered heroes like John Wayne in *The Big Trail* – who apparently carries all he owns in his saddlebags – and then by making a show of abandoning the inessential artifacts of civilization. In *The Big Trail*, chairs, tables, and heavy household furnishings litter the route before the travelers attempt to cross the Rockies. Meanwhile the genre slips back its principles about the importance of possession, primarily of land, but not only. After all, the vilest taunt in a Western is not "murderer"; it's "rustler" or "horse thief" – terms that label a man a thief of property.

Jeffersonian and Jacksonian democracy agreed fundamentally on the importance of expanding westward what Jefferson called the "empire of liberty" and Jackson called "the area of freedom."[9] Demands for territorial expansion by the twin forces of secular history and divine providence became encapsulated as the nation's "Manifest Destiny," a term for a hodgepodge of justifications coined by a Jacksonian newspaper editor shortly after the events depicted in *The Big Trail.* The catchphrase was ignored until being picked up for ridicule by a congressman denouncing the idea of acquiring the Oregon Country, and the term never caught on in the West itself.[10] Expansionism by many names had cycles of popularity in the United States, one such moment coming in the 1840s, the decade of the Mexican War and *The Big Trail,* and another at the turn of the century, at the time of the Spanish–American War and of the invention of the film Western. To some extent the film genre originates with an intentional confusion of the first era's expansionism with the second.

*The Big Trail*'s deepest, wordless argument for Manifest Destiny is carried by John Wayne's body. His youth, ease, and casually sensual buckskin costume set him off as the inheritor of the country's future, as opposed to his amusingly motley trio of antagonists: The heavily bearded Red Flack (Tyrone Power Sr.), with his uncountable layers of tattered clothes ("What does he know about water?" Wayne asks at a river crossing. "He never took a bath in his life"); the ferrety Lopez (Charles Stevens), lapsing into Spanish at moments of distress; and the mustachioed southerner Bill Thorpe (Ian Keith), who slowly sheds the formal black costume of a Mississippi riverboat gambler as he moves west.

Wayne's larger-than-life, all-American scout Coleman ("he comes from the plains, the mountains . . .") is the only major character not to be identified, at least by vocal accent, as originating in some European country or distinctive North American region, and the vague impression that he brings an Anglo-Saxon heritage is reinforced by his one statement about origins: "We're blazing a trail that started in England." (Among the little ironies here is "John Wayne's" – Marion Morrison's – own ancestry: His paternal great-great-grandfather Robert Morrison escaped to America in 1799 after his activity with Ulster's "United Irishmen" led to a English arrest warrant; his maternal grandmother emigrated after the Irish potato famine, which English policies had turned genocidal.)[11] The film imposes early-twentieth-century attitudes, more admiring of the English, onto the 1840s. The wittiest Western-film expression of this stance in the 1930s comes in Leo McCarey's *Ruggles of Red Gap* (1935) when the British manservant Ruggles (Charles Laughton) is alone among Washington State's pioneers in being able to evoke American democratic ideals, by reciting Lincoln's

Gettysburg Address. At the time when *The Big Trail* is set, in the early 1840s, it was not only that anti-English sentiment remained from the war of the 1810s and Jackson's presidency, but that it was from the British themselves that this "empty" Oregon Country would have to be claimed, relying loosely on the 1792 "discovery" of the Columbia River by Robert Gray – subject of that quiz question early in the film. The opposing claims of the Hudson's Bay Company – and its perhaps 750 British subjects then living north of the Columbia River – were being derided as "monopolistic," and soon President James K. Polk's expansionist 1844 presidential campaign targeted the Oregon Country with the slogan "54° 40′ or Fight" – which would have put the northern U.S. border just south of Russian Alaska.[12]

The British are evoked only as inspiration and never as antagonists in *The Big Trail.* The one collective impediment to westward progress are Cheyenne Indians who loom on the horizon just as the travelers are weakened from a tough river crossing. Breck Coleman has an ambiguous relationship to the Indians that in some ways looks back to an older style of 1920s Westerns and even to the lost opportunities of the earliest eastern Westerns but that also leads into the slaughters of the Hollywood years to come. The subject of Indians is introduced, for the first time in a John Wayne film, by a group of admiring children who gather around him, before the wagon train pulls out from the Mississippi, to ask, "Did ya ever kill a dead Indian?" (Fig. 28). "No, I've never killed any *dead* ones," he responds evasively until they press him further: "Before they was dead, did ya?" "No," he finally says, "you see, the Indians are my friends" – though evidence for this familiar old claim of "friendship" is more scant than in silent Westerns. He's seen in a two-shot flashback with an Indian companion when they come across the bones of the murdered trapper; he can "palaver" in sign language with Pawnee scouts he hires along the trail; and he negotiates peace with the first group of Cheyenne led, luckily enough, by "Black Elk, an old friend of mine." In all of this Wayne here is close to the Western hero played throughout the late 1910s and early 1920s by William S. Hart, who regularly conversed in fluid sign language with his friends the Indians, notably in *Wagon Tracks* (1919). In that film Hart also agrees to lead a wagon train west to follow his suspicions that a murderer –

**Figure 28.** "Did ya ever kill a dead Indian?" the children ask Breck Coleman (John Wayne) at the start of *The Big Trail.*

of his brother – is among the emigrants. Although Hart too so fully usurps the community's legal authority that he becomes "The Judge" in intertitles, he's pained to be cheated of personal vengeance by his respect for the tribal law of the Kiowas (to whom the murderer is given up for another claim against him).

Throughout his career, John Wayne's "sympathy" for Indians is internalized, which has its dangers too. The transference that we noted at the end of Part One – where Native Americans "vanish" on film at the same time that whites claim to become Indian themselves – nowhere reveals its price more than in Wayne's evolving career. A film such as *Hondo* (1953), where Wayne's title character is himself part Indian and has had an Apache wife, develops logically out of his *Big Trail* scout, who, when he is not struggling through those rhetorical monologues, tends to speak in vaguely "Indian" fashion ("Our paths fork here. . . .") and signals with a "Comanche yell" that others take for the cry of a panther. There was initially in America, as we saw in relation to the Pocahontas myth, an optimistic strand whereby such racial amalgamation offered national salvation, although Thomas Jefferson was its last politically powerful exponent and he was typically contradictory about it.[13] The pattern embodied in Wayne was darker: He identifies with the vanishing race while *also* dismissing any softheartedness toward their demise. After its slaughter of Indians, *Hondo*'s last lines are the briefest eulogy delivered in Wayne's offhand staccato: "Yep. End of a way of life. Too bad. Was a good way." He will sentimentalize the words a touch in *Chisum* (1970), regarding an old Comanche foe now confined to a reservation: "End of his way of life. Pretty good way too. I respect him. We're brothers." As Garry Wills pointed out in a comparison with Clint Eastwood, Wayne seldom has contempt for his adversaries,[14] and one reason is that Wayne's adversaries are so much a part of himself. John Wayne's greatest, late roles, all so self-destructive and convincingly death-haunted – in *Red River, The Man Who Shot Liberty Valance,* and especially *The Searchers* – develop out of his earlier identification with the race he slaughters. It is this deep identification that humanizes and makes tragic even the pathological racism of his character in John Ford's *The Searchers* (1956), the film that seems an inevitable culmination in retrospect.[15]

The legendary historical figures that Wayne's character in *The Big Trail* most resembles are Daniel Boone and Kit Carson, in their combinations of trail scout, Indian sympathizer, and Indian killer.[16] Recall that in the film of *The Vanishing American* (1925), Kit Carson is given the intertitle dialogue, "These Indians are my friends . . ." and finishes his sentence with ". . . but I must send them to their death." In *The Big Trail* Wayne doesn't qualify his claim that "the Indians are my friends," but, if we are to believe his story to the children that he has never killed them before, he makes up for lost time. The film justifies its unhistorical, grand-scale slaughter with a vague portrait of unreliable Indians.[17] Early in the film Wayne negotiates a carefully explained "Peace, so long as we march straight through the Cheyenne country without stopping to settle"; but a later attack by the Cheyennes, along with Crow allies, is given not the slightest motivation. To his character's credit, Wayne shows no surprise that an agreement with one band wouldn't necessarily carry over to others even within the same tribal group, but the film's emphasis is on the sacrifices of the white pioneers. After the attack, they leave behind a large cemetery, filled with crosses and one lone dog waiting faithfully at his master's grave.

**Figure 29.** Wayne's trio of antagonists in *The Big Trail:* The wagonmaster Red Flack (Tyrone Power Sr.) scratching his beard (29a); the southerner Bill Thorpe (Ian Keith) offering his arm to Ruth (29b); the Hispanic Lopez (Charles Stevens) backing from the raised knife (29c).

The Indians in the film remain collective and depersonalized. Other historical impediments to Manifest Destiny's progress are personalized in Breck Coleman's three antagonists: the western trapper, the Mexican, and the falsely chivalrous southerner (Fig. 29).

Of the three, Red Flack, the murdering wagon master, is the roughest and stands in for the older West of mountain men and hunters. As played by former Broadway star Tyrone Power Sr. – in his only sound film before his death in 1931 and thus in the only one to capture his extraordinarily deep voice – he's a barely civilized backwoodsman, face hidden under a mop of hair and an apparently lice-ridden beard that he scratches constantly. His lumbering walk is the furthest remove from Wayne's balletic ease, and Flack increasingly resembles a bear under the shaggy coat that he wears until Coleman finally throws a knife into his heart. Flack's theft of wolf pelts also reinforces that he's representative of the older fur-trading West, played out economically and illegitimate under any of those agricultural-based claims to legal ownership of the West. If Breck Coleman too has a past among trappers, his physical style and ability to talk to a woman – something Flack is never seen to do – reinforce how he moves with the times.

The second antagonist, Lopez, dressed vaquero-style with long scarf, tight pants, and sombrero, speaks Spanish when he's fearful of Coleman or superstitious of the knife that he and Flack have used to kill Coleman's old friend. He's played by Charles Stevens (of Apache ancestry) who had the genre's longest career playing Hispanics and Indians, from Douglas Fairbanks Westerns in the 1910s through the early 1960s. Coleman is curiously mild to Lopez, and doesn't kill him even after Lopez stabs what he thinks is Coleman's sleeping body. Lopez stands in for the Hispanic West otherwise unrepresented in *The Big Trail,* even though in the early 1840s the Oregon Trail travelers would be skirting the northern boundary of Spanish claims.

Bill Thorpe is the genteelly duplicitous southerner who twice tries to shoot Coleman in the back from afar, killing only his horse the first time and dying himself during the second attempt (at the hands of Zeke [Tully Marshall], who has overheard his plot with Flack). In his long dress coat, tie, and ruffled shirt, the well-groomed Thorpe makes a show of civilization so complete that he brags about his "old plantation" even to his coconspirators ("Your? Your plantation, huh? Lopez, he's hollered so much about that thar plantation of his, he believes it his self," Flack explains). Although Thorpe apparently wasn't party to the murder of Coleman's old friend, he falls into a rivalry with him over Ruth Cameron (Marguerite Churchill), one that also reads as a conflict of regions. Thorpe, as played smoothly by Boston-born Ian Keith, has a suspicious southern accent, and it may be that even southern roots are part of the character's lies. In regional terms, the film argues that Wayne's authentic West defeats an inauthentic South.

In so often and so stridently making this argument about the relative authenticity of the two regions, the Western genre protests too much. That is, the Western always claims as its own distinctive creation certain character traits and varieties of violence that historically in the United States were truer of the Old South, and to a certain extent remain true of the newer South – especially the high regard for "individualism," the valuation of rituals of "honor" as a justification for violence, and the long survival of a vigilante tradition of local justice.[18] Indeed, the types of murder that Western legends claim as so distinctive to the West – personal quarrels, barroom gunfights, killing over insults – remain statistically much more common in the South than in any other region, including the West.[19] There are a variety of reasons why the Western wouldn't admit how much it takes from the reality of the Old South, but chief among them is that to do so would be to admit how far such Western violence is from its mythic justification – as a temporary expedient needed for the historical advancement of the nation toward higher civilization. To see such gunplay as in any way merely "southern" would be to admit how much it looks not forward but backward toward a defeated traditionalism. It may be for such reasons that Thorpe is the least authentic character in *The Big Trail,* just as the southerner "Hatfield" (John Carradine) in *Stagecoach* (Wayne's other A-Western of the decade) is the one traveler who must die on the trip.

The genre's principle seems to be this: In Westerns, the visionary men who represent the West look forward and bring the nation together, whereas those who cling to an identification with the South look back and divide it – and almost inevitably die. This conflict also structures *Dark Command* (1940) – John Wayne's only other film for Raoul Walsh – which casts Wayne as a straight-talking Lawrence, Kansas, marshal against the historical figure of William Quantrill (slightly renamed "William Cantrell" and played by Walter Pidgeon), the Confederate guerrilla terrorist who is seen as bringing on the Civil War for gangster-style personal power ("I'm going straight to the top!"). In the 1930s the Western's contention about the two regions is argued out fully in *The Texans* (1938), where a southern belle (Joan Bennett) schemes for a post–Civil War aristocratic alliance with Mexico's briefly reigning Emperor Maximilian, but a former Confederate soldier (Randolph Scott) becomes the film's hero by turning visionary scout, recognizing that a new cattle trail through the West "would pull the North and the South back together. . . . It would mean a new future for Texas."[20] The same ideal of national unification lies behind *The Big Trail*'s pointed claim that the settlers include wagons "from every state in the union."

By the time the pioneers arrive "north of Oregon," all impediments to their Manifest Destiny have been routed or killed. The Indians are vanquished; the mountain man Flack, the Hispanic Lopez, and the southerner Thorpe are dead. Questions of ownership no longer need to be examined and, after those four lap dissolves establish farm life, the small community is settled. This ease of ownership reveals its full fantasy only when John Wayne leads another group of pioneers "hitting the trail to Oregon" in *Three Faces West* (1940), a version of the wagons-west, big-trail story set in contemporary America. "You'll hear history in the making!" a radio newscaster exclaims of the line of farm trucks that this time make the epic trip from the "dust bowl" middle states to what Wayne tells them is "new land" in Oregon (Fig. 30). (Again, only troublemakers – and Nazis! – want to cut south to California.) This time the improbabilities cannot be covered by labor theories of ownership by "good honest sweat," by the film's montage of land clearing, field plowing, and home building, nor by making a "temporary temple" under a tree with another final tilt shot to its highest branches. As the *New York Times* noticed in its review, "These settlers find an Eden which is apparently there for the taking. . . . And how a community supposedly ruined by dust storms manages to acquire rich bottomlands of Oregon with hardly any trouble isn't explained. An economic impasse can't be evaded by a trick with mirrors."[21] No, to be convincing to audiences, this argument had to remain the property of traditional Westerns set back in nineteenth-century history.

In its first decade of sound, then, the Western enlists America's social and political philosophies in some of the ways outlined above. Still, as a full explanation for the way Westerns argue about history or for the way they link history to modern life, such methods of analysis carry us only so far.[22] The dissatisfaction one may feel about this kind of historical analysis is difficult to disentangle from the dissatisfaction one feels about the thirties A-Western itself. It is partially that the films blithely refuse to admit just how contradictory are their ideas about nature, religion, and politics, and also that the decade's A-Westerns never discovered how to link fluidly their historical arguments to storytelling in any

**Figure 30.** John Wayne drives "the trail to Oregon" in *Three Faces West* (1940).

ways that didn't turn out to be ponderous. The "history lessons" stand out as awkwardly as do John Wayne's stolid speeches in *The Big Trail.* When one watches a lot of Westerns from the 1930s, the A-Westerns come to seem quite grimly dogged, and only the B-Westerns transcend their contradictions with verve. What is more surprising is that the lowly B-Western also crafts more convincing arguments about American history, without half trying.

# 15. Rambling into Surrealism: The B-Western

Kinda like history repeatin' itself, ain't it?
Harry Carey in *The Last Outlaw* (1936)

The thirties B-Western cuts through the genre's dilemma about history with liberating ease, but it doesn't do so directly. The historical era in which the films are set is often not so much imprecise as purposely odd and ambiguous. Stagecoach riders fall victim to a holdup while journeying to watch John Wayne compete in a 1930s rodeo in *The Man from Utah* (1934). The title trio of *The Three Mesquiteers* (1936) return from World War I to help out a covered-wagon train. Although the movies' towns often appear modern, filled with automobiles, radios, and well-tailored businessmen, just outside the city limits we invariably find the Old West of horse chases and six-gun shootouts.

The most knowingly droll of films set in such a divided world may be *The Last Outlaw* (1936), which draws on associations carried by its aging stars. Harry Carey, star notably of twenty-four John Ford silent Westerns (all but two now lost), is Dean Payton, the title's frontier bank robber who is released from prison and boards a bus to "Center City" to look up the sheriff, Cal Yates (Henry B. Walthall, star of *The Birth of a Nation* back in 1915), who had captured him and brought law to the town when it was known as "Broken Knee." Payton comes across a book published about his own exploits but can barely step off a curb without automobiles honking and drivers shouting, "Hey, where's your horse, Pops?" (Fig. 31a). The old sheriff is now reduced to "Under-Sheriff" below a "go-getter – younger, progressive." The escape car of some slick bank robbers, however, proves as unreliable as the squad car of the new sheriff, and the two pioneers ride horses to pin the robbers down at

**Figure 31.** *The Last Outlaw* (1936): Carrying his prison bundle, the released outlaw (Harry Carey) dodges automobiles in the city (31a), then uses his old skills to catch bank robbers alongside the "Under-Sheriff" (Henry B. Walthall, *at left;* 31b).

the same cabin where Payton had been captured years before. "You know, this sort of reminds me of old times," he says. "Kinda like history repeatin' itself, ain't it?" (Fig. 31b). The two are assisted by relative youngster Chuck Wilson (Hoot Gibson, who had appeared with Carey in Ford's 1917 *Straight Shooting*), a small rancher with credit problems. "These banks are the hardest things to get money out of. You ever try it?" he asks, momentarily forgetting Payton's bank-robbing past. Carey's bemused gravity allows him to voice a question that the film plays with: "What do you suppose everybody's risking their lives for nowadays?" Like the film itself, Carey's character knows only two disconnected eras – he spent the intervening years in prison – and for him the old ways are less nostalgic than practical.

Approached logically, B-Westerns seem irresponsibly cavalier about the era in which they are set. Some B-Westerns reveal a modern setting with a little punch of surprise, as in that 1939 version of *New Frontier,* with its joke about the Indians who turn out to be disguised white townsfolk. But B-Westerns usually play any leap in eras with a straight face. Among John Wayne's films, *The Lucky Texan* (1934) is the most leisurely about revealing itself fully. It seems to take place in the nineteenth century for the first fifty of its fifty-five minutes until Gabby Hayes hops into an automobile to chase crooks escaping by rail handcar – though Wayne finally beats them all on his white horse. *Overland Stage Raiders* (1938) gets its distinction by relying on every mode of Western transport *except* automobiles: To foil the robbery of gold carried on "the 3 o'clock stage" – which turns out to be a Greyhound bus – Wayne parachutes over to his horse. The same film manages to include scenes of cattle rustled off a train (foiled by cowboys on horses) and a race against mules hauling gasoline to the outlaws' downed plane. B-Westerns are often set in the world of fashion time warps, with women in the latest thirties gowns while men cling to Old West outfits and holsters.

Such films backed into their surrealism. The Western, that is, slowly evolved into what by the 1930s comes to look absurdist by its conservative refusal to give up the genre's defining belief that the "Old" West is intimately linked with our life. When the narrative Western film began in the first decade of the century, there was little distinction needed between films set in the nineteenth-century West and those set in contemporary America. Halfway through "Broncho Billy" Anderson's *A Ranchman's Rival* (1909), it's not particularly surprising when the city slicker and fake minister drive up in an automobile across the Colorado plains. Even the 1910 calendar on the back wall of the cavalry outpost in several Selig Westerns of that year seems only mildly odd. There is no exact year at which the claim that the Old West still surrounds us began to seem truly strange. Notwithstanding the technical "closing" of the "frontier" in 1890 (according to obscure census figures), more land was first brought into cultivation over the next thirty years than in the previous thirty, and more public land was taken up through Homestead Acts in the first two decades of the twentieth century than in all of the nineteenth.[1] In this sense "the frontier" remained open, whatever the economic problems for small farms. But by the 1920s a cycle of silent features – such as the Douglas Fairbanks vehicle *The Mollycoddle* (1920) and Buster Keaton's *Go West* (1925) – could find genuine comedy in the presumption that a traditional Old West could still be located somewhere. Within that cycle, the most pointed is Gregory La Cava's *Womanhandled* (1925), where Richard Dix desperately struggles to maintain the illusion of the frontier West for a woman hot on old-fashioned virility. After rounding up a few cattle with a touring car, the tennis-playing cowboys find appropriate costumes. "We snitched them out of the museum," they finally admit. It's not that ranch hands aren't still needed, but that "All the real cowboys have gone into the movies."

By the 1930s, as we have seen, the A-Western is slogging through its histories of nineteenth-century pioneers, while demanding, in ponderous dialogue and heavy symbols, acknowledgment of the value of their achievements for twentieth-century descendants. The decade's

**Figure 32.** John Wayne and his horse meet motor vehicles on their last miles in *Paradise Canyon* (1935) (32a) and *Somewhere in Sonora* (1933) (32b).

B-Westerns make that argument by leaping across the years. In these B-films, the nineteenth century generally solves the problems of the twentieth, the past usually resolves the conflicts of the present, the country sets straight the confusions of the city. The valorization of horses in B-Westerns has partly to do with the way horses stand in immediate visual contrast to the automobile and its centrality to the twentieth century. "Horses are a thing of the past," a Western hero often will be informed, as in *Desert Justice* (1936), where horses are threatened with the glue factory, but their association with the past is exactly the point for B-Westerns. "Looks like you need a couple of horses for this wagon, Doc," John Wayne tells the driver of a broken-down truck in *Paradise Canyon* (1935) (Fig. 32a). "We'll trade in this ol' crate for a hayburner," a woman announces in offhand slang to explain why she needs to buy just one final gallon of gas to drive to the ranch where Wayne works in *Somewhere in Sonora* (1933) (Fig. 32b). Motor vehicles are the transportation mode of gangsters, representatives of the city's individualist greed. "Yeah, using trucks for rustling's the latest thing," an up-to-date Chicago mobster instructs an underling in *Code of the Cactus* (1939). And when faced with a burro, "Pretty Boy Hogan" in *The Cowboy Star* (1936) whines, "I can't make that thing go." The most evocatively lunatic representation of this conflict may come in the 1932 Monogram Western *From Broadway to Cheyenne,* when gangsters out in California's Joshua-tree country halt their touring car to pull machine guns from violin cases and shoot a herd of cattle owned by a rancher who refuses to join their "Independent Cattlemen's Protection Association."

In a much-discussed 1932 presidential campaign speech in San Francisco, Franklin Roosevelt conceded that the Jeffersonian solution for urban unemployment was no longer tenable, although in arguing the need for an historical shift in government action, Roosevelt had motives for suggesting that it once had been:

> On the Western frontier, land was substantially free. . . . At the very worst there was always the possibility of climbing into a covered wagon and moving west. . . . Traditionally, when a depression came a new section of land was opened in the West; and even our temporary misfortune served our manifest destiny. . . . A glance at our situation today only too clearly indicates that equality of opportunity as we have known it no longer exists. . . . There is no safety valve in the form of a Western prairie to which those thrown out of work by the Eastern economic machines can go for a new start.[2]

Roosevelt might have carried the metaphor further, because by the 1930s the seldom-voiced truth had become demonstrably the reverse of Jefferson's principle about the value of open land to prevent urban discontent: It was the *cities* that had been serving for some years as "safety valves" to release *agrarian* discontent. Failing midwestern farmers had at least the possibility of moving to Chicago, and certain rural Kansas and Nebraska farm counties had lost more than half their populations to the growing cities in the turn-of-the-century decades, a pattern that accelerated after World War I.[3] In freeing itself of linear historical logic, however, the B-Western can obsessively retell a disconnected two-era fable in which the nineteenth century resolves the economic and ethical problems of modern urban life.

The B-Western valorizes the nineteenth-century West further by seeing it solve problems associated with every other era – from the eighteenth century to the twenty-first. In Westerns popular in the first years of the 1930s – alongside Universal Pictures' cycle of horror films – the Old West comes up against an even older, gothic world. The most compelling of these films must be *Mystery Ranch* (1932), where the title's ranch house is darkened by shadows (from cinematographer Joe August, three years before his expressionism for John Ford's *The Informer*) and a sinister, German-accented, piano-playing owner who lives in a time warp from the light-bathed Old West town. George O'Brien's smiling openness defeats Germanic shadows, with less angst than was required of him in Murnau's *Sunrise*. In John Wayne's entry in this cycle, *Haunted Gold* (1932), he's a friendly cowboy who laughs off vague threats from "The Phantom" and the grim, aged guardians of a mine whose faces too are shadowed (by cinematographer Nicholas Musuraca, a decade before his early film-noir mastery in *Cat People* and *Out of the Past*). The secret passageways and the heroine's sense that "there's something uncanny and weird about everything . . . like someone was always watching and spying" go against the bedrock values of the Western, which fights for an openness both visual and ethical. Visually the story is this: Sunny America defeats shadowed Europe.

Of thirties Westerns that use the Old West to fight the imagined hazards of the future, the most entertainingly bizarre remains Gene Autry's infamous Mascot serial *The Phantom Empire* (1935), which for twelve episodes pits "The Radio Riders from the Radio Ranch" against a technologically advanced underground civilization that relies on robot drones, ray guns, guided missiles, and wrist communication devices that convey orders from the "Queen of Murania." *Ghost Patrol* (1936) may be unique in managing a three-era conflict among the gothic past (in a "ghost town" below which the plotters work in expressionist caves), the future (where a "radium tube to control all electrical impulses" sends planes crashing), and the Old West, from which Tim McCoy rides to set the centuries straight. Among B-Western stars, it was Gene Autry who best demonstrated how to reconcile the Old West with modern life by casting new media as the people's communication, an understanding shared by President Roosevelt in his "fireside" radio chats. In *Public Cowboy No. 1* (1937), the rustlers rely, it's true, on refrigerator trucks and airplanes, while Autry sings his lament, "The West Ain't What It Used to Be" – with its ambiguous lyric about Roosevelt's farm efforts: "There's a new deal now in the West" – but Autry's ultimate means of foiling the rustlers is by short-wave radio ("Calling all cowboys! Calling all cowboys!") and the montage of responding bunkhouse men brings together a community on horseback.[4]

If the B-Western leaps across the centuries to locate a "safety valve" for modern pressures in an Old West, a place available for practical and ideological use just outside city limits, then what might the films be claiming by this double world? Is there anything to it beyond nostalgia? Or, to return to the questions we took up before, could such lowbrow Westerns be justifying themselves by drawing from any American intellectual traditions?

Revealingly, it is a particular kind of West that B-Western finds when it leaps back across the centuries, and the traits of that West correspond to an agrarian-centered argument about the essence of America, an argument most famously codified by historian Frederick Jackson Turner and from which Franklin Roosevelt drew in his campaign speech. As every older history of the West reminded us, Turner's "frontier thesis," initially delivered as a lecture at the 1893 Chicago World's Columbian Exposition and elaborated over the years, saw the West as a place whose essentially free natural abundance was what allowed for the prosperity of eastern American cities. Turner furthermore located the primary reason for America's distinction and the key to its democratic institutions in the fact that the nation possessed "that great supply of free lands" on the frontier, which, according to his citation of the census figures, had essentially "closed" after 1890. As a result of this logic, the nation's future could only look troubled.[5] The other major way of defining the essence of America in relation to the West centered on the Indian wars, an argument that, as we've seen, was made strongly in Theodore Roosevelt's historical writings and anticipated notably in Francis Parkman's. In this view, recall, democracy was carried forward by victors in a racial battle over the land. Among recent cultural historians, Richard Slotkin has most fully demonstrated how relatively little Turner's frontier thesis influenced or paralleled the twentieth-century pulp stories and films about the West, notwithstanding its centrality to academic historiography. Instead, as Slotkin traces in *The Fatal Environment* and especially *Gunfighter Nation,* Roosevelt's Indian-war reading of the past "is closer in style, emphasis, and content to the productions of industrial popular culture" and "Roosevelt's influence is paramount in the cultural realm."[6] Slotkin gets all of this unarguably right for the main path of the film genre, which also puts racial conflict at its center. However, something additional is first revealed by an unexpected trait of the thirties B-Western: the virtually complete absence of Indian characters or of plots that even touch upon wars against Native Americans.

As we saw in Part One, the film Western found its distinctive form after that shift from productions on the East Coast to those made in the West, and with this geographical change in locations came the fundamental shift in the way white–native relations were portrayed on film. As we also noticed, with the end of the silent film Native Americans "vanished" from the genre as anything like individualized characters. What becomes even clearer with the Western of the 1930s is that there were two distinct forms that this "vanishing" could take in Hollywood. In one, the Indian could become an unindividualized horde, war-whooping, seldom speaking, swooping down en masse from ominous hilltops, and then gunned down with godlike accuracy from long distance in uncountable numbers. This is the option seen in *The Big Trail* in 1930 and in virtually all of the decade's other A-Westerns through De Mille's *Union Pacific* and Ford's *Stagecoach* in 1939. In the other option, the Indian story could simply vanish from the screen altogether, elbowed out by other narratives; and this is the pattern taken by the decade's B-Westerns. Nothing more starkly separates the A- and B-Western than their use, or avoidance, of the Indian.

Although there are of course exceptions among the one thousand B-Westerns of the 1930s, it remains astonishing how completely absent Indian conflicts are from their interests and plots. Among the B-films of John Wayne, only *The Telegraph Trail* (1933) significantly involves battles against Indians, and even this seems due primarily to a production scheme by Warner Bros. to craft low-budget Westerns around footage reused from silent films obtained in their acquisition of First National productions. During the Indian attack in *The Telegraph Trail,* John Trent (Wayne) oddly disguises himself in a war headdress. His "motivation" can be understood only in production terms: With his face hidden by the headdress, his action can be intercut with footage from an excellent First National silent, *The Red Raiders* (1927), which is full of spectacular stunts and multiethnic wit, and in which cavalry officer Lieut. John Scott (Ken Maynard) sneaks into a Sioux camp disguised as a "medicine man." Thus *The Telegraph Trail*'s rare apparent casting in the 1930s of authentic Native Americans (Crows from Montana, impersonating Sioux) is only the result of its reuse of silent footage, and Trent/Wayne's curse against "those red devils" is also highly uncharacteristic of the B-form. In the few other cases where Native American characters appear marginally in Wayne's B-Westerns, he tends on the contrary to protect their interests – as with his adopted Osage daughter who is being cheated of payment for oil-lease land in *'Neath the Arizona Skies* (1934), or with his Tonto-like Indian companion in *The Star Packer* (1934), which opens with an unusual eastern Western shot of the canoeing Indian (named "Yak" and played by Yakima Canutt, the master stuntman, of Scots–Irish ancestry). The villain Wayne's character fights in *Lawless Frontier* (1934) – Pandro Zanti, alias Don Yorba (Earl Dwire) – is said to be "half-Apache," but it is his super-civilized Spanish manners that spell the threat.

It may be true that "the heart of the Western is," as Leslie Fiedler put it, "the encounter with the Indian."[7] But the thirties B-Western bestows its heart elsewhere – upon the land, and upon everything that working on the land can imply about the value of farming and ranching, and of water rights, bank credit lines, and other economic necessities for those occupations. The thirties B-Western is the one place in the history of the Hollywood genre that doesn't ignore the historic failure of small farming in America. Put this way, it is impossible not to claim that the B-Western, for all its crackpot plots and incompetent production values, is more sophisticated and even "intellectual" than the vastly more pretentious and straightfaced A-Western.

Both Theodore Roosevelt and Frederick Jackson Turner agreed that the frontier – that "meeting point between savagery and civilization," in Turner's words – was the key to understanding the exceptionalist character of American institutions, and both worried about what the frontier's "closing" meant for the nation's survival.[8] Where they diverged was in Roosevelt's sense that democracy was carried forward by favored races with the skills and "blood" to advance, so that he shared with Owen Wister that paradoxical Jeffersonian claim that democracy's survival rested on the efforts of "natural aristocrats." For Turner, the collective efforts of farmers, not of individual fighters, is at the center of the frontier story, and "democracy" is "born of free land."[9] The different contentions of the A-Western and B-Western in the 1930s reenact this argument, starting also from basic agreement about genre underpinnings, especially the importance of the "frontier" and the exceptional character of American democracy. At the time that Turner first proposed his hypothesis, he was not so much arguing with Roosevelt – who had published the first two volumes of *The Winning of the West* and wrote Turner a note praising him for having "struck some first class ideas" in the essay.[10] Rather, Turner was arguing for the sectional importance of the West against exclusive reliance on the more accepted idea – known as "the germ theory" and propounded notably by Turner's Johns Hopkins University dissertation director Herbert B. Adams – that American democracy grew on this continent from the germ of institutions brought over from England.[11] It is the A-Western that takes up the germ theory, and Wayne's Breck Coleman is advocating a germ-theory case in *The Big Trail* when he tells the pioneers, "We're blazing a trail that started in England." For Turner, on the contrary, the specific conditions of the frontier itself fostered the ways of thinking and the governmental institutions that had made America the country it was.

Although Theodore Roosevelt's West is more ruthless and racist, Turner's West can be faulted for generally evading the land dispossession of Native Americans and for placing their story back in some minor prelude to significant American history, the key to which comes in the struggle among Jefferson's yeoman farmers against impediments imposed by the demands of eastern cities, whose wealth is owed rightfully to the frontier land outside it.[12] Turner's notion that democracy is fostered innately by "free land" is easy enough to mock today, but his idea may be no less defensible than the accepted orthodoxy since the postcommunist 1990s – that democracy is born innately of "free markets" (an idea regularly applied, for instance, to China). The difference would be merely that the nineteenth century thought more easily of wealth in terms of land – "real" estate – rather than in that unreal, invisible concept of money. In the West of the 1890s whose changes Turner was lamenting, such "money" was seen as manipulated by untrustworthy eastern bankers and city businessman; hence all of those now arcane sectional debates about eastern-gold-versus-western-silver currency standards, propounded with a melodramatic fervor beyond any mere economic logic in which western farmers, as debtors, favored the inflation theoretically facilitated by silver (". . . you shall not crucify mankind on a cross of gold!"). Turner's particular sleight of hand, a conscious trick or unconscious failure noticed by innumerable subsequent historians, was to substitute a region – the West – for an economic interest group, farmers and others who work the land.[13] Notwithstanding his conflicted remarks about the political activism of the Populist movement, Turner essentially accepted both the special status of agricultural producers and the anti-eastern-monopolist platform of the Populist "People's Party," which was at the height of its fleeting power when Turner spoke in 1893.[14] Turner in this sense narrowed Populism by eliminating the key role played in that political movement by the South, whose cotton and tobacco farmers had, if more slowly, come to face the same troubles with credit and monopolistic rail rates.[15] Downplaying the role of the South as a region was also Turner's implicit argument against the school of historians who contended that slavery was the central issue for American history.[16] His elimination of the South in order to focus his argument about America's essential traits on the other two regions key for the Populist movement – the

Great Plains and the mountain West – was what allowed Turner's economic argument to become a regional one.

What is significant for us is that Turner's sleight of hand would be particularly welcomed by the Western film, which – as we noticed in connection with the character of the phony southerner Thorpe in *The Big Trail* – must always go out of its way to avoid anyone noticing that arguments the genre makes about its favored region might equally be made about the South. If, as Turner and the Western genre both claim, the region of the West fosters special high ethical values, especially noble democratic institutions, then to notice the similarities of the South's small-farm economics on which those claims are based presents terrible problems. The explicit exclusion of African-American farmers from the southern "Farmer's Alliance," the role of Populists in disenfranchising African Americans from voting, and the repeated eruptions of vigilantism within the movement are among the factors that prevented Populism from achieving anything like a unified national front.[17] The fragility of the Western genre's high ethical and democratic claims would become awfully clear were they to be made about the "Old South" instead of the "Old West."

With a little qualification then, the B-Western can be rightly labeled "Populist" – both in the sense that the political movement was understood in the 1890s and in the looser sense of the 1930s, a decade in which New Deal farm policies adopted many of the earlier People's Party demands.[18] The qualification is that the B-Western narrows the Populist arguments to make them regional rather than economic – a narrowing given intellectual sanction earlier by Frederick Jackson Turner.[19]

Among John Wayne's films of the thirties, *Wyoming Outlaw* (1939) may serve as the best guide to the Populist argument of the B-Western. This film opens, as usual, in some unspecified era that appears to be the Old West. Wayne is Stony Brooke, a cowboy herding cattle through a windstorm across cactus scrublands. (From *Stagecoach* and a few of his post–World War II films, we may think of Wayne as typically a lone, wandering gunman, but in his thirties B-films he is almost always employed, either as a working cowboy or as an agent of the government – this later role having other implications that we shall take up shortly.)

**Figure 33.** Old news and new media in *Wyoming Outlaw* (1939).

In *Wyoming Outlaw,* we subsequently learn that he's also part owner of the "3M Ranch," along with the two other "Three Mesquiteers" – heroes of a loose B-Western series with a shifting trio of stars and production companies. When the dust storm becomes too intense, Brooke and four cowboys take shelter with their horses in a large abandoned cabin. "I'm mighty glad we don't live in this country," one of them says, forcing the door closed on the blowing dust. "I wonder how it got this way?" Brooke has picked up in the cabin a tattered newspaper (Fig. 33a) and, in answer, cites its old news:

> Looks like the World War's to blame. . . . Listen to this. "March 9, 1918. Overseas demand sends wheat prices to new high. Panhandle country turns from cattle range to wheat fields. In this county alone eleven thousand acres of grassland are being plowed under this spring. Nora Higgins made a profit of over eighty dollars an acre last season and will plant three thousand acres this year. Luke Parker has just completed a fine home for his family and paid cash for an expensive automobile." Poor devils. Millions ruined at the end of the war. Wheat prices went down to nothing.

His fellow cowhands are less sympathetic, grousing about grazing range ruined in conversion to farmlands.

What is rare here for the B-Western is not the economic argument but having it spelled out so explicitly. Evidently we are not in the Old West but closer to the contemporary world, and one that will overtly dramatize the Populist argument. *Wyoming Outlaw* understands that the Great Depression of the 1930s had originated for farmers not long after World War I, during which the U.S. government – especially through Food Administrator Herbert Hoover, a decade before his presidency – had promoted huge increases in farm acreage to compensate for the wartime fall-off in European production. "Wheat Will Win the War!" the slogan went.[20] As Wayne's newspaper article notes, the problems came with the catastrophic underdemand and decline in prices after the war. (A bushel of wheat in 1932 brought thirty-eight cents, down from three dollars in 1919.)[21] Wayne's citation of the briefly prosperous farmer buying an automobile – always a worrisome sign in B-Westerns – hints also at the early-twentieth-century shift toward mechanized farming and the consequent conversion to salable crops of thirty million more acres previously used to grow feed grain for workhorses.[22] For the agricultural sector, the "depression" was nothing new. The abandoned house in which this scene is set reinforces also the population decline of farm communities.

When the dust storm abates, *Wyoming Outlaw* returns to a B-Western dual-era world. While other cowboys herd the cattle to water, Brooke/Wayne and his two partner "Mesquiteers" head for supplies to a town that appears to have reverted to the Old West (to judge from its tumbleweeds, horses, and eventually gunfights in the streets; Fig. 34a) but with touches of modern life (in jitterbug dancing and one apparently friendly man in an up-to-date thirties suit). Wayne has begun dancing, still packing his six-guns, with a young woman ("Something tells me we're staying over," one of his companions comments dryly), and he must win a fistfight over her, during which she takes the opportunity to steal from his wallet. Discovering the loss, Wayne's response is to say nothing but to insist upon walking her home, across barren fields. At the farmhouse, he's surprised to find his two partners already settled on the family sofa, awaiting dinner from the kindly if slightly befuddled mother. They too have taken the laid-back method of investigating a theft – the single steer rustled during the dust storm by a man who, from evidence of his tracks, dragged it off on foot. The rustler turns out to be this family's son – Will Parker – a bitter young man, quick to anger and to draw his guns. The Mesquiteers prove not unsympathetic to the reasons behind the double thefts, clearly motivated by the family's hunger and general need. Wayne chivalrously pretends that the daughter won his money in a "dance contest," and the Mesquiteers offer the son a job as cowhand with their outfit. But his modern style of sullen rebellion hints that a solution won't be quite so easy. (Don "Red" Barry – star of his own B-Western series in the 1940s – here manages to underplay even Wayne's soft-spoken intensity, a feat un-

**Figure 34.** The Western town in *Wyoming Outlaw:* gunfights (34a) and election posters (34b).

matched until Montgomery Clift in 1948's *Red River*.) The father of the family embodies the Populist bind that has aroused their sympathy. He is apparently the "Luke Parker" mentioned in the newspaper article, who bought his house and automobile in 1918's flush times (but the connection isn't underlined, since his first name goes otherwise unspoken). As a landowner, he ought not to be starving, and his problem is presented as monetary, involving bank credit and consequent lack of funds to replant after crop failures: "Did you ever try to borrow money on a thousand acres of dust and sand?" After an accident that has left him limping on a cane, he's also lost his government employment, "the only jobs there is, cleaning off the highway after the dust storms."

Again *Wyoming Outlaw* spells out the economic sympathies of the B-Western with rare directness. What Populists had long contended was not merely that farmers have a special value – as we've seen, the wider American political tradition long agreed on that – but also that farmers have an obligation to act politically and the right to expect special government response to their hardships.[23] It's more surprising that the Western promotes this second idea, especially if we come expecting the genre's apparently unqualified love of individualist gunfight solutions. Once *Wyoming Outlaw* has set up the situation of the family, it shifts into a plot around questions of voting – "There's an election comin' up!" – and about the response of elected leaders (see the campaign banner in Fig. 34b). When ultimately the Three Mesquiteers prove ineffectual bystanders to the resolution, that's only the result of the film's unusual choice not to cover over the contradictions of its Populist logic. It's not a good sign that the elected town boss turns out to be the man who stood out from everyone else by wearing a modern suit and tie at the dance. Among his schemes is to sell government jobs, disguising the payments as "campaign contributions." Only after Mrs. Parker makes her "contribution" does he inform her that the job for her husband is a return to day labor on the road gang, something his injury prevents. This piece of the plot also acts out one of Frederick Jackson Turner's rare concessions in his "Significance of the Frontier" paper about a regressive side of the democracy fostered by the West:

> But the democracy born of free land, strong in selfishness and individualism, intolerant of administrative experience and education, and pressing individual liberty beyond its proper bounds, has its dangers as well as its benefits. Individualism in America has allowed a laxity in regard to governmental affairs which has rendered possible the spoils system and all the manifest evils that follow. . . .[24]

*Wyoming Outlaw,* for all its parallels to Populist demands, also acts out what by the 1930s had become a Republican Party complaint about Roosevelt's Works Progress Administration jobs program: that it was a huge patronage machine to build up local bosses who in return would support FDR. In the closest parallel to *Wyoming Outlaw,* the Democratic mayor of Memphis, Tennessee, was revealed to have demanded political contributions from WPA workers as the price of their employment; in New Jersey, the required political contribution from WPA workers was an ongoing 3 percent of wages.[25] The question for the Western genre becomes what sort of response John Wayne should make to set this world right. His fistfight in the politician's office proves only a temporary solution. Wayne's ultimate response would be unthinkable in his later Westerns but is not uncharacteristic of the thirties Bs: "The best thing for me to do is go into the capital and have a talk with Senator Roberts," who runs Wyoming's "Committee on Public Welfare."

Especially in contrast to the political philosophies acted out in the A-Western, there is something jarring in the B-Western's way of expressing the genre's ongoing love of democracy by depicting faith in government action. In John Wayne's B-Westerns, there often comes a moment when his previously puzzling moves and motivations are explained by the revelation that he's an undercover "agent," usually sent by "the federal government" in Washington, D.C., to set things right out west. A few of his films hint at this ploy early, as in the unusual opening to *Rainbow Valley* (1935) where we watch him setting himself up in the outfit of a westerner: buying $210 worth of new clothes, guns, and a horse for his role as "special investigator to carry on undercover work." The typically harebrained schemes of the outlaws in this film are nevertheless built from everyone's agreement that elective government is the rightful and final authority: The outlaws steal the town citizens' petition to the governor – which asks for a new road into the isolated valley (paraphrasing the Populist argument against transportation monopolies) – and forge it into a petition asking for clemency for a member of their gang. One of the most surprisingly harsh moments in all of B-Westerns – in which children are almost never injured – comes in the "Three Mesquiteers" film *Santa Fe Stampede* (1938) when a ringleted, ten-year-old girl, who wants only to "grow up quick" so she can marry John Wayne, is killed in a wagon crashed to prevent the citizens' "petition of appeal" from reaching "Capital City." *Riders of Destiny* (1933) is easily the most engaging of Wayne's films of this type, if one accepts its bizarre mix of tones. "Ah, if that man from Washington would only come!" lament the townsfolk, who have written to the government to intercede against the local monopolist who controls water rights. There's little reason for them to suspect that the government man is already among them, because Wayne's character is so strange. As "Singin' Sandy Saunders," he takes the moment when he begins pacing forward in a main-street showdown to start singing (in dubbing by someone with a noticeably lower voice) a song with grim lyrics:

> Lace up your guns, outlaw, and cinch 'em on tight.
> There'll be blood a-runnin' in town before night.
> There'll be guns a-blazin' and singin' with lead.
> Tonight you'll be drinkin' your drinks with the dead.

Well might his black-garbed foe be fatally disconcerted! By the end, nature adds its own revenge when the monopolist drowns in the water he has hoarded while farmers frolic ecstatically in it (anticipating the watery frolic ending of King Vidor's depression fable *Our Daily Bread* [1934]). The restored natural order is overseen by Wayne, who finally admits proudly, "I was sent here by Washington."

Wayne's function in these films is not only to scale down destiny and give it a face but more surprisingly to reconcile the individualist philosophy of the Western with what ought to be its opposite: collective governmental solutions. That there *is* a conflict to overcome here is conceded by Wayne always acting initially "under cover." As he explains to his fellow agent in *The Lawless Nineties* (1936) after their "U.S. Dept. of Justice" briefing: "Boy, you better keep on foolin' them, 'cause where we're going, government men aren't exactly popular." Curiously again, the crackpot plots of these B-Westerns turn out to be fables truer to the authentic history of the West, as detailed by more recent historians, where the key to understanding the region has little to do with the "frontier" spirit and everything to do with federal intervention, especially in land distribution and water rights.[26]

One of the revealing curiosities of *Wyoming Outlaw* is how much it has to alter its historical inspiration to craft a Populist fable. In the film, the Mesquiteers are herding cattle into a national park – perhaps a less ecologically strange idea in the 1930s – and the park rangers refuse to allow in the newly hired cowhand: Will Parker is known to them as a "violator of the game laws." Apparently he has "poached" deer, just as he had rustled the steer, and the Mesquiteers are forced to let him go. The film nevertheless proceeds to come down on the side of Parker's poaching. "Sounds like pretty good sense to me," says a man at a lunch counter after reading in a newspaper Parker's defense that he set people's hunger above civilization's laws.

This and the resolution to *Wyoming Outlaw* draw from the story of one Earl Durand, who in March 1939 was being held in a Cody, Wyoming, jail for poaching elk when he managed to escape by grabbing the sheriff's gun and forcing the sheriff to drive him into the country. Durand was by all accounts an extraordinarily rugged outdoorsman, who regularly vanished for weeks into Yellowstone National Park carrying only a knife and rifle. His life and death read now as an early "survivalist" or protomilitia fable, anticipating elements of the Montana "Freemen," the Arizona "Viper Militia," or the 1980s Oregon outlaw Claude Dallas Jr. The nine-day pursuit of Earl Durand and siege in the inaccessible Beartooth Mountains, from which he escaped again, left five posse members dead. Durand was finally killed in a bank-robbery attempt in Powell, Wyoming, during which a hostage was also killed when Durand used him as a shield.[27]

The film version – whose production with typical B-film speed allowed it to be in theaters three months after these events – has this "Wyoming Outlaw" fighting more nobly and collectively for his impoverished family and for the basic rights of the farm community not to starve. The real Earl Durand seems to have simply chosen to live alone in a rough canvas-covered cabin away from his family of well-off ranchers. After his death, his father tried to justify his motivation: "The great outdoors was my son's god."[28] The story of his escape and mountain siege had been picked up by the *New York Times* and other national media, and the film uses a number of superficially close details, including the mountaintop-siege escape followed by his roadside kidnapping of a man who picked him up hitchhiking. The film is careful not to show any automobiles for the first forty-four of its fifty-five minutes, even during initial scenes of the town. But then modern life comes roaring in with unsympathetic vengeance, as mobile radio vans broadcast the siege of "Wild Man Parker" (see Fig. 33b) (in life, radio reporters dubbed Durand "The Tarzan of the Tetons"), anticipating the radio exploitation at the climax of Raoul Walsh's *High Sierra* (1941) or the multimedia frenzy in the New Mexico mountains of Billy Wilder's uncompromising *Ace in the Hole* (aka *The Big Carnival*, 1951). Durand's final shootout in a bank is also appropriated for the film's Populist fable – banks being standard villains for their control of credit – and Will Parker has gone to this one to settle scores with the town boss, who becomes the hostage appropriately killed in a hail of bullets at the entrance to the bank.

It is worth remembering, when we say that B-Westerns were Populist fables, that this is not unambiguously to their credit. The movement's support of outlaws, from Jesse James's attacks on railroads and banks in the 1870s onward (admired especially among the Missouri-centered "Grange" order), is a first reflection of what Richard Hofstadter described as the Populists' long heritage into the twentieth century of "an undercurrent of provincial resentments, popular and 'democratic' rebelliousness and suspiciousness, and nativism."[29] One of the fascinating traits of B-Westerns is how often they refuse to evade the logic that extends this admiration of outlaws into violent vigilantism. The repeated shout in the films of "Form a posse, men!" both evokes and softens vigilantism. "You're in a country now where you got to take it," westerners tell an eastern gangster at the end of *From Broadway to Cheyenne* (1932). "There'll be no lawyers here to pull a *habeas corpus*. . . . Yeah, we'll give ya a break. We'll give you a rope and a tree that ain't never been used before." In the event, this easterner escapes hanging by committing suicide.

Among John Wayne's thirties films, *Westward Ho* (1935) is the most explicit in its admiration, right from its opening dedication "to the Vigilantes." Wayne uniforms his gang – "We'll call ourselves vigilantes!" – in black outfits, fashionably set off with flowing white scarves and sleek white horses. The dark implications of living by law of their own making isn't so much softened as made more perverse by the deranged B-film presentation in which Wayne's vigilantes become known in newspaper headlines as "The Singing Riders" for the way they gallop in formation while singing rhyming lyrics in smooth harmonies about "the midnight dream of terror." Most astonishing among Wayne's B-films for its honoring of vigilantism, however, is the aptly titled *The Night Riders* (1939), in which the Three Mesquiteers themselves become "Los Capaqueros" – the hooded ones – in nineteenth-century Spanish California. Even when one of the Mesquiteers brings out his ventriloquist's dummy – "Don Elmer de Sliverola de Blockhead" – the tone isn't much lightened after Wayne and his vigilantes have galloped over the countryside in Klan-like white hoods and sheets to evict Spanish grandees from the state (Fig. 35). (The "Spanish" are revealed to be riverboat gamblers who forged their eighteenth-century land grants). To some extent, these films play to the sympathies of their primarily rural audiences. In 1933, the governor of Iowa placed part of the state under martial law after farmers, faces masked in blue kerchiefs, abducted a judge thought too willing to approve foreclosures.[30]

By 1939, this darker side of Populism was being tamed into a cycle of films sympathetic to "outlaws." *Wyoming Outlaw* is in the spirit of the A-Westerns in this cycle, best remembered through *Jesse James* and *Stagecoach*. Although *Jesse James*, as another biography of a historical figure, follows one of the standard options for the decade's A-Westerns, its appeal also came from the way it slanted the facts of the story into a Populist fable, with Jesse and Frank (Tyrone Power and Henry Fonda) initially fighting for their mother's farm against railroads, which the opening text titles concede were, "in some cases, predatory and unscrupulous." Among the fascinating B-films early in this outlaw cycle is *Renegade Ranger* (1938) with twenty-year-old Rita Hayworth, in one of the rare active female roles in 1930s Westerns, as the masked leader of a band of Hispanic vigilantes fighting Texas eviction laws.

**Figure 35.** John Wayne and his two compatriot "Mesquiteers" as heroic vigilantes in *The Night Riders* (1939).

When we arrive at *Stagecoach*, after a decade when the genre lived with its split personality, we can see what a breakthrough it was. On one hand, it's an entry in this outlaw cycle, with John Wayne, as the admirable Ringo Kid, apprehended after his jail break and determined upon justified vengeance. But *Stagecoach*'s unique trick was this: It discovered a way to bridge the chasm between the A- and B-Western formulas. John Ford's film is an A-Western in its inclusion of the Indian-war plot, as well as in length (97 min.), prestige (Ford had won the "Best Director" Academy Award for 1935; he would win again in 1940 and 1941), shooting schedule (eight weeks), and cost (though its $530,000 was on the low side for an A-film).[31] However, it falls into none of the tired categories that confined almost every other A-Western of the decade: It is not a biography of a legendary westerner, not a history of pioneering, not a remake of a successful silent. If *Stagecoach* comes to appear like the best of the B-Westerns, it's not only because it lacks then-major stars (John Ford declined David O. Selnick's offer to replace Wayne with Gary Cooper).[32] It is also due to its unpretentious verve and to the way that the concluding Lordsburg segment in particular feels like a separate B-film, an impression reinforced by the first appearance of the man said to have murdered Ringo's brother – Luke Plummer, played by Tom Tyler, nearly as familiar to rural audiences as John Wayne and like him the star of some forty B-Westerns in the 1930s, following a series of silents.[33] Although in retrospect Wayne's own casting seems inevitable, at the time it was a shorthand way to bring into *Stagecoach* the associations of B-Western heroism he had developed for audiences over the previous decade.

*Stagecoach*'s way of reconciling the A- and B-Western proved unrepeatable. Hollywood learned only the economic lesson taught by *Stagecoach*'s success, not its narrative one, and the A-Westerns that followed in 1940 returned to plodding histories, with one eye toward questions of military preparedness prompted by the new European war (especially in De Mille's *North West Mounted Police,* Vidor's *Northwest Passage,* and Curtiz's *Santa Fe Trail*). Nevertheless, *Stagecoach* brought the A-Western back from another near-death experience by arguing that the power of the genre had never been in the grand efforts to re-create history.

# 16. "Don't Cry, Pat, It's Only a Western": A Note on Acting

Christ, if you'd learn to act you'd get better parts.

John Ford to John Wayne, repeatedly throughout the 1930s.[1]

John Wayne's acting was long a subject for mockery and impressionists. Academic critics can still label him "a notoriously inept player," and even his admiring recent biographers are apologetic when looking back at his B-films of the 1930s: "In his early films his best as an actor was not very good."[2] Wayne in a later interview made a case for just how difficult was the sort of explanatory dialogue common to cost-cutting B-Westerns:

> Most anybody can play anger or hysteria but try to do a long boring speech like, "The stage from Albuquerque is due in at four and there's a shipment of silver and I hear that Joe and his gang are headin' for the Panamint so you take two men and be there to meet the stage and I'll keep an eye on Mike because he's fixin' to kidnap Maybelle because she thinks her claim is worthless but it's a silver mine," and you got trouble. The biggest difference between the B- and A-Western is how they tell the story.[3]

What happens with Wayne in *Stagecoach* is less a change in his abilities than in the dialogue he is given and, even more, in the way that he is filmed. John Ford famously treated his closest "friends" with what sounds from a distance awfully like cruelty, and his mockery of Wayne's ability as an actor in the thirties was expressed repeatedly in front of others. In *Stagecoach,* however, Ford lovingly set Wayne's performance within a visual context unknown in the B-Western (Fig. 36). The famous introductory shot of Wayne tracks in so rapidly to an extreme close-up of his face that the focus puller can't quite keep up (Fig. 37a).

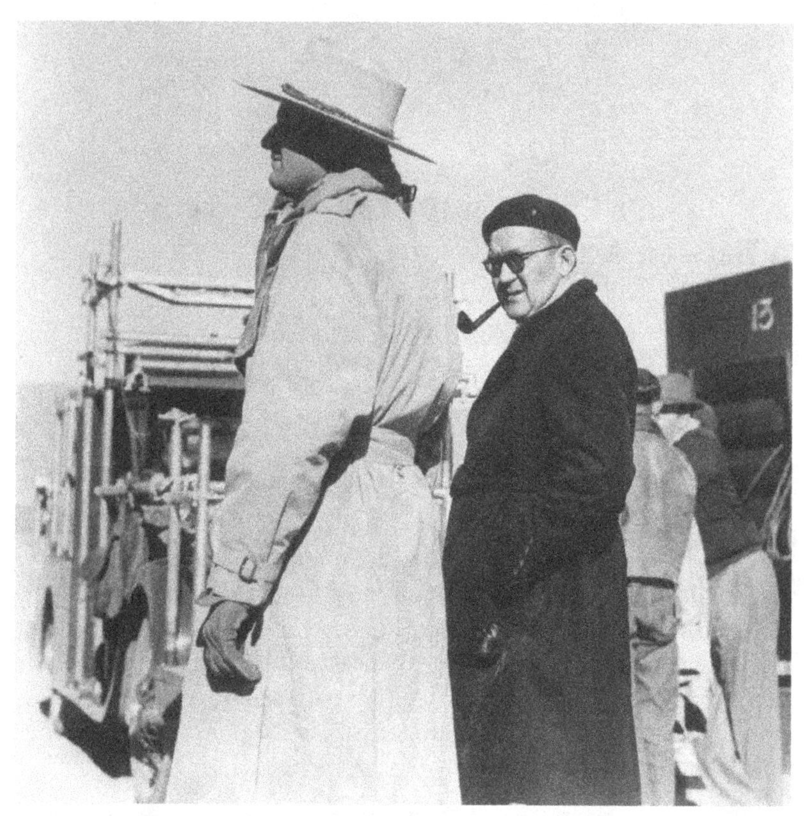

**Figure 36.** John Ford observing John Wayne on location for *Stagecoach* in 1938.

The change is in some ways as simple as the stylistic principle announced with this shot: *Stagecoach* may have more close-ups of Wayne's face than in *all* of his previous films combined. Even out in the landscape, as in the first confrontation with the sheriff following this introduction to Wayne's Ringo Kid, full-face shots both allow and justify his newly softened vocal style. Other scenes seem crafted to require speaking in whispers, as when Dallas urges him to escape during the journey, or when the Hispanic stage-stop proprietor (Chris-Pin Martin) informs him out of the sheriff's earshot about the whereabouts of the murderers of Ringo's family. Even when Claire Trevor as Dallas raises her throaty, cracking voice in the stage-stop kitchen – to play the scene where the woman must argue for evading the gunfight solution – Wayne's face looms in the left foreground, justifying his soft-spoken responses (Fig. 37b). The cramped quarters of the coach also justify a

**Figure 37.** *Stagecoach* (1939).

scene played by Wayne entirely in silent close-ups and droll double takes. The canteen he passes to Lucy Mallory, the pregnant Army wife, is called back by the southern gambler Hatfield so that the water can be offered more genteelly in his collapsible cup (Fig. 37c). As the scene's topper, Wayne is given two brief lines: "How about the other lady?" and, with a winning smile to Dallas, "Sorry, no silver cups" (Fig. 37d). In an interview Ford bristled – as usual – when Peter Bogdanovich offered the idea that "you made Wayne a star by not letting him talk too much." "No," countered Ford, "that isn't true at all – he had a lot to say, plenty of lines. . . . He didn't do any soliloquies or make any speeches."[4] Ford's point is well taken, and, as Sarah Kozloff details in *Overhearing Film Dialogue,* Wayne's taciturnity in *Stagecoach* is a relative thing, emphasized by a halting delivery, especially in contrast to Doc's extravagant vocabulary, Gatewood's political hectoring, Hatfield's smooth locutions, and the nervous chattering of the stage driver, Buck (Andy Devine). Dallas, bitter and pained by her eviction from the town of Tonto by the Law and Order League ladies, is also reserved of speech.[5] The bond between Ringo and Dallas grows through wordless intercut glances and later with tight two-shots. Surprisingly, Ford makes relatively little use of Wayne's full body and graceful walk, cutting away even from the climax of Ringo's showdown with Luke Plummer. The silences and close-ups that signify thought in *Stagecoach* are simple enough bits of film grammar, but they are almost unknown in B-Westerns for related budgetary and aesthetic reasons.

In contrast, it's true, the acting in B-Westerns, from Wayne and every other star, can often look barely competent. The old line was that B-Western actors had to master two expressions: hat on and hat off. If audiences of the 1930s didn't voice complaint, that is no doubt partly because acting didn't matter so much as action. It may also be, however, that there is an appeal to the acting itself in B-Westerns. To carp about Wayne's ineptitude is probably to rank him on an inappropriate scale, as if he were trying desperately to be Paul Muni or Fredric March and failing. His acting – and that of B-Western stars generally – may be working on a scale that in the thirties would instead include Al Jolson and the Marx Brothers. That is, there's a knowing theatricality, complicitous with the audience, that in B-Westerns is hidden in plain sight. The acting leans toward the presentational rather than striving for the representational, and the joke about hat on–hat off does catch how acting in Westerns begins as a series of codified gestures and conventional poses.[6]

*Stagecoach* is characteristic of A-Westerns for the way that many of its ostensibly outdoor dialogue scenes, including Wayne's introductory close-ups, are all clearly filmed inside a sound stage, complete with unconvincing cactus props and evidently painted backdrops. For better or worse, B-Westerns hadn't the budgetary luxury for this, and soft-spoken subtleties were difficult technically. The B-Western acting style is an innate part of the way that the form as a whole is unable – or refuses – to take itself as solemnly as the A-Western, and the clash between the genuine landscapes and the theatrical performances adds to the form's inadvertent surrealism. The B-Western always seems to be threatening to break cinema's fourth-wall convention and to let its audiences in on the joke.

An easy self-consciousness pervades both story lines and styles. For instance, Ken Maynard, originally a silent star and with a rather high-pitched voice, ends *Come On, Tarzan* (1932) with riding stunts (Tarzan is his horse) that are ludicrous as realism but astonishing as performance, including galloping along with one leg on the bad guys' horses while he tosses them off. The theatricality there is less that of the stage-play than of the Wild West show, and his self-conscious closing consolation to the heroine is to tell her, "Don't cry, Pat, it's only a Western." *Scarlet River* (1933), a minor David O. Selznick production, opens by staging one of the B-Western's era-leaping surprises: A lone covered wagon moving across a bleak desert seems in desperate straits when a wooden wheel breaks. "Looks like this is the end of the trail for us," says the driver ruefully. "Our horses are played out, and the water's gone. . . . There ain't a human being within miles of us." – at which point a bus roars past, honks its horn, and unloads real-estate salesmen. The pioneers turn out to be frustrated Hollywood filmmakers wondering, "Isn't there any place we can go to get away from civilization?" ("Sure, but who wants to go there?" asks the hard-bitten heroine.) When they find such a location, the ranch is facing just the sort of plot elements common in B-Westerns – a foreclosing bank, a crooked foreman, a kidnapped rancher – and where a cowboy would-be screenwriter is inordinately proud of avoiding in his unproduced scripts the clichés all around him ("The chief has a daughter and I *don't* call her Pocahontas!"). *Within* B-Westerns, complaints that the movies may not be living up to the demands of realism are played for laughs. In *Sioux City Sue* (1946) the filmmakers worry about their dialogue: "In real life, people just don't yell, 'Indians!'" – the comedy arising here from invoking "real life" at all as a touchstone for Western dialogue. After melodramatic plot convolutions, including a disgruntled cowhand set to blow up a dam to force Gene Autry's ranch into bankruptcy, *Sioux City Sue* ends with knowing circularity and complicity with the audience, as the cast watches a preview for a Gene Autry film called *Sioux City Sue.* When in *West of the Divide* (1934) John Wayne has to participate in a plot-explanatory dialogue like the one he complained of in the interview, it also includes a self-conscious reference to the conventional plotting of the film itself: "Oh, I see, like a dime novel. We eliminate the old gent, you marry the gal and get the ranch, is that it?"

Such self-consciousness could be a way for filmmakers to keep their self-respect by maintaining a slightly mocking distance from their material and winking at the audience. One suspects some such motivation in *Scarlet River* for David O. Selznick, who five years later turned down *Stagecoach* as "just another Western."[7] However, the films generally play too affectionately for that. Part of the serious, but never solemn, point behind all the self-referentiality may be hinted by the names of the lead characters. B-Western stars most often play characters with their given name the same as the actor's. Tom Keene, for instance, is "Tom Baxter" in *Scarlet River,* just as Ken Maynard is "Ken Benson" in *Come On, Tarzan.* In *Sioux City Sue,* Gene Autry plays a character called "Gene Autry," and Autry almost never played anyone else onscreen. John Wayne is "John" in more than half of his B-Westerns, although with Wayne there is the added irony that no one who knew him well in life ever called him that. ("I've always been either Duke, Marion, or John Wayne. It's a name that goes well together and it's like one word – Johnwayne. But if they say John, Christ, I don't look around.")[8] The naming tradition here goes back at least to 1872, when William F. "Buffalo Bill" Cody opened on the Chicago stage in Ned Buntline's *The Scouts of the Prairie* after one night trying to learn his lines – and failing, to judge from the Chicago *Times* review of the "execrable acting" – but who found a half-century of success with audiences by never playing anyone but a character called "Buffalo Bill."[9]

These names argue that the "actors" are only going so far in impersonation. Instead the B-Western stars are participating in something other than realistic representation, something more in the exaggerated tradition of the loosely structured western "tall tale," more a display of a tight-knit group having a grand time, to which we too have been generously invited. That tone may help explain why, within the thousand B-Westerns made in the decade, there were so relatively few lead actors, and why the establishment of a new B-Western star turned out to be so difficult. These are our friends, the films are saying, and we'll want to visit them again – in the same costumes, by the same names, with the same group of sidekicks and resurrected villains, fighting over the same small set of conflicts. Critics looking back on the B-Western generally see the plots as unforgivably routine and the acting as laughably inauthentic, and by standards of innovation and representation both points are inarguable. But the claim for authenticity may lie elsewhere, in men who offer up themselves with a certain directness. "He's not just a movie actor, he's a real guy!" his costar says of "Tom" in *Scarlet River.* No doubt Tom Keene's acting range limits the power of *Our Daily Bread* the next year, but in Westerns unconvincing acting is itself implicitly offered up as proof of the authenticity of men who would only half claim to be actors. As Tex Ritter put it when asked which actors had most influenced him, "I have been influenced by none because I don't act. For a good reason, I prefer to play myself."[10] In *The Cowboy Star* (1936), an old pal from Arizona compliments Spencer Yorke (Charles Starrett) – the cowboy star of the title – that he's come a long way in Hollywood. "You mean I've slipped a long way, don't you, Buckshot?" he responds, in amusing despair as he removes his makeup. "Can you imagine a cowboy dunking his face in cold cream and powder? . . . Did you think when I came to Hollywood I had any idea I'd wind up this kind of a guy?" The genuine westerner displays not some changeable role but his unalterable self. John Wayne returns to the name "John" in his last film, *The Shootist* (1976), which draws on his legend and his terminal cancer to claim, one final time, that the gap is narrow between actor and Western hero.

# 17. Time, Space, and the Western

My days were not days of the week, bearing the stamp of any heathen deity, nor were they minced into hours and fretted by the ticking of a clock; for I lived like the Puri Indians, of whom it is said that "for yesterday, to-day, and to-morrow they have only one word, and they express the variety of meaning by pointing backward for yesterday, forward for to-morrow, and overhead for the passing day."

Henry David Thoreau, *Walden*[1]

The long dispute about the place of the western man within America was succinctly encapsulated in the two words most often describing him: *backwoodsman* and *frontiersman*. The distinctions between the terms held both political arguments and philosophic ones.[2] Should America draw inspiration from Europe (making the westerner a *back*woodsman) or face toward the unknown (making him our advance-guard *front*iersman)? Did the West have a heritage more ancient than anything in Europe (as evidenced especially by anthropologic reports of the far Southwest) or did it allow for everything to be newer (as when, just after the Revolutionary War, Crèvecoeur found the American to be "the western pilgrim," who "leaving behind him all his ancient prejudices and manners, receives new ones from the new mode of life he has embraced . . .")?[3] This dispute settled easily into a paradox, a doubling of the power of the West, which could be admired for being simultaneously old and new, containing both our valued history and our best opportunities for the future.

It seems that hardly anyone who thought deeply about the West during the nineteenth century failed to arrive at some fanciful conceit about the relationship of chronological time to the region's vast spaces.

Thomas Jefferson, contemplating at age eighty the extent of his Louisiana Purchase, mused, "Let a philosophic observer commence a journey from the savages of the Rocky Mountains eastwardly towards our seacoast. . . . This, in fact, is equivalent to a survey, in time, of the progress of man from the infancy of creation to the present day."[4] Frederick Jackson Turner picked up that metaphor in his "Frontier in American History" address, and indeed the notion that travel into the West doubled as a reverse voyage into time could be found even in trail guidebooks, where it couldn't have been entirely encouraging.[5] Turner's bookish metaphor was this: "The United States lies like a huge page in the history of society. Line by line as we read this continental page from West to East we find the record of social evolution."[6] It may have required a novelist, Owen Wister, writing in 1895 and before penning *The Virginian,* to toy more fancifully with the relationship of time and space in the West:

> Never, indeed, it would seem have such various centuries been jostled together as they are today upon this continent, and within the boundaries of our nation. We have taken the ages out of their orderly processional arrangement and set them marching disorderly abreast in our wide territory, a harlequin platoon. We citizens of the United States date our letters 18—, and speak of ourselves as living in the present era; but the accuracy of that custom depends upon where we happen to be writing.[7]

In all of this, one gets the sense that the lowly B-Western again managed to vivify a long tradition of American thought. As we have seen, the B-Western's most distinctive way of relating time to space is to locate some version of the nineteenth century right outside the twentieth century's town limits, although occasionally one also finds the eighteenth century elbowing its way in with expressionist shadows and gothic villains or the twenty-first threatening with radium tubes and ray guns. The B-Western lightly jostles centuries together in a manner beyond the historical progress that obsesses the A-Western.

It may seem, however, that by intermingling centuries the B-Western falls back on only the simplest of nostalgic tricks to combat complex changes brought to rural societies by modern life. That a legendary Old West could exist conveniently near at hand, where the encroachments of modernity could be fought off with six-guns, is evoked often in the films as something genuine but merely forgotten. When a town's young men go overseas to World War I in *Cross Fire* (1933), some slick types take over – "They belong to this modern era" – until a trio of apparently feeble codgers begin to reminisce about their youth: "I propose we go back to the tried and true methods that were good enough when we fellas was startin' to settle this country. . . . Here's what I mean. You ain't forgot how to shoot, have ya?" Similarly, after a New Yorker loses his car over a cliff in *From Broadway to Cheyenne* (1932), Gabby Hayes reminds him of a mode of travel that he has only forgotten: "Like when you was a kid, by horseback." The nostalgia in these films is as "childlike" as the pastoralism of the eastern Western, which proved ultimately too simple to survive commercially much beyond 1911. What complicates things with the B-Western in the 1930s is that the ideal world functions in both spatial and temporal dramas. The ideal world is located spatially just outside the modern town and temporally under the more violent principles of the Old West. Pastoral poetry began of course as a purely spatial conceit, as with Virgil's Arcadian shepherds in the countryside just outside the court, but by the eighteenth century there had been enough of a shift toward thinking of actual countrysides as embodying the healing values of the past for beset city dwellers that young Alexander Pope felt obliged to remind his audience in the preface to his first published volume, *Pastorals, with a Discourse on the Pastoral,* that the city–country ethical distinction was only a thing of the imagination, that "we are not to describe our shepherds as shepherds at this day really are."[8] Although B-Westerns were also quite evidently imaginary constructs, they were following this centuries-long tendency to historicize the pastoral, through its ultimate politicization in the Populist movement's melodramatic economic rhetoric.

There is an undeniable fear of change confronted within the B-Western. Recall that in the 1939 version of *New Frontier,* after John Wayne rides from what seem to be Indians in the Old West, we find ourselves surprised to enter a 1930s town, "New Hope." Its jubilee celebrations include townsfolk bowing their heads in prayer: "The Lord has been so good to us that He hasn't left us much to ask for. Unless it's this. Keep us safe, O Lord . . . and if it's alright with You, we'd like to keep on just as we have in the past." Alongside this prayer for a changeless world is the citizens' fantasy of the Old West right outside town – one that they will rely upon in the film's later gun battles. The A-Western of the 1930s, for all its ponderous history lessons, must be said to be more concerned with the workings of memory, dramatized through linear stories of progress in which the past is logically linked to the present. The B-Western relies on nostalgia, finding no recoverable historical connection between the troubled present and an ideal past, and so leaps back and forth irrationally between the two.[9]

Still, there may be a little more to it than this. The A-Western claims, dishonestly, to bring us the facts of history, while the B-Western more readily admits its nostalgia. And with their twentieth-century towns and nineteenth-century outlands, many B-Westerns "spatialize time," to honor their world with an idea familiar from cultural critics of turn-of-the-century urban modernity, especially writers of the Frankfort School, who argued that new urban spaces, with their random "arcade" attractions, were related to fragmentation of individual memory and the loss of cultural tradition. As applied to cinema history with speculative brilliance by Miriam Hansen and synthesized deftly by Ben Singer, both drawing on Walter Benjamin, a case has been made for the "modernity thesis" as a way toward understanding how early narrative film styles as well as exhibition practices developed out of, and reflected the chaos within, city life in the first decades of the twentieth century.[10] Among the subsidiary arguments is that nickelodeon theaters and the films themselves, especially early melodramas, provided a public space for working through crises faced by new immigrants from preindustrial European regions, who brought with them agricultural tradition and a linear sense of time thrown into confusion by urban life. Without getting into the question of how much sentimentality might be found within this thesis itself – which may discredit the complexity of "peasant" thought and include its own nostalgia about the world before the Great War – it must be equally true that the B-Western, with its tales of jostled centuries, provided another space for coming to terms with the "competing temporalities" – in Miriam Hansen's phrase – of agricultural tradition and modernity. The Great Depression may not have been all that much less disorienting, even for those not spatially uprooted by it, than was turn-of-the-century Manhattan for new immigrants. The changes brought by World War I, which hovers behind the sophisticated nostalgia of "Lost Generation" writers such as Hemingway and Fitzgerald, was hardly less of a catastrophe for the rural West – as John Wayne reminds us through his commentary on the text of the tattered 1918 newspaper in *Wyoming Outlaw*.

It probably misses something to write off B-Westerns as *merely* nostalgic in the leap back in eras; or at least the nostalgia itself may have a certain positive complexity. It is clearly not missing from sophisticated European cultural critics and American novelists of the 1920s and 1930s. As Svetlana Boym has compellingly traced, nostalgia has a collective utopian dimension, not merely a regressive one; its yearning for a different time – or for a less rationalist concept of time and progress – is disguised as a yearning for a different place.[11] The temporal and spatial irrationality of the B-Western, however juvenile, reacts against the regimentation of time and space long imposed upon the West. For most of the nineteenth century, until standardization in 1883 by railroad corporations, agricultural communities kept their own time based on local high noon (the Sacramento valley was about four minutes ahead of San Francisco). Federal officials in the East were responsible for laying out all those neat squares (including such large ones as Yellowstone Park) and rectangles (such as Colorado) on the land.[12] While A-Westerns are often structured through the hero's travel across the landscape (as in both of John Wayne's A-Westerns of the 1930s), B-Westerns usually settle into stories of a single agricultural community (as in virtually all of Wayne's B-Westerns of the decade). Historians label two basic methodologies for describing the West: as "process" and as "place." That is, the historical study of the West has traditionally meant studying "the experience of going there" as well as the trans-Mississippi region itself.[13] Pre–World War II A-Westerns tend to see the West as "process": Even when they are not stories of heroic travel or the restless lives of legendary heroes, A-Westerns dramatize the processes of building up towns (*Dodge City,* 1939) and states (*Arizona,* 1940). B-Westerns almost invariably portray the West as "place," in economic melodramas about land or water use, and about outside forces impinging on previously settled areas.[14] And in this they are again closer to "New Western History," with its focus on land and water policies, than to earlier heroic histories of westward frontiering. By traveling only temporally back through jostled centuries, B-Westerns may come closer to finding "the true myth of America," at least as D. H. Lawrence saw it in James Fenimore Cooper based on the composition order of the Leatherstocking tales: "they go backwards, from old age to golden youth."[15]

In their insistent illogic about time and space, B-Westerns refuse to provide a rational narrative about history. To put this another way, their relation to the past is itself religious, in a broader sense than the A-Western's contending Christian creeds. That American history could be approached as a religion, a civil religion, may also hit closer to the popular spirit of the 1930s, when it seemed that every historical landmark or presidential home became a "shrine" for civil worship. At the 1930 dedication of the gigantic bust of George Washington on Mount Rushmore, the Sioux lands of fifty years earlier were declared "America's Shrine for Political Democracy"; the 1939 New York World's Fair dedicated a "patriotic shrine for patriotic societies from all parts of the United States."[16] Nineteenth-century historian Henry Adams, wrestling with his loss of faith, foresaw this coming "new religion of history" in the context of describing his giddy youthful disorientation while wandering in Rome, with its centuries jostled to within walking distances: "No law of progress applied to it. Not even time-sequences – the last refuge of the helpless historian – had value for it. The Forum no more led to the Vatican than the Vatican to the Forum."[17]

As we noticed, the Western is more comfortable including scenes of prayer than is any other Hollywood genre. Some of John Wayne's B-Westerns rest with a demonstration of the shift from sacred to secular law, as in *The Range Feud* (1931), where the pastor departs from his sermon text ("Thou shalt not kill, thunders the voice of God from Mount Sinai") to call upon the sheriff to give a lecture on the "law of man," which the sheriff then illustrates convincingly by aiming his six-gun from the pulpit. More often Wayne's B-films justify prayer scenes by tying them to the public story of America. True, this linkage goes back to Cotton Mather's lives of John Winthrop and other Puritan colony governors, but the priorities have reversed: American history itself now explains faith, instead of the other way around. The prayer "to keep on just as we have in the past" in 1939's *New Frontier* is a part of the community's "golden jubilee" invoked in front of a banner reading "NEW HOPE VALLEY. 50 YEARS OLD TODAY" and under the image of Lincoln, not Christ.

*New Frontier* pointedly does not rest with its nostalgia. With the coming flood of the valley because of the new dam for the city, the argument becomes whether it is time to "start making plans for the future." The original settlers choose to fight the surveyors with guns from behind barricades. As with the Populists of the late-nineteenth-century South – from where "New Hope's" pioneers emigrated, the Lincoln portrait notwithstanding – land has a value beyond monetary reckoning.[18] "Do you think that money can make up for what we put into this valley?" an old rancher asks. However, John Wayne and his two partner Mesquiteers are well satisfied with the $3,200 paid for their "3M Ranch." A dynamic montage of construction activity – invariably an emblem of hope in depression-era cinema – makes evident that the film itself also sees value in such change. Indeed, *New Frontier* comes around to dramatizing a debate about "progress." Wayne's heroism comes not in fighting progress but making sure that the right sort of progress prevails. The men initially promoting the dam are both too citified (calling the settlers "mule-headed hicks") and too savage (pulling a "lowdown Injun trick" by rolling flaming wagons down a hill into the defending settlers). As Wayne civilly asks them, "Letting loose those burning fuel tanks is your idea of progress, I suppose?" It becomes clear that fighting will still be required to keep the forces of progress honest (Fig. 38). The swindlers are convicted, and "the government" completes the water pipeline to a new community, tentatively named "New New Hope" (leading to the film's concluding dialogue: "Sounds like you're stuttering." "Well they named a town Walla Walla." "Yeah, and another one Sing Sing"). The settlers of *New Frontier* may have temporarily forgotten their own history of change, but their emigration fifty years earlier from the Old South to escape "reconstruction" (as an opening title and montage tell us), alongside the Western's usual need to deny its parallels to the history of violence in the Old South, may also explain why John Wayne still needs to school the settlers in the value of the right kind of progress.

There is little drama in nostalgia alone. B-Westerns get much of their dynamism from arguing about the relationship between looking backward and forward. Michael Kammen in *Mystic Chords of Memory* has traced encyclopedically how American culture as a whole can be understood as such a history of conflict between the values in "tradition" and those of "progress," but he also documents how communities reconciled the two by locating their "Tradition of Progress."[19] The oxymoron implies the compromise solution reached in so many B-Westerns. The films would look skeptically on the ecstatic slogan "Progress is God" – from William Gilpin, a celebrated nineteenth-century soldier, land speculator, and politician – which is closer to the way religion is hijacked by the Manifest Destiny of the A-Western.[20] The B-Western remains dubious about excess. The unalloyed happy conclusion to *New Frontier* is that the farmers and ranchers are able to purchase irrigated lands in "New New Hope" near double the size of their previous spreads. There is advancement here, but it's the progress of Populists,

**Figure 38.** Stony Brooke (John Wayne) confronts a foreman from the "Metropole Construction Co." in *New Frontier* (1939).

striving for what they would have called a "competency" – a sustainable piece of land for those with the skills to make a livelihood from it.[21] Of course, this dream of sustainable small-scale agricultural production has proven a solution possible only in the dreams of the B-Western – and in the more fantastic monetary schemes of the Populists. Frederick Jackson Turner's own nostalgia for the frontier turns out to have been misplaced. As the 2000 census confirmed, there are so many *more* official "frontier" counties – those with two to six persons per square mile – than when Turner lamented its "closing" in 1890 that they now amount to nearly nine hundred thousand square miles in the Great Plains states – about the size of Jefferson's original Louisiana Purchase.[22]

A handful of A-Westerns also compared the Old West to the new civilization of the 1930s, using the past to criticize the ethics of the present even as they praise material advancement. They made the comparison, however, not in the lightly jostled centuries of the B-Western but through linear structures. The most celebrated of these was *Cimarron* (1931), now among the least revived of "Best Picture" Oscar winners. It recounts "a nation rising to greatness" and "crude towns growing into cities" through an Oklahoma pioneer family, whose progress is measured off by a sequence of years: 1889, 1890, 1893 (the "Cherokee Strip land rush"), 1898 (the Spanish–American War), 1907 (an oil boom), 1929, 1931. The film could hardly be more insistent on its memory of history. When the hero's wife, Sabra (Irene Dunne), mentions as a possible subject of study for her women's club ". . . maybe early American history," he cuts her off impatiently: "Don't you know you're *making* it?" The film is not without interest, especially for how it's pulled one way by its celebrations of Manifest Destiny and the other by its unusual, if abstract, sympathy for Native Americans. (The hero, Yancey Cravat, is played by Richard Dix, who still carried associations from his Indian roles in *The Vanishing American* [1925] and *Redskin* [1929]; Yancey publishes *The Oklahoma Wigwam* newspaper with frequent "editorials about Indian's rights.")

While *Cimarron* makes room too for a Jewish pioneer, a "walking notion counter" named Sol Levy (George E. Stone) who becomes a retail merchant, his advancement is economic and so explicitly not part of history, as he says himself: "Ah, they will always talk about Yancey. He's going to be part of the history of the great Southwest. It's men like him that build the world. The rest of them, like me, we just come along and live in it." *Cimarron*'s prayer scenes are in line with its portrayal of history, striving to be all-inclusive. When Yancey conducts the first "divine service," he dubs the building "The Osage First Methodist Episcopalian Lutheran Presbyterian Congregational Baptist Catholic Unitarian . . . [pause, with a glance at Sol Levy] . . . Hebrew Church." By including so many chronological details of history, the film also claims to locate the inclusive democratic liberalism of the nation (countering de Tocqueville's fear that democracy would "seduce" American religions into a uniform and indolent pantheism).[23] Notwithstanding the wit in its opening sequences, the film's linear structure about its forty years of history forces a heavy-handed turn toward the visionary foresight of the pioneer ("Congress has passed all he asked for") until it ends with a final shot that embalms the pioneer in a statue of bronze.

Paramount made something of a studio style in the thirties of A-Westerns with the heaviest chronologic conscience about history. Best remembered are Cecil B. De Mille's epics for the studio, such as *The Plainsman* (1936), which limits itself to twelve years, from Lincoln proposing "the long furrows of the West" as just the place for newly unemployed Civil War soldiers (until interrupted by his wife, "Mr. Lincoln, we'll be late for the theater") to shortly after Custer's Last Stand; and *Union Pacific* (1939), which recounts five years from near the end of the Civil War to the "golden spike" ceremony uniting the transcontinental railroad. These were the sorts of film where by their last reels characters would be making formal speeches about the national importance of the events dramatized at their beginning. Paramount's *Wells Fargo* (1937), for instance, marks off its years with titles ("early 1840's"/1846/1850/1851/1857/1858/1860, and Lincoln penning his Second Inaugural to represent 1864) and closes with the hero's sidekick decked out in a tuxedo at a stockholders' meeting to testify that "The old Wells Fargo Company done its part in opening up the West. . . . [I]t helped keep the United States united."

Filmmakers seemed not unaware of the problems that resulted from trying to squeeze a half-century of history into two hours of screen time. There may be intentional wit in, say, a moment in *Wells Fargo* when scout Ramsay MacKay (Joel McCrea) finds city life too soft in the San Francisco of 1857 and yearns for the trail. His wife (Frances Dee) relents by saying, "After all, it's only for a year" – and, sure enough, the next shot takes us ahead one year to an "1858" title. Mary Pickford's career-killing role in Frank Borzage's *Secrets* (1933) requires her to voyage west from seacoast New England and on a wagon train to California, where she fights cattle thieves with vigilante justice and endures fifty years with her unfaithful husband (Leslie Howard), as a swinging pendulum overlays montages of passing years. "This is getting to be absurd," says their grown son near the end, in a comment that can't help but reflect also on the film's structure. As the gray-haired couple drive their car through city lights on a last journey west to California, a dissolve returns us to their covered wagon – and to the moral bedrock carried by that image.

*Cimarron* does its best to fight the ponderousness inherent in this way of structuring history. Still, the strain already shadows Yancey's opening visionary speech to his family about the two million acres "free for the taking" in Oklahoma and about the speed with which we'll see history unfold: "There's never been anything like it since creation! Creation? That took six days! This was done in one! History made in an hour!" Warner Bros.' aptly titled *The World Changes* (1933) has to be given credit for most actively sustaining the history-made-in-an-hour pace, if at the price of almost parodying the studio's no-nonsense style of the early 1930s. Opening with Scandinavian cattle pioneers settling in the Dakotas in the 1850s, it incarnates a seventy-year object lesson in Paul Muni's character, "The Refrigerator Car Czar" Orin Nordholm Jr. As a boy, he begins outside history, an ominous start: General Custer rides up to the family ranch in 1865 to tell them "some great news that I'm pretty sure you all ain't heard yet: The war's over!" "What war?" asks Ma. The issue for the film becomes distinguishing historical progress from mere economic drive. Muni's sweetheart admires, in Teddy Roosevelt terms, how ambition is "in his blood," and his father likewise links his ambition to the family's westward destiny: "The thing that brought us here, it's drivin' him." But his mother suspects otherwise: "That's what I been wishin', but it's not." At the end of his long life story, after his capital manipulations have precipitated the 1929 stock-market crash, his ancient mother returns to bury him, and final shots of pioneer covered wagons again bring back the moral bedrock.

The B-Western's refreshing way of leaping with miraculous illogic through time and space was lost not long after World War II, as the form itself was killed off by television and some less-than-charismatic stars. Alone among postwar B-Western stars, Gene Autry maintained his way of using modern technology to bridge the best values of both centuries: *The Last Round-Up* (1947) includes an Indian uprising and fatal shootings, but Autry sets things right by rigging up a television transmission to show the tribe that the land to which they are being removed isn't really all that bad after all. In the 1950s, the philosophy of time in the Western typically got simplified into dramas of man lost in existentialist space, a pattern that may reach a nadir in *Quantez* (1957), where a doomed outlaw (Fred McMurray) is reduced to lamenting, "There's nothin' to fight, nothin' to test yourself against, 'cept time." This was the era when R. W. B. Lewis's celebrated 1955 *The American Adam* would dehistoricize Cooper's Natty Bumppo into "the hero in *space*," who "seems to take his start outside time, or at the very outer edges of it, so that his location is essentially in space alone . . . the area of total possibility."[24] The 1950s, after all, liked to fancy itself the era of "adult" Westerns, and B-Westerns were nothing if not juvenile. The heritage of the B-Western doesn't arrive – with history again explored through miraculous leaps in time – until some imaginative "post-Westerns" of the 1990s, such as John Sayles's *Lone Star* (1996), with its distinctive tracking shots that locate in contiguous space a history of racial murders and generational secrets that still weigh upon the present. In the more fantastic, not to say New Age, *The Last of the Dogmen* (1995), an academic anthropologist (Barbara Hershey) and a police tracker of escaped convicts (Tom Berenger) ride horses through a secret passageway in a Montana waterfall into a green, nineteenth-century idyll where Cheyenne offspring of survivors from the 1864 Sand Creek massacre live in the old ways and where the white man's modern spiritual malaise can be cured.

There is a final apparent paradox about the ways that the Western represents the past. On the one hand the West is the region where we can go to find all that is deemed essential in American history, where the past is most treasured. On the other, the West is the place where men are allowed to have no past and to start life anew. Indeed, the very worst of social errors in a Western, fatally punishable, is to ask about a man's past or to try to investigate it. "What's past is past," someone will say, often insistently (as does the hero of *These Thousand Hills* [1959]), meaning that the past for an individual is best regarded as dead and gone.

Among John Wayne's Westerns of the 1930s, the film that makes the most of these tensions is undoubtedly *Stagecoach.* Questions about how to deal with the past revolve most complexly around his character, the sympathetic outlaw known as the Ringo Kid, whose way with the past will turn out to be liberating; but Ford's film also includes a character who demonstrates the genre's standard pattern about how men are allowed to begin anew in the West and how fatal it can be to inquire into a man's past. The southern gambler (John Carradine) has taken on in the West the name "Hatfield," although, as he admits with his dying breath, he is the son of a certain Judge Greenfield. With his reputation for shooting men – shooting them in the back, Doc Boone (Thomas Mitchell) suggests – he's not likely to have had close inquiries into his personal history. Lucy Mallory (Louise Platt), the cavalry wife who gives birth along the route, does question him about his background, puzzled by his knowledge of her father and by the initials on his silver cup, but as an upper-class southerner and a woman she has at least two excuses for not understanding the rules against questions about the past. "Hatfield's" touchiness about the slightest affront is contrasted with Ringo's calm refusal to find offense in the social slights directed at him, and "Hatfield's" formal chivalry toward "the lady" will be paralleled with Ringo's way of treating "the other lady," Dallas (Claire Trevor), the apparent prostitute in all but name.

Ringo from the start includes Dallas in the genre's principle about the place of the past, neither asking her about it nor investigating it. Applying this male prerogative to Dallas is what will eventually allow them to start life together afresh. Wayne's apparently new acting style, with its preponderance of close-ups and relatively few words, underlines Ringo's evident but unspoken confidence about both people and events to come. The plot tells us that he has vengeance – or justice – on his mind, so it is not that he forgets the weight of the past; but for Ringo the past is something to be fought where it impinges and then to be put behind him. He turns out to be neither deluded nor innocent, as the script makes him sound on the page and as the more knowing of the other passengers on the stagecoach worry. Doc Boone ("I'm not only a philosopher, sir, I'm a fatalist") and Sheriff Curly Wilcox (George Bancroft) fear Ringo's reaction when he comes to understand Dallas's sexual history. Their concern over Ringo's inexperience (he entered prison "going on seventeen") and some of Ringo's own comments ("this is no town for a girl like her") set up expectations of a "discovery scene," perhaps when Dallas leads him, as an unspoken confession, to Lordsburg's red-light district. But there is no such scene, nor even a hint of change registered in Wayne's face, when his character must have come to such knowledge.

Wayne's silent *gravitas,* so central to his subsequent career and first witnessed in *Stagecoach,* conveys a chivalry deeper than Hatfield's elaborate show of manners. Wayne's body language can say that women too will be allowed to start new in the West – even if the Production Code functioned to make this more difficult. "I know all I want to know," he finally tells Dallas, when pressed. "Things happen," they agree about their parallel histories of violent family death. (Her parents were "massacred" in Arizona's Superstition Mountains; his father and brother were murdered by the Plummer brothers.) Dallas seeks out ethical advice from Doc about the special force of a woman's history ("Is it right for a girl like me . . . ?"), but what count for more are ethics of the present, where she proves herself effortlessly selfless and competent, especially on the night when Lucy Mallory gives birth. Ringo's chivalry grows out of tacit acknowledgment of gender differences in the West even within their parallel tragedies ("It's tough, especially on a girl").

The Western genre claims this: We have a history in America, and we must celebrate it, but at our best we must also know when to leave it behind and to start afresh. In the 1930s, it was the B-Western that argued this philosophy with most vitality and wit, by leaping back to the past but also ahead to modest progress, by contending that pieces of the past, found right around that next rise, could be usable to remake the present. Among A-Westerns of the 1930s, *Stagecoach* is without rival the film least overtly concerned with the facts and legends of American history. Nevertheless, among the traits that advance it far beyond the decade's previous A-Westerns, among the things that unite it with the B-Western, is how it conveys a philosophy of history with the lightest touch. The philosophy is there even within John Wayne's silent look at Dallas, which is too unflinching to read as naïve. His gaze at her carries at its most concise and generous the genre's argument about how to remake history – and when to forget it.

John Ford on location in Arizona in 1938 for *Stagecoach,* with Tim Holt in cavalry costume as Lieutenant Blanchard. (Courtesy of the Academy of Motion Picture Arts and Sciences.)

PART THREE

# "That Sleep of Death"

## JOHN FORD AND THE DARKNESS OF THE CLASSIC WESTERN IN THE 1940S

In the middle of Don DeLillo's masterful 1982 novel *The Names,* Frank Volterra, a celebrated American filmmaker who is escaping Hollywood "genre crap," explains his plan for a "pure and simple" documentary about international death cultists, a film in which "the spoken word will be an element in the landscape." Last glimpsed, the filmmaker is still searching through remote Greek islands for any evidence of the cult's existence. Notwithstanding the futility of Volterra's quest and his annoying assurance, we might make a start into looking at what is innovative in Westerns of the 1940s by taking seriously his rant about the relationship of his current obsession to "classic" Westerns:

> People talk about classic westerns. The classic thing has always been the space, the emptiness. The lines are drawn for us. All we have to do is insert the figures, men in dusty boots, certain faces. Figures in open space have always been what film is all about. American film. This is the situation. People in a wilder-

ness, a wild and barren space. The space is the desert, the movie screen, the strip of film, however you see it. What are the people doing here? This is their existence. They're here to work out their existence. This space, this emptiness is what they have to confront.[1]

The Western, we've seen, always relished emptiness. The first film Westerns exploited a politics of space that went back to pioneers such as William Cooper who had a stake in portraying the land as empty. By the films of the 1940s, emptiness seems to seep into the characters themselves, who play out bitter conflicts on landscapes wiped clean for their testing. Volterra's intertwined obsessions about film, empty space, and rituals of killing argue also that the "classic Western" is darker than its reputation. He may have a point. It may be that what *saves* the Western in the 1940s from facile optimism is its very darkness – but that's something we'll have to explore as we go along.

"Classic" is a strange word to be linked so persistently to "Western." In the 1930s, John Ford and Merian Cooper had attempted to convince producer David O. Selznick that *Stagecoach* would be worthy project by arguing "that this was a *classic* Western with *classic* characters."[2] By the 1950s, influential critics were looking back fondly at "the classicism of the forties" from the vantage of a newer sort of Western that they had an awkward time naming.[3] Within Hollywood, "classic" has always been a relative term disguised as an absolute one, celebrating a genre's "golden age" before each complication or outrage. As hinted in Ford and Cooper's argument, a classic work of art is seen paradoxically as both superior and representative. By Latin etymology a classic is of the highest rank, but the implication has come to be that it is also typical ("that's a classic example of . . ."). A classic achieves quality while emptying its tradition, its genre, of all things extraneous, and a classic Western pares away the extraneous while evoking double nostalgia – for both the American past and the Hollywood tradition.

Notwithstanding the implication that a classic locates a genre's timeless essence, the "classic Western" turns out to label films from only a brief era in the genre's history, primarily the few years after World War II. *Stagecoach* is the single Western from before the war regularly called "classic" by critics, and the term also seems never to have been applied to films made *during* America's participation in World War II. In those years of 1941–5, western cattle barons developed the stray German accent and Native American swastikas could double for National Socialist ones. *Wild Horse Rustlers* (1943) found Nazi-saluting villains sabotaging the U.S. Army's procurement of horses.[4] "That man from Washington," a hero in thirties Westerns, makes a less surprising appearance during the war. "Ain't nothin' too tough fer the government," pronounces the wise grandpa in *Calling Wild Bill Elliott* (1943). When informed of who needs his help in *Enemy of the Law* (1945), Tex Ritter steps forward: "Oh, Uncle Sam, eh? Well count me in!" In *Gangsters of the Frontier* (1944), the response to domestic fascists is clear enough: "Our forefathers decided that some years ago. This is a free country, where nobody can set himself up as absolute ruler." In *Cowboy Commandos* (1943), the cowboys sing,

> I'm goina get der Führer sure as shootin'.
> When we cowboys go a huntin' we don't stop.
> I'll send his band of bandits all a scootin'
> And make a clean-up of the filthy lot.

These are all B-Westerns, with their surreal senses of historical time. If A-Westerns were insignificant in the war years – with one key exception, *The Ox-Bow Incident* (1943) – that's no doubt partly because the form's Indian-battle conventions were donated for the duration to combat films against the Japanese.[5] At war's end, the carrot of postwar bliss was hung just out of grasp. In Mervyn LeRoy's *Thirty Seconds over Tokyo* (1944), from a script by Dalton Trumbo, the pregnant wife of a flyer muses to other young women on a beach: "I sometimes wonder how we'll feel when it's all over. Just think, being able to settle down in a little house somewhere, and raise your children, and never be in doubt about anything." How disheartening were darkness to return to haunt postwar films.

If, as a way into the 1940s, we provisionally accept Volterra's contention that "the classic thing" in Westerns is their confrontation with "emptiness," it's necessary at this point to elaborate only slightly by noting that such emptiness would be two-sided. That is, the emptiness of classic Westerns would encompass things both positive and negative: Call them visual simplicity and social evasions. On the positive side, what still seems most impressive in Westerns of this era is their refinement of the genre's visual language, stripping it of the extraneous. It is often noted that the classic Western is conservative, and although this is usually meant politically, it's equally true visually. Just how Westerns managed to convert the genre's natural, religious, and political philosophies into apparently simple visuals, while maintaining too an enduring love of the dark sides of those philosophies, is something we'll give a shot at unraveling in the following pages. Movies learned to talk in the 1930s, but then Westerns had to learn to stop pontificating if they were to reconnect with the power of the silent film, if they were to earn back what had been glimpsed in the first productions in the landscape of the West itself: the evocation of visionary possibility and testing solitude. Westerns that achieve this in the postwar forties are regularly labeled "poetic," perhaps because whatever is going on in them is evidently not accomplished through the talky prose of the thirties.

When the best Westerns after World War II convert explicit philosophies into ambiguous visuals, the result is also that films leave their social contentions emptier than ever before. Classic Westerns are self-conscious (from perhaps the least so in *Stagecoach* to the most so in *Shane* [1953]) in the ways that they sum up the genre as it exists to that point, make new arguments, and then leave gaps for other films to fill. Exactly what it is that classic Westerns are refusing to say is also worth trying to pin down, although to do so we shall need to look (in the last chapters of this part) beyond the 1940s for answers that only later films were willing to provide.

Postwar classic Westerns are the most evasive films in our evasive genre, and yet they may also confront an evocative, darker emptiness not finally so far from that privileged in the era's abstract-expressionist paintings or in Samuel Beckett's deserts, where solitary men in greatcoat dusters wander encumbered only by pockets full of sucking stones.

# 18. *My Darling Clementine* and the Fight with Film Noir

I like a good Western. You can pick them up and put them down any time.
Sergeant Paine (Bernard Lee) in *The Third Man* (1949)

John Wayne was our trusty guide through the thickets of the 1930s' A- and B-Westerns, and there's an equally evident choice if we want to explore the Western of the 1940s: John Ford, clearly the master of classic Westerns, even if exactly what makes his best films succeed has always proven elusive. Among Ford's Westerns of the 1940s, his rendition of the Wyatt Earp legend, *My Darling Clementine* (1946), is the one most often labeled "classic." For Alan Lovell, it is "the perfect example of the classic Western," a characterization modified only slightly by others. In his seminal *Horizons West,* Jim Kitses links *My Darling Clementine* with *Shane* as two most closely approaching the "definitive model of the 'classical' western." Thomas Schatz, comparing *Stagecoach* to *Clementine,* finds the later film "the more overtly mythic, classical Western of the two" for its "positive light" on heroism and community. Influential French critics André Bazin and, later, Christian Metz tended to qualify the term "classic" when applying it to *Clementine,* but the film has settled into "an accepted 'classic'" that is often also "poetic" to a host of recent writers.[1] What's indisputable is that *My Darling Clementine* employs "emptiness" about as deeply as any Western – both in creating meaning from seemingly blank visuals *and* in historical evasions. Especially because it catches the genre at its next dynamic turning point, right after World War II, we'll be using it as our focus throughout Part Three.

The story line certainly is simple enough: On the desert outside Tombstone, Arizona, Wyatt Earp meets Old Man Clanton and turns down his purchase offer for cattle the Earp brothers are herding west. That evening, the three eldest brothers ride back from the "wide-awake, wide-open town" to find eighteen-year-old James Earp murdered and the cattle rustled. Wyatt accepts the job as Tombstone's marshal and, through a barroom confrontation, reaches an accommodation that leaves Doc Holliday in charge of the gambling. Arriving by stagecoach is Clementine Carter, Holliday's abandoned fiancée and nurse from his days as a surgeon in Boston. She incites distant admiration from Wyatt and quick jealousy from Chihuahua, the saloon singer who calls herself "Doc Holliday's girl." Clementine cannot persuade the apparently tubercular Doc to return east and makes plans to return alone.

Wyatt spots Chihuahua wearing the silver pendant stolen from James Earp at his murder. She claims it to have been a present from Doc but, when confronted by him, admits it was a gift from one of Clanton's four sons, Billy – who shoots her at the moment of her confession and is himself mortally wounded as he gallops from town. Pursuing Billy, Virgil Earp arrives at the Clanton ranch, where he is shot in the back by Old Man Clanton. Doc operates on Chihuahua and, later that evening, Virgil's body is dumped onto the main street by the Clantons. By sunup, Chihuahua has died of her wounds, and Doc joins the two surviving Earps for a showdown with the four surviving Clantons at the O.K. Corral. When the dust clears, Doc Holliday and all of the Clantons are dead. Wyatt bids farewell to Clementine – who remains as town schoolmarm – and rides down the long trail to the distant mountains.

Recounted thus, *My Darling Clementine* sounds ordinary enough, if a bit bleaker and more corpse-strewn than earlier Westerns. One might do better initially to watch the film without its sound. Then, one can't help but notice that the visuals tell another story, less a movement from crime to retribution than from darkness to light, and from constriction to openness. Although the plot heads toward a last-reel showdown, the visual climax comes earlier: a town of dark confusion, a crowded gambling hall deeply shadowed, gunshots in the night, a body face down in the mud and hard rain, a harshly lamplit hotel doorway, terse exchanges among men in dripping slickers. This confinement is fully brightened and opened by the arrival of Clementine a half-hour into the film.

The escape from film noir – that, put simply, is the first story that *My Darling Clementine* tells. This visual tale was told often in the movies in the first years after World War II: The family and community restore themselves from a maze of threats expressed through film-noir styles. The supreme expression of this battle between community satisfaction and noir fears is surely Frank Capra's *It's a Wonderful Life,* released in December 1946 – a month after *Clementine* – and sharing with it a defining, dark sequence of a small town gone hogwild with gambling nightlife. Especially because of James Stewart's intense way with anguish, Capra's film never entirely vanquishes its noir nightmare, notwithstanding the frantic final ecstasy.[2]

"What are the people doing here?" Don DeLillo's film director Volterra asks about "the figures" in classic Westerns: "This is their existence. They're here to work out their existence." Postwar A-Westerns did largely turn inward, away from grand historic processes and Manifest Destiny epics, and toward people who "work out their existence" within the confines of small communities. Rightly or not, Hollywood crafted postwar dramas under the assumption that audiences had lost their folk memories of larger depression-era problems, and even B-Westerns came to abandon agricultural discontent, moving closer to A-Westerns in gunfighter story lines and less threadbare production values. (The new independent companies that flourished after federal antitrust decisions of the midforties made many "Intermediates" – a term that itself emphasizes the breakdown of distinctions between A's and B's.) Filmmakers who insisted on the persistence of tensions had to take them up with a "social problem" bludgeon. More and more, the Western's political philosophies served to justify who would be included within America's ideal community – pictured as a small town – and who excluded. The genre's Puritanism turned to dividing the elect from the damned, something taken up by the "town-taming" subgenre so popular after the war and that we'll be exploring in this part.

To the extent that the classic Western is a story of inclusion and exclusion, then what it most has to exclude is everything now associated with film noir – at least if the opening of *My Darling Clementine* tells the whole story. Look at that strangely cloud-heavy shot of three Earp brothers first heading into Tombstone for the evening (Fig. 39). Leaving young James Earp with the herd, the other brothers are – so the plot line says – off for a night of fun on the town, relaxation from the work of the trail. But the dark visuals and downbeat acting already suggest something more like facing the music. Already the Earps seem to be doing the tough job that has to be done. Gazing down on the town, Wyatt utters the words "Let's go" in a weary, pleasureless tone, in two

**Figure 39.** *My Darling Clementine* (1946): Three Earp brothers ride into Tombstone for the night.

**Figure 40.** *My Darling Clementine:* Doc Holliday (Victor Mature) with his handkerchief at the O.K. Corral gunfight (40a); and clouds after the fight (40b).

falling notes that match the visuals even while contradicting the story motivation. (He'll return those words and tone to appropriate context before the showdown.)

The film closes, in counterpoint to the noir opening, with an array of whites. Among the oddest is a tilt shot at the end of the gunfight from fence rail up to . . . only white clouds (Fig. 40b). Doc has died, waving his white handkerchief like a flag of surrender, still spotless of

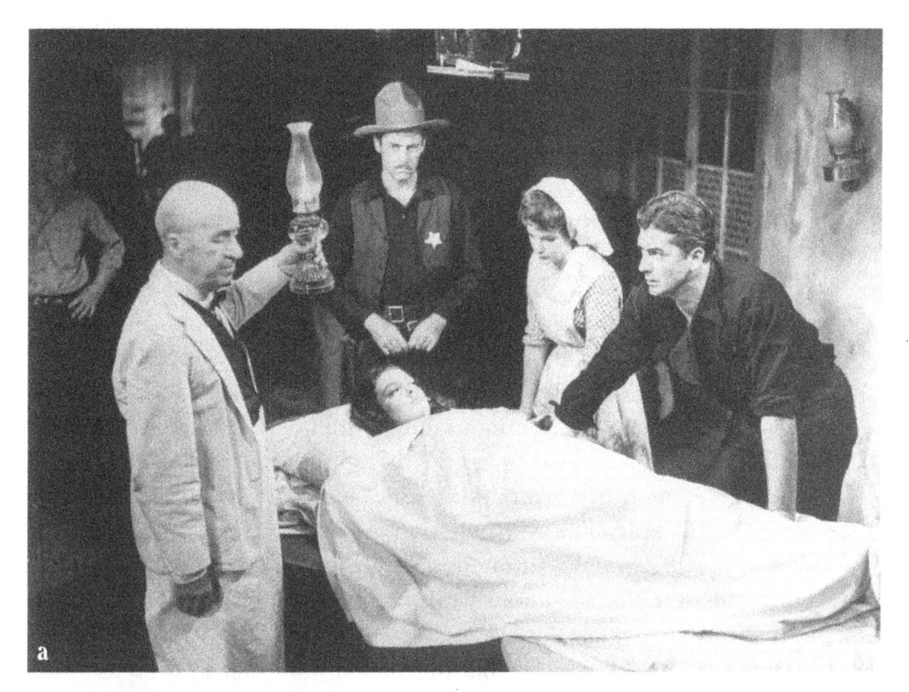

**Figure 41.** Doc Holliday returns to surgery to operate on Chihuahua in *My Darling Clementine.* A production photo taken during preparations for the scene (41a), with the spotlight for Chihuahua's face visible at top. Frame enlargements (41b,c) from the completed scene: Chihuahua (Linda Darnell) and Doc (Victor Mature).

blood notwithstanding his consumptive coughing into it (Fig. 40a).[3] Indeed, as body-strewn as the film becomes, it's bloodstain-free, even when Chihuahua (Linda Darnell) is gunned down at close range and operated on. Her stainless death is part of a shift in the representation of her character, from darkness to light, which underlines the unsettling racial component of the visual story. Chihuahua literally turns white because Mac the bartender brings a lamp near her face (Fig. 41), but the lighting draws from Catholic iconography of turning "virgin for Christ" – a whore washed of sins at the moment of her death.[4] In contrast, the nearly expressionless, very white face of twenty-two-year-old Cathy Downs as Clementine is seldom without direct lighting, made doubly stark in two-shots that contrast the shadows thrown onto the prominent facial bones of Victor Mature's Doc Holliday (Fig. 42). It is initially surprising that Clementine should bring an escape from film noir at the same time as she forces Doc to confront his past – a word he chokes on ("Forget the . . ."). A more typical female entrance into the Western in these years is that of Tess Millay (Joanne Dru) in Howard Hawks's *Red River* (1948), who shrouds herself in a black mantilla and brings fog and ominous music with her own insistent inquiries into the background histories of the fighting men. (*Red River* is the most celebrated film to combine noir elements with the older Manifest Destiny epic. The contradiction, especially within Tom Dunson, John Wayne's grandly tormented–easily tamed character, led Hawks into one of the most famously unconvincing endings ever to saddle a great film.)[5]

What is unsurprising is that John Ford would try to dispense with the world of film noir as soon as possible. The neuroses and perverse erotic yearnings of film noir are alien to most of his earlier films, even if he had been in the vanguard of protonoir expressionist styles in his German-influenced silents at the Fox studio and then in *The Informer* (1935), *The Prisoner of Shark Island* (1936), and *The Long Voyage Home* (1940). "What kind of town *is* this?" Wyatt Earp asks three times in *Clementine*'s dark opening, echoing the film's own bewilderment. The battle between the Western and film noir would be expected from film types long categorized as opposites: in visuals (the Western's open vistas against noir's confined shadows), narratives (linear stories of progress against convoluted flashbacks), and characters (clear good or evil against ambiguous heroes). In 1946 the earliest French essay to apply the term *films "noirs"* to Hollywood set their directors, notably John Huston and Billy Wilder, against such "museum pieces" as John Ford. In Raymond Borde and Étienne Chaumenton's landmark 1955 book *Panorama du film noir américain, 1941–1953*, John Wayne is put forward as the antithesis of the noir hero.[6] The retrospective voice-overs and ornate dialogue repartee of many Raymond Chandler–influenced noirs could hardly be further from the classic Westerner's straightforward taciturnity, nor have most noir heroes any but the most perfunc-

**Figure 42.** *My Darling Clementine:* The first conversation in Tombstone between Clementine (Cathy Downs) and Doc (Victor Mature).

tory and censor-demanded interest in bringing law and order to civilization.

Still, it may be revealing that film noir proved not quite so easy to evict from the classic Western as the opening of *My Darling Clementine* tries to argue. Even *Stagecoach* had ended with a long sequence – the confusing night battle in Lordsburg – that looks dropped from a darker film. *Clementine* is most evidently "classic" in the way that it wrings nostalgia from everywhere: from its landscape, from its pace, from its weight of time established through space, so to speak. (Henry Fonda, who plays Wyatt Earp, remembered that John Ford took pains to evoke such nostalgia from the cast as well: When a bugler was sent into the desert to blow taps at dusk on location in Monument Valley, "I tell you that people would cry with nostalgia; it was like being a child again. . . .")[7] The nostalgia is evoked in the film also in a repeated visual pattern that finds Fonda's Earp walking heavily from the camera, down covered boardwalks or through empty barrooms, carrying something like the burden of our past into his solitary darkness. Noir lighting also remains Doc Holliday's keynote until he finally surrenders with his white handkerchief. Indeed, if one gives visuals prominence over dialogue – which would be John Ford's own preference – then this classic Western remains more like a Josef von Sternberg film: slow, pictorial, nihilistic, with Victor Mature in the dark, sensual role played by Marlene Dietrich for Sternberg.[8]

Noir's essence is urban: stories of private eyes and city drifters; close-ups of disembodied, black wing tips down damp, lamplit streets. Those associations mean that *Clementine*'s dark-to-light progression can silently extend the Populist argument – the country reasserting its values over those of the city – that was talked through in earlier B-Westerns. This might seem the only way the Western could present its conflict with noir were it not that other Westerns of the time argued in just the reverse way. Elia Kazan's *Sea of Grass* (1947), for instance, finds Spencer Tracy relishing his warrior memories, as a fighter of buffalo and Indians on his vast grasslands, until Katharine Hepburn arrives from the East – a hard-jawed Clementine who sets Tracy's cowhands agog with her determination to reform her wild westerner and his ranch house ("This'll fix up nicely"). *Sea of Grass*'s progressing darkness was partly Kazan's solution to MGM's restraint on location shooting in favor of cost-cutting back-projected landscape, but for several reasons – including Kazan's growing resentment with MGM – the film progressively becomes the genre's most claustrophobic treatment of a great-outdoors theme.[9] The darkest sequences come with the entrance late in the film of Tracy and Hepburn's punk son (Robert Walker), whose amoral gunslinging points toward coming rebels without causes.

If film noir is clearly an urban form, one can also put it the other way: Noir revealed city life as the last frontier, where civilization and law is a veneered illusion and men must fight for whatever fragile order they care to invent. After all, such essential noir traits as the alien essence of woman and the brooding upon the nearness of death had long been developing within the Western. Style *is* theme, certainly, seldom more so than in film noir, but it may be that noir deepened, rather than simply opposed, certain anxieties that the Western had long contained and held at a distance. At its best, noir also carries a complex philosophy – label it existentialist with touches of absurdism – and like the classic Western, it represents much of its philosophy through a concise visual code. Raymond Chandler's ornate metaphors, after all, compete with another strain of film noir that draws its verbal inspiration instead from James M. Cain and, before him, Ernest Hemingway, giving us noir heroes who rival Westerners for uttering only the few, perfectly resonant words. All this is complicated by the fact that "film noir" and "classic Western" are both terms invented as a way of looking back upon film history. Both film types recovered in prestige from low origins in pulp fiction by being honored in the French journal pages of *Positif* and *Cahiers du cinéma* before finding respectability back home.

If the Western variety of noir appears less extreme, if Mom didn't have to send Junior to the lobby for the gundown, it's less because the noir in Westerns is stylistically tamer than because the landscape itself elegizes death and thus argues that murders committed there are less pointless and less perverse. Even the darkly looming cliffs in Raoul Walsh's haunted *Pursued* (1947) and the primordial boulders of his grim *Along the Great Divide* (1951) refer us to the roots of America, stabilizing qualms about deaths that even the characters question. There is some meaning in *these* killings, a meaning related at least indirectly to progress for civilization. John Ford's Monument Valley monoliths, as solid as the tombstones they resemble, can suggest a mocking hostility to human effort, especially by the time of *The Searchers* (1956); but in *Clementine* the monoliths keep their distance, are evidence of stability and witnesses to progress.[10]

Evidently there were any number of ways that Westerns could confront film noir, from *Clementine*'s escape to *Sea of Grass*'s progression into it. But these narrative options may disguise deeper affinities. The Western may have found in film noir a secret soul mate. If they are opposite, it may be in the sense that fighting brothers are said to be opposite: They are rivals over the same issues. There are revealing moments in several of the most masterful postwar films that suggest the blood brotherhood of the Western and film noir, and two are worth quick mention. In an early moment of expansive optimism in *It's a Wonderful Life*, George Bailey, played by James Stewart, had imagined lassoing the moon. However, when Mary (Donna Reed) draws him as a blue-jeaned caricature that she captions "George Lassos the Moon," her affectionate intentions also diminish his ambitions into a cowboy cartoon and ominously hint at the limitations to a westerner's aspiration within small communities that will lead George into his suicidal noir nightmare.[11] Carol Reed's *The Third Man* (1949), set on the damp cobblestones and in the dank sewers of Vienna and filmed with canted noir angles and giant shadows, is so stolen by Orson Welles's brief appearance that it is easy to forget that the film's lead is an American writer of pulp Westerns – *The Lone Rider of Santa Fe* and *Death at Double-X Ranch* among them – Holly Martins, played by Joseph Cotten. The film has fun with how lost culturally in Europe is Martins, who, when asked at the British Cultural Center about stream-of-consciousness techniques and "the place" of James Joyce, can only confess that his own greatest literary influence is Zane Grey. His confusion deepens after his old friend Harry Lime – Welles's character – shows up alive and brushes off with frightening charm the anonymous deaths that have resulted from his adulterated, black-market penicillin. However much Martins is in over his depth – he literally doesn't know the language of the place – we don't write him off completely because he's so doggedly relentless amid old Europe's world-weariness. "This isn't Santa Fe . . . and you're not a cowboy," he's reminded, but he turns out to be the only one capable of uttering the word "justice" and the one who must ultimately take on the gunfighter's role in shooting down his criminal friend. The morality here goes back to "the Virginian's" execution of his best-friend-turned-rustler, but dark complexities of postwar corruption now leave Martins empty. In *The Third Man*'s great final shot, his would-be romantic interest walks past him as if he has turned invisible.

For all film noir's affinity with city streets, it's worth remembering that some of the greatest noirs of the 1940s intensify their power by mixing dark visuals with western landscapes, notably the California Sierras of Jacques Tourneur's *Out of the Past* (1947) and the high New Mexican deserts of John Stahl's *Leave Her to Heaven* (1945), the first Technicolor noir. Raoul Walsh's *High Sierra* (1941) and John Huston's *The Treasure of the Sierra Madre* (1948) also set noir fatality under looming landscapes. In view of such films, it may be less surprising that the first classic Westerns turn out, on looking at their visual arguments, to be not so far from something usually labeled a mongrel "hybrid": the noir-Western.[12] If *My Darling Clementine* has been the easiest of all films to label a "classic Western," it may also be because it shuns film noir as rapidly as possible.

As a result of trying to evict everything related to noir, *Clementine* is left, after its first half-hour, almost with a visual and narrative tabula rasa. How it populates that "emptiness" with figures who "work out their existence" in an idealized community we'll explore in Chapters 21 and 22. For now, it's just worth pushing this line of argument about the relationship of the Western and film noir through to its implications. In the earlier two parts of this book, I've argued the value of groups of films usually ignored or assumed tangential to the mainstream history of the genre: eastern Westerns and B-Westerns. In this final part we arrive at the era where the genre at last apparently finds its bearings and settles into "classic" certainties, and yet here too a group of films often thought to be anomalous may be central to the genre's history. Indeed, with the partial exception of Ford's own films, it seems to me that all of the Westerns from this era that retain their force do so through incorporation of elements of film noir. If the key Westerns released in the five years after the war still remain relatively unappreciated, it may be because their links with noir have made them seem out of the mainstream – notably *Pursued* (1947), *Ramrod* (1947), *Blood on the Moon* (1948), *Yellow Sky* (1948), *Devil's Doorway* (1950), *The Furies* (1950) and the second Technicolor noir, *Duel in the Sun* (1946). For a full decade – from *The Ox-Bow Incident* in 1943 through *High Noon* in 1952 – Westerns confronted a darkness, a despair, and an emptiness that is never really held at bay by their routine genuflections to the progress of civilization. Whatever its didacticism *The Ox-Bow Incident* invented the dark tone that is unlike anything remotely seen in previous sound-era Westerns. *High Noon* retains its force less from its ambiguous political parable (intended as anti-McCarthyist but often taken at the time as pro–Korean War) than from the despair that Gary Cooper embodies in his face and his painfully long walks around the town, as he searches in vain for community solidarity.

Why should film noir fit smoothly into so many Westerns at this time? Partly it may be that because noir is about city life it slips more easily into stories about people who "work out their existence" within communities than into epics about advancing across the land. Many noir-Western are particularly dark (visually and morally) in intermittent clumps of space – in saloons, interiors, and the spaces between buildings – and this is where they most describe the hazards of community. *Only the Valiant* (1951) takes pains to maneuver its cavalry down a canyon, an enclosed space that permits the frontier enactment of an earlier snatch of dialogue: what the troops would do to despised Captain Richard Lance (Gregory Peck) if they ever got him down "a dark alley."

It's hard to avoid a sense that the classic Western invents itself through the encounter with film noir. If the classic Western is at its most compelling in the late 1940s, that may be precisely because Westerns of this era survive by incorporating homeopathic doses of darkness. *My Darling Clementine is* calm and assured – "classic" especially in its nostalgia – and yet held within it are the seeds of the collapse of all that it treasures.

# 19. Out of the Past

But if he does not know where he is going, Western man can at least look back and see where he came from.

Whittaker Chambers, writing anonymously for *Life* magazine (March 3, 1947)

*Stagecoach* had ended in 1939 by posing visually a question that it was unable to answer. The dark town of Lordsburg had shown none of the community spirit developed among the travelers on the stagecoach itself. The town, seen entirely at night during the film's last twenty minutes, is a series of confusing, crowded or confined spaces, filled with dark mysteries of action and motivation. On the set, cinematographer Bert Glennon had described the challenges of shooting with relatively few lights, including "the elimination of the conventional backlight or 'Hollywood halo'" except when the backlight was the primary illumination for foreground figures in shadow (Fig. 43a).[1] The suspicious, silent, and statically posed citizens of Lordsburg step back into shadows, awaiting violence, as John Wayne's Ringo Kid and Claire Trevor's Dallas walk through pools of light (Fig. 43b). The only resolution was to send the couple off into the night, away from the United States, across the Mexican border. However satisfying their escape from "the blessings of civilization," it was an evasive conclusion for the larger community. Ford's next Western – after Navy service in the war – was *My Darling Clementine*, which picks up visually where the expressionism at the end of *Stagecoach* left off, with the dark confusion of another night in a desert town a hundred miles further west, Tombstone. Ultimately *Clementine* is able to answer the questions – about the creation of American community – that *Stagecoach* approaches in the coach itself but then avoids in the Lordsburg finale.

The history of any genre can be looked upon as such a series of questions and answers. As suggested earlier, the Western's limited set of situations, landscapes, and actors make these questions and answers easier to follow than within other Hollywood genres, although those limitations have also made Westerns appear "all the same" to not a few viewers. The "classic Western" was defined along these lines in the most influential study of the genre in the 1970s, Will Wright's *Six-Guns and Society: A Structural Study of the Western,* which subdivided the genre into four basic patterns: "The Classical Western is the . . . one people think of when they say, 'All Westerns are alike.' It is the story of the lone stranger who rides into a troubled town and cleans it up, winning the respect of the townsfolk and the love of the schoolmarm." This certainly fits *My Darling Clementine,* and Wright's neat structural categorizations were tempting for the imprecise arts. He ended his book with the claim that his method allowed him to be "scientifically right."[2]

A structuralist reliance on binary oppositions in the human mind (following Claude Lévi-Strauss) along with inspiration from folktale analysis (following Vladimir Propp) and studies of the mythology of the American West (drawing especially from Henry Nash Smith) combined to pervade thinking about the Western film for several decades. Without getting sidetracked into a history of film criticism, it is worth noting the surprisingly enduring reliance on structural patterns within studies of the Hollywood Western. Henry Nash Smith's analysis of nineteenth-century thinking about the West in terms of "two myths . . . of exactly opposite meaning" represented in images of "the garden and the desert" was carried forward most influentially in Peter Wollen's 1969 reconciliation of structuralism, mythology, and auteurism, *Signs and Meaning in the Cinema,* which converted Smith's two myths into the "master antinomy" of John Ford's Westerns "between the wilderness and the garden" (taking the opposition also from the closing lines of Ford's *The Man Who Shot Liberty Valance*), a pattern said to be at its most "simple" and "uncomplicated" in *My Darling Clementine.*[3] Such categorizing itself, however, tended to make Westerns sound alike, partly because the folktale focus often relegated visual arguments to mere stylistic details and acting to mere "noise"[4] – which proved fatal for looking into Westerns, whose stories in outline are so numbingly repetitive.

By structural and mythic measures, the numerous films about Wyatt Earp tell substantially the same "classical Western" story, but such narrative categorizing blocks out almost everything of compelling interest

**Figure 43.** The dark town of Lordsburg at the conclusion of *Stagecoach* (1939): Luke Plummer (Tom Tyler) rises from the poker table (43a); Ringo (John Wayne) escorts Dallas (Claire Trevor) home (43b).

in any individual film, especially the arguments it takes up from previous films or sets up for further discussion. Michael Coyne in his 1997 *The Crowded Prairie: American National Identity in the Hollywood Western* can place *My Darling Clementine* next to *Duel in the Sun* and find that "close analysis of their narrative schematizations demonstrates that they share identical mythic and moral frameworks."[5] This is fair enough as far as it goes – Coyne finds both films enforcing "dominant cultural concepts of race, class and gender" – if not especially surprising. Such analyses tend to rule out quirky elements in any one narrative and to label similar story lines as "mere" variations on one another, rather than as rival arguments, which can well be mutually exclusive. Retellings of that most classic of tales, the Garden of Eden story, are variants of it, but, in being so, are arguments over it. Was Eve guilty? or Adam? or God? or the serpent? (and who is he?) And if guilty, of what exactly? (Disobedience? thirst for knowledge? sexuality? megalomania?) What both structural and mythic analyses take as variants are more compelling when seen as rivals engaged in a debate, declaring battle against one another.

In looking into the dialogue carried on among Westerns, cultural details prove more helpful than universal structures. *My Darling Clementine* rests calmly within long-standing arguments among critics – and also among filmmakers. Of course such a dialogue among films proves possible only when a sufficient number are made for an audience actively engaged with the genre, which is why in the post–World War II era and for a few decades thereafter we have the opportunity of tracing out the range of responses on film to *Clementine* and to the classic Western generally – as we shall try to do in the three final chapters of this part (24–26), after looking further into how Ford's film and other classic Westerns makes their argument, in the next four chapters (20–23).

Wyatt Earp's legend was never told in silent films, for the excellent reason that it had yet to be invented – primarily by two books, Walter Noble Burns's romantic history *Tombstone: An Iliad of the Southwest* (1927) and Stuart N. Lake's fitfully amusing but factually discredited biography *Wyatt Earp, Frontier Marshal* (1931). In the fifteen years before *My Darling Clementine,* there were a number of film versions of the Wyatt Earp–O.K. Corral story – as many as ten if one casts the net widely – and four are worth briefly introducing for the ways that they help differentiate the classic Western of the 1940s from the "same" story told in the 1930s.[6]

*Law and Order* (1932), coscripted by twenty-five-year-old John Huston, first mapped out on film the story of Wyatt Earp (with the names changed, partly from fear of Wyatt's widow, Josephine Earp, and her propensity for threatening lawsuits):[7] An ex-lawman is reluctant to put on the gun and badge again but is eventually brought round to the inevitability of a brothers-against-brothers showdown on the outskirts of Tombstone. What first strikes a viewer of *Law and Order* is not that story line, however "classic" its elements, but the gritty, crowded, off-center compositions filmed with a nervously prowling camera. Everywhere that *Clementine* is relaxed, *Law and Order* is tense. Walter Huston's Frame Johnson stands erect, shouting in evangelical cadences of a "reckoning" for the evil brothers. The film's source is the first novelization of the Earp legend, titled *Saint Johnson* and published in 1930. On the page, "Saint" is an ironic nickname for a lawman at the center of complicated double-dealings with outlaws and whose own less-than-classic gunplay includes shooting a man's horse to "slow him down some."[8] The film's title change to *Law and Order* foregrounds questions of social control, and the opening detail of Indians selling their votes for a dollar each initiates the kind of political melodrama found widely in other pre-Code thirties films (even if historically Arizona's Native Americans had no votes to cast, let alone to sell, until more than a half-century after the 1880s).[9] This Tombstone marshal expresses some regret over the necessity for violence; but his decision to force a showdown is played with teeth-grinding anger over lost options that leaves no time for soulful brooding. "As God is my judge, I'll get even with you to the last drop of blood!" Walter Huston shouts, echoing the flawed Old Testament moralists he made famous on stage in Eugene O'Neill's *Desire Under the Elms* in 1924 and on film in *Rain* later in 1932. "Saint" Johnson, his friends and brothers *all* dead, ends by throwing his tin star in the dust.

Visually, *Law and Order* would not look out of place twenty years later in the noir era and fits the spirit of *High Noon* – which also infamously ends with its sheriff throwing his tin star in the dust. But the darkness of *Law and Order* has other meanings arising from cross-formulations with other genres. The author of *Saint Johnson*, W. R. Burnett, was known for his gangster novels, especially *Little Caesar*, filmed to popular and critical success with Edward G. Robinson in 1930. *Law and Order* infuses into the Western the expressionist emotional bite of a hard-boiled gangster film and extends a pattern inaugurated in King Vidor's *Billy the Kid* (1930) – another ambiguous frontier gunman of no interest in the silent era – which had fused the gangster ethic to William S. Hart's Old Testament gunfighter morality. Also impressive in the pre-Code 1930s at Universal Studios, where *Law and Order* was produced, was the darkness of its horror cycle (*Dracula, Frankenstein* [both 1931], and their sequels). As we noticed with George O'Brien's fight against the German-accented, piano-playing villain in *Mystery Ranch* (1932), and as is equally the case for U.S. Marshal John Travers (John Wayne) in his battle against "The Shadow" in *The Star Packer* (1934), it's the dark forces within European expressionism that these lawmen must fight. Walter Huston's character doesn't merely evict darkness from Tombstone but recognizes it within himself, which contributes to his defeat as he rides from town, head bowed. *Law and Order* is an early argument for the suitability of darkness within the Western and its characters, but it is never relaxed or empty. It's full of explanations about the social and psychological meanings of its darkness.

The other versions of the Earp story on film in the 1930s are much less compelling, but collectively they have one fascination: They are what *My Darling Clementine* looks like as a B-Western, stripped of hesitations or lingering and each filled instead with around an hour of action virtues and lighter touches. *Frontier Marshal* (1934) is the first version of the Earp legend based on Stuart Lake's biography (called in the credits, with some honesty, a "novel"), although again it alters the names. George O'Brien is the no-nonsense ex-marshal, "Mr. Wyatt," who in Tombstone becomes a lawman again without any evident regret. Villainous businessmen are pitted against Wyatt and the reformed outlaw "Doc," who get a little help from a Jewish shopkeeper who prefers nonviolence. ("What, with business so rotten, you want I should kick customers?") Independently produced by Sol Lesser and released by Fox, the 1934 *Frontier Marshal* was a "Lesser Lesser," to Hollywood wags. Monument Valley, little seen on film before *Stagecoach,* appears here – as a stock-shot insert. *Law for Tombstone* (1937) hints at the surreal era leaps of B-Westerns when the Wyatt Earp figure (called "Alamo Bowie" and played by Buck Jones) gets his orders from a thirties-garbed man and his secretary with telephones on their desks; he heads off to Tombstone to find Doc Holliday faking drunkenness to disguise his work as "Government Agent Number 38." Allan Dwan's 1939 version, titled again *Frontier Marshal,* is his first sound Western after literally hundreds of silent ones and a vehicle for Randolph Scott – which may explain why this Wyatt Earp is played as such a traditional lone cowboy, without brothers. Although the dialogue requires this ex-lawman to say he's "had enough of gun-totin'," Scott's posture and persona convey little reluctance. Like Ford's film, this one was overseen by Darryl F. Zanuck for Twentieth Century–Fox, but only the story lines are close. Dwan's camera is very mobile, even in the saloon, and his mise-en-scène multilayered, which makes Tombstone, more historically, into a bustling boomtown.

John Ford claimed that his interest in the story came not from any previous film but straight from the source:

> When Wyatt Earp retired as a lawman, he went to some little town north of Pasadena. . . . We became quite friendly. . . . I didn't know anything about the O.K. Corral at the time, but Harry Carey knew about it, and he asked Wyatt and Wyatt described it fully. . . . As a matter of fact, he drew it out on paper, a sketch of the entire thing. . . . So in *My Darling Clementine,* we did it exactly the way it had been.[10]

It's a good tale, but whenever Ford is recorded saying "as a matter of fact," it almost always turns out to mean, "Here's a bit of blarney for a gullible journalist." The version of *My Darling Clementine*'s origin by its primary screenwriter, Winston Miller, is only marginally more reliable: "John Ford and I sat around for five or six weeks kicking this thing around, trying to cook up a story. Twentieth had once made a picture based on Wyatt Earp, and everybody in town had taken a shot at Earp, one way and another. But we disregarded that; we just started from scratch and made up our story."[11] John Ford is known to have screened the 1939 version *Frontier Marshal* in October 1945 – "Shit, I can do better than that," he told Henry Fonda – and both Ford and Winston Miller clearly made a study of it.[12] Large swatches of dialogue from the second *Frontier Marshal* survived into *Clementine*'s shooting script, but Ford followed his usual practice by cutting many lines on the set.

It would be futile to attempt to track down the discrepancies between *My Darling Clementine* and the historical events that took place in Tombstone, Arizona, in late October 1881. A shorter if less amusing catalog could be worked up the other way, as to the few places where *Clementine*'s story line has factual basis, assuming that such "facts" aren't lost forever in conflicting legend. Ford, in any case, would be the last director to disdain the tall tale. For any film fans who take *My Darling Clementine*'s visual hard edges for documentary truth, even a few facts are surprising: Wyatt Earp was never quite Tombstone's marshal, although his brother Virgil was. His whole past is cloudy, indeed shady, though his arrest for horse theft (on the one hand) and job as a deputy marshal in Dodge City (on the other) are matters of relatively undisputed record. Wyatt didn't merely "pass through" Tombstone but ran gambling at the "Oriental Saloon" while investing in real estate and mining. He lost an election for sheriff of Cochise County (newly created in 1881 with Tombstone as its seat), even though he and his brothers were Republicans and thus allied with the town businessmen. Set against them were the local cattle interests, primarily transplanted southern Democrats, among them N. H. "Old Man" Clanton and his three sons. If the Clantons were certainly cattle rustlers, they were also longer-standing residents of the region, closer to being true pioneers from before the silver discovery of 1877 and accustomed to an era when rustling cattle from Mexico was an honored, some would have said patriotic, activity. By most accounts, the O.K. Corral gunfight – which took place *after* Old Man Clanton's death – arose from a double betrayal: Ike Clanton revealed to Wyatt Earp the names of cohorts responsible for a stage robbery, and Wyatt let it be known who'd talked. On the Clanton side of the shootout, Billy Clanton and two friends were killed, while Ike and another escaped. On the Earp side, Virgil, Morgan, and Doc Holliday were apparently wounded slightly; Wyatt was unhurt.

Something about Wyatt Earp and the O.K. Corral has made the story the single most extreme example of a Western-history phenomenon we noticed in connection with Western painting: that truth consists of getting the details right, however dubious the underlying conception – at least to judge from the massive bibliography of ghostwritten memoirs, amateur histories, and feuding screeds about the Earps and their gunfights.[13] Messy history has never made good art, and few moments in frontier history are quite as messy as the O.K. Corral and its murderous revenges, which dragged on with disregard for the dramatic unities for more than a quarter century (not ending, arguably, until Virgil Earp in 1905 killed a man he held responsible for the death of another Earp brother, Warren). In *My Darling Clementine,* the grave marker of young James Earp may be a signpost of the filmmakers' attitude toward "the facts" at the time of the film's making: "Born 1864. Died 1882." As it happens, the real James Earp was perfectly "able to grow up and live safe," to quote Wyatt's lament over lost youth in the film's graveside speech. James, who was eight years *older* than Wyatt, survived from 1841 for three-quarters of a century to witness a completely changed world by the time of his death in 1926. His death date on the film's grave is a year *after* the O.K. Corral shootout (Fig. 44).

Early in the scripting Ford, aware of how far from the historical record his film would be, suggested fictionalizing the characters' names, but Zanuck disagreed and Ford relented, probably wisely.[14] It would change spectator response significantly had the film called Wyatt Earp's character, say, Frame Johnson, as had *Law and Order.* For those who have heard something of Wyatt Earp – and these would be virtually all of *My Darling Clementine*'s original audience – his name alone begins to fill in some of the emptiness of the film; the name brings its own back-story and provides a sort of fated suspense to the otherwise lackadaisical, seemingly lazy way that this man goes about avenging his first murdered brother. The audience already has the knowledge that, however much "Wyatt Earp" may delay or turn away from violence, that will be his legendary destiny.

What *My Darling Clementine* most obviously abandons, in comparison with the earlier film versions of Earp's story, is defining evil under the terms of Populism. In the earlier Earp films all of the bad guys evoke eastern styles or riches. *Law and Order*'s villains are the supercilious "Northrop" brothers with their gloves, pencil-line mustaches, and bags of money hanging from their belts. In the 1934 *Frontier Marshal,* the murdering double-dealer is Tombstone's rich mayor, a banker who robs his own bank. In *Law for Tombstone* rough Bull Clanton is only a

**Figure 44.** *My Darling Clementine:* Wyatt Earp (Henry Fonda) at his brother's grave.

front man for "the big boss," the mysterious "Twin-Gun" with his wall-safe loot. In the 1939 *Frontier Marshal,* slick businessmen again bring trouble.[15] Three of these 1930s films – all except *Law for Tombstone* – include variations on the same scene: Earp's character, new to the town of Tombstone, deals easily with a drunk barroom gunman and then is asked by the impressed townsfolk to stay on as sheriff or marshal. Thus one could use the motif (hero first cleans evil from a saloon before taking on the whole town) to line up the three earlier Earp tales alongside *My Darling Clementine* – which also includes the scene – as telling the same classic story about progress.[16] But what count for more than such narrative structures are distinctions of style and tone arising from production choices dominated by relatively brief social ideas. For Ford and the world of 1946, this meant opting to discuss *neither* the complicated gangster morality of *Law and Order* nor Populism's moneyed evil. *Clementine* begins with much precise discussion of money, including the "twenty-five American dollars worth of solid silver" represented in the necklace James Earp has bought for his girl back home and the offers Pa Clanton makes for the Earp cattle: "pay you in silver three dollars a head . . . might raise it to five dollars silver." But Ford's film soon eliminates, or evades, all economic explanation. Whatever the Clantons' criminal activity in the film, it evidently hasn't brought riches sufficient to alter their white-trash (southern Democratic) life-style in a cramped ranch house well outside the community.[17]

In place of the Populist social label, it's tempting to call *My Darling Clementine* a cold-war Western, if only for the way that a "cold" conflict matches its passive vengeance fable as well as the film's solemnity. Scripted early in 1946, filmed from April through June, and released in November, *Clementine* might instead be said to slip into the brief period after World War II but before the cold war (before, say, 1948, the year of the new peacetime draft and of *Fort Apache,* which shows Ford, at least, in a new mood).[18] In either case, a feeling among Americans that they needed to keep an eye on history may have been a factor in bringing Western films a newfound respectability after the war and in giving them their biggest box office to date in 1946 (and since, to speak in inflation-adjusted dollars).[19] Perhaps the importance of history at the time of *My Darling Clementine* lay not in fidelity to details, nor even to "the spirit of the West," but rather to a broader sense that history exists as an almost religious concept to which attention must be paid. *Life* magazine's major series throughout 1947 and into 1948 was a historical tour through "Western Civilization," which was seen to have "leapt the Atlantic Ocean" to reach its religious apotheosis in America. Classic Western films, with their double nostalgia for the American and Hollywood pasts, were one sort of reassurance against the jitters evident in the opening of that series: "But if he does not know where he is going, Western man can at least look back and see where he came from." In retrospect this reassurance is ominous, having been penned by Whittaker Chambers in his post as an editor for *Time–Life* shortly before he cast noir shadows over American life with his 1948 accusation of communism against State Department official Alger Hiss.[20]

In its refusal to answer historical questions, *My Darling Clementine*'s emptiness also fits the politics of the cold war. The confrontations within it are approached-and-avoided, a stance shared by the characters, the camera style, and the film's morality. *Clementine's* strange power to say nothing that can easily be pinned down may come from Ford's long-standing gift for projecting emotional atmospheres onto landscapes. If the film is evasive about matters of community, race, and militancy, it may be all the more revealing for that.

# 20. "Shakespeare? In Tombstone?"

Shakespeare, huh? He musta been from Texas.
John Wayne in *Dark Command* (1940)

The classic Western of the 1940s evidently relishes open space, darkness, and emptiness over the more explicit and upbeat social explanations of earlier sound films. We can make a start at looking into this transformation in *My Darling Clementine* by approaching it in an apparently roundabout way, via, of all things, *Hamlet.* Ford's film uses Shakespeare's words to further an almost exclusively visual argument. We shall come around to the way that this movement toward what *Hamlet* would call "dumb show" may help to get at the method of the classic Western as well as to the core of Ford's elusive cinematic genius, but (as again in the next three chapters) it should help to keep our focus by first recalling a single scene from the film:

**Scene No. 1:**

Wyatt Earp and Doc Holliday are sitting in box seats of Tombstone's Bird Cage Theater (Fig. 45a) above an audience grown rowdy over the nonappearance of the actors. Wyatt averts their plan to ride the theater manager around town on a rail by going himself in search of the missing players. Dissolve to a smoky saloon, where the lead actor, a certain Granville Thorndyke (Alan Mowbray), is in the middle of a tabletop performance forced by the four Clanton boys (Fig. 45b). The Clantons are unimpressed with the performance thus far and shoot at Thorndyke's feet: "Look Yorick, can't you give us nothin' but them poems?"[1] Puffing himself up, Thorndyke responds in his best drunken British dignity, "I have a very large repertoire, sir," and, swigging from a whiskey bottle – soon shot from his hand by a Clanton – begins Hamlet's soliloquy, for which he is ideally dressed by nineteenth-century convention (in black, with cape, pendant, and sheathed dagger; Fig. 45c).

Doc and Wyatt arrive, unnoticed, outside the swinging doors and are silhouetted in the night (Fig. 45d), but Doc softly holds Wyatt back: "Wait, I want to hear this." Thorndyke recites faultlessly, if bombastically, as Doc and Wyatt move silently closer (Fig. 45e):

> To be, or not to be – that is the question:
> Whether 'tis nobler in the mind to suffer
> The slings and arrows of outrageous fortune,
> Or to take arms against a sea of troubles,
> And by opposing end them? To die, to sleep –
> No more; and by that sleep to say we end
> The heartache and the thousand natural shocks
> That flesh is heir to – 'tis a consummation
> Devoutly to be wished: to die, to sleep.
> To sleep, perchance to dream. Ay, there's the rub;
> For in that sleep of death what dreams may come,
> When we have shuffled off this mortal coil, . . .

"That's enough!" shouts a Clanton, at the end of patience with such speechifying. "Leave him alone," says Doc with undisturbed intensity – as the Clantons whirl around to notice him – "Please go on, Mr. Thorndyke."

**Figure 45** *(here and facing). My Darling Clementine:* Hamlet in Tombstone.

"Thank you sir."

Must give us pause. There's the respect
That makes calamity of so long life.
For who would bear the whips and scorns of time,
The law's delay,
The insolence of office, and the spurns
That patient merit of the unworthy takes,
When he himself might his quietus make
With a bare bodkin? Who would fardels bear,
To grunt and sweat under a weary life . . . life. . . ."

Thorndyke, lost, finds a prompter in Doc ("But that the dread of something after death . . ."); however, it is no use, and Thorndyke begs Doc to carry on for him. Doc continues, as Wyatt watches (Figs. 45f, g):

The undiscover'd country, from whose borne
No traveler returns, puzzles the will,
And makes us rather bear those ills we have
Than fly to others that we know not of?
Thus conscience does make cowards of us all. . . ."[2]

One of Doc's fits of tubercular coughing interrupts him and he escapes into the night. As Wyatt helps Thorndyke off the table, the Clantons pull guns to make him stay. Wyatt swiftly clubs one with his gun and shoots the hand of another, after which the two others raise their hands. With the commotion, Old Man Clanton appears from among shrieking Mexican women in the back room ("Qué pasa! Qué pasa! Parece que hay banditos!") and apologizes to the marshal for his boys having "had a little whiskey." As soon as Wyatt is out of earshot, Clanton whips his cowering sons (Fig. 45h), bringing home his moral: "When you pull a gun, kill a man."

One's initial reaction to this scene has been anticipated by Doc Holliday: "Shakespeare? In Tombstone?" (part of a series of astonishments at incursions of civilization into the town; Clanton's "Marshaling? In Tombstone?" and the mayor's "Church bells! In Tombstone!"). Historically, however, the scene is not at all odd. Performances of Shakespeare would have been common enough in Tombstone, as they were throughout the mining towns of the West.[3] What's surprising is less Shakespeare in the Tombstone of 1882 than Shakespeare in the Hollywood of 1946, by which time the cultural split between the two sorts of "classics" was all but complete, with low-art Westerns separated from high-art Shakespeare.[4] The scene that opens *The Arizonian* (1935) projects a twentieth-century "highbrow–lowbrow" hierarchy back onto the nineteenth-century frontier: *Hamlet* so bores the audience of miners that they shoot the ghost of Hamlet's father off the stage. On the nineteenth-century mining frontier the problem was just the reverse. In 1863, the actor Frank Mayo initially resisted requests that he stage *Hamlet* for the miners of Virginia City, fearing that audiences were so familiar with the full text and action of Shakespeare's play that his performance would be anticipated with "preconceived ideas of correctness."[5] Nor is Doc Holliday's ability to combine Shakespeare with frontier gambling in *Clementine* merely a movie conceit. In 1861 a wager was published in Denver's *Daily Rocky Mountain News* that no one could play the part of Hamlet on less than three day's study. The "notorious gambler" C. B. Cooke took up the challenge and received a satisfactory newspaper review: "Mr. Cooke has not a strong voice, but his reading was most capital and his *action* graceful, artistic, and impressive. . . . With practice and study Mr. Cooke would make a most capital actor, but we suppose he prefers to *watch* and *prey*."[6] Historically, it was a member of the Clanton gang, Johnny Ringo, who reputedly spouted Shakespeare, although Wyatt Earp took to self-dramatization at the end of his life by comparing his frontier ordeals to Hamlet's.[7]

Shakespeare's plays may have been frequent visitors to the actual mining towns of the Old West, but that still doesn't explain what this scene is doing in *My Darling Clementine,* a film that in any case thoroughly rewrites the history of the region and the lives of the Earps. No doubt *Hamlet* and *My Darling Clementine* are alike family revenge tragedies, even Oedipal ones – as Wyatt too comes around, the long way, to killing an evil father figure (Old Man Clanton calls Wyatt "son" at their first meeting out among the cattle). But, in plot terms, it's easy enough to find other Westerns closer to *Hamlet:* take the spaghetti Western *Johnny Hamlet* (1968), whose title character returns from the Civil War to find "Uncle Claude" married to his mother and running roughshod over the family ranch; or the early independent feature *A Sagebrush Hamlet* (1919), where the title character returns from college to Arizona and pretends to have gone "plumb locoed" until uncovering his father's murderer. Wittiest among this undistinguished bunch is another silent feature, Universal's *The Phantom Bullet* (1926), in which shutterbug "Click" Farlane's father is murdered while Click (Hoot Gibson) is away. Returning, he dons foppish clothes (short pants, tweed jacket, and argyle socks) and Hamlet's antic disposition, bringing guffaws to the ranch hands and anxiety to his girl (whose genre label for the goings-on is "tragic farce") until he maneuvers the murderer to reveal himself.

The *Hamlet* connection to *My Darling Clementine* is looser but deeper. Doc chokes on the line "Thus conscience does makes cowards of us all."[8] And that becomes the text for one argument in the film. Will Wyatt be so rigorous in applying the letter of the law that he will let the Clantons escape? Will he lose his way in bickering with Doc Holliday, who is really his blood brother (as Hamlet loses his way with Laertes)? Will Wyatt, like Hamlet, let his disgust at corruption paralyze action? And will he take his vengeance in a way so roundabout and relaxed, so "lapsed in time and passion," that the Clantons will get the better of him? Thus will revenge itself – for many critics, a key trait of the classic Western – be lost in "the law's delay"?[9] Even as Thorndyke recites Hamlet's irresolution, the actor's prominent silver pendant reminds us of the silver pendant stolen at the time of his murder from Wyatt's still-unavenged brother.

*My Darling Clementine*'s shooting script drove home the relevance of *Hamlet* more heavily than in the final cut. In a scene that would have followed the one recounted above, Wyatt sends Thorndyke to the theater and goes in search of Doc, finding him in the Oriental Saloon. After Doc recites more lines from *Hamlet,* Wyatt responds, "First time I heard it. Parts I could understand make a powerful lot of sense – especially that last about conscience makin' cowards out of all of us." And in a later scene which may have been shot but cut before release, Clementine continues her argument with Doc about his refusal to return East, "You've become a coward, John. . . . A silly notion of self-sacrifice – of not wanting to hurt the people who love you – salves your conscience – and makes you think what you're doing is right."[10] These scenes may have been cut either by Ford or producer Darryl Zanuck, although evidence of their other films and some of Zanuck's comments suggest Ford's hand.[11] To what the shooting script calls this "quietly emotional" tirade of Clementine's, Doc would have responded, "Quite a speech" – and it does sound like exactly the sort of windy dialogue that Ford made no secret of despising. (Claire Trevor recalled her experience on the set of *Stagecoach* playing Dallas: "There was a nice intimate scene between Ringo and me. . . . Ford was reading the script – 'What *is* this?' It was me saying goodbye to Ringo and riding off – two pages. He read it and tore up the pages: 'It's too mushy.' It broke my heart." Often Ford would wait until an intrusive studio executive was present before making a show of ripping up offending script pages.)[12]

What seems to have happened in *My Darling Clementine* was this, and it is one key to the film's spirit and, more generally, to what happens as the classic Western of the 1940s takes over from the wordier 1930s: Hamlet's ethical and intellectual dilemma was transformed – between the script and the finished cut – from a dramatic dilemma, explored through dialogue, to a visual one. Such a transformation, I would suggest, comes close to the essence of John Ford's genius, which is always so difficult to pinpoint. *Hamlet* hangs over the film as a mood that is never quite argued out dramatically.

*My Darling Clementine* has a double hero, a doubled Hamlet – Wyatt *and* Doc – as would have been dramatized by those two omitted scenes, with their dual "conscience/coward" refrains. In place of those scenes, the film offers up the double hero with visual economy: as in the two-shots of Wyatt and Doc as they listen to the soliloquy, and then the almost-matching intercut close-ups (see Figs. 45d–g). It's more than that parts of the soliloquy reflect Wyatt (". . . to take arms against a sea of troubles, /And by opposing end them") while others reflect the self-destructive Doc ("'tis a consummation /Devoutly to be wished: to die, to sleep"); it's that the soliloquy presents a *choice*, which the film will illustrate doubly. Ultimately Wyatt will take one option, Doc the other.

If Wyatt seems more immediately Hamlet-like, it's partly because of his evident need to set right a political world turned dishonest, a world whose nature has been revealed by a family murder. Wyatt's graveside soliloquy, of the type that appears regularly in Ford, expands his burden beyond mere family revenge ("Maybe when we leave this country, young kids like you will be able to grow up and live safe"), although the dull expression of this sentiment and the duller studio backdrop representing Monument Valley make it unsurprising to learn that the scene was reshot under Zanuck's supervision by journeyman director Lloyd Bacon.[13] More resonant are certain essentially silent sequences, including Wyatt's slow walks into darkness, carrying his burden and ours.

In many ways, though, Doc is the clearer Hamlet figure, dressed in solemn black (if without the evening clothes and cloak given him by the shooting script). He's the supercivilized one, the champagne drinker who corrects his Hispanic girlfriend's English grammar, the intellectual who brings up – and perhaps thinks too deeply upon – the subject of "evil." Doc has "something in his soul /O'er which his melancholy sits on brood," evidentially a guilt turned death wish, but we never learn why. On paper, he sounds like an extension of Doc Boone in *Stagecoach*, another heavy drinking, Shakespeare-quoting frontier surgeon; but Doc Holliday is the darker figure, a noir Hamlet by dress and by Victor Mature's persona. This was Mature's first film in four years, but even in his early career from 1939 until war service in 1942, he is memorably dark and languid, especially in the early noir *I Wake Up Screaming* (where his style makes him the likeliest murder suspect) and Josef von Sternberg's *The Shanghai Gesture* (where he is "Doctor of Nothing," an ultimately appropriate degree for Holliday as well). His Doc Holliday in *Clementine* is a doctor turned gambler (intellect gone irresponsible), a doctor turned consumptive (a "city disease" in the West), a doctor who fails when his skills are tested (surely the only such instance in Ford). His cough cuts off his recitation of the next line of Hamlet's soliloquy, with its illness metaphor for intellectualized delay

("And thus the native hue of resolution/Is sicklied o'er with the pale cast of thought"). The excised dialogue between Doc and Clementine about cowardice and conscience derives from Allan Dwan's 1939 *Frontier Marshal,* where the parallel figures discuss how she'd read him Shakespeare's *Julius Caesar.* "Cowards die many times before their deaths, the brave but once." "I'm a coward?" this earlier Doc had asked. "You've become one, John. You're afraid of living and afraid of dying."[14] While such a diagnosis seems true also of *Clementine*'s Doc, it is discussed only visually. His counterpoint to Wyatt's measured walks are periodical frantic gallops off into Mexico, for reasons never explained. He remains a dramatically empty expression of one way of failing in the West, and it takes only a little willful distortion to call him (in John Baxter's words) "the true hero of the film."[15]

What is so central to Ford's method is the ways the film argues out explicitly Shakespearean dilemmas without expressing them through dialogue. Exactly how Ford accomplishes this shift toward "dumb show" is difficult to explain, since here as elsewhere in classic Westerns the arguments so often center on details of physiognomy, of gesture, of the placement of figures in landscape, of the pace of a stride or a ride. But in *My Darling Clementine,* we can hazard a few observations about this lyrical argument by looking at the shifts in Henry Fonda's *posture.*

At each moment of crisis, when by classic-Western convention one anticipates active vengeance, we find Wyatt recumbent. This purely visual argument turns out to be a more important subplot than any of those expressed through the dialogue. It is set up in the first scene in Tombstone when Wyatt stops into the barbershop after time on the trail. He sits upright in the barber chair, but, with a small surprise to both him and us, falls backward into a full horizontal ("I don't know how to work it so good," apologizes the barber), belying Wyatt's statement that he's "just passin' through here" – before gunshots burst the windows. The film's single most distinctive image comes in Wyatt's feet-up posture as he leans back in a chair on the covered boardwalk and emphasized when he does the strange little balancing-and-bicycling act that infuriates Chihuahua (Fig. 46a). Here, Wyatt's laid-back posture is set against surrounding verticals, especially the cacti (Fig. 46b) – which, as in a dream, were nowhere in the town when it was initially in its noir state.[16] At each moment that calls for gunfighting, Wyatt is seen leaning back precariously – at the poker table with the card cheat;

**Figure 46.** *My Darling Clementine:* Marshal Wyatt Earp (Henry Fonda) leaning back in his chair.

during the night in the jail office after the body of his second murdered brother, Virgil, has been dumped in the street. Is Wyatt waiting? weary? bored? lonely? self-absorbed? It is difficult to say, even alongside a similar pattern two years later in Laurence Olivier's noirish film *Hamlet* of 1948, in which each visitation of his father's ghost knocks him onto his back, from which apparently unsuitable posture he begins subsequent avowals of action and revenge. If in *My Darling Clementine* one thinks of these postures as visual questions, then they find an answer when Clementine invites Wyatt to the inauguration of the half-completed church, and he dances with an upright, stiff-backboned style, legs flung outward. It's gawky but somehow touching, a perfect escape from recumbency – and into community.

What *My Darling Clementine* may be arguing through this pattern of postures is perhaps made clearer by glancing back at *Young Mr. Lincoln* (1939), another story of nineteenth-century America that also united producer Darryl Zanuck with director John Ford and star Henry Fonda. Lincoln is introduced, unseen, through flowery electioneering rhetoric "on behalf of the great and incorruptible Whig Party, God bless it," but when the film cuts to a shot further down the porch, Lincoln is discovered leaning back in a chair, feet up on a barrel, and he only slowly ambles over for a self-effacing stump speech ("I presume you all know who I am. I'm plain Abraham Lincoln"). When his first love, Ann Rutledge, initially comes across him in the film, she expresses surprise at finding him recumbent – lying on the ground with his feet up against a tree ("Aren't you afraid you'll put your eyes out, reading like that upside down?"). Later in his law office, he typically extends his feet out the window or props them on his desk, while leaning back in his rocking chair. The temptation, or taint, of recumbency remains a threat within Lincoln's character too. And these arguments via posture are all aspects of his own Hamlet temptation. ("You've read poetry and Shakespeare," Ann reminds him.) How will Lincoln, the legalist and idealist, avoid the temptation of inaction, of excessive contemplation? Indeed, *Young Mr. Lincoln* virtually builds its plot, which climaxes with a lying witness at a trial where Abe is defense attorney, around this suspense. *How* will Lincoln square this temptation to passive recumbency with standing up for himself in a cynical and cheating frontier world? And how will he be not only an idealist but an active politician, with all the ethical compromises that entails? Recumbency looms as threat to Lincoln and Wyatt Earp both, if ultimately we suspect that their passivity is a consequence of admirable scruples of conscience.

The recumbency in Wyatt's posture suggests something additional as well, which arises from *My Darling Clementine*'s oblique but self-conscious position as a "postwar" narrative. The film isn't so blunt about that status as, say, *Dakota* (1945), with its opening crawl reminding audiences that "Those days were postwar too." Wyatt's fame as a fighter on behalf of frontier civilization has proceeded him to Tombstone, but he initially corrects the town mayor as to his profession: "*Ex*-marshal." (*Clementine* was the first film after war service for most of its principals: Not only for Ford, but also Henry Fonda, Victor Mature, and screenwriter Winston Miller.)[17] In William Wyler's definitive film about postwar readjustment to civilian life, *The Best Years of Our Lives* (released the same month as *Clementine,* in November 1946), Al Stephenson (Fredric March) returns from the war, props up his feet on his living-room coffee table, and sighs: "Last year it was 'Kill Japs,' this year it's 'Make Money.'"[18] Stephenson is weary, and the film admires his presumption of a well-earned rest, feet up, taking time off for contemplation between wartime and postwar modes of action. Has Wyatt "sicklied o'er with the pale cast of thought" and lost "the name of action," or has he earned such a postwar rest after taming those other frontier towns further east? Wyatt's posture *could* lead him to be taken for a member of the group of World War II veterans mocked in 1946 as "The Rocking Chair Club" – the eight-and-a-half million unemployed or semiemployed veterans who opted for a year of twenty-dollar-a-week "readjustment allowance," and who were paid (in the words of one who refused the money) for "sitting around on their dead asses."[19] Wyatt's passivity would thus be close to that of Henry Fonda's Peter Lapham, a returning veteran, in Otto Preminger's *Daisy Kenyon* (1947) – a convincing portrait of war weariness in which Peter's lazy lingering under the mothering love of a commercial artist (Joan Crawford) in her Greenwich Village apartment turns out to be necessary healing before a return to self-confidence. One of the tension points in Fonda's persona emerges in these years, and Ford will later exploit it: the threat within his heroism of inflexibility and stubbornness.

*My Darling Clementine* again credits Stuart Lake's fanciful 1931 biography as its source, but the book's governing image – "Wyatt Earp was a man of action" – could hardly be further from Fonda's Earp.[20] At the poker table, as Wyatt leans back precariously in his chair, Chihuahua is tauntingly explicit in her saloon song:

> Ten thousand cattle gone astray
> Left my range and wandered away,
> And the sons of guns, I'm here to say,
> Have left me dead broke today.
> In gamblin' halls delayin',
> Ten thousand cattle strayin'. . . .[21]

The oddity of Wyatt's resting his feet in town comes less in his failure to take rapid revenge (after all, like Hamlet, he needs evidence, only strongly suspecting the murderer's identity) and more in his failure to track down his rustled cattle, even though Virgil Earp has determined that the Clantons are moving cattle. Scriptwriter Winston Miller looked upon this doubly unjustified lingering as the construction flaw he was unable to solve, and his script – in lines cut from the finished film – had Morgan commenting on Wyatt's posture: "Can't figure you sometime, Wyatt. Here you sit – calm – just like you was fixin' to go to a picnic – all the time *my* blood's boilin' and racin'."[22] But lingering, roundabout vengeance is a trait of the Western throughout the history of the genre, even if the emptiness and slowed pace of the classic-era Western tend particularly to emphasize it. Recall that in *The Big Trail* even Wayne's Breck Coleman waited six months and two thousand miles to wreak revenge on his friend's murderers. And although Gary Cooper as *The Virginian* (1929) makes his own Shakespearean critique of inaction – he argues that Romeo brought his own tragedy by delaying – when the Virginian's own testing comes, he too delays in trusting his eyes' evidence that his pal is a rustler.[23]

*My Darling Clementine* seems part of a cycle of Westerns resting on something like postwar melancholy, with brooding cold warriors who move past simple demonstrations of heroics. Among the cycle's highlights would be *Along Came Jones* (1945), *Pursued* (1947), and *Angel and the Badman* (1947). Although the plot lines and dialogue of those three Westerns also argue that heroes are finding enemies difficult to locate, it's again primarily physical postures that convey a lingering confusion over how to take action. In *Along Came Jones,* Gary Cooper is the cowboy as postmodernist, comically deconstructing the mythic gunslinger: Mistaken for a wanted outlaw, he learns that he can impose fear on the town by replacing his common-man geniality and cheerful singing with silence – reinforced by measured, "unsmiling" dignity and an odd, stiff-necked posture. Raoul Walsh and Niven Busch's *Pursued* brings its hero back to New Mexico from the Spanish–American War with medals, wounds, and noir nightmares. The film rests on Robert Mitchum's weary way of moving, his passive but patient way of waiting for mysteries to unravel around him, as put to such good use in so many later noirs. His physical posture itself makes it impossible to imagine Mitchum a star of prewar Hollywood, and his first film roles as a dark heavy in Hopalong Cassidy B-Westerns during the war are retrospectively fascinating for their despair: "You don't know what it's like to be hunted and hounded," Mitchum laments shortly before Hoppy kills him in *Colt Comrades* (1943).

Similarly, one explanation for John Wayne having to ride out the thirties in all of those B-Westerns is that his wider stardom had to wait for an era that treasured his halting speech patterns and the considered weariness of his feline walk. Wayne's *Angel and the Badman* (his first independent production) finds its overall visual pattern in another escape from film noir. Feverishly ranting about his "past," the injured outlaw Quirt Evans (Wayne) falls from his horse and is rescued by a Quaker, then restored to consciousness by a kiss from the Quaker's daughter (Gail Russell). Evans lies recumbent in bed recovering from the unexplained gunshot wounds, caught between the daughter's penetrating gaze – which sexualizes Quaker optimism – and a doctor's dour pessimism about human nature in general and this outlaw's reformability in particular. On recovering, Evans attempts to regain the spirit of brawls and drinking – as do the veterans of *The Best Years of Our Lives* in their long night out – but learns instead ways of carrying, separately, a Bible and a baby.

*My Darling Clementine* has ambivalence about Wyatt's laid-back vengeance. On the one hand, he needs to brave the eastern effeteness symbolized by the perfume sprayed on him by the town barber and by his many self-reflections in mirrors and windows, if he is to cease being too wild for Clementine. On the other hand, Bill Nichols has a point in remarking that "town-lingering is a somewhat morbid state for Earp."[24] One could complete Nichols's thought in three ways:

1. on a *historical* level (Towns were dangerous for cowboys, who had been weeks in the saddle and were paid in lump sums; they could be fleeced by the Chihuahuas, the Doc Hollidays.)
2. on a *sociological* level (Wyatt could abandon himself to post–World War II comforts and become a "Rocking Chair Club" veteran like Claude, the pajama-lounging brother-in-law to Sam Clayton [Gary Cooper] in Leo McCarey's *Good Sam* [1948].)
3. on an *auteurist* level (A hazard for Ford's sailors in their *Long Voyage Home*, a 1940 film of his, is the English city, with its bars and shanghaiers.)

Still, if we're never too worried that Wyatt will succumb to these threats, it's because his aloofness is itself a defense mechanism against them. Indeed, it's as if hero and film *alike* blank out various temptations, and accept as the price of both the hero's *and* the film's passivity a sort of melancholy emptiness and stoic refusal of analysis. In that sense, *My Darling Clementine* is just the opposite of *Young Mr. Lincoln*, which is ingenious in its plotting and dialogue, a symbiosis of expressionist lyricism with "the well-made play." The once-fashionable expressionist style of *The Informer, The Long Voyage Home*, and other prewar Ford films is now usually dismissed as an arty deviation from his deeper concerns, but those films anticipate the darkness that Ford looks unable to shake in *My Darling Clementine* even after repudiating film noir.

Ultimately, Wyatt proves to be no Hamlet in inaction – any more than was Ford's Lincoln. *Young Mr. Lincoln* holds a knowing little joke about Lincoln's "passivity": In apparent indecision about his future vocation, he walks out to Ann Rutledge's grave to ask her spirit to choose for him via the direction a twig will fall. But a line of dialogue keeps the door open to his own willpower: "I wonder if I could have tipped it your way just a little?" It's a self-aware worry, and of course he did tip the twig; he isn't recumbent in the end. Ultimately neither he nor Wyatt resemble the indecisive postwar Hamlet of Laurence Olivier, announced in his opening voice-over, to the everlasting annoyance of Shakespearean scholars, as the "man who could not make up his mind." The Hamlet-soliloquy scene in *Clementine,* remember, ends with Clanton's advice to his boys, brought home with his whip: "When you pull a gun, kill a man." In the context of Hamlet's scrupulous worry over the relationship between action and mortality, the line earns an audience laugh every time: It cuts Hamlet's Gordian knot. But, of course, in having such a figure of evil do so, it legitimizes Hamlet's scruples and delays.[25]

If *My Darling Clementine* is both so conventional in its story line and yet so revealing in its visual arguments, it's because its underdramatized tensions result in a focus on moods and atmospheres. Land lost and family lost unite in the graveside scene and in Ford's acute topographical sense. Wagons and cattle moving across empty spaces counterpoint Ford's epic energy with a mourning for the loss of stable families on their own land, as evoked here in the Earp brothers' Sunday-morning memories of their mother and earlier by Ford in *The Grapes of Wrath* (1940) and *Tobacco Road* (1941). Neither literary-based criticism nor structural oppositions reckon with the ways that visual style can convey conflicts ignored in the story line. *My Darling Clementine*'s visual conflicts bring the film close to a lyrical tragedy (like *The Long Voyage Home*) even through it's not a dramatic tragedy (like *The Searchers*). The tragic tensions of *Clementine* are intimated within the visual atmosphere, instead of being argued out as in *The Searchers.* However, this alone would not establish the latter's greater stature. *Young Mr. Lincoln* is a dramatically complicated film, but the complications mystify an obvious issue (Lincoln as a great historical representative of America's "soul"). A film's visual atmosphere – we might call it "heroic melancholy" in *Clementine*'s case – can also initiate a dialogue of options. Thus apparently empty films may contest the absence of crucial issues from their plot.

It's natural to accept Bill Nichols's characterization of Wyatt's position as "town-lingering." Nevertheless, watched closely, the film specifies the time from Wyatt's and Doc's first meeting to the latter's death at the O.K. Corral as less than three days – from late on a Friday night to Monday dawn. Still, *Clementine* is hardly of the *High Noon* or *3:10 to Yuma* (1957) clock-watching school, and even to notice that most of the film consists of a long weekend is to violate its spirit. It *feels* unhurried. *Clementine*'s style – including acting style – suggests something more akin to Jean Renoir's philosophical sense of time, as in *The River*

(1951), where "Captain John" comes to savor his slow recovery from war wounds in an Anglo-Indian garden. In neither case is the lingering "morbid" exactly; it is more a sad sense of *temps-morts,* a sense of life flowing by as you observe it from a well-situated chair, a Proustian more than a Shakespearean sense of time.

This is the deeper trick of the most evocative classic Westerns: their replacement of historical time with the expanses of space. Ford's transformation of time in *My Darling Clementine* moves beyond the relatively simple if surreal era shifts we observed in 1930s B-Westerns and beyond the convention in American thought about the West that Owen Wister expressed as "the various centuries jostled together."[26] Unlike the historical Tombstone, Arizona, or most frontier towns known from photographs, Ford's Tombstone appears (after the noir opening) to be built entirely on one side of its main street. No bastion, it's open to the landscape. Wyatt, feet up and leaning back in his chair, gazes out at the blank grandeur of the Monument Valley monoliths. In doing so, he exemplifies the inward-and-outward gaze of Hollywood's historical figures generally: looking simultaneously forward and backward in time. Particularly but not exclusively in Ford, this gaze outward at the landscape implies a hero's knowledge of *our* past, hence a foreknowledge of his own future. That biblical burden of foresight adds to the *gravity* of Ford heroes, particularly those like Wyatt Earp and Abraham Lincoln whose very names reveal to us their historical destiny. If they seem not unaware of their responsibility to overcome evil, it's with a touch of Hamlet's self-dramatization ("heaven hath pleased it so/To punish me with this, and this with me/That I must be their scourge and minister"). In Ford, such self-dramatization, again free of dialogue, is starkest at the end of *Young Mr. Lincoln,* where Lincoln's slow walk to the top of a hill evokes (partly via the "Battle Hymn of the Republic" music) Lincoln's recognition of the burden of the Civil War to come; but Ford's Henry Fonda also silently conveys something of that knowledge of the American future in his heavy walks and unblinking gazes at the horizon at the ends of 1939's *Drums along the Mohawk* and even *The Grapes of Wrath,* just as Ford's John Wayne has it at the ends of *They Were Expendable* and *Fort Apache.* We leave Ford's horizon-gazing heroes with their burdens heavy, their tasks still to complete: "The readiness is all."

# 21. "Get Outta Town and Stay Out"

SHE: "Is it a Western custom to push yourself in on other people?"
HE: "Yes, Ma'am. That's how the West was settled."
SHE: "I'm not an Indian."

Alexis Smith and Errol Flynn in *San Antonio* (1945)

When classic Westerns focus on the formation of communities – where the "figures in open space . . . work out their existence" – the films are precise about dividing the damned from the elect, separating the excluded (the subject of this chapter) from the included (whom we'll take up in the next chapter). *My Darling Clementine*'s lack of economic explanations lets it smoothly incorporate a widespread transference within American narratives. Class conflicts in American fiction – and this is true as well for film – are regularly transfigured into battles among the races or battles between the sexes.[1] Historically, the Earp battle against the Clantons can be labeled as Republican versus Democratic. If there's little hint of such political or class battles in the film, it's in part because our attention is diverted twice, to race and to sex. Again, let's begin with a scene:

**SCENE NO. 2:**

On their first evening visit into Tombstone, Wyatt and two of his brothers head to the barbershop (Fig. 47a), but Wyatt's shave is disrupted by sounds of gunfire and a bullet into the shop (Fig. 47b). "What kind of a town *IS* this!?" he shouts. A gunman is shooting wildly inside a harshly shadowed saloon (Fig. 47c) as women run screaming through the doorway and men in serapes flee down the covered boardwalk. In a small gathering out of harm's way, the town mayor is reminding the current marshal of his duty – but he and his two deputies hand him their badges: "That's Indian Charlie in there drunk and I ain't committin' suicide on myself." Wyatt, still lathered for his shave, tosses the may-

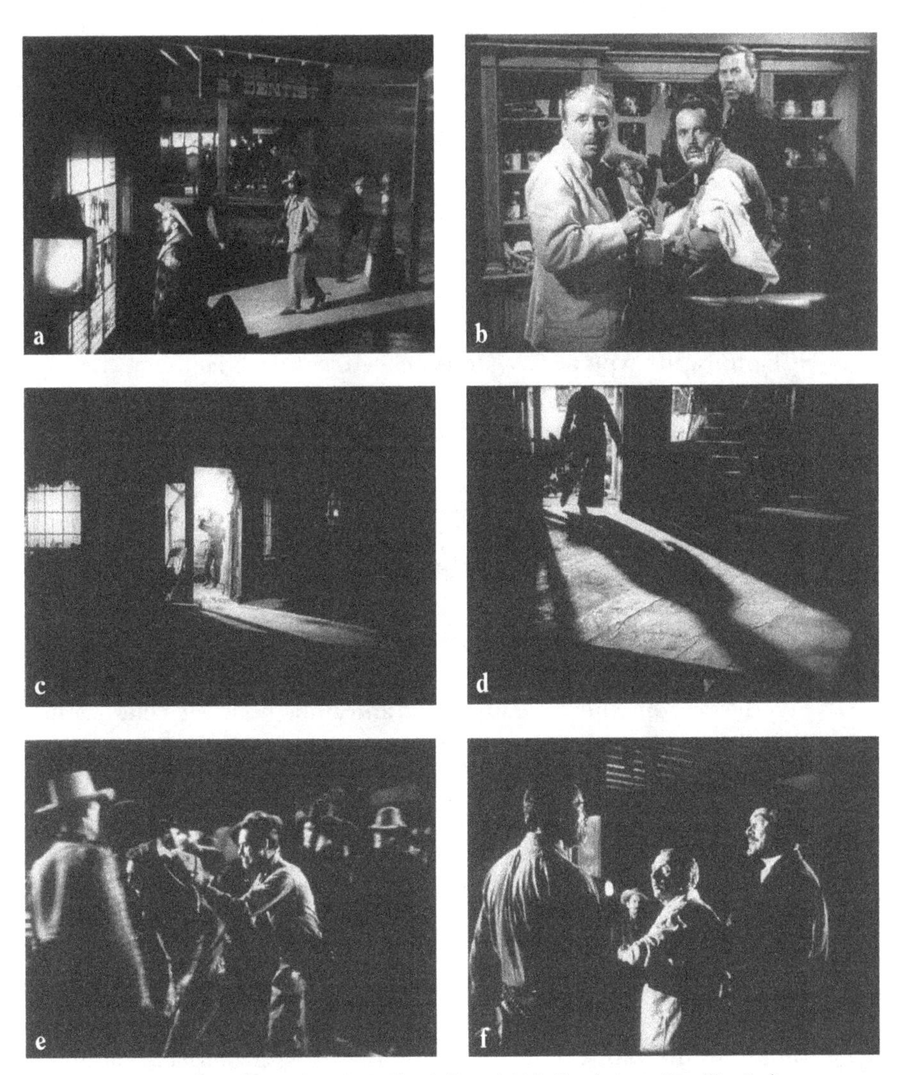

**Figure 47.** *My Darling Clementine:* Wyatt Earp's first night in Tombstone: Expelling Indian Charlie (Charles Stevens) from town (47c–e).

or the barber's sheet and heads toward the saloon. Our perspective remains with the townsfolk: We see Wyatt pick a large stone from the street, then enter the saloon through a second-floor window. After muffled sounds punctuate the silence, Wyatt reemerges in a shaft of light cast through the open saloon doors and drags a man out, feet first (Fig. 47d). "What kind of town is this, anyway? Selling liquor to Indians," he says to no one in particular. Hauling the Indian to his feet, he comments, "I put a knot on his head bigger than a turkey's egg." Turning him round, Wyatt shouts, "Indian, get outta town and stay out!" then kicks him to get him started (Fig. 47e). Impressed, the mayor offers Wyatt the job of marshal and is refused, twice. "I'm just passin' through tryin' to get me a relaxing little shave" (Fig. 47f).

*My Darling Clementine* tells of the cleaning up – or, strictly speaking, the cleaning *out* – of a small town: the type of violence associated with the Clantons, the type of despair associated with Doc Holliday, the type of sexuality associated with Chihuahua, and everything else associated with film noir. But before all these comes the Indian. As we've seen, the changing ways that the Western has found to make Native Americans "vanish" reveal much about the genre's history. The apparently off-hand racism of this scene now makes spectators squirm. In comparison to the Indian-war slaughters of earlier A-Westerns, however, Wyatt's gesture toward "Indian Charlie" is also ambivalent – contemptuous, certainly, but mild as well (considering that it's only by luck that Charlie's gunshots killed no one). Like so much in *Clementine,* Wyatt's response here is both simple and ambiguous: He takes neither the quick-bullet solution of the 1930s A-Western nor the "understanding" of the Indian "problem" that would appear rather suddenly in 1950.[2]

We haven't far to look for the older paradigm that *My Darling Clementine* avoids. This scene is based upon one in the 1939 *Frontier Marshal,* with the same actor – Charles Stevens – as Indian Charlie in both films. Charles Stevens (1893–1964), who also played the Mexican, Lopez, in *The Big Trail,* was a grandson of the Chiricahua Apache leader known to whites as Geronimo (1829?–1909), whose very name is enough to motivate the plot of *Stagecoach.*[3] In this *Frontier Marshal,* Randolph Scott's Wyatt Earp bests Indian Charlie in the saloon through a more traditional gunfight (Fig. 48), not with the rock than Fonda's Wyatt uses offscreen as his weapon. Charlie is shot – but not killed – before Scott's Wyatt drags him out feet first. In that film, Charlie's bullets *have* killed a bystander, prompting his arrest and presumably a punishment more severe than being kicked out of town. The sequence is of a piece with *Frontier Marshal*'s overall Populist social explanations: Indian Charlie has been plied with booze by a slick businessman (John Carradine) in a ploy to drive customers from the competing saloon.

**Figure 48.** Wyatt Earp (Randolph Scott) shoots Indian Charlie (Charles Stevens) in *Frontier Marshal* (1939).

Wyatt's mildness, relatively speaking, to Indian Charlie in *My Darling Clementine* no doubt draws something of its rationale from an attitude that far predates the postwar Western: that one needs to apply lower standards to lesser breeds. Even at the height of the savage cycle of Indian-war Westerns on the eve of America's entrance into World War II, this qualifier is seldom absent. In *Northwest Passage* (1940), French and Indian War soldier Hunk Marriner (Walter Brennan) muses, "They're peculiar people. You can't judge 'em like white folks." In *Hudson's Bay* (1940), Paul Muni as the French trapper and scout Pierre-Esprit Radisson gives a long speech about distinguishing Indian needs (food) from their wants (brandy); and in writings about the West, a seller of whiskey is always more reprehensible than the drunk Indian. Buffalo Bill, in William Wellman's 1944 film of that name, is cast as the defender of childlike Indians against a rabid Indian hater. Bill's argument: "The red man and whiskey don't mix, ma'am." If all this can sound pleasingly paternal, a more chilling variant has always existed, as in Benjamin Franklin's commonsensical prediction in his

*Autobiography* that rum, rather than bullets, will prove God's more practical annihilator of Native Americans.[4]

Still, *My Darling Clementine*'s perfunctory treatment of its Indian hints at a new embarrassment in post–World War II notions of just exactly what to *do* with Indians in Westerns. *Clementine* always chooses the emptiest option, and so it is unsurprising that one lone Indian stands in for tribes evicted from their land. But might there additionally be some relief in getting this whole issue out of both the town *and* the film so early? – particularly in a film shot on a Navaho reservation and featuring Geronimo's grandson? Like the exile of African Americans into the blaxploitation ghetto of the 1970s, emptiness too can reveal Hollywood's uncertainties. Another 1946 Western, Jacques Tourneur's *Canyon Passage*, has similar trouble when Andy Devine's character voices the sort of caveat about Native American rights seldom heard earlier in the sound era: "Well, it's their land and we're on it and they don't forget it." Since Tourneur's plot line has no idea how to accommodate that attitude, the line of dialogue becomes a lone qualm before the film proceeds traditionally.[5] With hindsight, it's evident that this aspect of the A-Western was near collapse. The choices soon became either to foreground the Indian "problem" or omit Indians completely. In the perfunctory nature of this *Clementine* encounter, one can glimpse why the scene will be missing entirely from the several Earp-legend remakes through the 1950s.

This early scene takes place at night, and it's worth noticing how the film's overall escape from film noir is reinforced by a curious spatial revision of the town of Tombstone itself. As if awakening from a nightmare, the town's whole layout will change for the rest of the film. Notice, for instance, that in the shot where we see Wyatt kicking Indian Charlie, the barbershop and Oriental Saloon (identified by its sign) are visible behind them, and through screen direction and actors' glances, we "know" that the two-story saloon that Charlie has been shooting up is on the other side of the street.[6] But any two-story saloon and indeed this whole side of the street will subsequently vanish. Instead, when Wyatt later situates his chair on the boardwalk in front of the barbershop and leans back, he gazes not upon buildings but an open landscape, with a few wagons and cattle pens in the foreground and the mountain buttes beyond. No random bullet shot from any such saloon could now enter the barbershop. Even viewers who don't consciously catch the "error" here are left with a sense that Tombstone has somehow become less constricting. The town is literally a different place after the Indian has been kicked out of it.

Drunk Indian Charlie isn't the last dark alien Wyatt Earp drags from a saloon. Wyatt shows the same ambivalence – the same mixture of contempt and mildness – in carrying out saloon singer Chihuahua and pushing her into a horse trough after catching her signaling his poker hand to a gambler. That's a capital crime in the Western, though not so for women – especially should she be Indian or Mexican and thus to be held to lower ethical standards. Chihuahua's own heritage is left ambiguous. Is she Mexican? Such is suggested by her name, clothing, and song selections. But preliminary to tossing her in the trough, Wyatt warns her, "If I catch you doing that again, I'll run you back to the Apache reservation where you belong." It's a strange line, worth briefly puzzling out. The apparent explanation is that she is "part-Indian," as some critics have taken her,[7] although how Wyatt would know her ethnic background is unclear: He's been in town too short a time even to have yet seen Doc Holliday, and when Doc later that evening introduces Wyatt to her, Wyatt implies that they've met just once before ("Sort of found ourselves together in an eight-handed poker game"). It may just be that hauling her out of a Tombstone saloon brings the Indian connection to *his* mind. There is also a residue here of film noir, where femmes fatales are dangerously irrational and thus, in the Western vocabulary, linked to primitivism and Indians. Thus the 1946 noir-Western *Duel in the Sun* intercuts shots of lizards with its avenging, part-Indian heroine. (For a positive view of this linkage of women and Indians, recall, we have to escape the noir era and return to silent films such as *Rose o' Salem-Town* and the modernism of D. H. Lawrence.)[8]

In Western films Mexicans and Native Americans compete in a racialist hierarchy tied to the progress of Manifest Destiny. Other things being equal, Mexicans are given a leg up. Thus in Edward Dmytryk's *Broken Lance* (1954), the mother (Katy Jurado) is called "Señora" to cover her Indian heritage,[9] and "Chihuahua" could be another instance of this. Still, the values were reversible whenever the United States found itself on bad terms with Mexico. When budding historian Francis Parkman explored the Oregon Trail in 1846, the United States was opening a war with Mexico, which may account for his hierarchy:

"The human race in this part of the world is separated into three divisions, arranged in the order of their merits: white men, Indians, and Mexicans; to the latter of whom the honorable title of 'whites' is by no means conceded."[10] In D. W. Griffith's two-reeler *A Temporary Truce* (1912), coming shortly after the Mexican Revolution and at another moment of U.S.–Mexican border tension, slouching "MEXICAN JIM, THE GOOD FOR NOTHING," is kicked from the town saloon by an Anglo prospector. When it comes to survival, however, the Anglos ally themselves with the Mexicans – hence the "temporary truce" of the title – to fight off an Indian uprising. While the Indians are more deadly, they're also more noble, with funeral ceremonies honored by Griffith in the closing shot. Only late in the history of the genre, with the Westerns of Sam Peckinpah, do Mexicans come to occupy the ethical high ground that the earliest silent Westerns had reserved for Native Americans: as representatives of ideal harmony (as in the Mexican village of *The Wild Bunch* [1969]) and sentimental wisdom (as in the old Mexican of *Pat Garrett and Billy the Kid* [1973]).

Whether Mexican, Indian, or some mix, Chihuahua is evidently set up as the dark reflection of Clementine, much as Doc is Wyatt's dark double. The opposition is prominent too in Ford's *Stagecoach,* between the fallen woman, Dallas, and Lucy Mallory, whom the chivalrous southern gambler Hatfield calls "an angel in the jungle, a very wild jungle." (Mrs. Mallory comes from the East to search for her man and finds a gambler instead, as will Clementine, suggesting a variation on a theme.) One would be tempted to see the shadow of Ford's Irish Catholicism in this split if that didn't narrow a wide cultural pattern. It's central even to *The Last of the Mohicans,* with dark Cora and light Alice as sisters *under* the skin. The 1929 film of *The Virginian* needs to add a character to Wister's novel to maintain the pattern, giving black-garbed Trampas (Walter Huston) a Mexican saloon girl (Nina Quartero) to set against the Virginian's schoolmarm from the East. However, the fact that even *Stagecoach* eventually elevates its fallen woman to a moral position above its "angel" alerts us to the difficulties in relegating this pattern to a simple structural division. Chihuahua too doesn't exactly play the "bad woman" to Clementine's good, even if her dialogue can like sometimes sound like a vestige of film noir. ("Why don't you go chase yourself up an alley!")[11] As a loose woman, Chihuahua means trouble, but she's not ignoble and may even show something like moral instinct in trying to attach herself to Wyatt, if in her sexual way. Ford wanted to honor her with a funeral procession through Tombstone until screenwriter Winston Miller pointed out that "it just doesn't work because she wasn't a whore with a heart of gold."[12] Chihuahua is already part way to spirited Maureen O'Hara in Ford's *The Quiet Man* (1952), allowing herself to be spanked by a patriarchal husband. As in *Drums along the Mohawk* (with its friendly Indian who advises farmer Gilbert Martin [Henry Fonda] to beat his wife) and *The Searchers* (with the temporary, servile Indian "wife" of part-Cherokee Martin Pawley [Jeffrey Hunter]), the combination of Native Americans, women, and discipline brings out the most stunted side of Ford's sexual politics.

Far from representing one pole of an opposition, Chihuahua may look not differentiated *enough* from Clementine, and both actresses play their roles coolly. The style is conventional for Clementine's easterner but seems odd for a Mexican spitfire. Their barely distinguishable emotional range might represent only Hollywood's madonna–whore split as characterized in another 1946 Western, George Sidney's MGM musical *The Harvey Girls:* "Well, it's all a matter of style," waitress Susan Bradley (Judy Garland) generously explains to saloon whore Em (Angela Lansbury). "Some people wear one kind of dress, some another." Chihuahua's style, however, reveals something more: the presence of another argument among filmmakers within the postwar Western. Her coolness appears to be Ford's answer to what was at the time a massively publicized new sensualization of the Western, first in Howard Hughes's *The Outlaw* (released in 1943 and more widely in early 1946) and then in King Vidor and David O. Selznick's *Duel in the Sun* (not released until the month following *Clementine* in 1946, although one needed to be blind in Hollywood to have missed the direction in which Selznick was pushing the genre after his two-year publicity campaign; see, for example, his prerelease advertisement for Jennifer Jones in "The Degradation Scene").[13] Wyatt's blank gaze of disinterest past Chihuahua's ankle on the poker table (prompting her retaliatory "cattle straying/delaying" song) looks like a response to this sensualization of the Western: Get this outta town and keep it out! Ford holds the classic line even in the face of Chihuahua's role as written. In the script, Linda Darnell's Chihuahua seems indistinguishable from Jane Russell's Rio McDonald in *The Outlaw* or Jennifer Jones's Pearl Chavez in *Duel in the Sun* – sultry "breeds" all, apparent mixtures of Mexican, Indian, and European blood. On screen, however, Jane Russell and Jennifer Jones play "hot," writhing their bodies at ground level in ways that generally denied their directors the static close-up (although Selznick brought in Josef von Sternberg to add some sensually sweaty close-ups of Jones). Linda Darnell's undynamic postures are further cooled by being observed in standing full-shots or face-only close-ups. There is a world view argued by Ford through these stylistic details: His film form holds the line against *The Outlaw*'s awkward visuals that reinforce its tricky Machiavellian cynicism. In its complicated pattern of betrayal topping homoerotic betrayal, *The Outlaw* tells the new story common to film-noir plot lines and to postwar power itself – from Howard Hughes through Joseph McCarthy to Richard Nixon – where treacheries are paranoid and lead ultimately to the Italian spaghetti Western. The classic Western's sense of treachery is, in comparison, reassuringly simple. *Clementine* pits the Earps' wide loyalty to family and community against the Clantons' clannish loyalty.

Wyatt's rejection of Chihuahua, at once priggish and jeering, carries a weight. He's rewarded for it, in that sexual complications don't alienate his eventually needed showdown partner, Doc Holliday. The other option had already been flamboyantly portrayed in *The Outlaw,* where *its* Doc Holliday (played by Walter Huston) faces repeated betrayals from his sometime partner Billy the Kid (Jack Buetel) due partly to their rivalry over "Doc's girl," Jane Russell's Rio. Wyatt's rejections keeps him freer. And so Chihuahua has to bear the film's share of a misogyny particularly overt in the film-noir era, onscreen and off. The most widely reported real-life eastern Western of 1947 featured American Legionnaires running amok in Manhattan, chasing women down Broadway with electric cattle prods.[14] *The Outlaw*'s Doc Holliday had lamented, "Women! Ah, they're all alike. . . . There isn't anything they wouldn't do for ya [spit] . . . or to ya [spit]." Though *Clementine*'s Doc avoids that universal condemnation, his own impatient rejection of Chihuahua (for squalling her "stupid little song" about the "broad sombrero") proves fatal, as it leads her to take up with Billy Clanton. Thus Wyatt's *and* Doc's double rejection of Chihuahua's sexuality and ethnicity has ramifications for the film that are explained only visually.

Where have they gone, all those Hispanic types that people the first half of the film: the serape-clad men in the street; the women selling tamales in the theater; the Mexican musicians in the saloon; the girls shouting in Spanish alongside Old Man Clanton? Like the lone, drunk Indian kicked from town, Chihuahua's death stands in for a culture exiled.

# 22. "A Lot of Nice People around Here"

This is no place for you. What do you know about building new worlds?

Spencer Tracy, captain of the *Mayflower,* to Gene Tierney in *Plymouth Adventure* (1952)

However soft her look, Clementine is evidently a tough traveler, having spent months searching "from cowcamp to cowcamp, from one mining town to another," for Doc Holliday, determined to free him from his film-noir despair. Her precursors are those fighting women in 1945 films who let nothing stand in the way of bringing their men out of noir-shadowed despondency, such as Ingrid Bergman in Hitchcock's *Spellbound* ("I'm going to fight and fight and get you free") or Jane Wyman in Wilder's *The Lost Weekend* ("I'm going to fight and fight and fight").[1] In *It's a Wonderful Life* (1946) the adolescent Mary announces her determination by whispering, "George Bailey, I'll love you 'till the day I die," into his deaf ear. However, the twist with Clementine's tough love is that she *fails* to bring Doc out of his demoralization. Noir remains *his* lighting style. His nightmare is to be unable to escape the domesticating woman of his eastern past. It is as if Rip Van Winkle had awakened from his long drunken sleep in the woods west of town only to find himself still ruled by Dame Van Winkle's "petticoat government" with its hectoring "household eloquence."[2] Doc makes another effort to escape by announcing "I'm moving on" if Clementine herself should fail to leave Tombstone on the stage for the East. She agrees, leading to the following Sunday-morning encounter:

**Scene No. 3:**

Into the silence of the hotel lobby, Clementine brings down her bags, finds no one at the front desk, and sits, dabbing her eyes with a handkerchief. Wyatt,

toying with his hat as he wanders in from the porch (Fig. 49a), does the smallest of double-takes on being caught whistling "My Darling Clementine." Clementine explains that she's waiting for the stage.

"I don't know, ma'am," Wyatt ventures, "if you ask me, I think you're giving up too easy" (Fig. 49b). "Marshal, if you ask me, I don't think you know too much about a woman's pride" (Fig. 49c). His admission to this is interrupted by, among others, the hearty mayor: "Bless my soul, he did it! Good morning, miss; good morning, Marshal. John Simpson said he'd have a church and he has. Church bells! In Tombstone!" Noticing the gravity of Wyatt and Clementine, the mayor too turns awkward and exits.

Wyatt and Clementine walk slowly onto the bright, vacant porch (Fig. 49d). "I love your town in the morning, Marshal," she says. "The air is so clean and clear. The scent of the desert flowers." "That's me. Barber," Wyatt admits, in reference to his cologne. Presuming that he intends to go to the church "services," Clementine asks him to accompany her. "Yes, ma'am, I'd admire to take you." Clem's arm in Wyatt's, the two make a measured walk down the boardwalk, then out toward the gathering as a choral "Shall We Gather at the River?" swells (Fig. 49e).

**Figure 49** *(here and facing). My Darling Clementine:* Sunday morning in Tombstone.

Our vantage shifts to a makeshift pulpit at the half-completed, still open-air church, where John Simpson, fiddle under his arm, declares the dedication of "the First Church of Tombstone": "Now I don't pretend to be no preacher but I've read the good book from cover to cover and back again and I've nary found one word agin dancin'. So we'll commence by havin' a dad-blasted good dance" (Fig. 49f). Long shots juxtapose American flags on one end of the church structure with a half-built bell tower on the other, dancers between, and the hotel and a wide mesa in the background (Fig. 49g).

Eventually an awkward Wyatt asks, "Oblige me, ma'am?" and they step onto the church flooring. "Sashay back," Simpson calls out, "and make way for our new marshal and his lady fair." Clementine's ease and Wyatt's high-legged formality center the gathering, surrounded by the music and rhythmic clapping (Fig. 49h). On a buckboard, Morgan and Virgil Earp, pausing on their way to visit James's grave, look on the scene with astonishment.

Dissolve to the hotel supper; Clementine has apparently given up immediate plans for any eastbound stage.

This is a scene of inclusion – the single most famous among Westerns – as the eviction of Indian Charlie was of exclusion. Its emotional resonance is reinforced by stylistic factors omitted above. (Among them is the restraint from tracking shots elsewhere in the film, so that the moving camera leading Wyatt and Clem along the boardwalk draws in viewers with an a half-conscious sense of some shift in the town's very ground.)[3] Just as Chihuahua's death cues the disappearance of a serape-clad culture, it's only after Clementine's arrival that the Earp brothers notice "a lot of nice people around here; we just ain't met 'em" (as Morgan says in the conversation being shot in Fig. 50). This classic celebration of the growth of a church-centered small town is, however, neither "mythic" nor timeless. It's primarily a reflection of post–World War II America.

Historically, Tombstone was a boomtown at the time the film depicts. From a few scattered ranches before silver discovery in 1877, it had grown to a population of perhaps eight thousand by the 1881 O.K. Corral shootout.[4] And rapid population growth tells only part of the story, since frontier towns – particularly on the mining frontier – had astonishingly transient populations.[5] The stately visuals of *My Darling Clementine* transmute Tombstone into a stable community, building itself up, but in a measured way. The real boom was closer to home for the film's audience. A few American seacoast port cities had grown rapidly during World War II, but the significant boom came after, when veterans returned to help spend accumulated personal savings, augmented by generous housing-loan laws.[6] *My Darling Clementine*'s escape from film noir, where dark gambling halls are replaced by families in open spaces, also reflects this story. The wartime homefront had been, after all, more of a gambling den than ever were the Roaring Twenties, because of the wartime scarcity of durable consumer goods on which to spend increased wages.[7] But as the war ended, homebuilding – which had been deferred first by the depression then by the war itself – could begin. The Long Island location for many of the earliest Westerns was buried in 1946 under the first mass-produced Levittown.[8] The "fresh-cut lumber" that Wyatt notices and Mr. Simpson's hope of raising "enough money to finish the church" are parts of the classic Western's portrayal of expansion as a moral activity, emptied of the corruption, the price-control violations, the outright fraud in the building trades so widely publicized after the war.[9] In its always-restrained way, *My Darling Clementine* exiles boomtown immorality to the same oblivion

**Figure 50.** Shooting the Sunday-morning scene of *My Darling Clementine* on location in Arizona. On the porch, from left, Ward Bond as Morgan Earp, Henry Fonda as Wyatt, and Tim Holt as Virgil.

as film noir and brings audiences a less obviously sentimental dream than that found in the 1947–8 cycle of homebuilding films (which includes *Apartment for Peggy, Good Sam, Mr. Blandings Builds His Dream House,* and the conclusion of *Miracle on 34th Street*). The Western's town-building argument is bluntest in a pair of Errol Flynn films that bracket the war years: *Dodge City* in 1939 and *San Antonio* in 1945.[10] Both anticipate *Clementine,* with Flynn each time a cattleman who becomes a reluctant marshal who then oversees small-town stability. In *Dodge City* (directed by Michael Curtiz), Flynn shepherds the town away from one that "knew no ethics but cash and killing." In the visually slack *San Antonio,* he stands in the ruins of the Alamo, inspired to build a town this time by the sacrifices of those who fought in war: "Those old-time Texans died for something pretty important."

The criticism – ethical and architectural – of the Levittowns and other low-cost suburban developments was that they were built without a community focal point, sometimes without even a store or park, let alone a town square or meeting place.[11] Such criticism evoked one of the bedrocks of the Western, the "small town," an ideal that linked Jefferson's small landowners, Jackson's small businesses, and Rousseau's social contract (where men would come together in sparsely populated rural societies). In the 1940s, a book of prescriptive sociology entitled *The Small Community: The Foundation of Democratic Life* informs us that civilization's "elemental traits" include "good will, neighborliness, fair play, . . . [and] patience. . . . They are learned in the intimate, friendly world of the family and the small community."[12] The evident fragility of a civilization based on such values is tested in another battle against film noir within William Wellman's tellingly titled *Magic Town* (1947), which, with a script by Robert Riskin, feels like a film by the screenwriter's frequent collaborator Frank Capra. After big-city pollsters discover the town to be statistically average – like "Middletown" (Muncie, Indiana) of sociologic fame – it turns so self-conscious as to become a joke to the nation. Townie Mary Peterman (Jane Wyman), accepting blame with pollster "Rip" Smith (James Stewart) for ruining the community spirit, expresses her anguish through a metaphor matching the noir darkness into which the town sinks before its recovery. Sounding as if she's come from a screening of *Double Indemnity* (1944) or *The Postman Always Rings Twice* (1946), she says that what they've done to the town is like when a man and another man's wife murder her husband but then discover their crime prevents happiness. *Magic Town* argues that (1) the best communities find their model in the nuclear family ("I feel as if my whole family is breaking up"); (2) the best communities = average towns; and (3) average towns = a secure United States. A U.S. senator in the film has become too restless for a foreign-policy conference because he's been denied the sustenance of lazing round the town hall's pot-bellied stove.

As a town-building Western, *My Darling Clementine* takes the relatively empty path that it took in discussing Native Americans and Hispanics: The single example stands in for the whole. It's not insignificant, however, that its one new building is a church, and the film again represents less the historical frontier than post–World War II history. Church attendance was notoriously "abysmal" on the mining frontier, but in the postwar decade church ties were more and more replacing ethnic ones as a public expression of social identity.[13] Too, *Clementine*'s church has "no name yet and no preacher neither," as Simpson tells the congregation. It's less a space for worshiping God than for demonstrating community – which is to say for demonstrating the newly unified Anglo community, as there's no evidence in the congregation of the earlier serapes and mantillas. "The First Church of Tombstone" is no longer the space for displaying the ethnic inclusiveness of a new town, as it was back in *Cimarron*'s "Osage First Methodist Episcopalian Lutheran Presbyterian Congregational Baptist Catholic Unitarian Hebrew Church." The hymn we hear the congregation sing, "Shall We Gather at the River?" is more appropriate for funerals – the recently deceased gather at what the lyrics suggest is the River Jordan before crossing over to the afterlife – but, as Kathryn Kalinak observed, it is also appropriate for this community gathering in *Clementine* because the lyrics are also implicitly about dividing chosen people from the damned.[14]

The hymn-singing and dancing townsfolk of *My Darling Clementine* form a collective character ("folk," like the crew of the battleship *Potemkin*), an ideal combination of the solo principals. The dance is decently hedonistic (a mild form of Chihuahua's sensuality), gregarious (a mild form of the Clantons' clannishness), justified as moral enough through cover-to-cover Bible reading (a mild form of Wyatt's Puritanism), and no doubt a touch corrupt (a mild form of Doc's corruption). Thus the dance convenes community by converging the temptations to individual martyrdom, finding a spirit that incorporates the best in otherwise destructive personal traits. The long shot of the gathering (see Fig. 49g), often discussed as having a dualistic "civilization-versus-wilderness" structure, is likewise a more lively disorder, combining the spirituality represented by the church belltower, the hedonism of the dance, the natural world of the clouds and mesa, the commerce of the saloon and hotel, and the nationalism of the flags.

When, earlier in the morning, Morgan Earp discovers what has brought all these folks together – "a camp meeting" – Mr. Simpson bristles at the description: "No such a dad-blasted thing! Regular church!" The moment seems to place the Earp family down among Ford's Irish and to underline differences in class background between Wyatt and

Clementine. It is also the church bell itself, the first she's heard "in months," that persuades Clementine from leaving on the eastbound stage. That church bell rang throughout the historical frontier as a signifier of the arrival of women's civilization, as in Phoebe Judson's mid-nineteenth-century recollections, *A Pioneer's Search for an Ideal Home:* With the church bell's first ring, "I realized that my 'ideal home' was one more step nearer completion."[15]

Clementine brings with her the domestication of the Western film that had been growing more prominent since the late 1930s. Even *Stagecoach* was *marketed* to women audiences, with a tie-in to Max Factor makeup, as a drama about romance.[16] Also in 1939 came *Destry Rides Again,* which carries within its comedy a castration Western: With nightmare logic, men keep losing their pants while being chased by women with rifles. Emblematic of the hapless men of this 1939 cycle is James Cagney in *The Oklahoma Kid.* Taking overmuch pleasure in killing (blowing smoke from his gunbarrel like the gangster implied in Cagney's casting), he needs to be taught the domestic logic buried within Manifest Destiny. "Empire building?" a woman questions, leaping on his phrase, "Well, it's a difficult thing to do by yourself. For an empire you've got to have people, and for people you've got to have children, and for children. . . ." Cut to her father, who by Freudian dream logic is a judge: "By the authority vested. . . ." Poor Cagney stands gape-mouthed, lacking gun or words. "I do," she says, "and he takes me, father, whether he likes it or not." The following year William Wyler's *The Westerner* (1940) dramatized the supplanting of Populist ideals of the thirties by the more genteel West of the forties. Wyler's relaxed style looks back to celebrate the small farmer on his plot of land, Gregg Toland's camera slowly tracking past careworn farmers as they stare out at their burnt corn. The choral music and praying to the crops is worthy of Ford's *The Grapes of Wrath,* also shot by Toland that year. But land as idyll is supplanted in *The Westerner* by woman as idol, both in the film's comic subplot (Walter Brennan's Judge Roy Bean is obsessed with portraits of actress Lillie Langtry) and in its main tale. Gary Cooper's Cole Hardin, the westerner of the title, is brought in from the cold to wash dishes alongside a woman who tempts him with visions of the home fires burning: lamplight, a dry bed under rain on the roof, the warm smell of coffee in the morning. She's a refreshingly undisguised "home-digger" who points out to Coop "that little knoll right there . . . just begging for a house."[17]

The godfather of the Western's evolution into domesticity was surely Cecil B. De Mille. Back in 1936 his *The Plainsman* had tried to resuscitate the big-scale Western by taming it. Indian killing is simple stuff for Wild Bill Hickok (Gary Cooper) compared to the double struggle to free his friend Buffalo Bill Cody from a life spent hanging his wife's curtains and to free himself from love-mad Calamity Jane. (She wins that last battle: After Hickok is shot dead, he "can't wipe off" her last kiss.) De Mille's *North West Mounted Police* (1940) bizarrely infused domesticity into the brutal Indian-slaughter cycle of just before World War II: A showdown is interrupted by shouts of "It's a boy!" After the war De Mille's *The Unconquered* (1947) trades its promising prerevolutionary motifs for a Cinderella story in which Captain Holden (Gary Cooper) takes erstwhile bondwoman Abby Hale (Paulette Goddard) to "The King's Birthday Ball." Cecil B. De Mille was known most intimately at this time less through his films than from his regular Monday-night hosting of CBS's highly popular *Lux Radio Theatre* from 1937 through 1945. His 1940 introduction to the hour-long dramatization of the Errol Flynn Western *Virginia City* employed this logic:

> Pioneering in the old West was exciting, and American women did more than their share of the job with a good deal less than their share of the ordinary conveniences. All of the gold in Virginia City couldn't have bought them a cake of Lux Toilet Soap because it took plenty of pioneering to develop that too. Pioneering both in science and the art of beauty.[18]

Before damning C. B. for taming the West to hawk soap, it is worth admitting that while a domesticated West flies in the face of the Western *myth*, it is not unhistorical. On the mining frontier at least, the demographics of sex ratios meant that single women, despite the rough work, could indulge in literary courtship rituals while choosing among suitors.[19] This unexpected cultural phenomenon arose also from the fact that it was not the least literate who went west but rather those who could raise the several hundred dollars necessary for such a move.[20] (If *this* fact is unacknowledged in the myth, it's because the *cost* of setting up a new life is the largest flaw in the idea of the West as a "safety valve" for the poor in teeming cities.) Indeed, the class of women who could afford to travel west may have been much the same as the class of women that Hollywood was seeking to attract to Westerns, notoriously the most actively disliked genre among women in audience surveys of the early 1940s.[21] In that respect, De Mille pinpointed his target audience when he calls Lux Toilet Soap "a product dedicated to the great-granddaughters of those hardy feminine pioneers."

*My Darling Clementine* doesn't ignore the hazards of such domestication. Indeed, it's exactly those temptations to softness that add to the threat in Wyatt's Hamlet-like recumbency. Such is hinted again in his "sweet-smelling" perfume, another referent that wouldn't have been lost on postwar audiences. ("Men's cologne," little known before the war, became familiar as a gift sent by women to servicemen overseas, because of its light weight.) The big secret of military service, kept by all veterans then and now, is that it spends most of its time teaching men traditionally female skills – cooking, washing, cleaning, clothes mending. . . .[22] Too, Ford's title is *My Darling Clementine.* While a third *Frontier Marshal* would have stretched even Zanuck's fondness for remakes, the change also downplays and disguises the film's status as a Western, at a time when market studies were finding women better informed about new films and making most of the decisions about which films couples would see.[23] (And to judge how rare the title is, try this game: Think of another Western whose title makes less evident that it is within the genre.) The title change places at the center of the empty film its emptiest figure, who lacks even the comic distinctiveness of her origin in the nineteenth-century song sung over the opening credits.[24]

The film's Clementine is based on characters in the two *Frontier Marshals*, especially the second, but her spiritual godmother is Owen Wister's schoolmarm in *The Virginian.* Revealingly, *The Virginian* also gets an adaptation, its fourth on film, in 1946, this time with a new stress on the schoolmarm, including an opening sequence of her leaving Vermont by train found in none of the earlier film versions. The 1914 Cecil B. De Mille version (starring Dustin Farnum) had featured scenes from the novel that played up the cowboy as unfettered trickster – including the Virginian's sham gunslinging "nightmare" to free beds in the overcrowded hotel, and his impish switching of babies at the community baptism and dance. By the 1923 B. P. Schulberg production (with Kenneth Harlan as the Virginian), the first of these sequences has vanished but the second remains. The 1929 Victor Fleming early-sound version, with Gary Cooper, also retains only the baby-switching comic sequence, and splits into lighthearted and solemn halves, delineated by the Virginian's midfilm lecture to his wayward pal: "This whole country's taking things more seriously." The

1946 version (directed by Stuart Gilmore and starring Joel McCrea) cuts *both* comic sequences, leaving in their wake only a shrillness to the moralism and a scolding schoolmarm in its Molly.

*My Darling Clementine* is in line with this movement – in its title change, in its elimination of Ford's usual roughhouse comedy, and in its casting of Cathy Downs as Clementine. Her unruffled looks and gliding walk suggest that she might be too refined for the West, just as her "woman's pride" turns her too quickly defeatist. But Ford also gives her traditionally masculine traits he admires elsewhere: She is unemotional in any demonstrative way and has been an undaunted searcher for Doc.[25] Cathy Downs had few other significant roles, but a revealing one is in Henry Hathaway's *The Dark Corner*, a film noir released earlier in 1946, where she is Mari, the coolly elegant trophy wife of a slimy art dealer (Clifton Webb), who married her for her resemblance to a Raphael portrait. Still, she eventually empties a six-gun into him – her coolness covering a toughness. Just as Chihuahua was not exactly the "bad woman," Clementine is not without a touch of the era's femme fatale. Her arrival and misplaced faith help to convince Doc to take up his scalpel when he hasn't the surgical skill and then to accept his suicidal role in someone else's family feud.

The gentle *Rachel and the Stranger* (1948), set at the turn of the nineteenth century, makes the most sophisticated postwar argument for the domesticating woman, as opposed to merely assuming her value. Rachel (Loretta Young) is pliant when bought out of bond servitude by widower David Harvey (William Holden), an isolated farmer who needs a mother for a son in danger of becoming one of the uncivilized "woodsy folk." David breaks manly silence only for the sort of lectures about homebuilding generally given by women in Westerns: "It's keeping up appearances no matter how deep you get in the wilderness." But, in one of the witty shifts here, David lets civilized "appearances" replace feeling, leaving space for mountain trapper Jim Fairways (Robert Mitchum) to sing his ballads and demonstrate courtly respect to Rachel. The film develops surprisingly clear parallels between "wife" and "bondwoman," and allows Rachel to grow into sarcastic disgust over both the taciturn and courtly variants of disengaged "Manhood!" while she sets about mastering the long rifle on her own. Visually, the film is *too* relaxed, finding neither the romanticism nor mournfulness of Ford, although the pace allows time, rare in the Western, for lingering on the cycle of seasons, the land, and the crops.[26]

*Rachel and the Stranger* is unusual. The usual problem, which the idealization of Clementine displays, is that such respect inhibits conflict and makes all of those 1950s town-cleaning Westerns built around Virginia Mayo or Rhonda Fleming more and more unwatchable. *My Darling Clementine* circumvents some of the problems of those films by giving its title character only about forty lines of dialogue (five of them "Thank you") and leaving her nearly as blank as when she first steps off the stagecoach. Cut were shooting-script scenes that would have made her more expressive: one where she breaks into tears during a visit to James's grave and another in which she physically fights Chihuahua.[27] Little wonder that she begins her final conversion in the released film with "There were so many things I wanted to say. . . ." The problem that the 1950s Westerns found in trying to dramatize such respect are evident in the frustrating near-miss of William Wellman's *Westward the Women* (1951), notwithstanding its typically witty Charles Schnee script from a story by Frank Capra. Scout Buck (Robert Taylor) has to stand around grinning at the spirit of Danon (Denise Darcel) and the rest of the quietly heroic wagon train of mail-order brides, and such conflicts as do come (lusting cowhands, treacherous mountain passes, Indians) are merely episodic. Wellman's camera is angled for heroism, whether shooting the women from below as they survey desert salt flats or from high booms as they cross. Certain sequences have the dream logic of protofeminist solidarity: A mass of women hold up the side of a broken wagon as another gives birth inside. But such strength is contextualized into "the will of a woman when there's a wedding ring in sight," the domestic version of Darwinist survival. One out of three will die, they're warned, but the remainder will be "fit stock" for the marriage bed.

The respect for women in Westerns presumes them to be demographic rarities – gold in the rough, or "like an angel in the jungle, a very wild jungle." Historically, women were not particularly rare in the nineteenth-century West – with the exception, mentioned above, of brief periods following gold or silver rushes. *Westward the Women* and *My Darling Clementine* can thus perform historical sleights-of-hand to justify their idolizations. *Westward the Women* opens with a "California 1851" title, when (after the 1849 gold rush) women did account for fewer than 10 percent of the population.[28] Well might a wagon train of Denise Darcels be idolized. Wellman's film further makes the bride-seeking men hard-working, Central Valley farmers – not a gold miner in the bunch. Through the genre's Jeffersonian ethical scale of occupations, these yeomen are raised to the level of the heroic women. By the start of the Civil War in 1861 – after which the great majority of Westerns are set – the ratio of the sexes on the frontier had nearly evened out (to around 106 men for every 100 women).[29] Although *My Darling Clementine* takes place in 1882, it is able to play the same double trick. It's set on a silver-mining frontier, and thus Tombstone's barber makes two reasonable guesses as to the Earps' profession – "Miners?" or "Prospectors, huh?" – and gets a gruff correction from Wyatt that elevates the Earps a notch in the genre's hierarchy of professions: "Cattlemen!" In this careful context, Clementine *is* a rare creature, and Wyatt is almost worthy of her.

# 23. "Who Do We Shoot?"

There's no better plan than a bullet.
Roy Rogers in *Young Bill Hickok* (1940)

The formation of the ideal community in *My Darling Clementine,* its exclusions and inclusions, can be said then to answer elaborately questions about community evaded in *Stagecoach. The Grapes of Wrath* (1940), another John Ford film from before U.S. entry into the war, had left hanging a more pointed question. A process server who has come with an eviction notice for an Oklahoma sharecropper named Muley and his family explains that he's a merely delivering it for the Shawnee Land and Cattle Company, which "ain't nobody, it's a company," itself being pressed by larger banking concerns. "Then who *do* we shoot?" demands Muley (John Qualen). "Brother, I don't know," responds the process server sympathetically before he drives off. "If I did, I'd tell you. I just don't know who's to blame." *The Grapes of Wrath,* with its epic trek of the dispossessed to California, evolves into something of a contemporary Western. Even out West, however, no one is able to tell Muley who exactly is culpable (and Native Americans, for once, are not a target: The Joads drive straight past them in Arizona). For the answer to his question, within Ford's work, we have to wait for *My Darling Clementine.* Its shootout at the O.K. Corral begins obliquely:

**Scene No. 4:**

Wyatt Earp, feet on his desk in the jail office at the edge of town, is reading a document when Morgan, his shirt off, opens the door for Tombstone's mayor and its church deacon, Mr. Simpson (Fig. 51). To their offer of help, Wyatt tells them that the fight is "strictly a family affair." Down at the O.K. Corral, Ike Clanton asks his father if the Earps are "too yellow" to come out and fight.

**Figure 51.** *My Darling Clementine:* The jail office on the night before the gunfight.

"They'll come," Clanton responds. Back at the jail office, Doc Holliday also enters, turns his face to the shadows as he announces Chihuahua's death and utters his medical title with disgust – "DOCTOR John Holliday!" He grabs a rifle off the rack and asks, "When do we start?" "Sunup," Wyatt says. Dawn finds all five men still in the office. Wyatt puts his badge in his pocket, gives two unloaded shotguns to the mayor and deacon, then asks, "Got everything straight?" After they leave the adobe jail, he tells them all, "Let's go."

By providing people to shoot, the Western scales down vexed problems of societal discontent into stories of individual violence. We don't want to feel helpless, and Westerns, with their identifiable villains, are one response to the social helplessness so movingly captured in *The Grapes of Wrath* after the process server drives off and the camera tilts down to find Muley clutching the land that he still calls his own. ("It's livin' on it, and dyin' on it, that's what makes it ours. And not no piece of paper!") John Ford is faithful to John Steinbeck's leftism to the extent that the film's Ma Joad (Jane Darwell) takes solace in the collectivist idea that "we're the people . . . they can't wipe us out." But the

Western provides something more: a structure to locate individual blame and to justify the right of the gunman to set the world straight. As Paul Zweig put it in discussing the popularity of pulp adventure stories after the First World War, "One wanted destiny scaled to the will of individuals, not cataclysms which made a joke of individuality, however brave or reckless."[1] In the week after the 2001 attack on the World Trade Center, President George W. Bush spoke of needing "Wanted Dead or Alive" posters "like they had in the Old West."[2]

As soon as Wyatt Earp announces his name ten minutes into *My Darling Clementine,* we know there will be people to shoot at the O.K. Corral. The shootout will be the final piece of the "get outta town" argument about necessary exclusions from civilization (the words are directed by Wyatt again to Old Man Clanton after his sons are dead [Fig. 52], although in the end Clanton pulls a gun and must be shot down by Morgan).[3] Partly because there is little suspense in this resolution, the film can carry its emptiness to extremes. Look a little more closely at the scene above. It holds within it a scheme, given not a word of dialogue, that leads Tombstone's mayor and church deacon to impersonate Doc Holliday and Morgan Earp by walking down the main street with Wyatt at the showdown, despite his having dismissed them earlier when he labeled the fight "a family affair." Old Man Clanton, making the same presumption that the fight is family business, mistakes the town leaders for Doc and Morgan – who have, in fact, snuck around to shoot from the side. The mayor and deacon pull their hats low and turn their collars up, the better to hide their faces, as they walk toward the O.K. Corral. Modern audiences, accustomed to having action plots spelled out more bluntly and reinforced with dialogue, often fail to notice the scheme at all.

Enough evidence survives from early versions of the script and film to see how Wyatt's scheme was slowly emptied of obvious explanation in the course of production. One of the reasons for his delay before the shootout is just hinted in the finished film when Clanton, waiting at the corral, says, "Easy on that keg, son." In lines Ford cut from the shooting script, Wyatt passes some of the night by explaining to Morgan that it's worth allowing the Clantons time to keep "worryin' and wonderin'. . . . Pretty soon they get to passin' the jug around. More they'll drink – more they'll need. First thing you know, you got 'em at a disadvantage – and all you've done to get it – is sit and wait."[4] Also, watching carefully, one can observe in the finished film that as Doc and

**Figure 52.** "Now get outta town, start wanderin'," Wyatt commands Old Man Clanton (Walter Brennan) after the gunfight in *My Darling Clementine.*

Morgan leave the jail office, they are without boots, the better to sneak quietly. In the rare surviving preview cut of *My Darling Clementine,* probably shown to a test audience in August 1946 – and preserved by the UCLA Film and Television Archive – that part of the scheme is underlined when Morgan later whispers, as they tiptoe down an alley, "Better watch out for nails in them stocking feet, Doc." Similarly, after the showdown, as Morgan gazes down at Doc's body, Wyatt speaks the last line in the preview version of this penultimate scene: "I'll get his boots" (so that, presumably, Doc can die with his "boots on"). The finished cut eliminates these lines and is everywhere sparer.

It's worth pointing out these details especially because of the mistaken assumption that classic Westerns must rely ethically on the open "walkdown," where antagonists stride in the clear sun toward each other down a town's main street, armed equally and weapons plainly visible. The rules for such a fair fight were explicated by no less than President Eisenhower in a 1953 televised speech about the cold war, drawing on stories of his boyhood in Abilene, Kansas, and "our marshal," Wild Bill Hickok ("If you don't know about him, read your Westerns more," Ike instructed the nation): You were allowed to "meet anyone face to face with whom you disagree," and "if you met him face to face and took the same risk he did, you could get away with almost anything as long as the bullet was in the front."[5] At a glance, *My Darling Clementine*'s showdown might look this straightforward, but it has not quite lost the darker schemes more associated with film noir.

If the Western is centrally about death, it is of a particular kind. Orson Welles, for instance, barely made a film that did not include imagining his own death. In contrast, Westerns in this era are less about one's own death than about inflicting it on others. Although *Clementine* plays its shootout with a ritual solemnity, there is nevertheless something of Monsieur Lange's discovery (in Jean Renoir's *The Crime of M. Lange* [1936]) that ultimately "it's easy" to gun down those who threaten a fragile ideal community – a lesson Lange learns through writing his "Arizona Jim" pulp Western serial. Notwithstanding Wyatt's line about the "family affair," the showdown as it finally plays out scrupulously balances personal vengeance with community service. Just before Wyatt unloads the two shotguns for the town citizens, he is seen receiving an unexplained piece of paper from the mayor – later revealed as an arrest warrant when he reads it to Clanton at the corral. With the World War II home front in memory, citizens turn out to play a backup role even if they can't wield usable weapons. Especially because the opening of the showdown is filmed in extreme long shot, it is difficult – both for us and the Clantons – to distinguish the gunmen from the nonviolent town leaders. And that is exactly the point for *My Darling Clementine*'s argument: Church (the deacon) and state (the mayor) turn out to validate the gunman. It can't just be a family affair. The problems that come with trying to justify gunfight heroism within a story of mere family revenge, even when enacted by Henry Fonda, are demonstrated by the maneuvers that Fritz Lang's *The Return of Frank James* (1940) must perform when Fonda's Frank James needs to avenge the murder of his brother Jesse by the Ford brothers: Bob Ford ends shot by someone else and Charlie Ford falls conveniently from a cliff.

The proper relationship between individual fighters and the larger community was regularly argued out among Westerns, including three of the best-known from the 1950s: *High Noon* (1952), *Rio Bravo* (1959), and the contemporary Western *Bad Day at Black Rock* (1955). All are variations on the story of a single-handed hero cleaning up a small town. Gary Cooper in *High Noon* is the most celebrated of lone Western heroes, but remember that he looks for and expects community support to help him fight the returning outlaws – an argument that itself attacks the single-handed hero myth, which achieved its apotheosis with *Shane* a year later. Cooper is offered a little support, but for a variety of reasons it's unacceptable (too young, too drunk, too many demands) until he gets unexpected and very violent help from his Quaker bride. *Bad Day at Black Rock* reinforces the single-handed hero myth literally, for Spencer Tracy's veteran has lost an arm in the war. Cooper had thrown his tin star in the dust to express his disgust with a community that accepted "one for all" but refused "all for one." Tracy, without much aid from anyone in the secretive town, nevertheless defeats the enemies within it, and then – rather than throwing a tin star in the dust – awards the town a war medal to help it "come back" from spiritual defeat. *Bad Day at Black Rock* responds with a liberal but militant optimism to *High Noon*'s dark pessimism, which had so troubled many in Hollywood. Howard Hawks said he made *Rio Bravo* in infuriated response to seeing Gary Cooper "go running around like a chicken with his head off asking for help" from his neighbors.[6] In *Rio Bravo* John Wayne is never quite single-handed; he's the kingpin of an exclusive group of community fighters. The presence of allies, whom Wayne selects, bullies, judges, and sustains, argues that the true civilizing lawman, if he's "good enough," wins by inspiring otherwise inadequate allies. This set of films reminds us that what may look like a similar classic structure may also be mutually exclusive options in an ongoing debate. When we remember *High Noon, Rio Bravo,* and *Bad Day at Black Rock* as films made in fifties America, the sheriff-cleans-up-town story turns out to hold cold-war arguments interpreted by everyone from President Eisenhower on down. Were we to look at a trio of films with the "same" classic plot line from before the war – say, *Dodge City, Destry Rides Again,* and *The Marshal of Mesa City,* all from 1939 – what we would find are films debating different topics. In those pre–World War II Westerns, each of the three newly appointed and reluctant sheriffs attempts to enforce an antigun ordinance or, more precisely, to test whether the idea of law and order is possible without violence. It's a focus that entails political questions of disarmament and isolationism that the later trio of cold-war films disdain to debate.

The gunfighting Earps in *My Darling Clementine* are seen first working as cowboys but forced by necessity out of that laboring occupation. This reluctant conversion-from-the-cowboy is another way that classic Westerns regularly justify the gunman's ethics. With its emphasis on the cowboy's physical skills, the Western alludes to, while evading the complexities of, ideals of the independent laborer.[7] Ford's postwar Westerns in that sense reenact, but in an empty way, the issues of his labor-force films that preceded them before the United States joined the war: *The Long Voyage Home* and *How Green Was My Valley*.[8] The first half-century of the Western film shows a gradual but relentless replacement of images of cowboys with gunfighters. The early silent Western regularly weaves plots around working cowboys, as in the earliest Tom Mix films or in the two-reelers directed by or starring Frank Borzage (surviving in such titles as *The Pitch o' Chance* [1915] or *The Pilgrim* [1916]). The relative prominence of cowboy labor in the B-Western of the 1930s is further diminished after the war. We won't catch the postwar John Wayne saying, "Well, I'm a cowhand. I chase cows" (as he does in the 1939 *Three Texas Steers*). The transference from cowboy laborer to gunslinger is encapsulated in a wry moment in a minor 1948 film called *Western Heritage:* "Oh, you got a job!" says a woman excitedly; to which the man slightly sheepishly replies, "Well, I *pulled* a job." The Western generally hides the irresponsibility of that reply by awarding to gunfight adventure the moral productivity of work. The Earps' origin in *Clementine* as cowboys soon gets lost, and they apparently forget completely about their rustled cattle.

By introducing Wyatt Earp as a cowboy, the film cannily denies one class conflict in the West. Historically, the O.K. Corral gunfight was a culmination of the wide conflict between more conservative mining and business interests in the town of Tombstone itself against the Democratic-leaning rural lands of Cochise Country that relied on the cattle-ranching business. The relatively large capital investments from the East required for hard-rock deep mining and ore processing meant that the Republican mining interests in town were keen on "law and order" so as not to discourage investment.[9] Wyatt Earp, a Republican who speculated in mineral properties, tried his hand at a number of western occupations – among them buffalo hunter, Wells Fargo stage guard, saloonkeeper, gambler, and lawman – but notably missing is the occupation he identifies so proudly in the film: "cattleman."

The most influential critical characterization of *Clementine*'s Earp was no doubt that of Peter Wollen, who, in *Signs and Meaning in the Cinema,* saw him moving "from wandering cowboy, nomadic, savage, bent on personal revenge, unmarried, to married man, settled, civilized, the sheriff who administers the law."[10] Insofar as Wyatt has vowed to avenge his murdered brother, one might concede that this is a "savage" type of justice. But the film implies no criticism of this duty, and the involvement of church and state before the showdown looks like a social ratification rather than some spurious reinforcement of Wyatt's personal reasons. He is never a savage in the Hobbesian sense, although he might be called a noble savage in Rousseau's sense: He's upright, dignified, self-controlled. The Earps open the film already looking more like pioneers than savages or "nomads," as they have driven their cattle from Mexico through what Wyatt critically labels this "rough lookin' country" bound for California. The low-angle shots of each of the four brothers, and the music accompanying the shots, honor them before a word is spoken. One of Wyatt's reasons for going to town in the first place is to get a shave – hardly a savage motivation – and what he finds is a town *more* savage than he. "What kind of a town *is* this?" he asks three times about a place where random gunshots fill the street. Compare *Abilene Town* (yet another sheriff-cleans-up-town film from 1946), in which Randolph Scott shouts, "What kind of town is this? Not a saloon on this side of the street"; or *The Hired Hand* (1971), in which director Peter Fonda perhaps hadn't forgotten his father when he has a young cowboy complain, "What kind of town is this, anyway?" – because it has no available women and, worse, no beer. These are among the responses to western towns that locate their speakers *further* along some scale of savagery than *Clementine*'s Wyatt – to consider only instances where his exact words are repeated. Still, if viewers and critics feel something savage within Wyatt, it is probably because the tinge of the nomad is conveyed stylistically, through his melancholy solitude. He needs the friendliness of the townsfolk to encourage him to join the community at the church dance and perhaps to begin to woo his darling Clementine.

The gunfight is not, after all, quite the end of *My Darling Clementine.* As Wyatt rides from Tombstone he encounters Clementine standing alone at the edge of town. She tells him that she's staying as town "schoolmarm," and he tells her that he "might" pass that way again (Fig. 53a). He parts from her – with a handshake in Ford's cut and a kiss on her cheek in a shot Zanuck added – and rides down the long road (Fig. 53b).[11] The film's way of evoking without explaining has tempted critics into reading this ending, with equal certainty, in diametrical ways. On one side, John Baxter, for instance, makes explicit what Peter Wollen and others imply: Wyatt is leaving "only for a short time" so as to explain the deaths to his "Pa" and will return to settle down as a "married" man with his schoolmarm Clementine.[12] On the other side, Tag Gallagher can speak for J. A. Place and others who presume that Wyatt is "destined to wander forever toward some mountainous fate as Clementine waits forever."[13] The ending thus demonstrably sums up the film's power of emptiness, its ability to specify almost nothing *without* disappointing its spectators – indeed suggesting much to critics who take the bait of the ending and run with it in either of two directions.

Those who envision Wyatt wandering forever in the wilderness are imposing onto *My Darling Clementine*'s emptiness a literary pattern established in Cooper's Leatherstocking novels (explicitly in *The Pathfinder* and hinted in *The Last of the Mohicans* and *The Deerslayer*) in which the hero, idealized though he may be, has internalized too much wildness of the West ever to find common ground with any eastern bride.[14] On the other hand, critics who see Wyatt happily settled and married are imposing onto *Clementine* a literary pattern first widely popularized in Wister's *The Virginian*, which marries its cowboy-gunfighter with its eastern schoolmarm – a match that, as the Virginian twice tells her, is "better than my dreams."[15] That latter option certainly *seems* to be the model toward which *My Darling Clementine* is heading: Wyatt will come in from the cold of his shattered cattleman family to be rewarded by the beautiful Clementine, the civilized/feminine East that has gone west to meet and complement him. In the twentieth century, the Cooper pattern lost out to the Wister one,[16] and *The Virginian* became the endemic model for pulp novels and thirties B-Westerns, with their "one-kiss" final shots. *The Dawn Rider* (1935), to take a B-Western story line with some resemblance to *Clementine*, concludes with John Mason (John Wayne) and a friend facing a pair of bad brothers; the friend (like Doc Holliday) dies in the showdown. Cut to the perfunctory coda: Wayne "hitched up" with his dead pal's girl. A little postwar sociology

**Figure 53.** Wyatt parts from Clementine in the final scene of *My Darling Clementine.*

of the movies also puts Wyatt's difficulty in perspective. As Martha Wolfenstein and Nathan Leites calculated from films of the 1940s, only 15 percent of Hollywood heroines reveal evidence of *ever* having loved before.[17] Clementine can hardly remain idealized *and* grab at Wyatt before her true love's body is cold. It is not just from lingering echoes of *Hamlet* that marriage to Clementine would seem "most wicked speed."

*My Darling Clementine* uses the Wister pattern as a bluff. Wyatt returns to the wilds – for how long is anybody's guess. Is he a loner because he's a judge figure, like Ford's Lincoln and his "Judge Priest"? Or does he personify celibate, late-marrying Irish habits beloved by Ford? Is he a scapegoat savior, like Shane? Or a tragic savior, like Hamlet? All of these explanations are plausible enough, but all are projections onto the film's evocative emptiness. The key may only be that *Clementine* is so clearly set up in the Wister pattern to end happily that it cries out for dissonance. It's tempting just to say that Ford, being Ford, chose melancholy.[18] The double reaction of *My Darling Clementine* – against film noir *and* against domestic complacency – is not contradictory. The film reacts against two options, *both* of which were in vogue after World War II.

# 24. The Revenge of Film Noir

Much obliged. I get awful scared in the dark.
Randolph Scott in *Coroner Creek* (1948)

If the celebrated scene in *My Darling Clementine* when the church community sings "Shall We Gather at the River?" is thought of as another question – or as a provocative statement – then responses would include scenes in Sam Peckinpah's *The Wild Bunch* (1969) and Arthur Penn's *Little Big Man* (1970). In the visceral opening of *The Wild Bunch,* that is, a temperance band marching to "Shall We Gather at the River?" through a south Texas town is slaughtered in the wild crossfire between bank robbers and vigilantes. Amid the massacre, Crazy Lee (Bo Hopkins), the last robber remaining in the bank, shouts to his hostages, "They was singing 'Shall We Gather.' You know that one? Sing it!" – before he shoots them. In *Little Big Man* the Reverend Pendrake's beautiful wife (Faye Dunaway) sings "Shall We Gather at the River?" as she feels up her new ward, Jack Crabb (Dustin Hoffman), in the bathtub ("the greatest bath I ever had," he tells us in voice-over). These moments are also shorthand ways for Peckinpah and Penn to announce their rebellion against the classic Western principles underlying Ford's film. One of *The Wild Bunch*'s arguments, after all, is that community cohesion may be *based* upon violence, not merely created after its eviction. For *Little Big Man,* the angelic woman is an artificial, indeed hypocritical, construct.

If there were so many answers to classic Westerns, it's not just because they can be so evasive. What's "classic" *is* in part the evasions. The visual emptiness can be genuinely evocative but typically at the expense of leaving social issues ambiguous or undiscussed. One way that we might look ahead briefly into the fate of the principles of the classic Western over the next decades, without losing our focus entirely, is to explore how subsequent films pick fights with *My Darling Clementine* – or to glance at a few films that might be considered in that light. We'll take several angles on such films to close out this book.

The earliest set of responses returns to what *My Darling Clementine* represses – or, rather, fails to repress fully: film noir. If the cycle of noir-Westerns in the five years after *Clementine* has one overall claim, it is that it is *not* so easy to evict noir, and thus not so easy to set aside all that the style represents. For instance, to take three quick examples, a number of films use noir to argue that the question "Who do we shoot?" doesn't necessarily have such self-evident answers. In the greatest noir-Western, *Pursued* (1947), that question turns arbitrary, beyond anyone's will, as emblematized by the coin tosses that determine turning points for the characters. For Robert Mitchum's character, Jeb Rand, gunfight violence proves disturbingly unavoidable, and when he turns over the corpse of someone he's been forced to shoot he's likely to stare into the face of a member of his family. Henry King's *The Gunfighter* (1950) uses the figure of Johnny (renamed Jimmy) Ringo, the Clanton-gang outlaw reputed to have spouted Shakespeare and to have tried unsuccessfully to force a showdown on the streets of Tombstone with Wyatt Earp and Doc Holliday in January 1882, a few months after the O.K. Corral shootout.[1] In the film Ringo (Gregory Peck) brags to his son, "The bunch I run with, we'd a spanked Wyatt Earp's britches with his own pistol." But the principle that a final showdown may be a man's duty – as announced in *Clementine* by Wyatt Earp's very name – is shifted in *The Gunfighter* toward film noir's sense of that it may be his doom. Gregory Peck's supercivilized but despondent gunman spends the film lingering morbidly in a small town, regretting his past, watching the swinging pendulum of a barroom clock, and doing everything to avoid the final fight that inevitably brings his death. In something of a mirror image, Quirt Evans, John Wayne's nightmare-haunted gunman in *Angel and the Badman* (1947), is also said to have taken part in the Tombstone fight against the Clantons, but on the side of Wyatt Earp. Thus, within the genre's interfilm arguments, he's a Doc Holliday figure who takes the active option offered by Hamlet's soliloquy, a Doc Holliday who allows *his* nurse (a Quaker daughter, played by Gail Russell) to ease him away from the doom implied by the noir sequence that introduces him. *Angel and the Badman* looks set to conclude with the most traditional of walkdowns in the town's main street, but Wayne turns around to give up his six-gun to the Quakers, and the film's concluding lines are spoken by Marshal Wistful McClintock (Harry Carey, who brings the authority of a Western star back to Ford's 1917 silents): "Only a man who carries a gun ever needs one," he pronounces, as he picks Wayne's forgotten gun from the dust. If this seems a stunningly pacifist argument against the classic Western's assumptions about gunfight solutions, especially in the first film produced by John Wayne, it may be partly a function of its production early in 1946, before the cold war fully kicked in.

The film that seems most elaborately twinned with *My Darling Clementine,* in the sense of arguing against it by an opposite visual movement across common themes, is William Wellman's *Yellow Sky,* released two years later, in 1948. Photographed again by *Clementine*'s Joseph MacDonald, it progresses *into* a film noir, even while it moves from a war film (men and their guns alone in a forbidding landscape) to a postwar one (enter the woman, the town, the temptations to soften). Wellman's film follows a taciturn band of outlaws who make easy pickings of a bank but find themselves chased by a posse into a harsh desert ("Let 'em go," the sheriff says. "Save us the trouble of hangin' 'em"). Near dead, they stumble into the abandoned mining town of Yellow Sky, where they are warily rescued – shown at riflepoint to water – by Anne Baxter (Fig. 54), who with her grandfather are the only residents of the place. (The plot draws from Shakespeare's "Western," *The Tempest* – influenced by early reports from the American colony – where another band with criminal secrets "come unto these yellow sands" to find only an old man and his lovely daughter.)[2] Visually, the film moves from harshly lit, *Greed*-like salt flats into the town, where the scenes grow darker and night-shrouded.

*Yellow Sky*'s apparent paradox is this: The film is brightest at the opening, when the human relationships are nearest savagery. Indeed, the harshest social-Darwinist philosophy is encapsulated in a wry snatch of dialogue delivered in blazing light when the outlaws are near death from thirst in the desert: "Look at that ol' lizard there. He's a heap better off than you, Walrus. Yes sir, a heap better off. That ain't right." Logically, the speaker shoots the offending reptile. Later, when a couple of the more reformable outlaws begin to see value in home and hearth, the shadows lengthen and the camera angles grow stranger (including an under-the-bed shot borrowed from the revelation moment in *Pursued*). But this growing darkness underlines the argument that *Yellow*

**Figure 54.** *Yellow Sky* (1948): Mike (Anne Baxter) defends the ghost town of Yellow Sky from the thirst-tortured outlaws (including Stretch [Gregory Peck], standing).

*Sky* picks with *My Darling Clementine* and suggests what makes the Wellman film more disturbing than the Ford. For *Yellow Sky,* the toughest conflicts are not the gunfights that male warriors fight on their own but the conflicts that come with their entrance into community, with greed over newfound prosperity, and with women – and thus with everything associated with noir. Set two years after the Civil War and filmed two years after World War II, *Yellow Sky* is self-conscious about "postwar" problems. Gramps is willing to give the outlaws the benefit of the doubt; Stretch (Gregory Peck) had, after all, watched his folks fall victim to Quantrill's Raiders along the Kansas border. "Ah, I guess the war has upset a lot of these boys," Gramps says, "set them off on the wrong foot." But once his gold stash is discovered, Gramps is full of darker warnings: "Gold's a mighty dangerous thing if you want it out of plum greediness." As a grizzled fast-talker (played by James Barton, originator onstage of the smooth-talking salesman at the center of Eugene O'Neill's *The Iceman Cometh*), he's twin to Walter Huston and *his* memorable warnings about gold greed in the same year's contemporary noir-Western *The Treasure of the Sierra Madre.* Indeed, noir-Westerns were regularly using greed-for-gold tales to warn of the postwar dangers of unbridled consumption, as again in John Sturges's *The Walking Hills* (1949), where a group of searchers, all hiding guilty secrets, seek wagons of gold lost under sand dunes along the Mexican border. Just as Walter Huston's commitment in *Sierra Madre* to "puttin' back" the mountain (a pantheist ecology that disturbs Humphrey Bogart's character) gives ethical permissibility to gold fever, so in *Yellow Sky* Gramps has a *use* for his gold: to "see the town come back to life again." *Yellow Sky* here locates another historical evasion of *My Darling Clementine.* As the ghost-town setting of *Yellow Sky* melodramatizes, late-nineteenth-century southwestern mining towns were usually not simply boomtowns but boom-*and*-bust towns. Tombstone, recall, had grown rapidly to a population of perhaps eight thousand by the time of the 1881 O.K. Corral shootout – but was down again to fewer than two thousand residents by the 1890 census.[3] *Yellow Sky*'s argument is that the maintenance of community and civilization is altogether more difficult than the one-time homebuilding implied by the "fresh-cut lumber" that Wyatt Earp admires.

Subsequent films used film noir also to argue with the exclusions that the classic Western claimed were necessary for civilization – to argue, that is, with *Clementine*'s "get outta town and stay out" scenes. For instance, *Return of the Bad Men,* a Randolph Scott vehicle from 1948, makes drama from the complications Ford's film evades in its treatment of Chihuahua when *its* ex-lawman turned reluctant new marshal (Scott) allows himself to become less interested in his genteel Anglo fiancée than in a wild outlaw named Cheyenne (Anne Jeffreys). This dangerous woman leads a historically absurd band that unites the Dalton and Younger brothers with Billy the Kid and the Sundance Kid, all of whom she keeps in line despite grumbles from the last about bank robbery being "man's work." Marshal Guthrie Oklahoma's treatment of Cheyenne, like Wyatt's of Chihuahua, is all the more humiliating for its condescending mildness. "You know," he tells her, "I think the best medicine for you would be an old-fashioned spanking." After the marshal nurses her bullet wound, Cheyenne's style begins to turn cooler; she loses most of her Texas accent and finally shifts north even the ethnicity of her name – to "Jeannie McBride."[4] The fiancée's style turns hotter in jealousy, away from flowered hats, and the two women come to look like sisters competing for the marshal's affections. By allowing the convergence of the two types of woman that *Clementine* had kept separate, *Return of the Bad Men* works its narrative into a corner from which only a deus ex machina permits escape. The film has been turning darker – it progresses again into a film noir – until a night-for-night battle in a ghost town ends with the backlit strangulation of

**Figure 55.** *Devil's Doorway* (1950): Men watch a saloon fistfight (55a); and "Broken Lance" Poole (Robert Taylor, in silhouette) meets with his lawyer (Paula Raymond) at his ranch (55b).

Cheyenne/Jeannie by the Sundance Kid, garbed in black and played by Robert Ryan, who brings further noir associations (especially from his anti-Semitic murderer in the previous year's *Crossfire*). *Return of the Bad Men* incidentally argues too against *Clementine*'s eviction of Indian Charlie, because *its* single Native American in town, Grey Eagle, is again played by Geronimo's grandson Charles Stevens. However, his death is now the opposite of any community service: Ryan's Sundance Kid shoots him down unarmed and at point blank for no evident reason beyond the fun of it.

The film unrivaled for employing the full force of noir against the easy "get outta town" kick at Indian Charlie is Anthony Mann's remarkable *Devil's Doorway* (1950). Made before but released two months after Delmer Daves's superficially similar and more commercially influential film about Native American rights, *Broken Arrow,* Mann's first produced Western looks like a transition from his late-1940s criminal-life noirs and remains surprisingly little known, partly because of its seemingly bizarre casting of Robert Taylor as a Shoshone and partly because the noir-Western has seemed a marginal hybrid. Yet, when shown, it's still able to speak to audiences by grappling with questions of racial assimilation and cultural identity far beyond *Broken Arrow*'s sympathetic but sentimental focus on whether whites and Indians can achieve "peace." *Devil's Doorway*'s triangular conflict is among Taylor's "Broken Lance" Poole (returning to Wyoming from the Civil War with a Congressional Medal of Honor), citizens of a claustrophobic, increasingly noir-shadowed town (Fig. 55a), and the lawyer who attempts to negotiate between them. Lance's father warns him (ostensibly in the Shoshone language, until Lance makes him speak English) that with war's end he's just another Indian. But Lance would have it that prewar social problems are solved, and sets out with color-blind capitalist drive to build up his cattle ranch: "No man, red or white, will ever be turned from our door." By fusing elements of Hollywood's tolerance cycle (Jews in 1947's *Crossfire* and *Gentleman's Agreement;* African Americans in 1949's *Intruder in the Dust* and *Pinky*) with the economics of veterans' homecoming (as back in *The Best Years of Our Lives*), Mann's Western becomes the rare Hollywood film to trace racism back to economic anxiety more than to one individual's neurosis. "Nobody likes a rich Indian," a friend warns Lance after a successful cattle sale.

Another slyly iconoclastic feature of *Devil's Doorway* is to make his lawyer a woman (Fig. 55b). Historically, she's probably an anachronism (there were no women lawyers in Wyoming before 1874),[5] but her sex also codifies for the genre her optimism ("I believe in people, Lance"). Her professional competence, however, is finally no match for the law's tilt. And likewise Lance's bright, idyllic valley is a setup; this is another Western pointedly *not* able to escape from noir (in hard-edged images and unsettling angles from master cinematographer John Alton in his last film with Mann). The town defeats both Lance and his lawyer: Their romance remains taboo; her humanist faith proves unfounded; he dies facing the U.S. Cavalry, his Civil War uniform an emblem of failed integration. Lance's grave prescience – "Maybe it would have worked in a hundred years" – is the bone thrown by the Western hero's regular biblical burden of foresight.

Film noir continues its love–hate relationship with the classic Western into the fifties. But one problem in moving with this topic too far ahead of the immediate postwar years is that although film noir does symptomize a changed mood, it also exaggerates it, as films came to target more specialized audiences. In the postwar forties, Ford's *My Darling Clementine* and Wellman's *Yellow Sky* could set up a dialogue over the nature of the peacetime transition to homebuilding. When Wellman in 1954 tried something along the same lines in *Track of the Cat,* the result is incoherently ferocious *and* domestic.[6] One mad extreme among these schizophrenic domestic noirs is the late B-Western *Crooked River* (1951). An outlaw helps his sister with the dishes while whining about his unregenerate gang, on whom he keeps an eye through a telescope installed over the kitchen sink. Soon a rebellious underling snarls to him, "So long; I don't think you'll be seeing anymore," and tosses lye in his face. This gets us into *The Big Heat*'s domestic terror and another noir argument altogether.

# 25. The Return of the Earps

The skinny fellow walked quickly to me and staring coldly from under his straight black eyebrows, says, "You have an objection?"

I allowed I did not, but I also requested he state a reason why in the god-damned hell he thought I might.

"You just spoke my name," he says.

"I don't know your name," says I.

"It," he says, "is Earp."

"Oh," I says, laughing, "what I done was belch."

He knocked me down.

Thomas Berger, *Little Big Man*[1]

At the box office, *My Darling Clementine* was a modest hit. It had cost slightly over \$2 million – expensive for a Western of the time – and grossed \$4½ million in its first release. It ranks among the top forty most successful Westerns, in inflation-adjusted rental-income dollars, but among 1946 releases alone it falls below *Duel in the Sun, California,* and *The Virginian.*[2] Its commercial reception was thus neither so spectacular as to call forth any cycle of slavish imitations nor so poor as to make box-office poison of Wyatt Earp. The Earp legend reappears with a certain regularity throughout the next twenty-five years and then makes a late return in two Westerns among the few produced in the 1990s. Although Earp's was the *type* of legend favored by filmmakers who clung to older formulas, the best postwar variants answer a few more questions evaded by the classic Western.

A full chronology of Wyatt Earp films after *My Darling Clementine* would begin unpromisingly with the 1953 remake of *Law and Order,* in which Ronald Reagan repeats Walter Huston's old role as Frame Johnson, again the ex-marshal (from Dodge City and Abilene) reluctant to take up the badge, until a brother is murdered. It steals from *My Darling Clementine* only to forget – or for legal reasons to pretend to forget – what made the film worth the compliment, even within the dialogue. Recall that in *Clementine*, Clanton bullwhips his sons to bring home his anti-Hamlet moral, "When you pull a gun, kill a man"; in *Law and Order*, Preston Foster's Kurt Durling punches his son to reinforce *his* slogan, "When you start a play, finish it." The complicated plot can't cover a slack style, which has none of the gangster grit that made the 1932 version compelling. Memories of Ronald Reagan's stint in the 1980s in "that job" – as he later referred to his presidency – throw up further barriers now to the film: "Maybe I shoulda gone into politics," a condemned outlaw muses to Reagan.

Less unwatchable is another 1953 film, *Powder River* (directed by Louis King), the closest of the follow-ups to being a strict remake of *My Darling Clementine.* If no less an admirer of the classic Western than Robert Warshow preferred *Powder River* to the Ford version, perhaps it's because the later Western spells out some of *Clementine*'s visual arguments. Warshow's claim in his celebrated 1954 essay "The Westerner" is that *Powder River* is "more concerned with drama than with style," and that is true enough – although "style," as we've been observing, may make for what's worth savoring in the classic Western.[3] Once again Darryl Zanuck had dusted off Stuart Lake's *Wyatt Earp, Frontier Marshal,* sending it for this update to Daniel Mainwaring (credited as "Geoffrey Homes"). The result is as if *Clementine* had been directed by a less talented Howard Hawks, with *Clementine*'s first terse barroom confrontation between Doc and the unarmed Wyatt ("Marshal, draw!" "Can't.") expanded, with echoes of *Red River,* into a masculine repartee over whether the Wyatt figure is "good enough." It's *Clementine* with the emptiness talked out: "Are you nervous?" Doc (Cameron Mitchell) inquires of the Wyatt figure (called "Chino Bull," played by Rory Calhoun) as he pushes a six-gun into his ribs. "If you cock it, I'll get nervous," he responds. Similarly *Powder River* reinserts those talky emotional scenes given to Clementine only in the shooting script for Ford's film: The Clementine figure – renamed, for the 1950s, Debbie (!) – breaks into sobs when Doc rejects her and rides the buckboard out with Chino Bull to mourn at the graveside (of his friend, not his brother).[4]

*Powder River*'s untroubled revision of *My Darling Clementine* arises too from its replacement of Ford's brooding black-and-white with a no-

nonsense Technicolor. Never shrouded in noir darkness, this town begins bright and slick – just the place for Chino Bull to stop off for his favorite snack, canned peaches. The later film is equally unbothered by dark races. For reasons suggested earlier, Henry Fonda kicked Indian Charlie not just from *Clementine* but from the Earp story line forever, and for a time after *Broken Arrow* ethnic anonymity kept the racial "problem" from cluttering classic plot lines. Thus the drunken gunman in *Powder River* is no longer an Indian, just as the Chihuahua figure is lightened into "Frenchie." Gone too is the *Hamlet* text and the questions it would bring of hesitation and conscience. (The touring actor offers up some poor juggling as gunpoint entertainment.) Even Doc's return to surgery proves successful this time around. One curious alteration, however, refuses to smooth over tensions and highlights an evasion within *My Darling Clementine.* What if, true to history, Doc Holliday had survived the gunfight? In *Powder River* he does, and thus the Clementine figure's two surviving suitors find themselves in a second showdown (doubly motivated by this Doc's criminal doings). The bind into which the plot line has worked itself is underscored by the unintentional comedy of the extrication: Doc shoots the gun from Chino Bull's hand but then proceeds to die of a fast-acting brain tumor! The ambiguous melancholy of *Clementine*'s coda is exchanged for the Owen Wister option: The Clementine figure settles down with Chino Bull in their nice clean town.

Jacques Tourneur's *Wichita,* two years later in 1955, goes after a more significant question evaded by *My Darling Clementine.* Ford's Tombstone, one recalls, is first glimpsed in rampant boomtown energy. What, we are left wondering, has happened to all that activity? Where are those men in serapes and women in mantillas spending their silver dollars, after Fonda's Wyatt cleans out the town? The argument that *Wichita* picks with *Clementine* is economic – taking capitalism for the ground on which frontier issues should be fought. Earp (Joel McCrea) is picked up earlier in his purported career (verified authentic by sixty-five-year-old Stuart Lake as "Technical Advisor"), but the town-taming pattern is the same further east. Rather than subduing a saloon gunslinger, this Wyatt's first-day-in-town heroism comes in foiling a robbery at the bank where he has gone to deposit his $2,400 savings. His refusal of the badge comes on these terms: "I'm honored, Mr. Mayor, but I'm a businessman not a lawman." The townsfolk show awe again, but it arises now from finding one businessman who does not consider himself a gambler, and thus to find in Wyatt the first businessman not to want to open a saloon. He has thoughts of starting a stage line, but the random shooting of a child by riotous cowboys convinces him to take the job as marshal. In responding to the violence with arrests of cowboys, Wyatt calms the town, cleans it up, makes the streets safe for children. But this classic resolution is exactly where *Wichita* locates its conflict. In cleaning up the town, Wyatt puts the lie to the town's reputation – "Wine, Women, and Wichita" – and thus stunts the cowboy commerce that, we learn, was fueling the building boom in evidence. The increasingly sinister "simple businessmen of Wichita" now see Wyatt's clean-up as far too drastic: "It's just a bit difficult for you to see the business side, that's all." The businessmen turn out to be genteel brothers of the slimy hotel clerk in *High Noon* who preferred his town overrun with outlaws because it was also "busier." And, as in *High Noon,* soon "the whole town's against" Wyatt in *Wichita.* Only with the help of his brothers and Bat Masterson can he establish *another* business ethic: that the interests of *good* capitalists and citizens are identical. Families too have money to spend. The theme song chirps, "No one fooled with the marshal of Wichita/And today it's a very nice town." The film's argument, sadly, plays better on paper than on the screen, with McCrea distractingly old for the lovesick Wyatt as written, and Jacques Tourneur (a noir master in *Out of the Past* and *Cat People*) paralyzed either by the Technicolor CinemaScope or Allied Artists' minuscule budget, which allowed only for north-of-L.A. locations.[5]

Commercially, the most successful version of the Earp legend was John Sturges's *Gunfight at the O.K. Corral* (1957), its episodic story line linked by the Frankie Laine–sung best-selling ballad and bloated with dialogue from Leon Uris, of "epic" novel fame. Particularly grim in this *Rebel without a Cause* era is the infusion of pop-Freudian phallicism ("It's not that I wanna be a gunfighter exactly, it's just that I get lonely sometimes"). But if *Gunfight at the O.K. Corral* is the Western gone defensive with overwrought explanations of motives, Sam Fuller's *Forty Guns* the same year opened a new line of Westerns, more fascinated with flamboyantly exploding the classic ideals than with justifying them. If *Gunfight* was the box-office success, *Forty Guns* proved the influential one, alluded to in films by everyone from Sergio Leone to Jean-Luc Godard, even if it's undeservedly forgotten today. Fuller's sullen Earp figure, Griff Bonnell (Barry Sullivan), is the U.S. Marshal who arrives with his two brothers to clean out the troubles in Tombstone. *Forty Guns* crossbreeds *Clementine* motifs with the high-camp matriarchal Western in which a self-made woman's sexuality erupts as a craving for domination – played here by Barbara Stanwyck and best remembered through Joan Crawford's saloon owner in Nicholas Ray's *Johnny Guitar* (1954). Where Ford's camera style in *Clementine* was unrelentingly static, Fuller's in *Forty Guns* is obsessively mobile. Where Ford's argument was cerebral, Fuller's is carnal and provides a demonstration of how to use fifties pop-Freudianism in entertainingly outrageous ways, right from the opening "High-Ridin' Woman with a Whip" theme song, sung by naked men in a row of bathtubs spread across the CinemaScope frame. As in *Clementine,* Fuller's Earp figure is pushed into a main-street showdown by the death of his brother at the hands of a brother from his antagonist's family, but the situation now separates the lawman from the law. In the iconoclastic shootout, Stanwyck's brother uses her as a shield, secure in the genre convention that the Western lawman never shoots a woman. The surprise on his face, just before his own death, matches that of the audience. (She'll recover from her bullet wound.) One of Fuller's topics here is the escalating appeal of violence. The marshal turns scapegoat, a self-described "freak," but he cannot persuade his surviving youngest brother to become an unglamorous "agricultural cowboy."

A decade later, in 1967, John Sturges takes up the story again in *Hour of the Gun.* Ostensibly it's a sequel, opening where his *Gunfight at the O.K. Corral* left off – with the gunfight. The new argument is that the locale for the West's true power struggle was never the street but the courthouse; and this is another historically valid complaint against the evasions of *My Darling Clementine* (even if *Hour of the Gun*'s grander claim – "This picture is based on fact. This is the way it happened" – proves bogus). Both Wyatt (James Garner) and a thoughtful Ike Clanton (Robert Ryan) are masters at legal maneuvering, and each avoids conviction in their court trials early in the film. What makes Ike the figure of evil is less Robert Ryan's noir persona than his "buying" law and murdering the voters' choice: "I won, didn't I?" asks newly elected Marshal Morgan Earp (Sam Melville) as he bleeds to death on a pool table. Both Fonda's Wyatt and this one are legalists; both are careful to read arrest warrants before they begin blazing away. But if Fonda's Wyatt wasn't above the showdown scheme, he was closer to the spirit of justice. James Garner's Wyatt skips moral shadings and shoots down a boy paid fifty dollars by the Clantons to keep watch. The ethical switchover between Wyatt and Doc (begun in *Gunfight at the O.K. Corral:* "At bottom, we're the same, Earp") is nearly complete. This Doc Holliday (Jason Robards Jr.), though confined to a tubercular sanitarium, is livelier than Wyatt and diagnoses his friend's despondency as arising from his abandonment of "the rules," the only thing that had sustained Wyatt's conception of himself.

Doc might have made this argument about the Western genre itself, which proved not infinitely flexible once the classic Western's rules were flouted by filmmakers, as the 1971 film *Doc* inadvertently demonstrated. Directed by Frank Perry, *Doc* fills in *Clementine*'s blankness with realpolitik, an angle explained by screenwriter Pete Hamill:

> I loved John Ford more than anyone else, for his stubborn belief in what he did, for the sheer pictorial beauty of his films, for the splendid economy of his craft. . . . But I didn't really begin to think about writing a western until I came into contact for the first time with Lyndon Johnson. I went to Vietnam in 1966. . . . I started to realize that within Lyndon Johnson, somewhere deep inside that darkly brilliant, Machiavellian, boorish and devious man, there was a western unspooling. . . . The Americans were some collective version of Wyatt Earp.[6]

This Doc (Stacy Keach) responds to one of Wyatt's many underhanded schemes by commenting, "We sound like bad people, Wyatt." "We are, John," agrees Wyatt (Harris Yulin), who turns political opportunist, gladhanding his way from U.S. Marshal (who has little jurisdiction in Tombstone) to town sheriff (a position lucrative for its bribes and kickbacks). When *Doc*'s Wyatt repeats the words that Old Man Clanton used in *Clementine* to describe Tombstone – "a wide-open town" – he means them in the identical sense, that the town is available for exploitation. Thus Wyatt exchanges moral position not only with Doc but with Clanton himself. In place of the private graveside vow to his dead brother in *Clementine,* this Wyatt turns the O.K. Corral showdown to public political speechifying: "My brother's death will not have been in vain if. . . ." As the Vietnam *Clementine,* there now *is* plenty of blood on Doc's handkerchief.

It took more than two decades to resurrect sufficient heroism for the legend to be recounted again on film. Of the competing retellings of the Earp legend in the 1990s, *Tombstone* (1993, directed by George P. Cosmatos, with Kurt Russell as Wyatt) and *Wyatt Earp* (1994, directed by Lawrence Kasdan, with Kevin Costner), the latter was the commercial extravaganza, but it is *Tombstone* that survives with something of a cult following for its lively wit, so rare in Westerns of any era, and for Val Kilmer's droll Doc Holliday. Regarding *Wyatt Earp,* the industry trade paper *Variety* opened its review with the deadpan observation, "If you are going to ask an audience to sit through a three-hour, nine-minute rendition of an oft-told story, it would help to have a strong point-of-view on your material and an urgent reason to relate it."[7] And it is true that this last theatrical Wyatt Earp film to date is the ultimate anti-*Clementine* in the sense of making painfully explicit everything that was evocatively suggestive in Ford's film. But *Wyatt Earp* is not without its own argument against the classic Western, one that it shares to some extent with the argument of *Tombstone.* That argument begins by shunning all of the questions about formation of *community* that had centrally animated *My Darling Clementine* and then been argued over by so many Westerns of the fifties (as we noticed in connection with *High Noon, Rio Bravo,* and *Bad Day at Black Rock*). In place of the possibilities for people to work together to create a society is an obsession with the isolated unit of the family.[8]

*Tombstone*'s Wyatt wants his brothers "to stop wandering and start to be a family," but that film at least has one eye beyond the nuclear family into something like blood brotherhood in its repeated links of Old West outlaws with modern urban gangs. *Wyatt Earp* begins more insistently with the Earp family patriarch (Gene Hackman) regaling Wyatt and his brothers around the dinner table: "The closer you keep your family the better. They're the only ones you can rely on. Remember this, all of you. Nothing counts so much as blood. The rest are just strangers." The kids smile at this; they've heard it all before; but the film proceeds to develop the idea with immense solemnity. Notwithstanding its three-plus hours and $60 million budget, *Wyatt Earp* cannot make room for a single scene that portrays a community larger than immediate family and friends, and its disinterest in community is reinforced by the episodic structure that tracks Wyatt Earp though every famous frontier town in his career. What drama the film has comes from squabbles within the family – especially by the shrill womenfolk – and from the question of whether (male) "friendship" might slightly expand the boundaries of family. "Everybody who's not family, get out!" shouts Wyatt through the confusion after the O.K. Corral shootout. An escape is offered by one woman: "I'll be your family, Wyatt. . . . We'll make our own place, where no one will find us." *Tombstone* and *Wyatt Earp* both conclude with information about this ostensibly saving union between Wyatt and Josephine. "In forty-seven years they never left each other's side," *Tombstone*'s narration tells us. "Their marriage lasted for forty-seven years," reads *Wyatt Earp*'s final onscreen text. This is Hollywood heroism for the 1990s, even if it wasn't exactly true.[9] One of the points of the subtle showdown scheme in *My Darling Clementine* was to suggest a productive symbiosis between family and community, but the two 1990s Earp films fall back on a more dispiriting claim: "Family values" serve as an escape from demands of community and from history itself.

# 26. Ford, Fonda, and the Death of the Classic Western

It seems to me we were all a bunch of romantic fools. . . .
Henry Fonda in *My Name Is Nobody* (1973)

In the figure of Wyatt Earp, John Ford offers up a hero, someone closer to being a Lincoln in the West than to a "savage." Ford's Wyatt is already famous before the Earps hit Tombstone, and Doc, on meeting him, suggests what he's famous *for* is moral righteousness: "You haven't taken it into your head to deliver us from all evil?" "I hadn't thought of it quite like that," Wyatt responds, "but it ain't a bad idea; it's what I'm getting paid for." A marshal would be paid presumably to enforce ordinances, but Wyatt's easy acceptance of the quasi-religious extensions of his job fits peacekeeping in the post–World War II era. In 1949, the U.S. Supreme Court shifted the requirements for government suppression of free speech from the need to show "a clear and present danger" to the presence of "grave evil."[1] Where Wyatt threatens for a time to prove less than ideal is in the Hamlet-like inaction that overtakes him, and if his delays get his second brother killed, it's more than a threat. But rather than anything in the script, it's Henry Fonda's aloof way of carrying himself that hints at something cold within Wyatt's heroism. John Ford himself seems increasingly to have viewed Fonda that way, or to have come to realize that the actor's gravity could be used more critically. If Ford crafted something like his own "responses" to *My Darling Clementine,* it is not only because he never accepted the final version of that film as his own but also because he, and America, had moved on.

From that angle, the first and most complex panel of Ford's loose "cavalry trilogy," *Fort Apache* (1948), suggests *My Darling Clementine*'s ideal gone awry – by pushing further that threat of disengagement within Henry Fonda's performance style. Fonda's Wyatt Earp had put his critique of the land into words in *Clementine*'s first scene: "Sure is rough looking country." Fonda opens *Fort Apache* with that critique as he stares out from a stagecoach: "What a country!" He remains the scrupulous traveler, never exactly at home in the wildness of the West. But this aloofness from his surroundings holds problems undiscussed in *Clementine,* where Fonda's character had to lead only by example, not by command.[2] As a cavalry officer sent from the East to oversee a western outpost, Fonda's inflexible character in *Fort Apache* can appreciate a paper on Genghis Khan's tactics but not Captain Kirby York's (John Wayne's) practical knowledge of the Apaches. That Fonda's Lieutenant Colonel Thursday keeps mangling the names of his Irish-American troops is a first clue, in Ford's universe, to deadly limitations.

*Fort Apache* ends with a disconnected coda that has proven of ongoing critical fascination. It takes place some years after the events recounted in the first two hours of the film, which had climaxed with, essentially, Custer's Last Stand – Fonda's character having, in his stated search for "glory," taken most of his troops with him to death at the hands of Indian warriors. In the coda, survivor John Wayne is talking with a group of newspapermen, who ask about Fonda's character – "the hero of the school books" – and about the celebrated painting of "Thursday's Charge." Notwithstanding Thursday's martinetlike actions, the years have, if not as he intended, fulfilled his dreams of glory. "He must have been a great man and a great soldier," comments one of the reporters. Surprisingly, Thursday's old antagonist York doesn't disabuse them, although he diverts discussion to the heroism of regular army troopers. Ford's stance seems to be this: If heroes don't live up to our myths, it's essential to reinvent them or, strictly speaking, to let them be invented by journalists whose business is such manufacture.[3]

One precursor to *Fort Apache*'s story line can be found back in Raoul Walsh's *They Died with Their Boots On* (1941), which, while not uncritical of Errol Flynn's Custer, credits him with winning the Civil War (his actions turn Gettysburg into a Northern victory) and with *knowingly* sacrificing his life for his country at Little Bighorn. His example teaches even a sneaky gunrunner (Arthur Kennedy) that there is something worth more than money: "Glory." You *can* take *that* with you. *Fort Apache*'s argument is more complex: It simultaneously reveals the deceit behind the ideals of the classic Western *and* reinforces the need for such ideals. *Fort Apache* stands alone among Westerns of the 1940s for its bold argument: Lies (even to the extent of a cover-up of military crimes) are one acceptable price to pay for the ideal of heroism and thus for the mythology that (presumably) binds together a nation. In this, *Fort Apache* proposes another question disguised by the blankness of the classic Western: Could heroism itself be a sleight of hand, offered to personalize and thus distract from failures of policy? – or even of ideology? Heroism here begins to look like a magician's trick, something to hold up with one hand while hiding history with the other.

Wyatt Earp as historical distraction? One would have said that this could never be *Ford's* Earp had the director not come around to worrying over just these issues in the one significant film portrait of Earp left unmentioned previously: James Stewart's wry Wyatt Earp in Ford's own *Cheyenne Autumn* (1964). That film is sometimes taken to be Ford's flip-flop revisionism, an apologia to Native Americans for their treatment in his earlier Westerns, an impression Ford himself promoted: "I've killed more Indians than Custer, Beecher and Chivington put together."[4] But Ford had also been in the advance guard for Hollywood's racial-tolerance cycles by his treatment of the Apache in *Fort Apache,* in which, whatever the final mythologizing, Cochise is the honorable figure, and responsibility for the massacre falls squarely on Fonda's cavalry commandant. Ford follows a skepticism long-standing among Irish Americans against blaming the Indian nations for their own demise.[5] Similarly the Wyatt Earp in his 1964 Western has also been mistaken as a flip-flop of the heroic portrait in *My Darling Clementine.* But Ford's revision is more measured: Wyatt is *still* admired, though in a significantly different way.

When we meet Marshal Wyatt Earp in *Cheyenne Autumn,* he's settled into a "little friendly game of poker" not unlike the "quiet game of poker" in *Clementine,* although this one is in Dodge City in 1878, a few years earlier in his life. Once again, Wyatt is contemplating a tophatted card cheat while again half-distracted by the loose woman behind him. The *tone* of the scene has turned tall-tale comic. Wyatt is paying no attention at all to Dodge City's mayor, who is shouting incoherently about the Cheyenne threat to the town, left unprotected by Army troops gone in search of them. Instead, Wyatt is apparently meditating on the deck of cards in his hand and – in James Stewart's stuttering deliberation – concluding that it "feels light," that it must have only fifty-one cards. While the mayor rants about the peril to women and children,

Wyatt confers with Doc Holliday (Arthur Kennedy), who advises, in reference to the nervous card sharp, "Wyatt, if we shoot him, we won't have anyone left to play with" (Fig. 56).

In its hour-and-a-quarter of running time before this Dodge City interlude, *Cheyenne Autumn* has portrayed a genocide by bureaucratic neglect, by disease, and by starvation. Wyatt Earp seems here concerned only with his gambling profits. When the mayor frantically loads an ammunition wagon in preparation to fight the Cheyenne, Wyatt argues, "Now Mayor, hold on, hold on. I've just been thinkin'. Seein' as how you control all of the gambling in this town and I get ten percent of the take, just exactly what would happen to my livelihood if you went out and got yourself shot?" In the context of the solemn pathos of the Cheyennes' long march north off their reservation, reluctantly pursued by duty-bound cavalry, this Wyatt Earp could sound exactly like the crafty Earp of *Doc.* Perhaps this is why even a critic so long attuned to Ford's sensibility as Joseph McBride refers to the character as "Ford's own portrayal of a thoroughly corrupt Wyatt Earp."[6] But to see James Stewart's Earp that way is, I think, to forget Ford's Irish-American fondness for politicians' blarney and for their roundabout manipulation of citizens toward their own best interests, as in *The Last Hurrah* (1958) and the film Ford often cited as favorite among his own, *The Sun Shines Bright* (1953). Ford's admiration of Wyatt Earp this time is as a man whose Western style – a deadpan Mark Twain or Bret Harte style, not a straight-faced Owen Wister or Fenimore Cooper one – masks his refusal to get caught up in anti-Indian hysteria. This is an Earp who is still eminently practical and apparently invincible. He is forced to shoot a loud cowboy, without rising from the poker table, and gives a fine look of stage petulance at the burn hole his derringer made in shooting through the pocket of his linen suit. Only a flash of fury – a James Stewart mastery that the cooler Fonda never approached – after the cowboy has thrown a Cheyenne scalp across his cards, breaks Wyatt's mask of unconcern. He's sensible, folksy, invincible with a gun, but classic heroics have been replaced by something drier. Far be it from this Marshal Earp to refuse to lead the drunken townsfolk, if they are determined to fight Injuns. But, as Wyatt and Doc ride from town (in a buggy, the West's woman's vehicle), their banter is mocking, arch, and ironic. Doc asks Wyatt:

"General, do you mind confiding your plan of campaign to your chief-of-staff?"

**Figure 56.** Ignoring Dodge City's mayor in *Cheyenne Autumn* (1964): from left, a gambler (John Carradine, in black tophat), the mayor (Judson Pratt), Wyatt Earp (James Stewart), and Doc Holliday (Arthur Kennedy).

"Not at all, not at all. From which direction are these bloodthirsty Cheyenne savages approaching?"

"Southwest, of course."

"And in which direction are we headed?"

"Northeast."

"That's my plan of campaign."

It is not that Wyatt Earp doesn't remain admirable, but he has drifted far from the center of history. Although now almost helpless to alter history's sweep, he functions within a comic-relief interlude that is quite pointed, and his achievement has been to make the would-be warrior townsfolk as irrelevant as he himself has become.[7] For larger heroism, *Cheyenne Autumn* searches, for a Western, into a very odd corner indeed. In Washington, D.C., it locates Secretary of the Interior Carl Schurz (Edward G. Robinson), who fights to keep the Indian Bureau out of the control of the "dollar patriots" of business expansion.[8]

There's little denying that *Cheyenne Autumn*, except for its Wyatt Earp interlude, is a failure as drama, sapped by CinemaScope pictorialism and as lacking in energy as the decimated Indians themselves. Almost everybody has good intentions – the Cheyenne, the cavalry, the Washington bureaucracy, Wyatt Earp – and Ford sets himself an insurmountable problem in trying to make movie adventure out of exterminationist policy. Still, the audacity of the argument is a surprise. This is, after all, the story of a long march not just for civil rights but for welfare. The Native Americans are demanding a handout, and they deserve it. *Cheyenne Autumn* looks like the Western-film version of the last event of consensus liberalism before the sixties exploded: the 1963 civil rights march on Washington, which President John F. Kennedy coopted and promoted.[9] Partly due to their shared Irish ancestry, John Ford had been a vocal supporter of Kennedy, who was assassinated while Ford was on location in Monument Valley for *Cheyenne Autumn*. The film's argument is admirable certainly, but the evident irrelevance of individual heroism in 1963 seems to have left Ford with nothing heartfelt to fall back upon.

For a decade, from 1939 to 1948, John Ford had found in Henry Fonda an ideal actor to incarnate and then to question American heroism, ending with the argument of *Fort Apache*. The team might well have advanced this line of thinking, but Fonda quit films for, as it turned out, seven years after 1948 following *Fort Apache* and his stage success on Broadway in *Mister Roberts*. Perhaps there was also some connection between that decision and the way Fonda was treated by Ford, onscreen and off. The more Ford stressed the disengagement within Fonda's characters, the more disrespectfully he seems to have treated him on the set. Their association came to an irreparable end after a conference in the midst of Fonda's return to filmmaking and to Ford for the adaptation of *Mister Roberts*, when Ford punched or pushed Fonda – hard enough to knock him to the floor by some accounts. (The film's direction was subsequently completed by Mervyn LeRoy and Joshua Logan.)[10]

Still, the classic-Western arguments laid out by Ford and Fonda within the emptiness of *My Darling Clementine* didn't end with a sock in the nose. Ford continued one line of elaboration, without Fonda, in *Chey-*

*enne Autumn.* As we have seen, other directors developed arguments around other Wyatt Earps, and for other Westerns the argument of film noir wasn't so easily exiled. A fourth line of response, Henry Fonda's own, may be the most complex. Unlike John Wayne, Fonda was not so exclusively associated with the Western genre, nor was he in the postwar years so politically conservative as most of John Ford's loose "stock company" of actors. For both reasons, Fonda's career was not so invested in maintaining the genre's classic certainties. For a sense of this, one need only listen in interviews to Fonda's genuine pleasure at the ways in which the best Western directors after his return to filmmaking in 1955 used his persona to undercut expectations, as in the way that Sergio Leone crafted Fonda's unforgettable entrance into *Once upon a Time in the West* (1968):

> If you remember my first scene, you get to the family, and they are happy, preparing some kind of picnic outside of their farmhouse. There's the father and the 18-year-old daughter and a 16-year-old son, and an 8- or 9-year-old son, and they are just as happy as you have ever seen a family be. They're piling food out there and suddenly they look up because there is silence. . . . But suddenly there is a shot and the girl falls with a bullet right there. The father looks up and then goes down. The boy, who has been out to get the buggy . . . pivots off and he falls dead. Then out of the house comes a boy about seven. He's carrying a couple jugs of wine or something and he looks up – and now you see the reverse – and you film the sagebrush and you see five sinister characters that have long dusters on and hats, and they all have side arms, either rifles or guns, and you can't recognize them; they're just converging from five different points very slowly toward the camera. Now you go back to one of these guys toward the little boy, who is just standing there with his dead father and his dead sister and his dead brother and looking up, and now this man stops – and the camera comes around very slowly until you can recognize the killer – and Sergio Leone was waiting for the audience to gasp, "Jesus Christ, it's Henry Fonda!"[11]

Fonda's associations as a Western-film hero – associations formed largely by Ford – were available for reuse or inversion by subsequent directors. And, as Fonda's glee in telling this story suggests, he was an enthusiastic collaborator in the revisions.

Take a simple example: Joseph Mankiewicz's *There Was a Crooked Man . . .* (1970), a striking moralist fable whose iconoclasm with Western conventions provoked surprisingly vitriolic outrage, ranging from the era's most prominent reviewer, Pauline Kael ("a new low in cynicism"), to Western novelist and scriptwriter Brian Garfield ("monumentally distasteful" and "nauseating").[12] The first question with which it toys is one unthinkable in *My Darling Clementine:* What if Fonda were to *lose* in that scene where he demonstrates invincibility by going into a frontier saloon to evict a wild gunslinger? "You're in a little trouble," Fonda says to him civilly, "Don't make it worse. Give me your gun." Here something of the punch comes from the scene's speed: The drunk outlaw responds to this speech by pulling out his gun – and shooting Fonda. Cut. The town elders' new worry is how to get rid of a "crippled" marshal, useless in the West.

This is a vicious little joke, but one worth telling for its serious edge. We *do* take invincibility for granted in the Western lawman when incarnated by Henry Fonda, who had walked into the saloon with his usual unhurried and understated assurance. Thus the little moment of shock, even in 1970. Of course, by that year, audiences were perfectly aware that heroism wasn't what it used to be, and the casting as the drunk gunman of Warren Oates, an actor so key to Sam Peckinpah's vision, suggests the defeat of the classic Western by grubbier new styles. (*There Was a Crooked Man* . . . was written by the team of David Newman and Robert Benton, celebrated for their era-defining *Bonnie and Clyde* three years earlier.) The coda of *Fort Apache* had been several times replayed, but shifted from Ford's balance of deconstruction *and* reinforcement into ham-fisted irony. Burt Kennedy and Niksa Fulgosi's *The Deserter* (also 1970), for instance, ends by awarding *its* cavalry officer an official "heroic death" as cover for atrocities, even while he lives on secretly. The collapse of Wyatt Earp's heroism had become more evident with in each postwar Earp variant through the unsatisfying *Doc* in 1971, where leveling disgust and soft-focus romanticism replace any interest in the process of mythmaking. Several of Henry Fonda's Westerns develop from *My Darling Clementine* on a divergent track, arguing against Ford's film by exploring the social interactions of violence with *fame* – which is to say mythic heroism deconstructed by recognition of its human authors. The subject is touched on in a number of Fonda's later Westerns, including Anthony Mann's *The Tin Star* (1957) and Burt Kennedy's noir-inflected *Welcome to Hard Times* (1967), but the most revealing two are *Warlock* (1959) and *My Name Is Nobody* (1973).

*Warlock* is the worried, liberal response to the classic Western. It sets up its situation as if it can be played out in the same manner as *My Dar-*

*ling Clementine.* Henry Fonda is again a fast-gun marshal, Clay Blaisdell, known again for having cleaned up a string of towns throughout the West. When the citizens of the town of Warlock recover from cowering behind shutters after watching yet another of their weak town sheriffs run out by the ruling outlaw gang, they determine to hire Blaisdell, who soon arrives with his sidekick, Tom Morgan, played by Anthony Quinn. Fonda's marshal is the figure of true fame (he's had a book written about him) whereas Quinn's Morgan (a bit put out at having been the subject only of magazine articles) is something of a Doc Holliday, a heavy-drinking gambler, quick to anger. As he rides into Warlock, Fonda carries himself heavier, a bit wearier, with considerably more wariness, but with as much assurance as when he entered Tombstone in *Clementine.* Completely confident, he again comes out on top in the opening saloon confrontation. If we think we know this classic lawman, that is part of the film's trick. The new marshal is ready to clean up the town, and the film never suggests he couldn't do so. However, director Edward Dmytryk (drawing largely on Oakley Hall's well-regarded novel) comes to focus on the nature of "law and order" imposed in such a way – which is to say that this film sees trouble at exactly the point where *My Darling Clementine* assumes a solution. To dramatize this, Dmytryk adds another character on the side of the law, one who accepts, when all the other townsfolk refuse, a job as deputy – Johnny Gannon. The casting in this role of Richard Widmark, with his antiheroic noir associations, reinforces how markedly this third lawman is *not* larger than life. He has begun the film as a lowly member of the outlaw gang, tolerated because he's a brother of the leader but usually to be found unconscious beside the horse trough or drinking to erase the torment of his participation in a massacre of Mexicans. But, whatever his personal weakness, he's part of the local community, and strong enough later to tell his brother, "I'm the law."

A hero isn't someone who has performed a socially beneficial deed but rather one who is *known* for such a deed. *My Darling Clementine* had touched on this principle with its usual shorthand, when the camera remained fixed on Old Man Clanton's double take as Wyatt Earp announces his name. But *Warlock* refuses to let the convention stay so blank. When the outlaw gang rides in for the showdown with Gannon – wounded in his gun hand after the gang had pinned it to a table with a knife – Fonda's Blaisdell is set to back him up. But sidekick Morgan (Quinn) pulls a gun on him to keep him in his hotel room, explaining apologetically that it's necessary for Gannon to be shot down so that the town will recognize its need for Blaisdell's heroics: "After he's dead they'll come beggin' for you to protect 'em." But Morgan's scheme backfires when Gannon, surprisingly, wins the showdown, backed by a few town citizens, thus reinforcing a sense that "the law" is exactly as strong as the support it receives from the community. By placing the two lawmen side by side, *Warlock* dramatizes the long-held recognition – indeed, Aristotle argues it in *The Politics* – that the lone hero hasn't the qualities that make for "the good citizen."[13] Fonda's determination to resign his now-unnecessary job doesn't reckon with his sidekick's determination to continue to manufacture a hero. Quinn's character drunkenly proclaims his own skill ("I'm the all-time champion cowboy killer!"), calls himself by his magazine name ("The Black Rattlesnake"), and fires randomly at citizens ("I'll kill anything that moves!") until Blaisdell has little choice but to shoot his friend down – which is exactly Morgan's backup plan. "I won," he whispers, dying, having forced Fonda's marshal to extend his town-saving reputation.

Edward Dmytryk knew quite a lot about the complexities of heroism from his imprisonment as one of the "Hollywood Ten" and subsequent recantation, but *Warlock*'s sophisticated deconstruction of heroism is ultimately subverted by its overcomplicated plot line and plodding visuals.[14] (The film has none of *Clementine*'s way with physicality and landscape, notwithstanding cinematography again by Joseph MacDonald.) The argument about the manufacture of heroism is, however, carried forward with renewed verve in *My Name Is Nobody*. Where *Warlock* is heavily worried, *Nobody* is lightly witty. Direction of the multinational 1973 European production is credited to solely to Tonino Valerii, but everywhere is the master touch of Sergio Leone (credited onscreen as producer and with the original "idea"), making his final Western.[15] The film's first sequence – directed by Leone – opens another argument with *My Darling Clementine*, Henry Fonda's fullest. Again his character, Jack Beauregard, walks gingerly into a frontier barbershop for a relaxing little shave, but the commonplace is now pervaded by spaghetti-Western textures of threat: CinemaScope close-ups of his lathered neck, agonizingly slow and loud scrapes of the razor. Again the shave is interrupted by gunfire, confusing to the film audience but clearly not so to Beauregard, who kills his attackers outside the shop and in. One underlying distinction is this: Fonda has none of his old Wyatt

Earp's civilized amazement ("What kind of town *is* this?"); violence has become the expected state of the world. With the (impostor) barber dead, Fonda toys with a variation on *Clementine,* spraying *himself* with cologne and taking time to examine his image in the mirror (as Wyatt does in a window after his haircut). "Jack Beauregard, the only hope for law and order in the West" is, like the actor who plays him and the genre itself, evidently reaching its end. If in the barbershop shootout Fonda is still invincible, his eyesight is later represented in hazy-focus point-of-view shots. The film is set in 1899, but Fonda's "best year" for gunfighting is said to have been back in 1882, when *Clementine* is set. "Pa, ain't nobody faster than him?" marvels the (real) barber's son, when they untie themselves. "Nobody," he's told.

*My Name Is Nobody* combines low jokes with sophisticated legend. "Nobody" is the name taken by Fonda's baby-blue-eyed doppelgänger, a lower-class trickster fast enough on the draw to catch fish barehanded. Played by the Italian star "Terence Hill" (the *nom de cinéma* of Mario Girotti), Nobody's insouciant persona draws from Hill's highly popular comic Italian-Western "Trinity" series, with inspiration from *The Odyssey* (where Odysseus calls himself Nobody to befuddle the Cyclops). Hill's hyperactive character shadows the steady Beauregard, taunts him, protects him, comes to stage-manage his showdowns, all the while insisting he is himself nobody. "You're sure tryin' hard to make a hero out of me," Beauregard can't help but notice. "You're that already," Nobody tells him. "You just need a special act, something that will make your name a legend." *My Name Is Nobody* demystifies the classic Westerner by casting Nobody as a conscious creator of legends, but in a flamboyant and optimistic way sharing nothing with the devious cynicism of those dime novelists who cringe around the edges of so many heavily didactic revisionist Westerns from *The Left-Handed Gun* (1958) through *Buffalo Bill and the Indians* (1976).

"We live in a society bound together by the talk of fame." So Leo Braudy begins *The Frenzy of Renown* with deadpan iconoclasm.[16] This simple idea, self-evident to supermarket point-of-purchase checkout browsers, flies in the face of cherished notions in academic cultural studies that American society is bound together by enduring myths. *My Name Is Nobody* argues against Fonda's figure in *My Darling Clementine* by underscoring the distinctions unacknowledged there between private self and public performance. Fonda's Beauregard in *My Name Is*

*Nobody* has set out to avenge a murdered brother (although the narrative obliqueness characteristic of Leone's films holds this *Clementine* pattern a mystery for a time). Eventually he tires of that resolve, recognizing that his brother was "a grade-A skunk" anyway. But Nobody won't have him abandoning the vengeance requirement of the classic Western so easily: "My, my, how modern the old folks have become, but a hero can't run away from his destiny." Setting up a showdown to end all showdowns, Nobody makes certain that Fonda is alone to face down the 150-man "Wild Bunch." (The film is also arguing with Sam Peckinpah, whose surname graces a gravestone in an earlier scene; Fig. 57.) With the smallest of assists from Nobody (who obliquely reminds him that the Wild Bunch are carrying dynamite in their saddlebags: a good target), Fonda wins, horses flailing, gray dusters flapping, Ennio Morricone choral music swelling. "You'll end in history!" Nobody shouts in triumph.

The sequence has all the stylistic trappings of an ending, especially when engraved pages of a history book flip forward in montage. But Fonda's character now recognizes that the classic showdown, no matter how escalated the numbers of defeated opponents, evades further questions:

"Well, you got me into the history books. How do I quit?"

"There's only one way. You gotta die."

"Where?"

"Where there's lots of people."

Fonda's furrowed brow, in a long silent gaze at Nobody after this exchange, hints at a growing awareness of the Western hero's contract with his audience. Nobody arranges a last, main-street walkdown – himself against Beauregard. Throughout, Nobody has been comically "faster," and he wins, Beauregard falling into the dust. Nobody becomes, apparently, a superior somebody, defeating the defeater of the Wild Bunch, and the film thus also concludes another argument: that Italian styles could reinvigorate the dying American genre (something that proved true, and provided the final full flowering of the Western genre). The transference of fame requires validation by the public, and there are plenty of Gilded Age spectators at the shootout, further recorded by a photographer for whom Nobody obligingly reframes himself on the main street. If newspaper journalists were responsible for manufacturing heroism in *Fort Apache,* this is now 1899, the turn of the

**Figure 57.** *My Name Is Nobody* (1973): "Nobody" (Terence Hill) and Jack Beauregard (Henry Fonda) at his brother's grave (in a scene shot in Acoma Pueblo, New Mexico).

century in which film will take over responsibility for purveying the myth. As it happens, this shootout is entirely staged for the camera, faked to allow Fonda an exit from the West, from the film, and – as it turned out – from the genre. In a film that has made its points through visual wit, Henry Fonda's concluding critique in *My Name Is Nobody* – the actor's last words in a Western – is blunt, but perhaps not overly so, considering the enduring and mystifying power of the Western myth. From shipboard to Europe, he puts on his glasses to write a letter (Fig. 58), ruminating on mistakes that reflect back also on the basic assumptions of the Western: "Dear Nobody. . . . It seems to me we were all a bunch of romantic fools, who still believed that a good pistol and a quick showdown could solve everything. . . ."

**Figure 58.** *My Name Is Nobody:* Henry Fonda as a "dead" gunfighter, with his farewell letter to "Nobody," on shipboard east to Europe after retiring from the American West.

# Notes

## Preface: The Western and the West

**1.** James Fenimore Cooper, *The Last of the Mohicans,* in *The Leatherstocking Tales,* vol. 1, Blake Nevius, ed. (New York: Library of America, 1985), 502.

**2.** Carson's *Memoirs* are quoted in Thelma S. Guild and Harvey L. Carter, *Kit Carson: A Pattern for Heroes* (Lincoln: University of Nebraska Press, 1984), 186–7; see also Richard White, *"It's Your Misfortune and None of My Own": A History of the American West* (Norman: University of Oklahoma Press, 1991), 616.

**3.** William S. E. Coleman, *Voices of Wounded Knee* (Lincoln: University of Nebraska Press, 2002), 206; Robert M. Utley, *The Indian Frontier of the American West 1846–1890* (Albuquerque: University of New Mexico Press, 1984), 253–6; Utley, *The Last Days of the Sioux Nation* (New Haven: Yale University Press, 1963), 160.

**4.** Brian W. Dippie, "American Wests: Historiographical Perspectives," in Patricia Nelson Limerick, Clyde A. Milner II, and Charles E. Rankin, eds., *Trails: Toward a New Western History* (Lawrence: University Press of Kansas, 1991), 112–13; Brian W. Dippie, *The Vanishing American: White Attitudes and U.S. Indian Policy* (Middletown, Conn.: Wesleyan University Press, 1982), 201–3.

**5.** For applicability of the word "genocide" uniquely to California within Western history, see comments by historians Richard White in the PBS television documentary *In Search of the Oregon Trail* (1996, Michael Farrell, producer-director) and Patricia Nelson Limerick in "Less to Celebrate at This Gold Rush Anniversary," *New York Times,* Mar. 22, 1998: A16.

**6.** Jenni Calder, *There Must Be a Lone Ranger: The American West in Film and Reality* (New York: McGraw–Hill, 1977); Michael Wayne Sarf, *God Bless You, Buffalo Bill: A Layman's Guide to History and the Western Film* (Rutherford, N.J.: Fairleigh Dickinson University Press, 1983); Ward Churchill, *Fantasies of the Master Race: Literature, Cinema, and the Colonization of American Indians* (Monroe, Maine: Common Courage Press, 1992); Jon Tuska, *The American West in Film: Critical Approaches to the Western* (Lincoln: University of Nebraska Press, 1988), esp. xiii.

**7.** Jane Tompkins, *West of Everything: The Inner Life of Westerns* (New York: Oxford University Press, 1992), 45; Peter A. French, *Cowboy Metaphysics: Ethics and Death in Westerns* (Lanham, Md.: Rowman & Littlefield, 1997), xi; Janet Walker, "Introduction: Westerns through History," in Walker, ed., *Westerns: Films through History* (New York: Routledge/American Film Institute, 2001), 7–8.

**8.** Jon Tuska, *The Filming of the West* (Garden City, N.Y.: Doubleday, 1976), xviii.

9. In its opening weekend at 402 theaters nationwide, *Texas Rangers* collected in ticket sales "an abysmal $300,000. Repping only $746 per playdate . . ."; "Oater Misfires," www.variety.com, Dec. 2, 2001.

### PART ONE: "MY FRIEND, THE INDIAN": LANDSCAPE AND THE EXTERMINATION OF THE NATIVE AMERICAN IN THE SILENT WESTERN

1. Exact statistics for the number of Westerns made in these years are impossible to determine, especially because roughly 80 percent of the films are now lost, but production companies would often promise to "balance" their releases among three large genre groups – dramas, comedies, and Westerns – and a similarly "balanced" showing by theater exhibitors required one Western in each program; Eileen Bowser, *The Transformation of Cinema, 1907–1915* (New York: Charles Scribner's Sons, 1990), 167–9. From trade-paper reviews, Robert Anderson calculated that "one out of every five" films released in the United States was a Western in 1910; "The Role of the Western Film Genre in Industry Competition, 1907–1911," *Journal of the University Film Association* 31.2 (1979): 19–26, at 25. In 1911, a commentator for *Moving Picture World* (hereafter abbreviated *MPW;* Oct. 21, 1911: 189) estimated that a third of the films shown in U.S. theaters were Westerns, although Anderson calculated a decrease in production that year to 12 percent.
2. Brian W. Dippie, *The Vanishing American: White Attitudes and U.S. Indian Policy* (Middletown, Conn.: Wesleyan University Press, 1982), 218. See also Richard Ohmann, "Out West," *Selling Culture: Magazines, Markets, and Class at the Turn of the Century* (New York and London: Verso, 1996), 329–37.
3. For instance, *MPW,* Jan. 22, 1910: 82. Unless noted otherwise, all of the films mentioned in Part One survive in film archives in 2002.
4. See Richard White, "Discovering Nature in North America," in David Thelen and Frederick E. Hoxie, eds., *Discovering America: Essays on the Search for an Identity* (Urbana: University of Illinois Press, 1994), 40–57, at 47.
5. All except about 15 of Griffith's approximately 495 films survive in archives, although many are not yet viewable; see Paolo Cherchi Usai, ed., *The Griffith Project,* vols. 1–6 (London: British Film Institute, 1999–2002). For no other director of Westerns in this era have even 10 percent of films survived.
6. "The Passing of the Western Subject," *The Nickelodeon,* Feb. 18, 1911: 181; W. Stephen Bush, "The Overproduction of 'Western Pictures,'" *MPW,* Oct. 21, 1911: 189.

### 1. Indians to the Rescue

1. *MPW,* Jan. 22, 1910: 82; rpt. in Stanley Kauffman and Bruce Henstell, eds., *American Film Criticism: From the Beginnings to "Citizen Kane"* (Westport, Conn.: Greenwood Press, 1979), 35–6.
2. *New York Herald,* Sept. 25, 1894: 12; rpt. in Charles Musser, *Edison Motion Pictures, 1890–1900: An Annotated Filmography* (Pordenone, Italy: Le Giornate del Cinema Muto, and Washington, D.C.: Smithsonian Institution Press, 1997), 125–9, which also distinguishes *Sioux Ghost Dance* from another short film shot the same morning with which it is often confused, *Buffalo Dance;* see also Musser, *Before the Nickelodeon: Edwin S. Porter and the Edison Manufacturing Company* (Berkeley: Uni-

versity of California Press, 1991), 50. Nearly a hundred Sioux survivors of Wounded Knee had been recruited by William F. "Buffalo Bill" Cody for his Wild West show for a season after 1890, when the Commissioner of Indian Affairs was apparently happy to see them leave the reservation; twenty-three of Buffalo Bill's Sioux performers had been designated "prisoners of war"; see Joy S. Kasson, *Buffalo Bill's Wild West: Celebrity, Memory, and Popular History* (New York: Hill & Wang, 2002), 191–5; Marcus Klein, *Easterns, Westerns, and Private Eyes: American Matters, 1870–1900* (Madison: University of Wisconsin Press, 1994), 73; and L. G. Moses, *Wild West Shows and the Images of American Indians, 1883–1933* (Albuquerque: University of New Mexico Press, 1996), 106–28.

3. Leah Dilworth discusses the conversion of the Hopi ceremony into a tourist attraction in "Representing the Hopi Snake Dance," *Imagining Indians in the Southwest: Persistent Visions of a Primitive Past* (Washington, D.C.: Smithsonian Institution Press, 1996), 21–75; Alison Griffiths analyses Edison's snake-dance films in "Playing at Being Indian: Spectatorship and the Early Western," *Journal of Popular Film and Television* 29.3 (Fall 2001): 100–11.

4. Two similar 1897 Edison films survive under this title, both produced by James White and photographed by Fred Blechynden. The one described is preserved at the Library of Congress under the title *Serving Rations to the Indians #1.*

5. Because these films were copyrighted as a series of separate shots, their relative "epic" status has been easy to ignore.

6. See Charles Musser, *The Emergence of Cinema: The American Screen to 1907* (Berkeley: University of California Press, 1994), 227. For a revisionist argument proposing less of a commercial slump in these years, see Richard Abel, *The Red Rooster Scare: Making Cinema American, 1900–1910* (Berkeley: University of California Press, 1999), 1–12.

7. Edwin S. Porter and Wallace McCutcheon also produced in 1906 the atmospheric *Daniel Boone; or, Pioneer Days in America.* Its middle section, involving an Indian girl who helps Boone's daughter to escape from capture, survives only through still images; see the Museum of Modern Art reconstruction.

8. *Film Index,* Sept. 1, 1906: 16; quoted in Musser, *Before the Nickelodeon,* who discusses the narrative problems with *Life of a Cowboy* more fully (359–63).

9. For the "Panic of 1907," see Nell Irvin Painter, *Standing at Armageddon: The United States, 1877–1919* (New York: W. W. Norton, 1987), 212–15. Eileen Bowser discusses the 1907 "crisis of film narrative" in *The Transformation of Cinema, 1907–1915* (New York: Charles Scribner's Sons, 1990), 19.

10. See Jack Weatherford, *Indian Givers: How the Indians of the Americas Transformed the World* (New York: Fawcett Columbine, 1988).

11. *MPW,* Jan. 22, 1910: 82.

12. Robert Anderson, "The Role of the Western Film Genre in Industry Competition, 1907–1911," *Journal of the University Film Association* 31.2 (1979): 19–26; Edward Buscombe, "Inventing Monument Valley: Nineteenth-Century Landscape Photography and the Western Film," in Patrice Petro, ed., *Fugitive Images: From Photography to Video* (Bloomington: Indiana University Press, 1995), 87–108; Richard Abel, "'Our Country'/Whose Country?: The 'Americanization' Project of Early Westerns," in Edward Buscombe and Roberta E. Pearson, eds., *Back in the Saddle Again: New Essays on the Western* (London: British Film Institute, 1998), 77–95, revised in Abel, *Red Rooster Scare,* 151–74.

**13.** This idea is most thoroughly explored in Richard Slotkin, *Regeneration through Violence: The Mythology of the American Frontier, 1600–1860* (Middletown, Conn.: Wesleyan University Press, 1973); see also Michael Kammen, *Mystic Chords of Memory: The Transformation of Tradition in American Culture* (New York: Vintage Books, 1993), 187.

**14.** Theodore Dehon (1807), quoted in Martin Barker and Roger Sabin, *The Lasting of the Mohicans: History of an American Myth* (Jackson: University Press of Mississippi, 1995), 30. For other early arguments about the centrality of the Indian to a new American national literature, see Susan Scheckel, *The Insistence of the Indian: Race and Nationalism in Nineteenth-Century American Culture* (Princeton, N.J.: Princeton University Press, 1998), esp. 8–9, 16–17. The British mockery of American literature is cited in Alan Taylor, *William Cooper's Town: Power and Persuasion on the Frontier of the Early American Republic* (New York: Vintage Books, 1996), 409. On the relationship of early nineteenth-century "Indian dramas" to American identity, see also Don B. Wilmeth and Christopher Bigsby, eds., *The Cambridge History of American Theatre,* vol. 1: *Beginnings to 1870* (Cambridge: Cambridge University Press, 1998), 272–5.

**15.** Anne Farrar Hyde, *An American Vision: Far Western Landscape and National Culture, 1820–1920* (New York: New York University Press, 1990), 229.

**16.** As Jack Weatherford points out, the sculpture was originally planned to represent "freedom" though the classical figure of a freed female Roman slave (*Indian Givers,* 149–50), but because *that* symbolism was objectionable to Secretary of War Jefferson Davis, sculptor Thomas Crawford added what he called "a bold arrangement of feathers, suggestive of the costumes of our Indian tribes"; quoted in Brian W. Dippie, *The Vanishing American: White Attitudes and U.S. Indian Policy* (Middletown, Conn.: Wesleyan University Press, 1982), 91. The sculpture is illustrated and discussed further in Dippie, "The Moving Finger Writes: Western Art and the Dynamics of Change," in Jules David Prown et al., *Discovered Lands, Invented Pasts: Transforming Visions of the American West* (New Haven: Yale University Press, 1992), 89–115, at 99. Further use of the Indian as symbol in pre–Civil War art in the U.S. Capitol is discussed in Scheckel, *Insistence of the Indian,* 127–51.

**17.** E. McClung Fleming, "Symbols of the United States: From Indian Queen to Uncle Sam," in Ray B. Browne et al., eds., *Frontiers of American Culture* (Lafayette, Ind.: Purdue University Studies, 1967), 6–9.

**18.** For a full study of Pathé-Frères in America, see Abel, *Red Rooster Scare;* also Richard Abel, *The Ciné Goes to Town: French Cinema, 1896–1914* (Berkeley: University of California Press, 1994), 44–5.

**19.** Kevin Brownlow, *The War, the West, and the Wilderness* (New York: Alfred A. Knopf, 1979), 235–7; Abel, *Red Rooster Scare,* 138.

**20.** *MPW,* Oct. 21, 1911: 190; Brownlow, *War, the West, and the Wilderness,* 235; Abel, *Red Rooster Scare,* esp. 151–74. See also the British trade journal *The Bioscope,* "Topics of the Week: The Popularity of Western Films," Aug. 18, 1910: 4–5: "A run round at any of the London picture theatres – no matter where situated and in spite of different conditions – will convince the observer that undoubtedly Western films are the favorites of an audience; and the same holds good in the provinces. . . . Let us have more of these films, . . ."

**21.** Dippie, "Moving Finger Writes," 96.

**2. The Eastern Western**

1. Almost all of D. W. Griffith's surviving Biograph films released before October 1909 are missing their original intertitles. However, the *Biograph Bulletins* – one-page flyers for exhibitors – recount details of the narratives sometimes unclear without the lost intertitles and are incorporated into my plot descriptions. The flyers from Griffith's years at the company are reprinted in Eileen Bowser, ed., *Biograph Bulletins, 1908–1912* (New York: Farrar, Straus & Giroux, 1973).

2. The white actor playing the Indian, Charles Inslee, subsequently made a specialty of Indian roles for several companies. His director at the New York Motion Picture Company, Fred Balshofer, much later suggested one other obvious appeal of this gesture of throwing away European clothing: "Inslee made a striking appearance on the screen, and the ladies simply went gaga over him. Oh's and ah's came from them whenever he appeared on the screen in one of his naked Indian hero roles . . ."; Fred J. Balshofer and Arthur C. Miller, *One Reel a Week* (Berkeley: University of California Press, 1967), 40.

3. *New York Dramatic Mirror*, Aug. 8, 1908: 7; rpt. in George C. Pratt, *Spellbound in Darkness: A History of the Silent Film* (Greenwich, Conn.: New York Graphic Society, 1973), 56. *Variety*, Aug. 1, 1908: 13; quoted in Tom Gunning, *D. W. Griffith and the Origins of American Narrative Film: The Early Years at Biograph* (Urbana: University of Illinois Press, 1991), 69–70.

4. John G. Cawelti, *The Six-Gun Mystique* (Bowling Green, Ohio: Bowling Green University Popular Press, 1970), 34. See also Leslie A. Fiedler, *Love and Death in the American Novel*, rev. ed. (New York: Dell, 1969), 181: "Cooper invented not only the 'Western'. . . ."

5. *The Last of the Mohicans*, Cooper's best-known novel, is also partially an exception for the way its landscape can be terrifying; see David Morgan, "Frontier Myth and American Gothic," *Genre* 14 (Fall 1981): 329–46; also Roderick Nash, "A Wilderness Condition," *Wilderness and the American Mind* (New Haven: Yale University Press, 1973), 23–43.

6. John Mack Faragher, *Daniel Boone: The Life and Legend of an American Pioneer* (New York: Henry Holt, 1992); Richard Slotkin, *Regeneration through Violence: The Mythology of the American Frontier, 1600–1860* (Middletown, Conn.: Wesleyan University Press, 1973), 268–312.

7. James Fenimore Cooper, *The Last of the Mohicans*, in *The Leatherstocking Tales*, vol. 1, Blake Nevius, ed. (New York: Library of America, 1985), 678. On Cooper's treatment of the landscape, see particularly Blake Nevius, *Cooper's Landscapes: An Essay on the Picturesque Vision* (Berkeley: University of California Press, 1976); and H. Daniel Peck, *A World by Itself: The Pastoral Moment in Cooper's Fiction* (New Haven: Yale University Press, 1977).

8. Cooper, *Last of the Mohicans*, 744. On the convention in painting, see Barbara Novak, *Nature and Culture: American Landscape and Painting, 1825–1875* (New York: Oxford University Press, 1980), 228

9. James Fenimore Cooper, *The Deerslayer*, in *Leatherstocking Tales*, vol. 2, 497.

10. Ibid., 514–15.

11. James Fenimore Cooper, *The Pioneers*, in *Leatherstocking Tales*, vol. 1, 302.

12. Thomas Cole, "Essay on American Scenery," *American Monthly Magazine* 1 (Jan. 1836); rpt. in Cole, *The Collected Essays and Prose Sketches*, Marshall Tymn, ed.

(St. Paul, Minn.: John Colet Press, 1980), 11. Barbara Novak discusses this passage from Cole in *Nature and Culture,* 39.

**13.** Kevin Brownlow, *The War, the West, and the Wilderness* (New York: Alfred A. Knopf, 1979), 332.

**14.** Cole, "American Scenery," 9.

**15.** Cooper, *The Oak Openings,* quoted and discussed in Nevius, *Cooper's Landscapes,* 98. Cooper, *Deerslayer,* 524–5. Lee Clark Mitchell convincingly argues that such stasis in Cooper is also a way of creating heroic characters by unifying them with the silent and unmoving landscape; "Still Landscapes and Moral Restraint," *Westerns: Making the Man in Fiction and Film* (Chicago: University of Chicago Press, 1996), 28–54. Tony Tanner deeply explores the implications of such scenes in the title essay of his collection, *Scenes of Nature, Signs of Men* (Cambridge: Cambridge University Press, 1987), 1–24.

**16.** Henry David Thoreau, *Walden; or, Life in the Woods* [1854], in *"A Week"; "Walden; or, Life in the Woods"; "The Maine Woods"; "Cape Cod,"* Robert F. Sayre, ed. (New York: Library of America, 1985), 473; also quoted in Novak, *Nature and Culture,* 41.

**17.** Brian W. Dippie reproduces and compares this Remington painting to De Witt Clinton Boutelle's *Indian Surveying a Landscape* (ca. 1855) in "The Moving Finger Writes: Western Art and the Dynamics of Change," in Jules David Prown et al., *Discovered Lands, Invented Pasts: Transforming Visions of the American West* (New Haven: Yale University Press, 1992), 89–115, at 109–11.

### 3. Our Friends, the Indians

**1.** James McLaughlin, *My Friend the Indian* [1910] (Lincoln: University of Nebraska Press, 1989), 2.

**2.** On Indians as immature children of nature, an idea more pronounced in eighteenth-century Europe than in nineteenth-century America, see Robert E. Bieder, *Science Encounters the Indian, 1820–1880: The Early Years of American Ethnology* (Norman: University of Oklahoma Press, 1986), esp. 5–6; Michael Paul Rogin, "Children of Nature," *Fathers and Children: Andrew Jackson and the Subjugation of the American Indian* (New York: Alfred A. Knopf, 1975), 113–25; and Brian W. Dippie, *The Vanishing American: White Attitudes and U.S. Indian Policy* (Middletown, Conn.: Wesleyan University Press, 1982), 97–8.

**3.** *Views and Film Index,* Jan. 21, 1911: 3; cited in Richard Abel, *The Ciné Goes to Town: French Cinema, 1896–1914* (Berkeley: University of California Press, 1994), 479.

**4.** In a 1928 survey of 10,052 children, Westerns were the favorite genre among ten choices for "delinquent girls" – 36.2 percent – versus only 7.4 percent for Girl Scouts. For boys Westerns were both the first (20.4%) and second choices (16.4%), but again "delinquent boys" favored Westerns (36.6%) more than did Boy Scouts (16.7%); Alice Miller Mitchell, *Children and Movies* (Chicago: University of Chicago Press, 1929), 104–5, 107, 167.

**5.** *MPW,* Oct. 21, 1911: 189–90.

**6.** *The Land beyond the Sunset,* preserved by the George Eastman House, can be seen in the *Treasures from American Film Archives* DVD set, which includes my further notes on the film (San Francisco: National Film Preservation Foundation, 2000), 98–100.

7. Paul Alpers, *The Singer of the "Eclogues": A Study of Virgilian Pastoral, with a New Translation of the "Eclogues"* (Berkeley: University of California Press, 1979), 15. Leo Marx makes the point about the restoration of harmony in Virgil in *The Machine in the Garden: Technology and the Pastoral Ideal in America* (New York: Oxford University Press, 1964), 21, 31; he extends the argument about the pastoral as a political ideology in "Susan Sontag's 'New Left' Pastoral: Notes on Revolutionary Pastoralism in America," *TriQuarterly* 23–4 (Spring 1972): 552–75, and in "Pastoralism in America," in Sacvan Bercovitch and Myra Jehlen, eds., *Ideology and Classic American Literature* (Cambridge: Cambridge University Press, 1987), 36–69.

8. Hannah Cooper to Isaac Cooper, June 25, 1798; quoted in Alan Taylor, *William Cooper's Town: Power and Persuasion on the Frontier of the Early American Republic* (New York: Vintage Books, 1996), 339.

9. James Fenimore Cooper, *The Pioneers,* in *The Leatherstocking Tales,* vol. 1, Blake Nevius, ed. (New York: Library of America, 1985), 13–14.

10. Taylor, *William Cooper's Town,* esp. 86.

11. Cooper, *Pioneers,* 262.

12. James Fenimore Cooper, *The Last of the Mohicans,* in *Leatherstocking Tales,* vol. 1, 877.

13. Leslie A. Fiedler, *Love and Death in the American Novel,* rev. ed. (New York: Dell, 1969), 182.

14. D. H. Lawrence, *Studies in Classic American Literature* [1924] (Harmondsworth, U.K.: Penguin Books, 1971), 59–60.

15. Cooper, *Last of the Mohicans,* 877.

16. On McLaughlin's role in Sitting Bull's death, see Robert M. Utley, *The Last Days of the Sioux Nation* (New Haven: Yale University Press, 1963), 146–66; and Dee Brown, *Bury My Heart at Wounded Knee: An Indian History of the American West* (New York: Bantam Books, 1972), 390–412.

17. Hart Crane, "The Dance," in the "Powhatan's Daughter" section of *The Bridge* (1930), in Brom Weber, ed., *The Complete Poems and Selected Letters and Prose of Hart Crane* (Garden City, N.Y.: Anchor Press, 1966), 70–5.

18. Henry David Thoreau, *The Maine Woods* [1864], in *"A Week"; "Walden; or, Life in the Woods"; "The Maine Woods"; "Cape Cod,"* Robert F. Sayre, ed. (New York: Library of America, 1985), especially his second and third trips and pp. 657, 696.

19. If there is an American literary tradition about *this* use of the Indian, it goes back through Crèvecoeur's "Farmer James," who, horrified by the Revolutionary War, makes elaborate plans to move his extended family hundreds of miles west into a tribe whose "honest chief will spare us half his wigwham until we have time to erect one"; J. Hector St. John de Crèvecoeur, *Letters from an American Farmer* [1782] (New York: Oxford University Press, 1997), 206.

20. Virginia Wright Wexman in "The Family on the Land: Race and Nationhood in Silent Westerns," in Daniel Bernardi, ed., *The Birth of Whiteness: Race and the Emergence of U.S. Cinema* (New Brunswick, N.J.: Rutgers University Press, 1996), 129–69, has looked at the relationship of Indians and landscape in this way, concentrating on Westerns of the 1920s. See also Wexman, *Creating the Couple: Love, Marriage, and Hollywood Performance* (Princeton, N.J.: Princeton University Press, 1993), 67–129. When Cooper inserts a woman between the men of the wilderness, the result is usually confusion, havoc, and violence; see Donald J. Greiner, *Women Enter the Wilderness: Male Bonding and the American Novel of the 1980s* (Columbia: University of South Carolina Press, 1991), 7–20.

**21.** Lawrence, *Studies in Classic American Literature,* 55.

**22.** Thomas Campbell, *"Gertrude of Wyoming" and Other Poems* (London: Longman, Hurst, Rees, Orme & Brown, 1814) [part 1, stanza 26], 25; Campbell's "Wyoming" is not the state but the "Valley of Wyoming" in Pennsylvania. The division between the two sorts of Indian is not precise: Rousseau also credits the savage with "natural pity" and "compassion"; *Discourse on the Origin of Inequality,* in Donald A. Cress, ed. and trans., *On the Social Contract and Other Works* (Indianapolis: Hackett, 1983), 133–4. See also Robert F. Berkhofer Jr., *The White Man's Indian: Images of the American Indian from Columbus to the Present* (New York: Vintage Books, 1979), 72–80.

**23.** Griffith's infamous racism complicates discussion of his Indians, including the question of how representative his apparent feminization of them might be. Three quick points are worth making. First, as Marianna Torgovnick has traced in *Gone Primitive: Savage Intellects, Modern Lives* (Chicago: University of Chicago Press, 1990) and especially in *Primitive Passions: Men, Women, and the Quest for Ecstasy* (New York: Alfred A. Knopf, 1997), there is a long history to the linkage of the primitive with the female. Second, as I've argued in *The Films of D. W. Griffith* (Cambridge: Cambridge University Press, 1993), 47–9, 111–15, Griffith's attitudes are more representative of his era than it's now comfortable to admit. Third, in comparison at least to his portraits of other non-European races, his Indians are not extraordinarily self-sacrificing. Certainly, there is nothing among his images of Native Americans to correspond to the stupefying self-sacrifice of the ex-slave in *His Trust Fulfilled* (1911) or, among his Westerns, of the emigrant Chinese laundryman in *That Chink at Golden Gulch* (1910), who cuts off his queue to tie up a bandit and bestows his money on a young white couple before wandering off alone.

**24.** For instance, *MPW,* Oct. 8, 1910: 813. I discuss this response to *Rose o' Salem-Town* in Paolo Cherchi Usai, *The Griffith Project,* vol. 4: *Films Produced in 1910* (London: British Film Institute, 2001), 177–80. Charlie Keil provides a thorough formalist look at the film in *Early American Cinema in Transition: Story, Style, and Filmmaking, 1907–1913* (Madison: University of Wisconsin Press, 2001), 181–6, 223–6.

**25.** Cooper's *The Wept of Wish-ton-Wish* (1829), a captivity narrative set in the late seventeenth-century colonies, is a partial exception. A heroic Indian chief marries a white woman, and they live for a time in apparent happiness with their child; but by the novel's end he has been executed for his role in "King Philip's War," and she dies of the distress of living between racial cultures.

**26.** Louis Owens, situating Costner's film within this tradition of the "vanishing" Native American, finds that "*Dances with Wolves* is one of the most insidious moments yet in the history of American film"; "Apocalypse at the Two-Socks Hop: Dancing with the Vanishing American," in *Mixedblood Messages: Literature, Film, Family, Place* (Norman: University of Oklahoma Press, 1998), 113–31.

**27.** Robert Baird makes this point in "Going Indian: Discovery, Adoption, and Renaming toward a 'True American,' from *Deerslayer* to *Dances with Wolves,*" in S. Elizabeth Bird, ed., *Dressing in Feathers: The Construction of the Indian in American Popular Culture* (Boulder, Colo.: Westview Press, 1996), 195–209, at 197–8.

**28.** For an engaging examination of this image, see the title essay of Rennard Strickland's *Tonto's Revenge: Reflections on American Indian Culture and Policy* (Albuquerque: University of New Mexico Press, 1997), 17–45.

**29.** *Chingachgook, die große Schlange* (1967, a DEFA production from East Germany directed by Richard Groschopp) uses the outlines of Cooper's *The Deerslayer* for an anticapitalist parable (the "red" tribes are the internally divided Eastern Bloc) with anti-Nazi echoes (the heel-clicking colonial English plot to "eliminate" the "minorities"). In comparison with this jaw-dropping film, even Bela Lugosi's portrayal of Chingachgook looks conventional in the 1920 German silent *Der Wildtöter und Chingachgook,* another adaptation of *The Deerslayer.* On the West German Western, see Robin Bean, "Way Out West in Yugoslavia," *Films and Filming* 11.2 (Sept. 1965): 49–51; Tassilo Schneider, "Finding a New *Heimat* in the Wild West: Karl May and the German Western of the 1960s," *Journal of Film and Video* 47.1–3 (Spring–Fall 1995): 50–66; and Christopher Frayling, *Spaghetti Westerns: Cowboys and Europeans from Karl May to Sergio Leone* (London: Routledge & Kegan Paul, 1981), 103–17.

**30.** Willa Cather, *The Professor's House,* in Cather, *Later Novels,* Sharon O'Brien, ed. (New York: Library of America, 1990), 247–8. As Walter Benn Michaels has argued in relation to this passage and others, such a claim is also paradoxically an argument for racial purity; *Our America: Nativism, Modernism, and Pluralism* (Durham, N.C.: Duke University Press, 1995), 32.

**31.** On the relationship of *Hiawatha* to Indian removal, see Richard Slotkin, *Regeneration through Violence: The Mythology of the American Frontier, 1600–1860* (Middletown, Conn.: Wesleyan University Press, 1973), 354–68; also Michael Kammen, *Mystic Chords of Memory: The Transformation of Tradition in American Culture* (New York: Vintage Books, 1993), 82–3.

**32.** *MPW,* Aug. 5, 1911: 271.

**33.** Most of Young Deer's production and directorial credits are impossible to confirm, but such a number is suggested by *Moving Picture World*'s mention in 1912 that he had just completed his one-hundredth film for Pathé; *MPW,* June 29, 1912: 1218. Only eight of his films are thought to survive in U.S. archives. *White Fawn's Devotion,* preserved by the Library of Congress, can be seen on the *Treasures from American Film Archives* DVDs, with my additional notes: 69–71.

**34.** *MPW,* Mar. 25, 1911: 656.

**35.** *MPW,* July 1, 1911: 1508.

**36.** Young Deer was accused in late 1913 by the Los Angeles County sheriff of being part of a "white slave ring," and, although charges were eventually dropped, the publicity seems to have led to the end of his employment with Pathé in the United States. He directed briefly in Britain in the mid-1910s and later in France and, according to Kevin Brownlow, acted in and directed a few low-budget films in the United States into the 1930s; *The War, the West, and the Wilderness* (New York: Alfred A. Knopf, 1979), 331–4. See also Jim Sleeper, *Great Movies Shot in Orange County* (Trabuco Canyon: California Classics, 1980), 29–33; "James Young Deer," *MPW,* May 6, 1911: 999; and Angela Aleiss, "Native Americans: The Surprising Silents," *Cinéaste* 21.3 (1995): 34–5.

## 4. The Death of the Western, 1911

**1.** W. Stephen Bush, "The Overproduction of 'Western Pictures,'" *MPW,* Oct. 21, 1911: 189; see also *MPW,* Dec. 2, 1911: 700.

**2.** W. Stephen Bush, "Moving Picture Absurdities," *MPW,* Sept. 16, 1911: 733; partial rpt. in Gretchen M. Bataille and Charles L. P. Silet, eds., *The Pretend Indian: Images of Native Americans in the Movies* (Ames: Iowa State University Press, 1980), 60.

3. *MPW*, Oct. 21, 1911: 190.

4. "Public Opinion Controls," *MPW*, Apr. 22, 1911: 873–4.

5. George C. Pratt, "The Posse Is Ridin' Like Mad," *Image* 7.4 (Apr. 1958): 76–84, at 80. On Selig's first films in the West, see also Robert Anderson, "The Role of the Western Film Genre in Industry Competition, 1907–1911," *Journal of the University Film Association* 31.2 (1979): 19–26, at 22–3.

6. On Essanay in the West, see Pratt, "Posse Is Ridin' Like Mad," 80; Eileen Bowser, *The Transformation of Cinema, 1907–1915* (New York: Charles Scribner's Sons, 1990), 151, 171; George C. Pratt, *Spellbound in Darkness: A History of the Silent Film* (Greenwich, Conn.: New York Graphic Society, 1973), 127–30; "Essanay Producers in Texas and Mexico," *MPW*, Dec. 4, 1909: 801.

7. Linda Kowall Woal, "Romaine Fielding: The West's Touring Auteur," *Film History* 7 (1995): 401–25; Linda Kowall Woal and Michael Woal, "Romaine Fielding's Real Westerns," *Journal of Film and Video* 47.1–3 (Spring–Fall 1995): 7–25.

8. Richard Abel, *The Ciné Goes to Town: French Cinema, 1896–1914* (Berkeley: University of California Press, 1994), 50.

9. Again, one must judge tentatively from few surviving examples; see *When the Tables Turned* (1911), a story of a tough woman, played by Edith Storey, who tames a group of cowboys, including Francis Ford; see also Frank Thompson, "The First Picture Show: Gaston Méliès's Star Film Ranch, San Antonio, Texas, 1910–1911," *Literature/Film Quarterly* 23.2 (1995): 110–13; Bowser, *Transformation of Cinema*, 30, 104–5, 156.

10. See Peter Bogdanovich, *Allan Dwan: The Last Pioneer* (New York: Praeger, 1971), 19; Fred J. Balshofer and Arthur C. Miller, *One Reel a Week* (Berkeley: University of California Press, 1967), 59–63; Bowser, *Transformation of Cinema*, 150.

## 5. The Far-Western

1. Henry David Thoreau, "Walking," in *Excursions* [1863] (New York: Corinth Books, 1962), 176.

2. Peter Stanfield makes a similar point in "The Western, 1909–1914: A Cast of Villains," *Film History* 1.2 (1987): 97–112, at 101.

3. See Roderick Nash, "An Unprecedented Landscape: The Problem of Loving the Arid West," in Christopher S. Durer et al., eds. *American Renaissance and American West: Proceedings of the Second University of Wyoming American Studies Conference* (Laramie: University of Wyoming, 1982), 69–77, at 70–1; David W. Teague, "A Barren Wild," *The Southwest in American Literature and Art: The Rise of a Desert Aesthetic* (Tucson: University of Arizona Press, 1997), 13–50; and Peter Wild, *The Opal Desert: Explorations of Fantasy and Reality in the American Southwest* (Austin: University of Texas Press, 1999), esp. chap. 2, "William L. Manly: The Classic Account of Deserta Horribilis," 19–34.

4. The literary precursors, such as John C. Van Dyke (*The Desert*, 1901) or Mary Austin (*Land of Little Rain*, 1903), may be more widely known today than in the 1910s; see Peter Wild, "Sentimentalism in the American Southwest: John C. Van Dyke, Mary Austin, and Edward Abbey," in Michael Kowalewski, ed., *Reading the West: New Essays on the Literature of the American West* (Cambridge: Cambridge University Press, 1996), 127–43; and Wild, *Opal Desert*, 61–87.

5. As Anne Farrar Hyde points out, even the Grand Canyon was not widely seen

until William Henry Jackson made the first successful commercial series in 1892; Hyde, *An American Vision: Far Western Landscape and National Culture, 1820–1920* (New York: New York University Press, 1990), 219.

**6.** Remington's interestingly dark fiction, pessimistic about racial and regional reconciliations, is likewise surprisingly evasive about western land. He seldom attempts to describe what he is likely to characterize simply as "the interminable landscape"; *John Ermine of the Yellowstone* (1902), in Peggy and Harold Samuels, eds., *The Collected Works of Frederic Remington* (New York: Doubleday, 1979), 499. On his depiction of "nature as an oppressive force" in his earliest published sketches, see G. Edward White, *The Eastern Establishment and the Western Experience: The West of Frederic Remington, Theodore Roosevelt, and Owen Wister* [1967] (Austin: University of Texas Press, 1989), 103–6. Late in his short life (1861–1909), Remington discovered European impressionism and began to pay more attention to landscape.

**7.** The shot is illustrated in Scott Simmon, *The Films of D. W. Griffith* (Cambridge: Cambridge University Press, 1993), 83.

**8.** See Chon Noriega, "Birth of the Southwest: Social Protest, Tourism, and D. W. Griffith's *Ramona*," in Daniel Bernardi, ed., *The Birth of Whiteness: Race and the Emergence of U.S. Cinema* (New Brunswick, N.J.: Rutgers University Press, 1996), 203–27.

**9.** See Hyde, *American Vision*, "Packaging the American Indian," 229–38.

**10.** Joni Louise Kinsey, *Thomas Moran and the Surveying of the American West* (Washington, D.C.: Smithsonian Institution Press, 1992), 36.

**11.** E. H. Gombrich, *Art and Illusion: A Study in the Psychology of Pictorial Representation* (Princeton, N.J.: Princeton University Press, 1960); John Berger, *Ways of Seeing* (New York: Viking Press, 1972).

**12.** Susan Hegeman, "Landscapes, Indians, and Photography in the Age of Scientific Exploration," in Leonard Engel, ed., *The Big Empty: Essays on Western Landscapes as Narrative* (Albuquerque: University of New Mexico Press, 1994), 55; Kinsey, *Thomas Moran*, 29–35.

**13.** On O'Sullivan's use, but inversion, of traditional classical poses, see Olaf Hansen, "The Impermanent Sublime: Nature, Photography and the Petrarchan Tradition," in Mick Gidley and Robert Lawson-Peebles, eds., *Views of American Landscapes* (Cambridge: Cambridge University Press, 1989), 31–50, at 42. See also Jonathan Rabin's discussion of the Montana landscape experiments in British émigré Evelyn Cameron's turn-of-the-century photographs; *Bad Land: An American Romance* (New York: Vintage Books, 1996), 57–95.

**14.** Blake Nevius, *Cooper's Landscapes: An Essay on the Picturesque Vision* (Berkeley: University of California Press, 1976), 27–31.

### 6. Wars on the Plains

**1.** Theodore Roosevelt, 1886; quoted in Martin E. Marty, *Righteous Empire: The Protestant Experience in America* (New York: Dial Press, 1970), 12.

**2.** James Fenimore Cooper, *The Last of the Mohicans*, in *The Leatherstocking Tales*, vol. 1, Blake Nevius, ed. (New York: Library of America, 1985), 542.

**3.** See Jenni Calder, *There Must Be a Lone Ranger: The American West in Film and Reality* (New York: McGraw–Hill, 1977), 93.

**4.** See Mody C. Boatright, "The Beginnings of Cowboy Fiction," in William T. Pilkington, ed., *Critical Essays on the Western American Novel* (Boston: G. K. Hall,

1980), 41–55; Boatright, "The Cowboy Enters the Movies," in Wilson M. Hudson and Allen Maxwell, eds., *The Sunny Slopes of Long Ago* (Publications of the Texas Folklore Society, no. 33) (Austin, Texas: Southern Methodist University Press, 1966), 51–69.

**5.** Gregory S. Jay provides a reading of *The Massacre,* along with *The Call of the Wild* and *A Romance of the Western Hills,* in "'White Man's Book No Good': D. W. Griffith and the American Indian," *Cinema Journal* 34.4 (Summer 2000): 3–26. My further discussion of *The Massacre,* a film that was held back from release in the United States until 1914, is in Paolo Cherchi Usai, ed., *The Griffith Project,* vol. 6: *Films Produced in 1912* (London: British Film Institute, 2002), 86–90.

**6.** James Fenimore Cooper, *The Deerslayer,* in *The Leatherstocking Tales,* vol. 2, Blake Nevius, ed. (New York: Library of America, 1985), 835, 1003, 1005; see Michael Kowalewski, *Deadly Musings: Violence and Verbal Form in American Fiction* (Princeton, N.J.: Princeton University Press, 1993), 75–9; and Philip Fisher, *Hard Facts: Setting and Form in the American Novel* (New York: Oxford University Press, 1987), 59–61.

**7.** Over a hundred dime-novel series were issued in the nineteenth century from several publishing houses, some series with as many as a thousand titles, including, for instance, 550 Buffalo Bill novels. See Daryl Jones, *The Dime Novel Western* (Bowling Green, Ohio: Bowling Green University Popular Press, 1978), 18, 27, 32, 127, 140; Richard Slotkin, *Regeneration through Violence: The Mythology of the American Frontier, 1600–1860* (Middletown, Conn.: Wesleyan University Press, 1973), especially for his discussion (409–11) of the earlier John McClung, *Sketches of Western Adventure* (1832); David Reynolds, *Beneath the American Renaissance: The Subversive Imagination in the Age of Emerson and Melville* (New York: Alfred A. Knopf, 1988), esp. 191–210, 346–51, 450–7; Christine Bold, *Selling the Wild West: Popular Western Fiction, 1860–1960* (Bloomington: Indiana University Press, 1987), 2–36. For reprinted samples, see Bill Brown, ed., *Reading the West: An Anthology of Dime Westerns* (Boston: Bedford Books, 1997).

**8.** James Fenimore Cooper, *The Prairie,* in *Leatherstocking Tales,* vol. 1: "hard and unyielding," 890; "comparative desert," 883; "naked plains," 1101; "I often think . . . ," 903; "Amid the monotonous . . . ," 973; "friend," 1176.

**9.** For instance, King's *The Deserter* features several examples of "the devil in petticoats"; in Charles King, *"The Deserter" and "From the Ranks"* (Philadelphia: J. B. Lippincott, 1898), 150.

**10.** Quoted in R. W. B. Lewis, *The American Adam: Innocence, Tragedy and Tradition in the Nineteenth Century* (Chicago: University of Chicago Press, 1955), 166.

**11.** Francis Parkman, "The Works of James Fenimore Cooper," *North American Review* 74 (Jan. 1852): 147–61; rpt. in George Dekker and John P. McWilliams, eds., *Fenimore Cooper: The Critical Heritage* (London: Routledge & Kegan Paul, 1973), 249–61, at 252.

**12.** By "hunting" Indians Parkman primarily means seeking them out, but the chapter includes such sentiments as this: "The Indians kept close within their lodge, except . . . the old conjurer. . . . Surely, I thought, there could be no harm in shooting such a hideous old villain, to see how ugly he would look when he was dead, . . ."; Francis Parkman, *The Oregon Trail* [1849], in *"The Oregon Trail" and "The Conspiracy of Pontiac,"* William R. Taylor, ed. (New York: Library of America, 1991), 176, 155.

**13.** Quoted in Francis Jennings, "The Vanishing Indian: Francis Parkman versus His Sources," *Pennsylvania Magazine of History and Biography* 87 (1963): 306–23.

**14.** For Parkman's most extensive characterization of what he takes to be the Indian character, see the first chapters of *The Jesuits in North America in the Seventeenth Century* [1867], in *France and England in North America,* vol. 1, David Levin, ed. (New York: Library of America, 1983). See also Russell B. Nye, "Parkman, Red Fate, and White Civilization," in Clarence Gohdes, ed., *Essays on American Literature in Honor of Jay B. Hubbell* (Durham, N.C.: Duke University Press, 1967); and Robert Shulman, "Parkman's Indians and American Violence," *Massachusetts Review* 12 (1971): 221–39.

**15.** Richard Slotkin, *Gunfighter Nation: The Myth of the Frontier in Twentieth-Century America* (New York: Atheneum, 1992), 76–86; Joy S. Kasson, *Buffalo Bill's Wild West: Celebrity, Memory, and Popular History* (New York: Hill & Wang, 2002), 244–8; William G. Simon and Louise Spense, "Cowboy Wonderland, History, and Myth: 'It Ain't All That Different than Real Life,'" *Journal of Film and Video* 47.1–3 (Spring–Fall 1995): 67–81.

**16.** Quoted in Brian W. Dippie, "The Visual West," in Clyde A. Milner II, Carol A. O'Connor, and Martha A. Sandweiss, eds., *The Oxford History of the American West* (New York: Oxford University Press, 1994), 675–705, at 690.

**17.** The writing on Custer and the imagery of the "last stand" is immense, but see in particular Richard Slotkin, *The Fatal Environment: The Myth of the Frontier in the Age of Industrialization, 1800–1890* (Middletown, Conn.: Wesleyan University Press, 1985), 3–32, 371–477; and William H. Goetzmann and William N. Goetzmann, *The West of the Imagination* (New York: W. W. Norton, 1986), 217–27. On the relationship of this image to the later Western, see Edward Buscombe, "Painting the Legend: Frederic Remington and the Western," *Cinema Journal* 23.4 (Summer 1984): 12–27.

**18.** For instance, "To push the frontier westward in the teeth of the forces of the wilderness was fighting work, such as suited well enough many a stout soldier . . ."; Theodore Roosevelt, *The Winning of the West,* vol. 3: *The Founding of the Trans-Allegheny Commonwealths 1784–1790* [1894] (Lincoln: University of Nebraska Press, 1995), 4. On Roosevelt's use of the word "blood," see Gail Bederman, *Manliness and Civilization: A Cultural History of Gender and Race in the United States, 1880–1917* (Chicago: University of Chicago Press, 1995), 178–80. *Fighting Blood,* previously viewable only in a corrupt version with intertitles added years later, was restored in 2001 by the George Eastman House.

**19.** Edmund Morris, *The Rise of Theodore Roosevelt* (New York: Ballantine Books, 1979), 411; Bederman, *Manliness and Civilization,* 189. "The weakling" is also a favorite term in *The Virginian* and its many film adaptations; Owen Wister may have developed his fondness for the term from Roosevelt, to whom the novel is dedicated.

**20.** Roosevelt, *Winning of the West,* vol. 3, 30, 45. TR uses "border" to mean any frontier.

### 7. The Politics of Landscape

**1.** Priscilla Sears, "A Pillar of Fire to Follow: Myths of the American Indian Dramas, 1808–1859," in Christopher S. Durer et al., eds., *American Renaissance and American West: Proceedings of the Second University of Wyoming American Studies Conference* (Laramie: University of Wyoming, 1982), 15–30; Brenda Murphy, *American Realism and American Drama, 1880–1940* (Cambridge: Cambridge University Press,

1987), 11; Kathryn C. Esselman, "From Camelot to Monument Valley: Dramatic Origins of the Western Film," in Jack Nachbar, ed., *Focus on the Western* (Englewood Cliffs, N.J.: Prentice–Hall, 1974), 16; Gordon M. Wickstrom, "Buffalo Bill the Actor," *Journal of the West* 34.1 (Jan. 1995): 62–9; Don B. Wilmeth and Christopher Bigsby, eds., *The Cambridge History of American Theatre,* vol. 1: *Beginnings to 1870* (Cambridge: Cambridge University Press, 1998), 272–5.

2. Daryl Jones, *The Dime Novel Western* (Bowling Green, Ohio: Bowling Green University Popular Press, 1978), 27, 121. The early dime novel was widely influenced by the characterization of the pathological Puritan Indian fighter in Robert M. Bird's *Nick of the Woods* (1837).

3. Blake Nevius, *Cooper's Landscapes: An Essay on the Picturesque Vision* (Berkeley: University of California Press, 1976), 120; Allen J. Koppenhaver, "The Dark View of Things: The Isolated Figure in the American Landscapes of Cole and Bryant," in Mick Gidley and Robert Lawson-Peebles, eds., *Views of American Landscapes* (Cambridge: Cambridge University Press, 1989), 183–98, at 189.

4. William Cooper, *A Guide in the Wilderness; or, The History of the First Settlements in the Western Counties of New York, with Useful Instructions to Future Settlers* [1810] (Cooperstown, 1986), 13–14; quoted in Alan Taylor, *William Cooper's Town: Power and Persuasion on the Frontier of the Early American Republic* (New York: Vintage Books, 1996), 32.

5. Taylor, *William Cooper's Town,* 34–56. Even Francis Parkman interrupts his description of the "warlike hearts" of the nearby Iroquois to note their settled life in New York in 1779, including "the old apple orchards"; Parkman, *The Conspiracy of Pontiac* [1851], in *"The Oregon Trail" and "The Conspiracy of Pontiac,"* William R. Taylor, ed. (New York: Library of America, 1991), 369, 371.

6. See William H. Goetzmann, *New Lands, New Men: America and the Second Great Age of Discovery* (New York: Viking Books, 1986), 411.

7. John C. Van Dyke, *The Desert: Further Studies in Natural Appearances* [1901] (New York: Charles Scribner's Sons, 1918), 114, 41.

### 8. Pocahontas Meets Custer: *The Invaders*

1. Fred J. Balshofer and Arthur C. Miller, *One Reel a Week* (Berkeley: University of California Press, 1967), 54–67; Richard V. Spencer, "Los Angeles as Producing Center," *MPW,* Apr. 8, 1911: 768; rpt. in George C. Pratt, *Spellbound in Darkness: A History of the Silent Film* (Greenwich, Conn.: New York Graphic Society, 1973), 88–90. Balshofer and Miller's book reproduces a production still crediting James Young Deer and "Red Wing" with roles in *Little Dove's Romance* (63), but the still probably depicts another (unidentified) film.

2. *The Invaders,* preserved by the Library of Congress, can be seen in the DVD set *Saving the Silents: 50 More Treasures from American Film Archives* (San Francisco: National Film Preservation Foundation, available July 2004). In the most definitive volume on Ince to date, Paolo Cherchi Usai and Livio Jacob, eds., *Thomas H. Ince: Il profeta del western* – the special issue of *Griffithiana* published for the Third Pordenone Silent Film Festival (nos. 18–21 [Oct. 1984]) – direction of *The Invaders* is credited to Ince by Steven Higgins ("I film di Thomas H. Ince," 155–94, at 161) and to Ford by Tag Gallagher ("Francis Ford – Una filmografia," 205–20, at 210).

**3.** "Bison Company Gets 101 Ranch," *MPW*, Dec. 9, 1910: 810; Thomas H. Ince, "The Early Days at Kay Bee," *Photoplay Magazine*, Mar. 1919; rpt. in Richard Koszarski, ed., *Hollywood Directors, 1914–1940* (London: Oxford University Press, 1976), 62–70; Michael Wallis, *The Real Wild West: The 101 Ranch and the Creation of the American West* (New York: St. Martin's Press, 1999), 357–76; Kevin Brownlow, *The War, the West, and the Wilderness* (New York: Alfred A. Knopf, 1979), 253–62; Steven Higgins, "Thomas H. Ince: American Film Maker," in Richard Dyer MacCann, ed., *The First Film Makers: New Viewpoints on the Lives and Work of D. W. Griffith, Thomas Ince and Erich Von Stroheim* (Metuchen, N.J.: Scarecrow Press, 1989), 69–71, at 70–1; George Mitchell, "Thomas H. Ince," *Films in Review* 11.8 (Oct. 1960): 464–84.

**4.** The reason for their attack is not clear from the film as it survives, in two slightly incomplete reels (reel 1 at the UCLA Film and Television Archive; reel 2 at the Library of Congress). A week earlier Ince had made a now-lost one-reel nonfiction film about the Miller Bros. 101 Ranch entitled *The Wild West Circus.* As is the case with all early filmmakers except Griffith, the great majority of Ince's films are lost, but of his key Westerns of 1911–12, a good representative sample survives: approximately 20 percent, including most of his first two- and three-reelers.

**5.** Many thousand other Native Americans had previously been declared citizens, as members of the so-called Five Civilized Nations or through homestead allotment; Brian W. Dippie, *The Vanishing American: White Attitudes and U.S. Indian Policy* (Middletown, Conn.: Wesleyan University Press, 1982), 192–6; Brownlow, *War, the West, and the Wilderness,* 261.

**6.** Tag Gallagher, "Brother Feeney," *Film Comment* 12.6 (Nov.–Dec. 1976): 12–18, at 13.

**7.** Janet Staiger, "Dividing Labor for Production Control: Thomas Ince and the Rise of the Studio System," in Gorham Kindem, ed., *The American Movie Industry: The Business of Motion Pictures* (Carbondale: Southern Illinois University Press, 1982), 94–103, at 99.

**8.** "Bison-101 Feature Pictures," *MPW*, Jan. 27, 1912: 298.

**9.** Louis Reeves Harrison, "*The Invaders*," *MPW*, Nov. 9, 1912: 542.

**10.** "Bison-101 Feature Pictures," 298.

**11.** Brian W. Dippie, "The Visual West," in Clyde A. Milner II, Carol A. O'Connor, and Martha A. Sandweiss, eds., *The Oxford History of the American West* (New York: Oxford University Press, 1994), 675–705, at 679. For a characterization of Ince's Westerns as "authentic," see, for instance, Pratt, *Spellbound in Darkness,* 142.

**12.** Wallis, *Real Wild West,* 455–60. On Sitting Bull's association with Cody, see Joy S. Kasson, *Buffalo Bill's Wild West: Celebrity, Memory, and Popular History* (New York: Hill & Wang, 2002), 169–83. See also Thomas L. Altherr, "Let 'er Rip: Popular Culture Images of the American West in Wild West Shows, Rodeos, and Rendezvous," in Richard Aquila, ed., *Wanted Dead or Alive: The American West in Popular Culture* (Urbana: University of Illinois Press, 1996), 77–89; Joseph Schwartz, "The Wild West Show: 'Everything Genuine,'" *Journal of Popular Culture* 3.4 (Spring 1970): 656–66; and Richard Slotkin, *Gunfighter Nation: The Myth of the Frontier in Twentieth-Century America* (New York: Atheneum, 1992), 76–86.

**13.** Quoted in Richard J. Walsh and Milton Salsbury, *The Making of Buffalo Bill: A Study in Heroics* (Indianapolis: Bobbs–Merrill, 1928), 260. A slightly different version of Twain's testimonial was published in the *New York Times;* Kasson, *Buffalo Bill's Wild West,* 62.

**14.** As Corey K. Creekmur suggests, the 1912 *Life of Buffalo Bill* "doesn't recognize the distorting quality of dreams," and presents the body of the film as Cody's memory, and "given the national status of this particular dreamer, these memories might be described as history"; "Buffalo Bill (Himself): History and Memory in the Western Biopic," in Janet Walker, ed., *Westerns: Films through History* (New York: Routledge / American Film Institute, 2001), 131–47, at 138. For a description and production photos of Cody's lost *The Indian Wars* (1914; aka *Wars of Civilization*), centered around a controversial reenactment of the 1890 "battle" at Wounded Knee, see L. G. Moses, *Wild West Shows and the Images of American Indians, 1883–1933* (Albuquerque: University of New Mexico Press, 1996), 228–51; Brownlow, *War, the West, and the Wilderness*, 224–35; and Kasson, *Buffalo Bill's Wild West*, 257–63.

**15.** Sarah J. Blackstone, *Buckskins, Bullets, and Business: A History of Buffalo Bill's Wild West* (New York: Greenwood Press, 1986), 93.

**16.** For a suggestive history of the newly widespread valuation of "the real" in American artistic culture at this time, see Miles Orvell, *The Real Thing: Imitation and Authenticity in American Culture* (Chapel Hill: University of North Carolina Press, 1989). See also discussion of the "dilemma of authenticity" in Slotkin, *Gunfighter Nation*, 234–5.

**17.** "*Chief Blackfoot's Vindication*," *MPW*, May 21, 1910: 834. See also "The 'Make-Believe' Indian," *MPW*, Mar. 4, 1911: 473; rpt. in Gretchen M. Bataille and Charles L. P. Silet, eds., *The Pretend Indian: Images of Native Americans in the Movies* (Ames: Iowa State University Press, 1980), 59.

**18.** Tom Mix to W. N. Selig, Sept. 26, 1910; cited in Richard Dale Batman, "The Founding of the Hollywood Motion Picture Industry," *Journal of the West* 10.4 (Oct. 1971): 609–23, at 612.

**19.** Mark Twain, *Roughing It* [1872], in *"The Innocents Abroad" & "Roughing It,"* Guy Cardwell, ed. (New York: Library of America, 1984), 634.

**20.** Dippie, *Vanishing American: White Attitudes*, 91–2; Robert M. Utley, *The Indian Frontier of the American West 1846–1890* (Albuquerque: University of New Mexico Press, 1984), 122.

**21.** See Craig D. Bates, "Dressing the Part: A Brief Look at the Development of Stereotypical Indian Clothing among Native Peoples of the Far West," *Journal of California and Great Basin Anthropology* 4.2 (1982): 55–66.

**22.** On the long-suppressed ethnic heritage of "Iron Eyes Cody," see Angela Aleiss, "Native Son," *New Orleans Times–Picayune*, 26 May 1996: D1.

**23.** "We did not think of the great open plains . . . as 'wild.' Only to the white man was nature a 'wilderness' . . . ," Luther Standing Bear, *Land of the Spotted Eagle* [1933] (Lincoln: University of Nebraska Press, 1978), 38.

**24.** Standing Bear heard more about the battle against Custer when Crazy Horse, a distant relative, visited his family in 1877; *My People the Sioux* [1928] (Lincoln: University of Nebraska Press, 1975), 82–5. On his name-choosing, see Standing Bear, *Land of the Spotted Eagle*, 231–8; also Standing Bear, *My Indian Boyhood* [1931] (Lincoln: University of Nebraska Press, 1988).

**25.** *Exhibitors' Herald*, Dec. 20, 1924: 31; quoted in Brownlow, *War, the West, and the Wilderness*, 261.

**26.** Louis Reeves Harrison, "The 'Bison-101' Headliners," *MPW*, Apr. 27, 1912: 322. Alexander Pope, *An Essay on Man* [1733–4] (New Haven: Yale University Press,

1964), 27: "Lo! The poor Indian, whose untutor'd mind/Sees God in clouds, or hears him in the wind; . . ."

**27.** Edward Abbey, *Desert Solitaire: A Season in the Wilderness* (New York: McGraw-Hill, 1968), 37.

**28.** The lake had been constructed by damming earlier in 1912, primarily to give the company access to water during summer shooting; "Western Operations of the New York Motion Picture Company," *MPW,* Aug. 24, 1912: 777.

**29.** Jean Mitry, "Thomas H. Ince: His Esthetic, His Films, His Legacy" [1965], trans. and adapted by Martin Sopocy and Paul Attallah, *Cinema Journal* 22.2 (Winter 1983): 2–25.

**30.** *MPW,* Oct. 21, 1911: 189.

**31.** On the provisions of the 1851 Fort Laramie treaty and the Sioux treaty of 1868, see Donald E. Worcester, "Treaties with the Teton Sioux," in Worcester, ed., *Forked Tongues and Broken Treaties* (Caldwell, Idaho: Caxton Printers, 1975), 214–52, at 215–19; and Francis Paul Prucha, *American Indian Treaties: The History of a Political Anomaly* (Berkeley: University of California Press, 1994), 237–40, 282–4.

**32.** Richard White, *"It's Your Misfortune and None of My Own": A History of the American West* (Norman: University of Oklahoma Press, 1991), 90, 96; Utley, *Indian Frontier,* 103–5, 121; Arthur King Peters, *Seven Trails West* (New York: Abbeville Press, 1996), 208, 214.

**33.** Robert M. Utley, ed., *Life in Custer's Cavalry: Diaries and Letters of Albert and Jennie Barnitz, 1867–1868* (New Haven: Yale University Press, 1977), 115; quoted in Sherry L. Smith, *The View from Officers' Row: Army Perceptions of Western Indians* (Tucson: University of Arizona Press, 1990), 123.

**34.** Gen. George Crook, *His Autobiography,* Martin F. Schmitt, ed. (Norman: University of Oklahoma Press, 1960); quoted in Smith, *View from Officers' Row,* 125. See also Michael L. Tate, "In Defense of 'Poor Lo': Military Advocacy for Native American Rights," *The Frontier Army in the Settlement of the West* (Norman: University of Oklahoma Press, 1999), 237–59.

**35.** Richard Slotkin explores some reasons for the resurgence in cavalry films in the late forties in *Gunfighter Nation,* 328–43.

**36.** Smith, *View from Officers' Row,* 37; White, *It's Your Misfortune,* 338–40.

**37.** The classic texts are William H. Whyte, *The Organization Man* (New York: Simon & Schuster, 1956); and David Riesman, with Reuel Denny and Nathan Glazer, *The Lonely Crowd: A Study of the Changing American Character* (New Haven: Yale University Press, 1950).

**38.** Steven Higgins has made this point about Ince's work generally in "The Films of Thomas H. Ince"; film screening notes – Mary Pickford Theater, 1983; Thomas Ince subject file; Motion Picture, Broadcasting, and Recorded Sound Division; Library of Congress.

**39.** James Fenimore Cooper, *The Last of the Mohicans,* in *The Leatherstocking Tales,* vol. 1, Blake Nevius, ed. (New York: Library of America, 1985), 667.

**40.** Richard Slotkin, *The Fatal Environment: The Myth of the Frontier in the Age of Industrialization, 1800–1890* (Middletown, Conn.: Wesleyan University Press, 1985), 60; see also Dippie, *Vanishing American: White Attitudes,* 257–9.

**41.** Ray H. Mattison, ed., "An Army Wife on the Upper Missouri: The Diary of Sarah E. Canfield, 1866–1868," *North Dakota History* 20.4 (Oct. 1953): 191–220, at 217; quoted in Smith, *View from Officers' Row,* 19.

42. Utley, *Indian Frontier,* 105.

43. Robert S. Tilton, *Pocahontas: The Evolution of an American Narrative* (Cambridge: Cambridge University Press, 1994), 35.

44. Ibid., 7–8. For Pocahontas as "our first celebrated traitor to her own race," see Leslie A. Fiedler, *The Return of the Vanishing American* (Briarcliff Manor, N.Y.: Stein & Day, 1968), 63–83.

45. Rodman W. Paul, *The Far West and the Great Plains in Transition: 1859–1900* (New York: Harper & Row, 1988), 129.

46. Tilton, *Pocahontas,* 184.

47. Rayna Green, "The Pocahontas Perplex: The Image of Indian Women in American Culture," *Massachusetts Review* 16.4 (Autumn 1975): 698–714, at 704.

48. Howard Chandler Christy, *Liberty Belles: Eight Epochs in the Making of the American Girl* (Indianapolis: Bobbs–Merrill, 1912); Christy's "Pocahontas" is also reproduced in Martha Banta, *Imaging American Women: Idea and Ideals in Cultural History* (New York: Columbia University Press, 1987), 495.

49. See Jane Tompkins, *Sensational Designs: The Cultural Work of American Fiction, 1790–1860* (New York: Oxford University Press, 1985), 110–11.

50. The celebrated account is Theodora Kroeber, *Ishi in Two Worlds: A Biography of the Last Wild Indian in North America* (Berkeley: University of California Press, 1961); see also Dippie, *Vanishing American: White Attitudes,* 207–8.

**9. "No Indians Wanted"**

1. Ernest A. Dench, *Making the Movies* (New York: Macmillan, 1915), 92–3.

2. "No Indians Wanted," *MPW,* Oct. 18, 1913: 258.

3. Louis Reeves Harrison, "Wake Up! This Is 1912!" *MPW,* Jan. 6, 1912: 21.

4. Jane Tompkins, *West of Everything: The Inner Life of Westerns* (New York: Oxford University Press, 1992), 7–10.

5. Kevin Brownlow, *The War, the West, and the Wilderness* (New York: Alfred A. Knopf, 1979), 263–4; Michael Wallis, *The Real Wild West: The 101 Ranch and the Creation of the American West* (New York: St. Martin's Press, 1999), 438–9.

6. *MPW,* Dec. 5, 1914: 1390.

7. See Virginia Wright Wexman, *Creating the Couple: Love, Marriage, and Hollywood Performance* (Princeton, N.J.: Princeton University Press, 1993), 3, which cites statistics from David Bordwell, Janet Staiger, and Kristin Thompson, *The Classical Hollywood Cinema: Film Style and Mode of Production to 1960* (New York: Columbia University Press, 1985): 85 percent of pre-1960 Hollywood films have romance as their main plot and 95 percent as a main or secondary plot.

8. Roberta E. Pearson discusses these intertitles, although without noting them as later additions, in her otherwise excellent "The Revenge of Rain-in-the-Face? or, Custers and Indians on the Silent Screen," in Daniel Bernardi, ed., *The Birth of Whiteness: Race and the Emergence of U.S. Cinema* (New Brunswick, N.J.: Rutgers University Press, 1996), 273–99.

9. Zane Grey, *The Vanishing American* (New York: Grosset & Dunlap, 1925), 16. The Navaho tribe is given the fictional name "Nopah" in both the film and novel as a sop to the government agents and missionaries criticized; the film was shot primarily on Navaho lands in northeastern Arizona.

10. Richard Slotkin, *Gunfighter Nation: The Myth of the Frontier in Twentieth-Century*

*America* (New York: Atheneum, 1992), 211–13. See also Angela Aleiss, "Hollywood Addresses Indian Reform: *The Vanishing American*," *Studies in Visual Communication* 10.4 (Fall 1984): 53–60. For Grey's sympathy to Indians, see especially his early novels *Betty Zane* (1903) and *The Spirit of the Border* (1906), which had little readership until he achieved popularity in 1912 with *Riders of the Purple Sage.* Grey ended his original draft of *The Vanishing American* with the marriage of the Indian man and white woman, which Nophaie recognizes as the other, assimilationist way to vanish: "In the end I shall be absorbed by you – by our love – by our children"; quoted in Christine Bold, *Selling the Wild West: Popular Western Fiction, 1860–1960* (Bloomington: Indiana University Press, 1987), 89.

**11.** As a civilization Anasazi seem to have been forced to move south or were slowly decimated by a fifty-year drought beginning in the late thirteenth century; Peter Nabokov and Robert Easton, *Native American Architecture* (New York: Oxford University Press, 1989), 364.

**12.** Grey, *Vanishing American,* 136.

**13.** On Fairbanks, masculinity, and the West, see Linda Podheiser, "Pep on the Range, or Douglas Fairbanks and the World War I Era Western," *Journal of Popular Film and Television* 11.3 (Fall 1983): 122–30; and Gaylyn Studlar, "Wider Horizons: Douglas Fairbanks and Nostalgic Primitivism," in Edward Buscombe and Roberta E. Pearson, eds., *Back in the Saddle Again: New Essays on the Western* (London: British Film Institute, 1998), 63–76.

**14.** The native cast of *The Silent Enemy* included one impostor: The role of the main hunter was played by "Buffalo Child Long Lance," who claimed Blackfoot ancestry and in 1928 had published *Long Lance: The Autobiography of a Blackfoot Indian Chief.* He was unmasked, while the film was in production, by Chauncey Yellow Robe (Sioux), who delivers the film's spoken prologue; see Donald B. Smith, *Long Lance: The True Story of an Impostor* (Lincoln: University of Nebraska Press, 1982).

### 10. The West of the Mohicans

**1.** Quoted in Richard Drinnon, *Facing West: The Metaphysics of Indian Hating and Empire Building* (New York: Schocken Books, 1990), xiii.

**2.** Jan-Christopher Horak suggests that "Tourneur 'improves' on Cooper's novel" because of the film's sophisticated use of Cora, rather then of Natty, to reconcile wilderness and civilization; "Maurice Tourneur's Tragic Romance," in Gerald Perry and Roger Shatzkin, eds., *The Classic American Novel and the Movies* (New York: Ungar, 1977), 10–19.

**3.** Mark Twain, "Fenimore Cooper's Literary Offenses" [1895]; rpt. in Donald McQuade et al., eds. *The Harper American Literature,* 2d ed., vol. 2 (New York: HarperCollins, 1993), 307.

**4.** Quoted in Gary Edgerton, "'A Breed Apart': Hollywood, Racial Stereotyping, and the Promise of Revisionism in *The Last of the Mohicans,*" *Journal of American Culture* 17.2 (Summer 1994): 1–17, at 7, 13.

**5.** Marianna Torgovnick explores this aspect of Mann's film in *Primitive Passions: Men, Women, and the Quest for Ecstasy* (New York: Alfred A. Knopf, 1997), 144–50.

**6.** Gary Edgerton discusses this borrowing and precisely quantifies the marginalization of the Native American characters in this version; "A Breed Apart," 1–17. For a full discussion, with plot synopses, of all of the film versions mentioned above except *Der Letzte Mohikaner,* see Martin Barker and Roger Sabin, *The Lasting of the Mohicans: History of an American Myth* (Jackson: University Press of Mississippi, 1995), 56–120. Jeffrey Walker provides a brief overview of the films, with emphasis on the divergences of Mann's version from Cooper's novel, in "Deconstructing an American Myth: *The Last of the Mohicans* (1992)," in Peter C. Rollins and John E. O'Connor, eds., *Hollywood's Indian: The Portrayal of the Native American in Film* (Lexington: University Press of Kentucky, 1998), 170–86.

**11. Desert Places**

**1.** Robert Graves, ed., *Selected Poems of Robert Frost* (New York: Holt, Rinehart & Winston, 1963), 195.

**2.** For a critique of the pastoral mode along these lines, see John Seelye, "Some Green Thoughts on a Green Theme," *TriQuarterly* 23–4 (Winter–Spring 1972): 576–638. James Fenimore Cooper, *Home as Found* (1838); quoted in Alan Taylor, *William Cooper's Town: Power and Persuasion on the Frontier of the Early American Republic* (New York: Vintage Books, 1996), 426.

**3.** D. H. Lawrence, *Studies in Classic American Literature* [1924] (Harmondsworth, U.K.: Penguin Books, 1971), 61.

**4.** Richard Poirier quotes these lines from Emerson's *Journals* (Oct. 27, 1851) and explores the virtues of bareness in literary traditions in *The Renewal of Literature: Emersonian Reflections* (New Haven: Yale University Press, 1987), 71, 3–67.

**5.** Mather is quoted in Patricia Nelson Limerick, *Desert Passages: Encounters with the American Deserts* (Albuquerque: University of New Mexico Press, 1985), 5; and in Martin E. Marty, *Righteous Empire: The Protestant Experience in America* (New York: Dial Press, 1970), 6. For Mather's view of Indians, see Charles M. Segal and David C. Stineback, *Puritans, Indians, and Manifest Destiny* (New York: G. P. Putnam's Sons, 1977), 182. Roderick Nash notes how the Puritans drew their "desert" descriptions of New English from the Old Testament imagery; *Wilderness and the American Mind* (New Haven: Yale University Press, 1973), 38–41.

**6.** James Fenimore Cooper, *The Last of the Mohicans,* in *The Leatherstocking Tales,* vol. 1, Blake Nevius, ed. (New York: Library of America, 1985), 722.

**7.** Alexis de Tocqueville, *Democracy in America,* vol. 1, Phillips Bradley, ed. (New York: Vintage Books, 1954), 26.

**8.** William Shakespeare, *The Two Gentlemen of Verona,* V.iv.2, in Stephen Greenblatt, ed., *The Norton Shakespeare* (New York: W. W. Norton, 1997), 127. On the evolution in the meaning of "desert," see also Peter Wild's introduction to his *The Opal Desert: Explorations of Fantasy and Reality in the American Southwest* (Austin: University of Texas Press, 1999), 1–4.

**9.** *American Poetry: The Nineteenth Century,* vol. 1: *Freneau to Whitman,* John Hollander, ed. (New York: Library of America, 1993), 162–5.

**10.** Nathaniel Hawthorne, *The Scarlet Letter,* in *Collected Novels,* Millicent Bell, ed. (New York: Library of America, 1983), 290. Sacvan Bercovitch discusses this passage and Hawthorne's use of Indians in *The Office of The Scarlet Letter* (Baltimore: Johns Hopkins University Press, 1991), 28–9.

**11.** Zane Grey, "What the Desert Means to Me," *The American Magazine* 98 (Nov. 1924): 5–6. Grey's connection of his desert conversion into "a savage" with an intensified manhood reinforces David Anthony Tyeeme Clark and Joane Nagel's argument about the uses of native symbols in "White Men, Red Masks: Appropriations of 'Indian' Manhood in Imagined Wests," in Matthew Basso, Laura McCall, and Dee Garceau, eds., *Across the Great Divide: Cultures of Manhood in the American West* (New York: Routledge, 2001), 109–30. For a full history of the evolving meanings of white men acting out American Indian identities, see Philip J. Deloria, *Playing Indian* (New Haven: Yale University Press, 1998).

**12.** "Indian and Western subjects": e.g., "What Is an American Subject?" *MPW*, Jan. 22, 1910: 82. "Indian and cowboy pictures": e.g., the December 1910 letter to "a trade paper," quoted in "Where Do We Ride From Here?" *Photoplay* 15.3 (Feb. 1919): 37. "Western and Indian films": e.g., "Los Angeles as a Producing Center," *MPW*, Apr. 8, 1911; rpt. in George C. Pratt, *Spellbound in Darkness: A History of the Silent Film* (Greenwich, Conn.: New York Graphic Society, 1973), 89.

### PART TWO: "IT'S TIME FOR YOUR HISTORY LESSON, DEAR": JOHN WAYNE AND THE PROBLEM OF HISTORY IN THE HOLLYWOOD WESTERN OF THE 1930S

**1.** For instance, *Photoplay* editorialized in April 1929: "Lindbergh has put the cowboy into the discard as a type of the national hero. . . . Within the past two years, Western pictures, always surefire profit earners, have lost their popularity"; quoted in George N. Fenin and William K. Everson, *The Western*, rev. ed. (New York: Grossman, 1973), 174.

**2.** Edward Buscombe, who has published the most complete calculations, finds 44 A-Westerns made from 1930 through 1939, out of a total of 1,063 U.S. feature-length Westerns; *The BFI Companion to the Western* (New York: Atheneum, 1988), tab. 5: 427. Others have calculated even fewer A-Westerns; see Randy Roberts and James S. Olson, *John Wayne: American* (New York: Free Press, 1995), 150. I add a few to Buscombe's total because he doesn't include the handful of A-efforts by minor studios (such as Republic's *Man of Conquest*, 1939) and apparently keeps to a strict genre definition (excluding, e.g., *Viva Villa!*, 1934). By any estimate, B- or "series" Westerns comprised more than 95 percent of the decade's Westerns. In total, about 5,500 U.S. feature films were made in the 1930s. Westerns thus comprised about 20 percent of the decade's titles but significantly less than that in terms of total production costs.

**3.** John Wayne's Westerns for Warner Bros. in 1932–3 were budgeted at $28,000 (and made an average profit for the studio of over $60,000 each). His Monogram and "Lone Star" Westerns of 1933–5 were budgeted at $15,000 or less, including Wayne's $2,500-per-film salary. For these and other dollar figures for B-Westerns, see Karl Thiede, "The Bottom Line: Low Finance in the Reel West," in the extremely useful anthology, Packy Smith and Ed Hulse, eds., *Don Miller's Hollywood Corral: A Comprehensive B-Western Roundup* (Burbank, Calif.: Riverwood Press, 1993), 407–25. Costs for *The Big Trail* are reported in "*The Big Trail*," *Variety*, Oct. 29, 1930; rpt. in *Variety Film Reviews* (New York: Garland, 1983), vol. 4, n.p.

**4.** On the B-film in the thirties, see Brian Taves, "The B Film: Hollywood's Other Half," in Tino Balio, ed., *Grand Design: Hollywood as a Modern Business Enterprise, 1930–1939* (Berkeley: University of California Press, 1995), 313–50; Charles Flynn and Todd McCarthy, "The Economic Imperative: Why Was the B Movie Necessary?" in Flynn and McCarthy, eds., *King of the Bs: Working within the Hollywood Sys-*

*tem – An Anthology of Film History and Criticism* (New York: E. P. Dutton, 1975), 13–43.

**5.** In an opening newspaper headline, the 1935 *New Frontier* confuses, or conflates, the 1889 rush with the 1893 "Cherokee Strip" rush.

**6.** In rerelease and on some videos, the 1939 *New Frontier* is retitled *Frontier Horizon,* presumably to distinguish it from the 1935 film.

**7.** Henry Wallace also published a book titled *New Frontiers* in 1934; see David M. Wrobel, "The New Deal Frontier," *The End of American Exceptionalism: Frontier Anxiety from the Old West to the New Deal* (Lawrence: University Press of Kansas, 1993), 122–42.

**8.** Garry Wills, *John Wayne's America: The Politics of Celebrity* (New York: Simon & Schuster, 1997), 29.

## 12. *The Big Trail* and the Weight of History

**1.** Alexander Bakshy, "The Romantic Western," *The Nation,* Nov. 12, 1930: 534–6. "*The Big Trail,*" *Variety,* Oct. 29, 1930.

**2.** For the full context of these experiments, see John Belton, *Widescreen Cinema* (Cambridge, Mass.: Harvard University Press, 1992), 48–62. *The Big Trail* in its 70mm "Grandeur" version (aspect ratio of 2:1) was restored onto 35mm CinemaScope in 1985 by the Museum of Modern Art, although only the standard version is available on video at the time I write. On the restoration, see Ronald Haver, "Trail Blazing," *American Film* 11.7 (May 1986): 17–18. The widescreen version of *Billy the Kid* is not known to survive; for a still frame from that version, see Raymond Durgnat and Scott Simmon, *King Vidor, American* (Berkeley: University of California Press, 1988), 181.

**3.** The standard-aperture version of *The Big Trail* runs 107 minutes; the Grandeur version is listed as 125 minutes in initial reviews and runs 120 minutes as restored by MoMA. Unless otherwise noted, my quotations of the film's dialogue and intertitles are from the Grandeur version, which is sometimes slightly different even in scenes included in both versions because of use of alternate takes.

**4.** Raoul Walsh, *Each Man in His Time* (New York: Farrar, Straus & Giroux, 1974), 241.

**5.** "Raoul Walsh Talks about D. W. Griffith," *Film Heritage* 10.3 (Spring 1975): 1–4; Kevin Brownlow, *The War, the West, and the Wilderness* (New York: Alfred A. Knopf, 1979), 99–102.

**6.** See Roger McNiven, "The Western Landscape of Raoul Walsh," *Velvet Light Trap* 15 (Fall 1975): 50–5.

**7.** A replica wagon train had left St. Louis on April 10, 1930, and arrived at the Idaho–Oregon border October 10 – declared "Oregon Trail Day" by Idaho teachers – two weeks before the release of *The Big Trail.* That 1930 became the year to celebrate the Oregon Trail seems to have been due primarily to a grizzled Oregonian named Ezra Meeker. He had crossed the plains by wagon in 1852 and spent the twenty-five years before his death at age ninety-seven giving speeches about the historical importance of the Oregon Trail while repeatedly crossing the country by covered wagon, light plane, and auto – in which he died on the "trail" in 1928. His efforts convinced a number of municipalities to proclaim 1930 as "Covered Wagon Centennial" year, confused somewhere along the way with the centennial of Meeker's own birth; see Michael Kammen, *Mystic Chords of Memory: The Transformation of Tradition in American Culture* (New York: Vintage Books, 1993), 397–400.

**8.** As Robert Rosenstone notes in discussing these traits of Hollywood historical films, even such apparent exceptions as mainstream films about the Holocaust are structured optimistically to leave us feeling that things are getting better: "Aren't we lucky we did not live in those benighted times? Isn't it nice that certain people kept the flag of hope alive?"; Robert A. Rosenstone, *Visions of the Past: The Challenge of Film to Our Idea of History* (Cambridge, Mass.: Harvard University Press, 1995), 56. See also Rosenstone, ed., *Revisioning History: Film and the Construction of a New Past* (Princeton, N.J.: Princeton University Press, 1995); Mark C. Carnes, ed., *Past Imperfect: History According to the Movies* (New York: Henry Holt, 1995); Marcia Landy, *Cinematic Uses of the Past* (Minneapolis: University of Minnesota Press, 1996); and Landy, ed., *The Historical Film: History and Memory in Media* (New Brunswick, N.J.: Rutgers University Press, 2001).

**9.** Patricia Nelson Limerick, "The Adventures of the Frontier in the Twentieth Century," in James Grossman, ed., *The Frontier in American Culture* (Berkeley: University of California Press, 1994), 72–3.

**10.** Rick Altman, *The American Film Musical* (Bloomington: Indiana University Press, 1989), 19.

**11.** For instance, see the discussion of John Wayne in Virginia Wright Wexman, *Creating the Couple: Love, Marriage, and Hollywood Performance* (Princeton, N.J.: Princeton University Press, 1993), 67–129.

**12.** Garry Wills discusses these conflicts in *John Wayne's America: The Politics of Celebrity* (New York: Simon & Schuster, 1997), 48, 52. See also Deborah Thomas, "John Wayne's Body," in Ian Cameron and Douglas Pye, eds., *The Book of Westerns* (New York: Continuum, 1996), 75–87, at 79.

**13.** Sandra L. Myres, *Westering Women and the Frontier Experience, 1800–1915* (Albuquerque: University Press of New Mexico, 1982), 160. See also Julie Roy Jeffrey, "Ladies Have the Hardest Time, That Emigrate by Land," *Frontier Women: The Trans-Mississippi West, 1840–1880* (New York: Hill & Wang, 1979), 25–50. The most complete treatment is John Mack Faragher, *Women and Men on the Overland Trail* (New Haven: Yale University Press, 1979), which emphasizes how fully male and female spheres still remained separate even on the trail.

**14.** "*The Big Trail*," *Variety*, Oct. 29, 1930.

**15.** This series of shots in *The Big Trail* can at least claim something over the way such linkage is typically expressed in B-Western dialogue: "Sorry I called you a heifer, ma'am," as a cowboy apologizes in *Sunset Range* (1935).

**16.** See Randy Roberts and James S. Olson, *John Wayne: American* (New York: Free Press, 1995), 127. This pattern was invariable until Wayne became for a time in 1938 and 1939 one of the "Three Mesquiteers"; no kissing there, the three men ride off together in the final shots. Richard D. McGhee notices that in *The Dawn Rider* (1935), as Wayne rides off with his bride on a buggy, the focus shifts to two watching men: the doctor and the undertaker. "The doctor expects to deliver their babies, but the undertaker is here to drive a nail in the coffin of the romantic hero"; *John Wayne: Actor, Artist, Hero* (Jefferson, N.C.: McFarland, 1990), 65.

**17.** The sequence in which she makes this admission explicit is cut from the standard-aperture version.

**13. What's the Big Idea?**

1. Claude Lévi-Strauss, *Myth and Meaning* (New York: Schocken Books, 1978), 42–3.

2. See Henry Steele Commager, *The Empire of Reason: How Europe Imagined and America Realized the Enlightenment* (New York: Anchor Books, 1978); Robert A. Ferguson, "The American Enlightenment, 1750–1820," in Sacvan Bercovitch, ed., *The Cambridge History of American Literature,* vol. 1: *1590–1820* (Cambridge: Cambridge University Press, 1994), 347–537, at 378–82.

3. Thomas Hobbes, *Leviathan,* J. C. A. Gaskin, ed. (New York: Oxford University Press, 1996), 84; Hobbes makes this argument in his chap. 13, "Of the Natural Condition of Mankind as Concerning Their Felicity and Misery." He admits that historically such a violent state of nature is rare but gives the example of "many places in America" (85) – in 1651! For how Hobbes's ideas were manipulated to conform with social Darwinism and other justifications for imperialism, see Michael Nerlich, *Ideology of Adventure: Studies in Modern Consciousness, 1100–1750,* 2 vols., trans. Ruth Crowley (Minneapolis: University of Minnesota Press, 1987), vol. 1, 200–9.

4. Richard Hofstadter, *The American Political Tradition* (New York: Vintage Books, 1948), 3–5.

5. Zane Grey, *The Man of the Forest* [1920] (New York: Forge Books, 2000), 114.

6. Herbert Spencer, *First Principles* (1862); quoted in Richard Hofstadter, *Social Darwinism in American Thought* [1945] (Boston: Beacon Press, 1992), 37. For discussion of how Spencer was misunderstood in America, see also T. J. Jackson Lears, *No Place of Grace: Antimodernism and the Transformation of American Culture, 1880–1920* (New York: Pantheon, 1981), 20–2.

7. Hobbes, *Leviathan,* 85. Before the arrival of "spaghetti Westerns" in the mid-1960s, the most complete denials of man's nobility in the face of a brutally survivalist world tend to be found on the fringes of the Western genre, such as Nicholas Ray's "Eskimo" drama *The Savage Innocents* (1959) or the Death Valley finale of Erich von Stroheim's *Greed* (1924).

8. The most memorable such social-Darwinist image announces the philosophy of Sam Peckinpah's *The Wild Bunch* (1969) in the opening hierarchy of children giggling above ants swarming over a scorpion. There are witty examples too in the subsequent Peckinpah film, *The Ballad of Cable Hogue* (1970), as when Cable apologizes to a Gila monster for killing it ("Sorry, old timer, but you're only part poison and I'm hungry for meat"). See also the desert scenes of William Wellman's *Yellow Sky* (1948), discussed in Part Three.

9. See Lears, *No Place of Grace,* 137; also Marianna Torgovnick, *Gone Primitive: Savage Intellects, Modern Lives* (Chicago: University of Chicago Press, 1990).

10. The seminal study is John Higham, "The Reorientation of America Culture in the 1890s," in John Weiss, ed., *The Origins of Modern Consciousness* (Detroit: Wayne State University Press, 1965), 25–48; see also Gail Bederman, *Manliness and Civilization: A Cultural History of Gender and Race in the United States, 1880–1917* (Chicago: University of Chicago Press, 1995); and Jane Tompkins, *West of Everything: The Inner Life of Westerns* (New York: Oxford University Press, 1992).

11. Roosevelt condemned "that baleful law of natural selection which tells against the survival of some of the most desirable classes"; quoted in Edmund Mor-

ris, *Theodore Rex* (New York: Random House, 2001), 34. "The view that acquired characteristics cannot be inherited . . . is hardly worthy of serious reflection," Roosevelt wrote; quoted in Thomas G. Dyer, *Theodore Roosevelt and the Idea of Race* (Baton Rouge: Louisiana State University Press, 1980), 39, within a discussion of Roosevelt's commitment to the genetic theories of French naturalist Jean Lamarck: 37–44.

**12.** Theodore Roosevelt, *An Autobiography* [1913] (New York: Da Capo Press, 1985), 52, 100, 125. See also John A. Barsness, "Theodore Roosevelt as Cowboy: The Virginian as Jacksonian Man," *American Quarterly* 21.3 (1969): 609–19.

**13.** Quoted in William Henry Harbaugh, *Power and Responsibility: The Life and Times of Theodore Roosevelt* (New York: Farrar, Straus & Cudahy, 1961), 50.

**14.** David McCullough, interviewed in the PBS television documentary *TR, The Story of Theodore Roosevelt* (1996, prod. David Grubin; aired on *American Experience*). Films caught on early to the contradictions within Roosevelt's image and took their cue from newspaper editorial cartoons. In the Edison Company's 1901 *Terrible Teddy, the Grizzly King*, the TR figure shoots a house cat from a tree while being trailed by two men wearing signs reading "MY PHOTOGRAPHER" and "MY PRESS AGENT."

**15.** On wages for cowboys, see David Dary, *Cowboy Culture: A Saga of Five Centuries* (New York: Avon Books, 1981), 191–2, 297–8. Roosevelt is quoted in Dee Brown, *The Westerners* (New York: Holt, Rinehart & Winston, 1974), 265. The frontispiece to *Hunting Trips of a Ranchman* is reproduced in Bederman, *Manliness and Civilization*, 177.

**16.** György Lukács, *The Historical Novel* [1955], trans. Hannah and Stanley Mitchell (London: Merlin Press, 1962); see also Philip Fisher, *Hard Facts: Setting and Form in the American Novel* (New York: Oxford University Press, 1987), 14–21.

**17.** The debate between the gangster film and the Western at this time is discussed in Raymond Durgnat and Scott Simmon, *King Vidor, American* (Berkeley: University of California Press, 1988), 183–5.

**18.** See Christopher Lasch, *The True and Only Heaven: Progress and Its Critics* (New York: W. W. Norton, 1991), 78–81; and Tomkins, *West of Everything*, 125–8.

**19.** Estwick Evans, *A Pedestrious Tour of Four Thousand Miles, through the Western States and Territories, during the Winter and Spring of 1818* (Concord, N.H.: Joseph C. Spear, 1819), 6. Evans's little-known book is discussed in Roderick Nash, *Wilderness and the American Mind* (New Haven: Yale University Press, 1973), 56–7.

**20.** Evans, *Pedestrious Tour*, 6, 102. Estwick Evans was a member of the New Hampshire bar at the time of his long walk through the West – he turned south at Michigan and ended in New Orleans – fought in Greece in the 1820s, and returned to become a New Hampshire legislator. He published a broadside promoting his (failed) election as secretary to the U.S. Senate in 1836 and, at age 77, another pamphlet "offering myself for the Presidency," which he admits "may be termed eccentric"; *Mr. Evans for the Presidency* (Washington, D.C., 1864).

**21.** John Wayne, however, doesn't go as far in promoting the gentle view of westward wagon travel as the WPA guidebook *The Oregon Trail*, published in 1939: "the pioneering forefathers were not different from their descendants; they enjoyed the overland journeys in exactly the same way that modern Americans enjoy their holiday cruises and week-end ski trips"; Federal Writers Project of the Works Progress Administration, *The Oregon Trail* (New York: Hastings House, 1939), xi.

22. James Fenimore Cooper, *The Prairie*, in *The Leatherstocking Tales*, vol. 1, Blake Nevius, ed. (New York: Library of America, 1985), 898.

23. Much of Peter A. French's *Cowboy Metaphysics: Ethics and Death in Westerns* (Lanham, Md.: Rowman & Littlefield, 1997) elaborates this idea; see esp. chap. 2, "The Mount and the Mountains," 13–46. It is also succinctly argued in Tompkins, *West of Everything*, 28–45.

24. Owen Wister, *The Virginian: A Horseman of the Plains* [1902] (Boston: Houghton Mifflin, 1968), 146–54.

25. See Sydney E. Ahlstrom, *A Religious History of the American People* (New Haven: Yale University Press, 1972), esp. 295–313, 388–402; Emory Elliott, "New England Puritan Literature," in Bercovitch, *Cambridge History of American Literature*, vol. 1, 169–306, at 279–306.

26. Yvor Winters, "Maule's Curse, or Hawthorne and the Problem of Allegory" [1938], in Winters, *In Defense of Reason* (Denver, Colo.: Allan Swallow, 1947), 157–75, at 158.

27. "Inner-direction" was introduced in *The Lonely Crowd* to describe a post-Renaissance, premodern ideal, said to be found especially in societies strong in "exploration, colonization, and imperialism"; David Riesman, with Reuel Denny and Nathan Glazer, *The Lonely Crowd: A Study of the Changing American Character* (New Haven: Yale University Press, 1950), 15. Wayne's interview and the sequence from *Straight Shooting* are in the film *Directed by John Ford* (1971, dir. Peter Bogdanovich).

28. Sacvan Bercovitch, *The American Jeremiad* (Madison: University of Wisconsin Press, 1978), xiv, 9, 24, 63. Bercovitch was arguing against Perry Miller's then-influential emphasis on the vehemence of denunciations of the present and the sense of doom in Puritan jeremiads.

29. Sacvan Bercovitch, *The Puritan Origins of the American Self* (New Haven: Yale University Press, 1975), 88–9; on the Puritan theory of "plain style," see 29–31.

30. Robert Warshow, "Movie Chronicle: The Westerner," *Partistan Review* 21.4 (Mar.–Apr. 1954): 190–203; rpt. in Jim Kitses and Gregg Rickman, eds., *The Western Reader: Selected Readings in the Western American Film* (New York: Limelight, 1998), 35–47.

31. See Bercovitch, *Puritan Origins*, 5–6.

32. Quoted in Albert K. Weinberg, *Manifest Destiny: A Study of Nationalist Expansion in American History* (Baltimore: Johns Hopkins University Press, 1935), 74.

33. Arminian motto quoted in Martin E. Marty, *Righteous Empire: The Protestant Experience in America* (New York: Dial Press, 1970), 53.

34. Letter to Mrs. Samuel H. Smith, Aug. 6, 1816, in Thomas Jefferson, *Jefferson: Political Writings*, Joyce Appleby and Terence Ball, eds. (Cambridge: Cambridge University Press, 1999), 399.

35. "The Motion Picture Production Code" [1930] as reprinted in Gerald Gardner, ed., *The Censorship Papers: Movie Censorship Letters from the Hays Office, 1934–1968* (New York: Dodd, Mead, 1987), 207–12; variant versions are in Thomas Doherty, *Pre-Code Hollywood: Sex, Immorality, and Insurrection in American Cinema, 1930–1934* (New York: Columbia University Press, 1999), 347–67.

36. The film combines elements of "The Outcasts of Poker Flat" with "The Luck of Roaring Camp," both in Bret Harte, *The Luck of Roaring Camp and Other Stories*

[1870], and rpt. in John Seelye, ed., *Stories of the Old West: Tales of the Mining Camp, Cavalry Troop, & Cattle Ranch* (New York: Penguin Books, 1994), 17–36.

**37.** James Fenimore Cooper, *The Deerslayer,* in *The Leatherstocking Tales,* vol. 2, Blake Nevius, ed. (New York: Library of America, 1985), 948–9.

**38.** Washington Irving, *A Tour of the Prairies* [1835], in William P. Kelly, ed., *Selected Writings of Washington Irving* (New York: Modern Library, 1984), 436.

**39.** See Edmund Wilson, *Apologies to the Iroquois* [1959] (Syracuse, N.Y.: Syracuse University Press, 1992), 46–8; Jack Weatherford, "The Founding American Fathers," *Indian Givers: How the Indians of the Americas Transformed the World* (New York: Fawcett Columbine, 1988), 133–50.

**40.** Increase Mather, *An Earnest Exhortation to Inhabitants of New-England* (Boston: John Foster, 1676), 9; quoted in Richard Slotkin, *Regeneration through Violence: The Mythology of the American Frontier, 1600–1860* (Middletown, Conn.: Wesleyan University Press, 1973), 86.

**41.** Thomas Jefferson, *Notes on the State of Virginia,* in Jefferson, *Writings,* Merrill D. Peterson, ed. (New York: Library of America, 1984), 290–1. Also: "I repeat it again, cultivators of the earth are the most virtuous and independent citizens," 301. The earlier passage is thoroughly discussed in Leo Marx, *The Machine in the Garden: Technology and the Pastoral Ideal in America* (New York: Oxford University Press, 1964), 121–44, and Roy Harvey Pearce, *Savagism and Civilization: A Study of the Indian and the American Mind* (Berkeley: University of California Press, 1988), 66–70.

**42.** Letter to Rev. James Madison, Oct. 28, 1785; quoted in Henry Nash Smith, *Virgin Land: The American West as Symbol and Myth* [1950] (New York: Vintage Books, 1957), 144. Jefferson's comment on morals in cultivators is from the same passage in *Notes on the State of Virginia,* 290.

**43.** Letter to "Mr. Lithson," Jan. 4, 1805; quoted in Smith, *Virgin Land,* 237.

**44.** Under the economic principles of the physiocrats, only agriculture produces a surplus, which other economic activities merely distribute; hence agriculture is the basis for all true wealth; see John Rennie Short, *Imagined Country: Environment, Culture and Society* (London: Routledge, 1991), 34–5. For Jefferson's belief that the American continent provided greater opportunities for European physiocratic principles, see Gilbert Chinard, "Introduction on Jefferson and the Physiocrats," in his edition of *The Correspondence of Jefferson and Du Pont de Nemours* (Baltimore: Johns Hopkins University Press, 1931), ix–cxxiii; also Richard Hofstadter, *The Age of Reform* (New York: Vintage Books, 1955), 28; Marx, *Machine in the Garden,* 126.

**45.** The 1862 Homestead Act extended Jefferson's assumption – based on eastern modes of agriculture – that western land would be used for farming, for which the 160 acres given for a small fee and five years residence was adequate size in a few places, such as Nebraska and parts of the Dakotas. But, again like Jefferson, the act refused to consider that sustenance in most of the Great Plains and the desert West would have to rely on using land for grazing, mining, or logging. For a particularly evocative look at the failure of homesteading on arid lands, in eastern Montana, see Jonathan Rabin, *Bad Land: An American Romance* (New York: Vintage Books, 1996). Jefferson's governing assumption about population growth also proved false. As Richard White notes, the U.S. population grew by thirty-two million between 1862 and 1890, but only two million settled on farms created by the Homestead Act; White, *"It's Your Misfortune and None of My Own": A History of the American West* (Norman: University of Oklahoma Press, 1991), 142–7.

**46.** Several bills were introduced in the U.S. Congress in 1842 offering a square mile (640 acres) of land to American men over age eighteen who settled in Oregon. After the U.S. Oregon Territory was created, the Donation Land Law of 1850 gave 320 acres to single men and 640 acres to married couples; Dean L. May, *Three Frontiers: Family, Land, and Society in the American West, 1850–1900* (Cambridge: Cambridge University Press, 1994), 148–9. The joke about the "Parting of the Ways" is quoted in John D. Unruh Jr., *The Plains Across: The Overland Emigrants and the Trans-Mississippi West, 1840–60* (Urbana: University of Illinois Press, 1982), 61; see also Arthur King Peters, *Seven Trails West* (New York: Abbeville Press, 1996), 85–116; and the PBS documentary *In Search of the Oregon Trail* (1996, prod.-dir. Michael Farrell).

**47.** See Joseph J. Ellis, *American Sphinx: The Character of Thomas Jefferson* (New York: Vintage Books, 1998), 161–6; Myra Jehlen, "The Literature of Colonization," in Bercovitch, *Cambridge History of American Literature*, vol. 1, 11–168, at 140.

**48.** Ellis, *American Sphinx*, 252.

**49.** Robert Remini, *Andrew Jackson*, vol. 2: *The Course of American Freedom, 1822–1832* (Baltimore: Johns Hopkins University Press, 1998), 34.

**50.** The characterization of Jeffersonian democracy is Richard Hofstadter's in *American Political Tradition*, 19.

**51.** Quoted in Arthur M. Schlesinger Jr., *The Age of Jackson* (New York: Mentor Books, 1949), 32–3.

**52.** Remini, *Andrew Jackson*, vol. 2, 193.

**53.** Sen. Hugh Lawson White spoke of Jackson's natural schooling in 1827; quoted in John William Ward, *Andrew Jackson: Symbol for an Age* (New York: Oxford University Press, 1962), 31, which also discusses the similar positioning of Jackson in the 1828 presidential campaign: 63–71. See also Richard Slotkin, *The Fatal Environment: The Myth of the Frontier in the Age of Industrialization, 1800–1890* (Middletown, Conn.: Wesleyan University Press, 1985), 122–3; and Slotkin, *Regeneration through Violence*, 395.

**54.** Remini, *Andrew Jackson*, vol. 1: *The Course of American Empire, 1767–1821* (Baltimore: Johns Hopkins University Press, 1998), 178–86; Remini, *Andrew Jackson*, vol. 2, 1, 92.

**55.** See Schlesinger, *Age of Jackson*, 131.

**56.** The line has long been attributed to Jackson in his 1832 presidential reelection campaign, but it's not clear when or even if he spoke it publicly.

**57.** Letter to John Adams, Oct. 28, 1813, in Jefferson, *Political Writings*, 187. Richard Slotkin applies Jefferson's idea to Jackson in *Fatal Environment*, 123.

**58.** On the contradictory politics of *Our Daily Bread*, see Durgnat and Simmon, *King Vidor, American*, 148–64.

**59.** Wister, *Virginian*, 93.

**60.** Letter to Thomas Seymour, Feb. 11, 1807, in Jefferson, *Political Writings*, 273.

**61.** Carl N. Degler, *Out of Our Past* (New York: Harper & Row, 1970), 139; Remini, *Andrew Jackson*, vol. 2, 366, see also 45, 117, 229.

### 14. Manifestations of Destiny

**1.** Jean-Jacques Rousseau, *Émile; or, On Education*, trans. Allan Bloom (New York: Basic Books, 1979), 98–100; Bloom analyzes the episode in his introduction, 13–

14; see also Philip Fisher, *Hard Facts: Setting and Form in the American Novel* (New York: Oxford University Press, 1987), 30.

2. The book-length study of the political implications of this landscape tradition is Albert Boime, *The Magisterial Gaze: Manifest Destiny and American Landscape Painting, c. 1830–1865* (Washington, D.C.: Smithsonian Institution Press, 1991).

3. On this principle, "still much in vogue in playground disputes: 'It's mine; I got here first,'" see Patricia Nelson Limerick, *The Legacy of Conquest: The Unbroken Past of the American West* (New York: W. W. Norton, 1987), 66–73.

4. William Bradford, *Of Plymouth Plantation* [written 1630–46]; quoted in Richard Slotkin, *Regeneration through Violence: The Mythology of the American Frontier, 1600–1860* (Middletown, Conn.: Wesleyan University Press, 1973), 38. Paramount's *Desert Gold* (1936), from the Zane Grey novel, makes a concession rare for this era on this point: To the question of whether a mine is already owned by Indians, an assessor replies, "You know how these things are. It belongs to the first white man who finds it. We used to have quite a nation of Indians in this territory, but they're dying out."

5. Franklin is quoted in Richard Hofstadter, *The Age of Reform* (New York: Vintage Books, 1955), 27; see also Anders Stephanson, *Manifest Destiny: American Expansionism and the Empire of Right* (New York: Hill & Wang, 1995), 24–6; Henry Nash Smith, *Virgin Land: The American West as Symbol and Myth* [1950] (New York: Vintage Books, 1957), 141–2, 195–6; Slotkin, *Regeneration through Violence*, 556.

6. Quoted in Albert K. Weinberg, *Manifest Destiny: A Study of Nationalist Expansion in American History* (Baltimore: Johns Hopkins University Press, 1935), 74–5.

7. Alexis de Tocqueville, *Democracy in America*, vol. 1, Phillips Bradley, ed. (New York: Vintage Books, 1954), 26.

8. Robert Warshow, "Movie Chronicle: The Westerner," *Partistan Review* 21.4 (Mar.–Apr. 1954): 190–203; rpt. in Jim Kitses and Gregg Rickman, eds., *The Western Reader: Selected Readings in the Western American Film* (New York: Limelight, 1998), 35–47, at 37.

9. John William Ward, *Andrew Jackson: Symbol for an Age* (New York: Oxford University Press, 1962), 146–8; Richard White, *"It's Your Misfortune and None of My Own": A History of the American West* (Norman: University of Oklahoma Press, 1991), 74; Stephanson, *Manifest Destiny*, 31.

10. On the term, see Stephanson, *Manifest Destiny*, 5, 38–9, 43; White, *It's Your Misfortune*, 73–5; on its lack of use in the West, see Sherry L. Smith, *The View from Officers' Row: Army Perceptions of Western Indians* (Tucson: University of Arizona Press, 1990), 132–3.

11. On Wayne's ancestry, see Randy Roberts and James S. Olson, *John Wayne: American* (New York: Free Press, 1995), 7–14.

12. White, *It's Your Misfortune*, 69–77; John D. Unruh Jr., *The Plains Across: The Overland Emigrants and the Trans-Mississippi West, 1840–60* (Urbana: University of Illinois Press, 1982), 15–16.

13. Of Native Americans, Jefferson wrote, "The ultimate point of rest and happiness for them is to let our settlements and theirs meet and blend together, to intermix, and become one people"; quoted in Anthony F. C. Wallace, "'The Obtaining Lands': Thomas Jefferson and the Native Americans," in James P. Ronda, ed., *Thomas Jefferson and the Changing West* (Albuquerque: University of New Mexico Press, 1997), 25–41, at 30.

**14.** Garry Wills, *John Wayne's America: The Politics of Celebrity* (New York: Simon & Schuster, 1997), 25.

**15.** For a sociological study of the reverse pattern of identification – contemporary Native Americans identifying with John Wayne in *The Searchers* – see JoEllen Shively, "Cowboys and Indians: Perceptions of Western Films among American Indians and Anglos," *American Sociological Review* 57.6 (Dec. 1992): 725–33. For a more biting view of Wayne's destructiveness from a Native American perspective, see Louis Owens, "The Invention of John Wayne," in his *Mixedblood Messages: Literature, Film, Family, Place* (Norman: University of Oklahoma Press, 1998), 99–112.

**16.** On Boone's place, in John Filson's version of his story, between white and Indian worlds ("I was exceedingly familiar and friendly with them"), see Slotkin, *Regeneration through Violence*, 278–94. For a reliable life of Carson, see Thelma S. Guild and Harvey L. Carter, *Kit Carson: A Pattern for Heroes* (Lincoln: University of Nebraska Press, 1984), which, notwithstanding its subtitle, recounts Carson's less-than-heroic battles against the Navahos. The fullest account, which defends Carson from previous charges of genocide, is Tom Dunlay, *Kit Carson and the Indians* (Lincoln: University of Nebraska Press, 2000), esp. 306–24.

**17.** The actual chance of being killed by Native Americans on the California and Oregon Trail seems to have been about one-fiftieth of the chances of dying from less dramatic causes. Somewhere between two hundred fifty thousand and four hundred thousand travelers made the trip by wagon, and about twenty thousand died while on the trail; of these, as many as four hundred were reported killed by Indians, but even that figure is probably exaggerated; see Arthur King Peters, *Seven Trails West* (New York: Abbeville Press, 1996), 88–94. As John Unruh discusses, a number of murders originally attributed to Indians proved to have been committed by whites who hoped to disguise their crimes; thus the melodramatic basis of *The Big Trail*'s revenge plot – a murder made to look like the work of Indians – is not without authenticity; *Plains Across*, 154–5.

**18.** See W. J. Cash, *The Mind of the South* [1941] (New York: Vintage Books, 1969), esp. 32–5, 43–6; Bertram Wyatt-Brown, *Southern Honor: Ethics and Behavior in the Old South* (New York: Oxford University Press, 1982).

**19.** "Southern Curse: Why America's Murder Rate Is So High," *New York Times*, July 26, 1998, sec. 4: 1, 16.

**20.** In a subtle look at the function of the South in late-1930s Westerns, Peter Stanfield notes how often fictional westerners *begin* as southerners, from "the Virginian" onward, and discusses how the West becomes the site where national tensions are resolved. As he argues in connection with Gene Autry, southern "hillbilly" music too was made respectable and marketable in the 1930s by its move west into the singing cowboy; *Hollywood, Westerns and the 1930s: The Lost Trail* (Exeter, U.K.: University of Exeter Press, 2001), 56–77, 193–224. See also Stanfield, "Dixie Cowboys and Blue Yodels: The Strange History of the Singing Cowboy," in Edward Buscombe and Roberta E. Pearson, eds., *Back in the Saddle Again: New Essays on the Western* (London: British Film Institute, 1998), 96–118; and Stanfield, *Horse Opera: The Strange History of the 1930s Singing Cowboy* (Urbana: University of Illinois Press, 2002), 71–7.

**21.** Theodore Strauss, "*Three Faces West*," *New York Times*, Aug. 19, 1940; rpt. in *The New York Times Film Reviews* (New York: Arno Press, 1970), vol. 3, 1727.

22. See Jane Tompkins's related complaints about the methodologies traditionally used for discussing the genre's popularity and origins; *West of Everything: The Inner Life of Westerns* (New York: Oxford University Press, 1992), 27–8, 39, 43–4.

## 15. Rambling into Surrealism: The B-Western

1. Robert G. Athearn, *The Mythic West in Twentieth-Century America* (Lawrence: University Press of Kansas, 1986), 32; and Richard Slotkin, *Gunfighter Nation: The Myth of the Frontier in Twentieth-Century America* (New York: Atheneum, 1992), 29–30.

2. "Campaign Address on Progressive Government at the Commonwealth Club, San Francisco, Calif. September 23, 1932," in *The Public Papers and Addresses of Franklin D. Roosevelt*, vol. 1: *The Genesis of the New Deal*, comp. Samuel I. Rosenman (New York: Random House, 1938), 746–50. The metaphor of western lands as "a safety valve to the great social steam engine" was initially Edward Everett's in the 1830s; Richard Slotkin, *The Fatal Environment: The Myth of the Frontier in the Age of Industrialization, 1800–1890* (Middletown, Conn.: Wesleyan University Press, 1985), 117. See also Henry Nash Smith, "The Garden as Safety Valve," *Virgin Land: The American West as Symbol and Myth* [1950] (New York: Vintage Books, 1957), 234–45.

3. Gabriel Kolko, *Main Currents in Modern American History* (New York: Pantheon Books, 1984), 28; Richard Hofstadter, *The Age of Reform* (New York: Vintage Books, 1955), 110–11.

4. In easily the most sophisticated analysis of Gene Autry, Peter Stanfield suggests how Autry and other Western stars mediate between an older world and modernity. My sense is, however, that this is not accomplished exactly through "his battles against modern technology," which Autry, uniquely among B-Western stars, tends to embrace; *Hollywood, Westerns and the 1930s: The Lost Trail* (Exeter, U.K.: University of Exeter Press, 2001), 78. See also Stanfield, *Horse Opera: The Strange History of the 1930s Singing Cowboy* (Urbana: University of Illinois Press, 2002), esp. 83–8, 102–9. 149–54.

5. Frederick Jackson Turner, "The Significance of the Frontier in American History" [lecture, July 12, 1893], in George Rogers Taylor, ed., *The Turner Thesis* (Lexington, Mass.: D. C. Heath, 1972), 3–28; and Turner, "Contributions of the West to American Democracy," *Atlantic Monthly* 91 (Jan. 1903): 83–96, rpt. in Taylor, *Turner Thesis*, 28–48, at 30.

6. Slotkin, *Gunfighter Nation*, 26–61; see also Slotkin, *Fatal Environment*, 33–47, 52.

7. Leslie A. Fiedler, *The Return of the Vanishing American* (Briarcliff Manor, N.Y.: Stein & Day, 1968), 21.

8. Turner, "Significance of the Frontier," 4.

9. Ibid., 24. For Turner's sense that he was broadening history to include the common frontiersman – beyond the Great Man histories of the Francis Parkman tradition – see Kerwin Lee Klein, *Frontiers of Historical Imagination: Narrating the European Conquest of Native America, 1890–1990* (Berkeley: University of California Press, 1999), esp. 11–12, 82–8.

10. Edmund Morris, *The Rise of Theodore Roosevelt* (New York: Ballantine Books, 1979), 466; see also Slotkin, *Gunfighter Nation*, 29–32.

11. Turner, "Significance of the Frontier," 4–5, 17; Smith, *Virgin Land*, 291–2; Klein, *Frontiers of Historical Imagination*, 78–9.

**12.** See Slotkin, *Fatal Environment*, 51–2. As Lee Kerwin Klein discusses in connection with Turner's master's thesis, he *began* his career with analysis of the importance of the encounter of European Americans with Native Americans; *Frontiers of Historical Imagination*, 129–44.

**13.** See Slotkin, *Gunfighter Nation*, 58–9.

**14.** On Turner's conflicted and evolving ideas about the Populist movement, see Ray Allen Billington, *Frederick Jackson Turner: Historian, Scholar, Teacher* (New York: Oxford University Press, 1973), 438–9.

**15.** For the role of the South in the movement, see Steven Hahn, *The Roots of Southern Populism: Yeoman Farmers and the Transformation of the Georgia Upcountry* (New York: Oxford University Press, 1983), esp. "Epilogue: The Contours of Populism," 269–89.

**16.** In "The Problem of the West" (*Atlantic Monthly* 78 [Sept. 1896]: 289–97) – 1896 also being the year of William Jennings Bryan's "Cross of Gold" speech – Turner allows that the level of discontent in the West had risen to a level to unite the region with farmers and workers of the South and East; rpt. in John Mack Faragher, ed., *Rereading Frederick Jackson Turner* (New Haven: Yale University Press, 1994), 61–76, at 74. See also Smith, *Virgin Land*, 291–2.

**17.** African-American farmers founded a separate group, the Colored Farmers' National Alliance; Robert C. McMath Jr., *American Populism: A Social History, 1877–1898* (New York: Hill & Wang, 1993), 57, 92–4, 206–7.

**18.** David M. Kennedy makes this argument in *Freedom from Fear: The American People in Depression and War, 1929–1945* (New York: Oxford University Press, 1999), 202; and this connection was also something like the view of Populism in histories written around the start of the New Deal. John Chamberlain, in *Farewell to Reform: The Rise, Life and Decay of the Progressive Mind in America* [1933, 2d ed.] (Gloucester, Mass.: Peter Smith, 1958), made the comparison negatively by predicting that the New Deal wouldn't survive prosperity (which he saw as right around the corner in 1933), vii–xi. John D. Hicks ends *The Populist Revolt: A History of the Farmer's Alliance and the People's Party* (Minneapolis: University of Minnesota Press, 1931) by claiming that "the old Populist panaceas" are receiving "the enthusiastic support of Hooverian Republicans and Alsmithian Democrats," 422. In short, Populism shifted from a minority grievance in the 1890s to something not so far from a patriotic set of agreed principles in the 1930s.

**19.** In an interesting essay, "The New Western American Historiography and the Emergence of the New American Westerns," Rick Worland and Edward Countryman track "the divergence" of academic historians from film Westerns, which they see intersecting only in the 1990s. If both their premises about Turner and conclusions are finally a bit too easy, it's because they bypass not only B-Westerns but also the ways that "spaghetti Westerns" and Sam Peckinpah's films anticipate New Western historiography in abandoning the "frontier" to take up stories and iconography of the "border." In Edward Buscombe and Roberta E. Pearson, eds., *Back in the Saddle Again: New Essays on the Western* (London: British Film Institute, 1998), 182–96.

**20.** Athearn, *Mythic West*, 39.

**21.** Robert S. McElvaine, *The Great Depression: America, 1929–1941* (New York: Times Books, 1993), 135; Kennedy, *Freedom from Fear*, 207.

**22.** Kennedy, *Freedom from Fear*, 17; McElvaine, *Great Depression*, 35–6.

**23.** See Hofstadter, *Age of Reform,* 24; McMath, *American Populism,* 110.
**24.** Turner, "Significance of the Frontier," 24.
**25.** Kennedy, *Freedom from Fear,* 253.
**26.** For a complete overview of "New Western History," see Richard White, *"It's Your Misfortune and None of My Own": A History of the American West* (Norman: University of Oklahoma Press, 1991). White's book is also famous, or infamous, for being a history of the West that avoids the word "frontier" except when citing its use by others.
**27.** George Morrill, "The West's Most Incredible Outlaw," *American History Illustrated* 18.8 (Dec. 1983): 40–4.
**28.** Ibid., 42.
**29.** Hofstadter, *Age of Reform,* 5; see also 82–93. On Jesse James and the Grange movement, see McMath, *American Populism,* 56–65.
**30.** Kennedy, *Freedom from Fear,* 196.
**31.** Edward Buscombe, *Stagecoach* (London: British Film Institute, 1992), 18.
**32.** Ibid., 14.
**33.** That Tom Tyler's character is misidentified in filmographies in most of the books about John Ford may say something about the separation of the realms of A- and B-Westerns among critics also: e.g., Tag Gallagher, *John Ford: The Man and His Films* (Berkeley: University of California Press, 1986), 527; Peter Bogdanovich, *John Ford* (Berkeley: University of California Press, 1967), 130; J. A. Place, *The Western Films of John Ford* (Secaucus, N.J.: Citadel Press, 1974), 30. For an accurate filmography, see Buscombe, *Stagecoach,* 92.

### 16. "Don't Cry, Pat, It's Only a Western": A Note on Acting

**1.** Randy Roberts and James S. Olson, *John Wayne: American* (New York: Free Press, 1995), 149.
**2.** Joe Fisher, "Clarke [*sic*] Gable's Balls: Real Men Never Lose Their Teeth," in Pat Kirkham and Janet Thumin, eds., *You Tarzan: Masculinity, Movies and Men* (New York: St. Martin's Press, 1993), 35–51, at 49. Roberts and Olson, *John Wayne: American,* 135.
**3.** Quoted in Maurice Zolotow, *Shooting Star: A Biography of John Wayne* (New York: Simon & Schuster, 1974), 122.
**4.** Peter Bogdanovich, *John Ford* (Berkeley: University of California Press, 1967), 70.
**5.** Sarah Kozloff, *Overhearing Film Dialogue* (Berkeley: University of California Press, 2000), 155–62. Claire Trevor recalled Ford's method with Wayne on *Stagecoach:* "He would stop in the middle of a rehearsal, take Duke's chin in his hand, and say, 'What are you doing? Don't act with your chin. It's *here* [the eyes] – *here's* where you think'"; quoted in Joseph McBride, *Searching for John Ford: A Life* (New York: St. Martin's Press, 2001), 297.
**6.** For a history of these conventions, see James Naremore, *Acting in the Cinema* (Berkeley: University of California Press, 1988), 36, 50–67.
**7.** Edward Buscombe, *Stagecoach* (London: British Film Institute, 1992), 14.
**8.** Roberts and Olson, *John Wayne: American,* 84–5.
**9.** Gordon M. Wickstrom, "Buffalo Bill the Actor," *Journal of the West* 34.1 (Jan. 1995): 62–9, at 63–4. The Chicago *Times* is quoted in Edward Buscombe, *The BFI*

*Companion to the Western* (New York: Atheneum, 1988), 75. "Ned Buntline" was the pen name of Carroll Judson. On Buffalo Bill as an actor, see also Joy S. Kasson, *Buffalo Bill's Wild West: Celebrity, Memory, and Popular History* (New York: Hill & Wang, 2002), 20–7.

**10.** Quoted in Peter Stanfield, *Horse Opera: The Strange History of the 1930s Singing Cowboy* (Urbana: University of Illinois Press, 2002), 114.

## 17. Time, Space, and the Western

**1.** Henry David Thoreau, *Walden; or, Life in the Woods* [1854], in *"A Week"; "Walden; or, Life in the Woods"; "The Maine Woods"; "Cape Cod,"* Robert F. Sayre, ed. (New York: Library of America, 1985), 412.

**2.** The linguistic and literary implications of the two terms are also discussed in Edwin Fussell, *Frontier: American Literature and the American West* (Princeton, N.J.: Princeton University Press, 1965), 13–18.

**3.** J. Hector St. John de Crèvecoeur, *Letters from an American Farmer* [1782] (New York: Oxford University Press, 1997), 44.

**4.** Letter to William Ludlow, 1824. *The Writings of Thomas Jefferson* (Washington, 1904–5), vol. xvi, 74–5; quoted in Fussell, *Frontier,* 46–7.

**5.** For instance, in William Darby's early *Emigrant's Guide* (1818) a voyage west to Texas would reveal to the traveler "man in every stage of his progress, from the most civilized to the most savage"; quoted in Michael Kammen, *Mystic Chords of Memory: The Transformation of Tradition in American Culture* (New York: Vintage Books, 1993), 51.

**6.** Frederick Jackson Turner, "The Significance of the Frontier in American History" [lecture, July 12, 1893], in George Rogers Taylor, ed., *The Turner Thesis* (Lexington, Mass.: D. C. Heath, 1972), 11.

**7.** Owen Wister, preface to *Red Men and White* (New York: Grosset & Dunlap, 1895), vi; quoted in Christine Bold, *Selling the Wild West: Popular Western Fiction, 1860–1960* (Bloomington: Indiana University Press, 1987), 65–6.

**8.** Alexander Pope, *Selected Poetry and Prose,* William K. Wimsatt, ed. (New York: Holt, Rinehart & Winston, 1951), 9.

**9.** This distinction between nostalgia and memory is developed by Christopher Lasch, *The True and Only Heaven: Progress and Its Critics* (New York: W. W. Norton, 1991), esp. chap. 3, "Nostalgia: The Abdication of Memory," 82–120.

**10.** Miriam Hansen, "Chameleon and Catalyst: The Cinema as an Alternative Public Sphere," *Babel and Babylon: Spectatorship in American Silent Film* (Cambridge, Mass.: Harvard University Press, 1991), 90–125; Ben Singer, "Making Sense of the Modernity Thesis," *Melodrama and Modernity: Early Sensational Cinema and Its Contexts* (New York: Columbia University Press, 2001), 101–30. The "modernity thesis" is David Bordwell's skeptical term in *On the History of Film Style* (Cambridge, Mass: Harvard University Press, 1997), 139–49, 295.

**11.** Svetlana Boym, *The Future of Nostalgia* (New York: Basic Books, 2001), esp. 7–18, 33–55.

**12.** Thomas J. Schlereth, *Victorian America: Transformations in Everyday Life, 1876–1915* (New York: HarperCollins, 1992), 29–31; Jon Roush, "Square Places, Round Wholes," in Deborah Clow and Donald Snow, eds., *Northern Lights: A Selection of New Writing from the American West* (New York: Vintage Books, 1994), 22–5.

13. See, for instance, John Mack Faragher, "Afterword: The Significance of the Frontier in American Historiography," in Faragher, ed., *Rereading Frederick Jackson Turner* (New Haven: Yale University Press, 1994), 225–41.

14. On the West primarily as "place" in recent historical writings, see Patricia Nelson Limerick, "What on Earth Is New Western History?" in Limerick, Clyde A. Milner II, and Charles E. Rankin, eds., *Trails: Toward a New Western History* (Lawrence: University Press of Kansas, 1991), 81–8. For an argument that analyzing the West as "process" remains vital, see William Cronon, George Miles, and Jay Gitlin, "Becoming West: Toward a New Meaning for Western History," in their edited volume *Under an Open Sky: Rethinking America's Western Past* (New York: W. W. Norton, 1992), 3–27.

15. D. H. Lawrence, *Studies in Classic American Literature* [1924] (Harmondsworth, U.K.: Penguin Books, 1971), 60. Lawrence is not strictly accurate about Cooper's composition order, but he catches a general truth. Natty starts old (in *The Pioneers,* 1823) and ends young (in *The Deerslayer,* 1841), although he dies in *The Prairie* (1827).

16. Kammen, *Mystic Chords of Memory,* 486.

17. Henry Adams, *The Education of Henry Adams* [1904] (Boston: Houghton Mifflin, 1961), 91.

18. Steven Hahn describes a "distaste for the power of the marketplace" within land transfers in the South and land ownership itself as a symbol of distinction, especially from landless African Americans, beyond measurement in dollars; *The Roots of Southern Populism: Yeoman Farmers and the Transformation of the Georgia Upcountry* (New York: Oxford University Press, 1983), 81–9.

19. Kammen, *Mystic Chords of Memory,* esp. 14, 132, 136–7, 145.

20. William Gilpin, *Mission of the North American People* (Philadelphia, 1873); quoted in Roderick Nash, *Wilderness and the American Mind* (New Haven: Yale University Press, 1973), 41.

21. This is Turner's usage as well: "So long as free land exists, the opportunity for a competency exists, . . ."; "Significance of the Frontier," 24; see also Lasch, *True and Only Heaven,* 531.

22. It's true that Turner was also lamenting the census report of the disappearance of a frontier "line," replaced by "isolated bodies of settlement," although such a line was always more of a metaphor or fantasy; "Significance of the Frontier," 3. On the increase in "frontier" counties in the 2000 census, see Peter Kilborn, "Bit by Bit, Tiny Morland, Kan., Fades Away," *New York Times,* May 10, 2001: A1, A22; and Timothy Egan, "As Others Abandon Plains, Indians and Bison Come Back," *New York Times,* May 27, 2001: A1, A18.

23. Alexis de Tocqueville, "What Causes Democratic Nations to Incline Towards Pantheism," *Democracy in America,* vol. 2, Phillips Bradley, ed. (New York: Vintage Books, 1954), 32–3. As Peter Stanfield discusses, the significant exclusion from this scene of ecumenical liberalism in *Cimarron* is the "black child-fool," Isaiah, a representative of the Old South; *Hollywood, Westerns and the 1930s: The Lost Trail* (Exeter, U.K.: University of Exeter Press, 2001), 210–12.

24. R. W. B. Lewis, *The American Adam: Innocence, Tragedy and Tradition in the Nineteenth Century* (Chicago: University of Chicago Press, 1955), 91.

**PART THREE: "THAT SLEEP OF DEATH": JOHN FORD AND THE DARKNESS OF THE CLASSIC WESTERN IN THE 1940S**

1. Don DeLillo, *The Names* (New York: Vintage Books, 1983), 140, 198–9. DeLillo touches on the same themes in his biting first novel, *Americana* (New York: Penguin Books, 1971), structured through the narrator's escape from Manhattan into the far Southwest. Catching part of "a Kirk Douglas western on TV," he comments (239–40), "I loved the landscapes, the sense of near equation called forth by man and space, the cowboy facing silent hills; there it was, the true subject of film, space itself, how to arrange it and people it, time hung in a desert window, how to win out over sand and bone. (It's just a cowboy picture, I reminded myself.)"

2. Merian Cooper, quoted in Ronald Haver, *David O. Seznick's Hollywood* (New York: Alfred A. Knopf, 1980), 224 (emphasis in original).

3. André Bazin, "The Evolution of the Western," in *What Is Cinema?*, vol. 2, ed. and trans. Hugh Gray (Berkeley: University of California Press, 1971), 149–57, at 150; Bazin's term "superwestern" for what immediately followed never caught on.

4. Ray White discusses *Wild Horse Rustlers* in "The Good Guys Wore White Hats: The B Western in American Culture," in Richard Aquila, ed., *Wanted Dead or Alive: The American West in Popular Culture* (Urbana: University of Illinois Press, 1996), 135–59, at 154.

5. Richard Slotkin discusses *Bataan* (1943) and *Objective, Burma!* (1945) in these terms; *Gunfighter Nation: The Myth of the Frontier in Twentieth-Century America* (New York: Atheneum, 1992), 318–28.

## 18. *My Darling Clementine* and the Fight with Film Noir

1. Alan Lovell, "The Western," in Bill Nichols, ed., *Movies and Methods: An Anthology* [vol. 1] (Berkeley: University of California Press, 1976), 164–75, at 169. Jim Kitses, *Horizons West: Anthony Mann, Budd Boetticher, Sam Peckinpah – Studies of Authorship within the Western* (Bloomington: Indiana University Press, 1969), 17. Thomas Schatz, *Hollywood Genres: Formulas, Filmmaking, and the Studio System* (New York: Random House, 1981), 67. For André Bazin *Clementine* is a "baroque embellishment" on the purer "classicism" of *Stagecoach;* "The Evolution of the Western," in *What Is Cinema?*, vol. 2, ed. and trans. Hugh Gray (Berkeley: University of California Press, 1971), 149–57, at 150. Christian Metz finds an "accent of parody" within "the classic Western" of *My Darling Clementine; Language and Cinema,* trans. Donna Jean Umiker-Sebeok (The Hague: Mouton, 1974), 151–2. Douglas Gomery calls the film "an accepted 'classic'" in "Mise-en-scène in John Ford's *My Darling Clementine,*" *Wide Angle* 2.4 (1978): 14–19, at 14. See also Michael Coyne, *The Crowded Prairie: American National Identity in the Hollywood Western* (London: I. B. Tauris, 1997), 34: "*My Darling Clementine* is today considered a genre classic, . . ." *Clementine* has been labeled "poetic" by, for instance, Andrew Sarris, "*My Darling Clementine,*" *Village Voice,* Aug. 12, 1986: 61, and Elizabeth Pincus, "Film Pick of the Week: *My Darling Clementine,*" *L.A. Weekly,* June 17, 1994: 57.

2. With intentional perversity or unintentional blindness, Frank Krutnik in his book on film noir cites *My Darling Clementine* and "the sentimental comedy-drama" *It's a Wonderful Life* to demonstrate the "diverse" range of nonnoir 1946 films; *In a Lonely Street: "Film Noir," Genre, Masculinity* (London: Routledge, 1991), 56. For a

full argument for the bleakness of *It's a Wonderful Life*, see Robert Ray, *A Certain Tendency of the Hollywood Cinema, 1930–1980* (Princeton, N.J.: Princeton University Press, 1985), 179–215.

**3.** In the shooting script for *My Darling Clementine* (as well as in the 1939 film version of the Earp legend, Allan Dwan's *Frontier Marshal*), Doc uses his handkerchief as a trick weapon of sorts: While holding one end of it, he makes his opponents hold onto the other, thus assuring a "fair" drop as both go for their guns. In Ford's completed film, the handkerchief remains only an emblem of mortality. The finished film's divergences from the shooting script are usefully cataloged in Robert Lyons, ed., *My Darling Clementine* (Brunswick, N.J.: Rutgers University Press, 1984).

**4.** There's a point to Robin Wood's complaint that Ford treats Chihuahua with racist contempt for the first hour of the film until "she is shot and dying, whereupon he promptly sentimentalizes her"; "*Shall* We Gather at the River?: The Late Films of John Ford," *Film Comment* 7.3 (Fall 1971): 8–17, at 13. The heritage of Ford's visual shift from darkness to light can be seen, for instance, in a legend set down in the seventeenth century by Canadian Catholic priests about their Mohawk convert Kateri Tekakwitha, whose face was said to have miraculously turned white at the moment of her death and who became known as "the Lilly of the Mohawks"; see John Demos, *The Unredeemed Captive: A Family Story from Early America* (New York: Vintage Books, 1995), 128; and Leslie A. Fiedler, *The Return of the Vanishing American* (Briarcliff Manor, N.Y.: Stein & Day, 1968), 79. A similarly "miraculous" change to white at the moment of his Indian hero's death was also the iconographic solution forced on Zane Grey by editors of *The Ladies' Home Journal* for serialization of *The Vanishing American*. His original ending for the novel, where the Indian settles into happy married life with a white women from the East, proved unpublishable in his lifetime. For a fascinating comparison of his original version, the serialized version, and a compromise in the published novel, see Christine Bold, *Selling the Wild West: Popular Western Fiction, 1860–1960* (Bloomington: Indiana University Press, 1987), 89–91.

**5.** For brief discussion of the critical response to this ending and a strained postmodern defense of it ("the director made a deliberate decision to make fun of the conventions of narrative verisimilitude"), see Suzanne Liandrat-Guigues, *Red River* (London: British Film Institute, 2000), 12–13.

**6.** Nino Frank's early essay "Un Nouveau Genre 'policier': L'Aventure criminelle," *L'Écran français* 61 (Aug. 28, 1946): 8–14, is translated in Alain Silver and James Ursini, eds., *Film Noir Reader 2* (New York: Limelight Editions, 1999), 15–19. Alain Silver and Elizabeth Ward note some of film noir's oppositions to the Western in their *Film Noir: An Encyclopedic Reference to the American Style* (Woodstock, N.Y.: Overlook Press, 1979), 325. Borde and Chaumenton's use of John Wayne in *Panorama du film noir américain, 1941–1953* (Paris: Édition de Minuit, 1955) is discussed in James Naremore's superb *More Than Night: Film Noir in Its Contexts* (Berkeley: University of California Press, 1998), 18–22.

**7.** Henry Fonda, interviewed by Peter Bogdanovich in his film *Directed by John Ford* (1971).

**8.** "No, don't look at the fucking script," Ford advised Elia Kazan in 1945. "That will confuse you. You know the story. Tell it with pictures. Forget the words. . . . Direct it like you were making a silent"; Elia Kazan, *A Life* (New York: Alfred A.

Knopf, 1988), 255–6. Thinking of the visuals of *My Darling Clementine* as resembling a von Sternberg film would also reinforce Corey K. Creekmur's sophisticated gay reading, "Acting Like a Man: Masculine Performance in *My Darling Clementine*," in Creekmur and Alexander Doty, eds., *Out in Culture: Gay, Lesbian, and Queer Essays on Popular Culture* (Durham, N.C.: Duke University Press, 1995), 167–82.

**9.** Kazan, *Life*, 304–16.

**10.** "This land!" laments Lars Jorgensen (John Qualen) in *The Searchers* over the cause of his son's death; see Richard Hutson, "Sermons in Stone: Monument Valley in *The Searchers*," in Leonard Engel, ed., *The Big Empty: Essays on Western Landscapes as Narrative* (Albuquerque: University of New Mexico Press, 1994), 187–205. For a survey of how film noir was attacked in the 1940s for the immorality of its violence and a look at how noir represents death, see Paul Arthur, "Murder's Tongue: Identity, Death, and the City in Film Noir," in J. David Slocum, ed., *Violence and American Cinema* (New York: Routledge/American Film Institute, 2001), 153–75.

**11.** Robin Wood details the implications of Mary's caricature within his discussion of how Hollywood genres interact in "Ideology, Genre, Auteur," *Film Comment* 13.1 (Jan.–Feb. 1977): 46–51, at 48–9.

**12.** For example, Silver and Ward, *Film Noir*, 325.

## 19. Out of the Past

**1.** Bert Glennon's interview in *American Cinematographer* (Feb. 1939) is quoted in Edward Buscombe, *Stagecoach* (London: British Film Institute, 1992), 57. See also Richard Slotkin, *Gunfighter Nation: The Myth of the Frontier in Twentieth-Century America* (New York: Atheneum, 1992), 310–11.

**2.** Will Wright, *Six-Guns and Society: A Structural Study of the Western* (Berkeley: University of California Press, 1975), 32, 201. His other three types of Western are labeled the Vengeance Variation, the Transition Theme, and the Professional Plot.

**3.** Henry Nash Smith, *Virgin Land: The American West as Symbol and Myth* [1950] (New York: Vintage Books, 1957), 202. Peter Wollen, *Signs and Meaning in the Cinema*, rev. ed. (Bloomington and London: Indiana University Press, 1972), 96. As Kerwin Lee Klein argues, "Smith's opposition of nature and civilization . . . *could* be assimilated to structuralist equations," but his appeal "to consciousness, free will, and individual agency would not survive the operation"; *Frontiers of Historical Imagination: Narrating the European Conquest of Native America, 1890–1990* (Berkeley: University of California Press, 1999), 244.

**4.** Wollen, *Signs and Meaning*, 104–5.

**5.** Michael Coyne, *The Crowded Prairie: American National Identity in the Hollywood Western* (London: I. B. Tauris, 1997), 37.

**6.** Among the other pre-*Clementine* Wyatt Earp films are the 1937 serial *Wild West Days* and a 1940 remake of *Law and Order*, both with Johnny Mack Brown. *The Arizonian* (1935) and *Tombstone, the Town Too Tough to Die* (1942) both star Richard Dix as Wyatt Earp types. Errol Flynn's character in *Dodge City* (1939) is also based loosely on Earp.

**7.** According to W. R. Burnett, author of *Law and Order*'s source novel *Saint Johnson* (New York: Dial Press, 1930), Josephine Earp "objected very strenuously to the publication of my book. She came out to Universal Studios to try to stop them from filming it"; "W. R. Burnett Interviewed by Ken Mate and Pat McGilligan," *Film Com-*

*ment* 19.1 (Jan.–Feb. 1983): 58–70, at 62. Producer Darryl Zanuck called Josephine Earp's bluff for the 1939 *Frontier Marshal* and appeased her with a $5,000 payment. As he suspected, she wasn't really all that eager for a courtroom airing of the facts about the Earps; see Jon Tuska, *The American West in Film: Critical Approaches to the Western* (Lincoln: University of Nebraska Press, 1988), 191–2; and John Mack Faragher, "The Tale of Wyatt Earp," in Mark C. Carnes, ed., *Past Imperfect: History According to the Movies* (New York: Henry Holt, 1995), 154–61, at 160.

**8.** Burnett, *Saint Johnsom*, 61. C. L. Sonnichsen takes the title without irony and thus finds that "the novel is misnamed" in his negative critique; *From Hopalong to Hud: Thoughts on Western Fiction* (College Station: Texas A&M University Press, 1978), 45–7.

**9.** In 1948 the Arizona Supreme Court voided a provision of the state constitution that prevented Native Americans from voting; see Library of Congress, "American Memory" Voting Project http://memory.loc.gov/ammem/ndlpedu/features/election. About his inspiration for the novel, W. R. Burnett said, "I got the idea it was a political thing: Republicans versus Democrats. The Earps were Republicans, and the Sheriff and the other gang were all Democrats"; "W. R. Burnett Interview," 62.

**10.** Quoted in Joseph McBride and Michael Wilmington, *John Ford* (New York: Da Capo Press, 1975), 90.

**11.** "Interview with Winston Miller," in Robert Lyons, ed., *My Darling Clementine* (Brunswick, N.J.: Rutgers University Press, 1984), 141–50, at 141. According to Miller, the other credited writer (also the film's producer), Samuel Engel, made his additions to the script on location. Engel's name was added to the screen credits after two Screen Writers Guild arbitrations, and the controversy resulted in a subsequent tightening of the rules regarding producers crediting themselves as screenwriters.

**12.** Joseph McBride, *Searching for John Ford: A Life* (New York: St. Martin's Press, 2001), 430.

**13.** Three serious books do their best to sort out the truth, although they don't abandon the feuding: Paula Mitchell Marks, *And Die in the West: The Story of the O.K. Corral Gunfight* (New York: Simon & Schuster, 1989); Casey Tefertiller, *Wyatt Earp: The Life behind the Legend* (New York: John Wiley & Sons, 1997); and Allen Barra, *Inventing Wyatt Earp: His Life and Many Legends* (New York: Carroll & Graf, 1998).

**14.** McBride, *Searching for John Ford*, 431–2.

**15.** The Western's actors also engage in the debate carried on within the genre. In the 1934 *Frontier Marshal*, the scheming mayor who robs his own bank is played by Berton Churchill, who blusters, "That's what's the matter with this town – no respect for the law." In *Stagecoach*, Berton Churchill plays the similarly thieving, right-wing banker, who rants that "What this country needs is a businessman for president." The business sneak who gives liquor to the gun-toting Indian in the 1939 *Frontier Marshal* is played by John Carradine, who introduces himself with "Yup, drove me out of Lordsburg," as if he'd been resurrected in the same costume after *Stagecoach*, released five months earlier. Russell Simpson plays essentially the same role as solid Tombstone citizen in three of these first four versions of the Earp legend. (He's missing only from the 1939 version.) The reliable Ward Bond earns promotions: Beginning as the drunk gunslinger in the 1934 *Frontier Marshal*, he has by 1939 become the weak-willed sheriff who refuses to face down the drunk; by 1946 he's an Earp brother.

**16.** This scene goes back on film to *The Return of Draw Egan* in 1916, where William S. Hart plays the lone westerner who demonstrates his prowess by gunning down a barroom ruffian and is asked to stay on as sheriff – only to run up against townsfolk who find in his criminal past an excuse to deny him community support when he needs it most.

**17.** As Peter Lehman argues, "it is only by repressing the role of money, trading, and capitalism in the West that Ford can represent his ideal communities and families"; "How the West Wasn't Won: The Repression of Capitalism in John Ford's Westerns," in Gaylyn Studlar and Matthew Bernstein, eds., *John Ford Made Westerns: Filming the Legend in the Sound Era* (Bloomington: Indiana University Press, 2001), 132–53.

**18.** If one sees the atomic blasts of Hiroshima and Nagasaki as demonstrations to the Soviets as well as to Japan, then such a post–World War II, pre-cold-war historical moment vanishes; for that argument, see Howard Zinn, *A People's History of the United States* (New York: Harper & Row, 1980), 413–16. The term "Cold War" wouldn't be coined – by Bernard Baruch – until after *Clementine*'s release, but several key events in cold-war psychology predate its filming, including Stalin's Communist Party Congress speech of February 1946 (which William O. Douglas called "the declaration of World War III") and Churchill's "Iron Curtain" speech of March 1946; see William L. O'Neill, *American High: The Years of Confidence, 1945–1960* (New York: Free Press, 1986), 64–8; Geoffrey Perrett, *A Dream of Greatness: The American People, 1946–1963* (New York: Coward, McCann & Geoghegan, 1979), 130; and Joseph C. Goulden, *The Best Years: 1945–1950* (New York: Atheneum, 1976), 256–8. *My Darling Clementine* has been read as "a Cold War Western" by Stanley Corkin in "Cowboys and Free Markets: Post–World War II Westerns and U.S. Hegemony," *Cinema Journal* 39.3 (2000): 66–91; Peter Biskind in *Seeing Is Believing: How Hollywood Taught Us to Stop Worrying and Love the Fifties* (New York: Pantheon Books, 1983), 34–40; and Thomas H. Pauly in "The Cold War Western," *Western Humanities Review* 33.3 (Summer 1979): 257–73.

**19.** Phil Hardy, *The Film Encyclopedia: The Western*, rev. ed. (London: Aurum Press, 1991), 375. The year 1946 was also the most successful for Hollywood studios generally, both in inflation-adjusted box-office revenue and in profits; Thomas Schatz, *Boom and Bust: American Cinema in the 1940s* (Berkeley: University of California Press, 1999), 289–91, 465.

**20.** "The Protestant Revolution," *Life*, June 14, 1948: 59–94, at 94; "The History of Western Culture: Renaissance Man," *Life*, Mar. 3, 1947: 69–83, at 69. The *Life* series was unsigned. Whittaker Chambers wrote the first seven installments and collaborated on the rest; Terry Teachout, ed., *Ghosts on the Roof: Selected Journalism of Whittaker Chambers, 1931–1959* (Washington, D.C.: Regnery Gateway, 1989), xxiv, 195–253. Richard Hofstadter, in the opening sentence of *The American Political Tradition* (New York: Vintage Books, 1948), picks up on the same phrasing and mood to arrive at less sanguine conclusions: "Since Americans have recently found it more comfortable to see where they have been than to think of where they are going, their state of mind has become increasingly passive and spectatorial" (v).

### 20. "Shakespeare? In Tombstone?"

**1.** The Clantons' name for Thorndyke is a vestige of an earlier comic sequence, apparently cut by producer Darryl Zanuck, in which Thorndyke drunkenly misplaced his "Yorick's" skull prop for *Hamlet.* The omitted sequence also explains why Thorndyke performs alone: He has lost not only Yorick's skull but his entire acting company, who have run out on him, presumably for the same lack of payment that he floridly demonstrates later in leaving the hotel. See Robert Lyons, ed., *My Darling Clementine* (Brunswick, N.J.: Rutgers University Press, 1984), 115–16.

**2.** Granville Thorndyke has forgotten, or the filmmakers have omitted, a line-and-a-half missing between a cut to a closer view: ". . . and scorns of time, /The oppressor's wrong, the proud man's contumely, /The pangs of disprized love, the law's delay. . . ." Punctuation and spelling follow G. R. Hibbard, ed., *Hamlet* (New York: Oxford University Press, 1987).

**3.** Clair Eugene Willson, *Mimes and Miners: A Historical Study of the Theater in Tombstone,* University of Arizona Bulletin 6.1 (Tucson, 1935), 128.

**4.** For this evolution in perceptions of Shakespeare, see Lawrence W. Levine, *Highbrow/Lowbrow: The Emergence of Cultural Hierarchy in America* (Cambridge, Mass: Harvard University Press, 1988), 13–81.

**5.** Quoted in Margaret G. Watson, *Silver Theater: Amusements of the Mining Frontier in Early Nevada, 1850–1864* (Glendale, Calif.: Arthur H. Clark, 1964), 164–5.

**6.** *Daily Rocky Mountain News,* July 29, 1861; quoted in Melvin Schoberlin, *From Candles to Footlights: A Biography of the Pike's Peak Theater, 1859–1876* (Denver, Colo.: Old West, 1941), 61–2 (emphasis in original).

**7.** Adela Rogers St. Johns, "I Knew Wyatt Earp," *American Weekly,* May 22, 1960: 10; cited in Paul Andrew Hutton, "Showdown at the Hollywood Corral: Wyatt Earp and the Movies," *Montana* 45.3 (Summer 1995): 2–31, at 6. Richard Slotkin, *Gunfighter Nation: The Myth of the Frontier in Twentieth-Century America* (New York: Atheneum, 1992), 384. For Walter Noble Burns in *Tombstone: An Iliad of the Southwest* [1927] (New York: Penguin Books, 1942), "John Ringo stalks through the stories of old Tombstone like a Hamlet among outlaws . . ." (94).

**8.** Although "conscience" for Shakespeare generally means something closer to consciousness, he also inflects the word with our modern – and Western film – meaning of moral scruples (as in "thy conscience /Is so possessed with guilt"; *The Tempest,* I.ii.471–2).

**9.** For revenge as essential to the "complete classical form" of the Western, see Alan Lovell, "The Western," in Bill Nichols, ed., *Movies and Methods: An Anthology* [vol. 1] (Berkeley: University of California Press, 1976), 164–75, at 169.

**10.** Lyons, *Clementine,* 116, 117.

**11.** After seeing Ford's first cut of *My Darling Clementine,* Zanuck complained, "I think certain elements have been already eliminated that were absolutely essential if we are going to put on the screen *all* of the story we started to tell"; Darryl Zanuck to John Ford, June 25, 1946, in Rudy Behlmer, ed., *Memo from Darryl F. Zanuck: The Golden Years at Twentieth Century–Fox* (New York: Grove Press, 1993), 104.

**12.** Quoted in Joseph McBride, *Searching for John Ford: A Life* (New York: St. Martin's Press, 2001), 299. Frank S. Nugent, "Hollywood's Favorite Rebel," *Saturday Evening Post,* July 23, 1949; rpt. in Gaylyn Studlar and Matthew Bernstein, eds., *John Ford Made Westerns: Filming the Legend in the Sound Era* (Bloomington: Indiana University Press, 2001), 260–71, at 263.

**13.** See the memo from Zanuck to Bacon, July 13, 1946, in Behlmer, *Memo from Darryl F. Zanuck,* 106.

**14.** Caesar: "Cowards die many times before their deaths; /The valiant never taste of death but once." *The Tragedy of Julius Caesar,* II.ii.32–3.

**15.** John Baxter, *The Cinema of John Ford* (New York: A. S. Barnes, 1971), 101. Doc's function as Wyatt's dark double is also underscored by another moment of British poetry on the frontier. Granville Thorndyke's grand flourish of departure – to cover running out on his hotel bill – includes applying a couplet from Joseph Addison to a grizzled character called "Dad" (played by Francis Ford, John's older brother and director of *The Invaders,* 1912):

Great souls by instinct to each other turn,
Demand allegiance, and in friendship burn.

Addison writes "Demand alliance. . . ." Wyatt and Doc's "friendship" is not much in evidence until the showdown; cf. Addison:

In hours of peace content to be unknown,
And only in the field of battel shown.
To souls like these, in mutual friendship join'd,
Heaven dares entrust the cause of human-kind.

*The Campaign* (1705), in A. C. Guthkelch, ed., *The Miscellaneous Works of Joseph Addison,* vol. 1 (London: G. Bell & Sons, 1914; rpt. St. Clair Shores, Mich.: Scholarly Press, 1978), 159–60.

**16.** For instance, after Wyatt gets his Sunday haircut, notice the large saguaro cactus directly in front of the Oriental Saloon. It is not there in the night shots near the opening of the film (and would take at least fifty years to grow to that height!). Not native to Monument Valley, the saguaro cacti are part of the purposeful set decoration. As Douglas Gomery observed, they appear only after Clementine's arrival; "Mise-en-scène in John Ford's *My Darling Clementine,*" *Wide Angle* 2.4 (1978): 14–19, at 18–19.

**17.** Ford was still on active duty in the U.S. Navy when he made his great PT-boat film *They Were Expendable* in 1945.

**18.** Fredric March's character is recalling a celebrated sign posted in fleet headquarters in the South Pacific, attributed to Admiral "Bull" Halsey: "KILL JAPS. KILL JAPS. KILL MORE JAPS"; James T. Patterson, *Grand Expectations: The United States, 1945–1974* (New York: Oxford University Press, 1996), 7; Slotkin, *Gunfighter Nation,* 325.

**19.** Joseph C. Goulden, *The Best Years: 1945–1950* (New York: Atheneum, 1976), 50–1.

**20.** Stuart N. Lake, *Wyatt Earp, Frontier Marshall* [1931] (New York: Pocket Books, 1994), vii.

**21.** The song was composed for the 1904 stage adaptation of *The Virginian,* with words and music credited to Owen Wister himself. After a preview of *Stagecoach* Ford had cut a scene where Doc Boone leads the passengers in singing this song; see Kathryn Kalinak, "'The Sound of Many Voices': Music in John Ford's Westerns," in Studlar and Bernstein, *John Ford Made Westerns,* 169–92, at 177–81. *The Texans* (1938) anticipates *Clementine* in using the song's lyrics to communicate a personal double meaning when post–Civil War southerner Joan Bennett sings it to signal to her aunt that she'll be sneaking their cattle away from carpetbagger taxes.

**22.** "Actually, if you analyze that picture, there were a lot of flaws in the construction. Earp stays in town to get his brother's killer, and we vamp around for about sixty pages with what we hope are interesting scenes"; "Interview with Winston

Miller," in Lyons, *Clementine,* 141–50, at 148. For Morgan's line, see Lyons, *Clementine,* 130.

**23.** The Virginian in Owen Wister's novel too finds Shakespeare a cowboy's ideal companion. He's seen several Shakespeare plays and borrows the schoolmarm's complete Shakespeare to read *Othello, Romeo and Juliet,* and *Henry IV* until he is able to buy the volume for himself; Wister, *The Virginian: A Horseman of the Plains* [1902] (Boston: Houghton Mifflin, 1968), 89, 171–2, 211. Lee Clark Mitchell argues that Wister's "*The Virginian* presents a hero who triumphs not only through bullets but through words . . ."; *Westerns: Making the Man in Fiction and Film* (Chicago: University of Chicago Press, 1996), 98.

**24.** Bill Nichols, "Style, Grammar, and the Movies," *Film Quarterly* 28.3 (Spring 1975): 33–49; rpt. in Nichols, ed., *Movies and Methods: An Anthology* [vol. 1] (Berkeley: University of California Press, 1976), 607–28, at 617.

**25.** Wyatt's way of lingering when confronted with evil thus moves beyond the tradition of hair-trigger action as represented through another meeting of John Ford and Shakespeare in *The Man Who Shot Liberty Valance.* Drunken newspaper editor Edmund O'Brien fractures *Henry V* in anticipating the routing of outlaw Liberty Valance:

> But those in England now asleep
> Shall think themselves accursed they were not here
> Whiles any lives
> That fought with us upon Saint Crispin's day.
> But when the blast, the blast of war blows in our ears,
> Then we summon up, Liberty Valance.

This Shakespearean relish for testing in battle is missing from Wyatt. In its place is a certain regret and a risky nonviolence. Responding to Doc's leveled gun for the first time, he smoothly flip open his coat to reveal himself weaponless. For the unfractured version of O'Brien's Shakespeare, see *Henry V,* III.i and IV.iii, and Sonnet 30. Ford's 1962 film probably discovered these lines through President Kennedy's fondness for quoting them; Patterson, *Grand Expectations,* 460.

**26.** Owen Wister, preface to *Red Men and White* (New York: Grosset & Dunlap, 1895), vi; cited in Christine Bold, *Selling the Wild West: Popular Western Fiction, 1860–1960* (Bloomington: Indiana University Press, 1987), 65.

### 21. "Get Outta Town and Stay Out"

**1.** For the most influential – and entertaining – discussion of this process, see Leslie A. Fiedler, *Love and Death in the American Novel,* rev. ed. (New York: Dell, 1969); and, for its particular application to the Western, Fiedler, *The Return of the Vanishing American* (Briarcliff Manor, N.Y.: Stein & Day, 1968). For the most historically detailed analyses, see Richard Slotkin, *Regeneration through Violence: The Mythology of the American Frontier, 1600–1860* (Middletown, Conn.: Wesleyan University Press, 1973); and Slotkin, *The Fatal Environment: The Myth of the Frontier in the Age of Industrialization, 1800–1890* (Middletown, Conn.: Wesleyan University Press, 1985).

**2.** The key 1950 films are *Broken Arrow* and *Devil's Doorway,* and even the Hollywood industry's Production Code Administration seemed to develop a new conscience that year. The PCA returned the script for Ford's *Rio Grande* (1950) with an overcall complaint: "It is our considered opinion that it behooves the industry to see to it that Indians in Motion Pictures are fairly presented"; quoted in Joseph McBride, *Searching for John Ford: A Life* (New York: St. Martin's Press, 2001), 505. As Steve Neale points out, there were hints toward this shift in a few 1949 films; "Vanishing Americans: Racial and Ethnic Issues in the Interpretation and Context of Post-war 'Pro-Indian' Westerns," in Edward Buscombe and Roberta E. Pearson, eds., *Back in the Saddle Again: New Essays on the Western* (London: British Film Institute, 1998), 8–28, at 16.

3. Charles Stevens's mother was Geronimo's daughter Eloisa; for a brief biography, see Diane MacIntyre, "Charles Stevens," *The Silents Majority: The On-Line Journal of Silent Film,* www.mdle.com/ClassicFilms/.

4. "And, indeed, if it be the design of Providence to extirpate these savages in order to make room for the cultivators of the earth, it seems not improbable that rum may be the appointed means. It has already annihilated all the tribes who formerly inhabited the sea-coast"; Benjamin Franklin, *Autobiography* [1788], Larzer Ziff, ed. (New York: Holt, Rinehart & Winston, 1959), 125.

5. As in *Clementine, Canyon Passage* mounts a community dance in celebration of new building in its mining town, but this dance is disrupted by Indians savage enough to smash Hoagy Carmichael's character's mandolin.

6. Douglas Gomery was the first to describe these discontinuities; "Mise-en-scène in John Ford's *My Darling Clementine,*" *Wide Angle* 2.4 (1978): 14–19, at 14–15. Granville Thorndyke recites from *Hamlet* in a third saloon, identifiable in a shot cut from the film's release version as the "Silver Strike."

7. For example, McBride, *Searching for John Ford,* 563.

8. For a convincing defense of Lawrence's Mexican novel *The Plumed Serpent* on these terms, see Marianna Torgovnick, *Gone Primitive: Savage Intellects, Modern Lives* (Chicago: University of Chicago Press, 1990), 159–74.

9. John H. Lenihan discusses this aspect of *Broken Lance* in *Showdown: Confronting Modern America in the Western Film* (Urbana: University of Illinois Press, 1980), 67.

10. Francis Parkman, *The Oregon Trail* [1849], in *"The Oregon Trail" and "The Conspiracy of Pontiac,"* William R. Taylor, ed. (New York: Library of America, 1991), 274–5.

11. Edward Gallafent notices this film-noir connection in "Four Tombstones, 1946–1994," in Ian Cameron and Douglas Pye, eds., *The Book of Westerns* (New York: Continuum, 1996), 302–11, at 305.

12. "Interview with Winston Miller," in Robert Lyons, ed., *My Darling Clementine* (Brunswick, N.J.: Rutgers University Press, 1984), 141–50, at 144.

13. Reproduced in Raymond Durgnat and Scott Simmon, *King Vidor, American* (Berkeley: University of California Press, 1988), 242.

14. Geoffrey Perrett, *A Dream of Greatness: The American People, 1946–1963* (New York: Coward, McCann & Geoghegan, 1979), 62.

### 22. "A Lot of Nice People around Here"

1. Cited by Barbara Deming in her pioneering look into the postwar fighting helpmate cycle, "I've Got to Bring Him Back Home Where He Belongs (A Holly-

wood Ariadne)," *Running Away from Myself: A Dream Portrait of America Drawn from the Films of the 40's* (New York: Grossman, 1969), 39–71.

**2.** Washington Irving, *The Sketch Book of Geoffrey Crayon, Gent.* [1820], in Irving, *History, Tales and Sketches*, James W. Tuttleton, ed. (New York: Library of America, 1983), 771, 783.

**3.** There are some car-mounted, much faster traveling shots during Wyatt's later chase through the desert after Doc, and the one angle-correction move earlier – illustrated in the production photo shown as Fig. 50 in the present volume – but this is the single extended tracking or dolly shot as such. Ford seldom used camera movement in this era – there are only a couple of tracking shots in, for instance, *How Green Was My Valley* (1941) – and when Fred Zinnemann, after recovering from Ford's backhanded compliment ("You know, you could be a pretty good director if you'd stop fooling around with that boom and quit moving the camera so much"), asked him when you *should* move the camera, Ford told him simply, "When there's a cause for it"; quoted in Joseph McBride, *Searching for John Ford: A Life* (New York: St. Martin's Press, 2001), 161–2.

**4.** The 1880 U.S. Census had put the population of Tombstone at 973; Richard Lingeman, *Small Town America: A Narrative History, 1620–The Present* (Boston: Houghton Mifflin, 1980), 213. Stuart N. Lake claims that the town grew by five thousand during the first six months alone of Wyatt's residence in early 1880; *Wyatt Earp, Frontier Marshal* [1931] (New York: Pocket Books, 1994), 234. The more reliable Work Projects Administration guide, *Arizona: A Guide to the Sunset State* (New York: Hastings House, 1940), 244–5, cites the 1881 population at between seven thousand and fourteen thousand. As Allen Barra notes, "no one was entirely clear about what constituted a resident"; *Inventing Wyatt Earp: His Life and Many Legends* (New York: Carroll & Graf, 1998), 94.

**5.** Take Roseburg, Oregon, a county seat and called by an 1862 visitor "a gem of a village" with "neat, white frame cottages," and yet only 15 percent of those in the 1860 census were still there in 1865; Julie Roy Jeffrey, *Frontier Women: The Trans-Mississippi West, 1840–1880* (New York: Hill & Wang, 1979), 81–3. Even Western cities that grew from mining booms were remarkably transient: Only 25 percent of the residents of San Francisco in 1850 were still there in 1860; Richard White, *"It's Your Misfortune and None of My Own": A History of the American West* (Norman: University of Oklahoma Press, 1991), 186.

**6.** By 1945 personal savings in the United States had grown to $37 billion (from "near zero" before the war), to be spent down to $5 billion by 1947; Gabriel Kolko, *Main Currents in Modern American History* (New York: Pantheon Books, 1984), 316–17. For boomtown cities during the war, see Alonzo Hamby, *The Imperial Years: The United States since 1939* (New York: Weybright & Talley, 1976), 90–1.

**7.** Geoffrey Perrett, *A Dream of Greatness: The American People, 1946–1963* (New York: Coward, McCann & Geoghegan, 1979), 32.

**8.** Ibid., 71; Joseph C. Goulden, *The Best Years: 1945–1950* (New York: Atheneum, 1976), 138–9; James T. Patterson, *Grand Expectations: The United States, 1945–1974* (New York: Oxford University Press, 1996), 72–6.

**9.** See especially Perrett, *Dream of Greatness*, 28, 36; Goulden, *Best Years*, 132–42.

**10.** Errol Flynn's *Virginia City* (1940), despite its title, does not follow the same pattern. For an argument that *Dodge City* is "the source of the thematic ideas worked out by Ford himself from *My Darling Clementine* to *The Man Who Shot Liberty Valance*," see David Morse, "Under Western Eyes: Variations on a Genre," *Monogram* 6 (Oct. 1975): 34–9; rpt. in Don Whittemore and Philip Alan Cecchettini, eds., *Passport to Hollywood: Film Immigrants Anthology* (New York: McGraw–Hill, 1976), 202–15.

**11.** See, for instance, Goulden, *Best Years*, 140–2.

**12.** Arthur E. Morgan, *The Small Community: The Foundation of Democratic Life – What It Is and How to Achieve It* (New York: Harper & Bros., 1942), 6. For an encyclopedic history of the ideal and practice, see Lingeman, *Small Town America.*

**13.** For church attendance on the mining frontier, see Jeffrey, *Frontier Women,* 128–9. As she notes, mining towns had "flourishing counterinstitutions" of social cohesion in saloons, whorehouses, and gambling halls; "The Reverend James Pierpoint reported a Sunday attendance of only 40 out of a total mining population of 3,000–4,000, and his report was not atypical." For the growing social, as opposed to spiritual, role of church affiliations after World War II, see Stephen J. Whitfield, *The Culture of the Cold War,* 2d ed. (Baltimore: Johns Hopkins University Press, 1996), 82–7.

**14.** Kathryn Kalinak, "'The Sound of Many Voices': Music in John Ford's Westerns," in Gaylyn Studlar and Matthew Bernstein, eds., *John Ford Made Westerns: Filming the Legend in the Sound Era* (Bloomington: Indiana University Press, 2001), 169–92, at 175. See also Joseph W. Reed, *Three American Originals: John Ford, William Faulkner, & Charles Ives* (Middletown, Conn.: Wesleyan University Press, 1984), 20–1.

**15.** Phoebe Goodell Judson, *A Pioneer's Search for an Ideal Home* (Tacoma: Washington State Historical Society, 1966); quoted in Jeffrey, *Frontier Women,* 179.

**16.** Edward Buscombe, *Stagecoach* (London: British Film Institute, 1992), 78–80.

**17.** The term "home-digger" comes from Martha Wolfenstein and Nathan Leites's still suggestive 1950 cultural study of American films – primarily from the 1940s – misleadingly titled *Movies: A Psychological Study* (Glencoe, Ill.: Free Press, 1950), 39.

**18.** Transcribed from a Library of Congress recording; Motion Picture, Broadcasting, and Recorded Sound Division. On *Lux Radio Theatre* and its popularity, see John Dunning, *Tune in Yesterday: The Ultimate Encyclopedia of Old-Time Radio, 1925–1976* (Englewood Cliffs, N.J.: Prentice–Hall, 1976), 378–81.

**19.** Jeffrey, *Frontier Women,* 66–78. For the literary sources of these rituals, see also Annette Kolodny, *The Land before Her: Fantasy and Experience of the American Frontier, 1630–1860* (Chapel Hill: University of North Carolina Press, 1984), esp. chap. 8: "The Domestic Fantasy Goes West," 161–77.

**20.** Early guidebooks estimated costs to travel west by wagon train for a family of four at over $600, although the costs fell after the Civil War; Jeffrey, *Frontier Women,* 28.

**21.** Leo A. Handel's valuable *Hollywood Looks at Its Audience: A Report of Film Audience Research* (Urbana: University of Illinois Press, 1950) draws its evidence from surveys made in the 1940s. Among two thousand respondents in forty-five towns in a 1942 survey, Westerns were the most disliked by women among eighteen genre choices (121). Preference for Westerns also decreased with higher income (126), although this result was not broken out by gender.

**22.** See Perrett, *Dream of Greatness,* 70.

**23.** According to Leo A. Handel's surveys, when decisions were not made mutually, "the wife was usually more responsible for the particular motion picture visit in question than the husband. An almost identical situation prevails when a man and his girl friend are planning to see a picture"; *Hollywood Looks at Its Audience*, 113, also 100–2. Darryl Zanuck, in Nunnally Johnson's words, "was a nut about rewrites and redoing old film plots. He never liked to waste old standbys"; quoted in Leonard Mosley, *Zanuck: The Rise and Fall of Hollywood's Last Tycoon* (Boston: Little, Brown, 1984), 139. In a November 1945 memo to Ford, Zanuck himself suggested the problem with a third *Frontier Marshal:* "If possible I would like to get more or less of a neutral title and not be tied down to *Boom Town* or *Tombstone* or anything that sounds like a typical western"; Rudy Behlmer, ed., *Memo from Darryl F. Zanuck: The Golden Years at Twentieth Century–Fox* (New York: Grove Press, 1993), 101–2.

**24.** Authorship of the song is uncertain but often attributed to Percy Montross, ca. 1880; see Denes Agay, *Best Loved Songs of the American People* (Garden City, N.Y.: Doubleday, 1975), 200, 384. Wyatt's and Doc's darling Clementine is no daughter of a "miner forty-niner," so rustic her shoes are "herring boxes, without topses." The film's Clementine is a daughter of Boston and as genteel as the song's Clementine fails to be – except in the song's one line of comic contradiction and exaggeration, where she hits her foot against a splinter and drowns in the foaming brine. The song ridicules exactly what the film admires: the toughness of pioneer women *and* Victorian sentimentality.

**25.** Gaylyn Studlar argues that "Ford's Westerns frequently present us with women characters who meet the demands of frontier life in unexpected ways"; "Sacred Duties, Poetic Passions: John Ford and the Issue of Femininity in the Western," in Studlar and Bernstein, eds., *John Ford Made Westerns*, 43–74, at 50.

**26.** As Jane Tompkins convincingly argues, "The Western *answers* the domestic novel. It is the antithesis of the cult of domesticity that dominated American Victorian culture"; *West of Everything: The Inner Life of Westerns* (New York: Oxford University Press, 1992), 39. *Rachel and the Stranger* plays out this argument *within* the Western genre. Its script is by one old-time leftist, Waldo Salt, based on a novel by another, Howard Fast.

**27.** Robert Lyons, ed., *My Darling Clementine* (Brunswick, N.J.: Rutgers University Press, 1984), 128, 129.

**28.** Walter Nugent, "Frontiers and Empires in the Late Nineteenth Century," in Patricia Nelson Limerick, Clyde A. Milner II, and Charles E. Rankin, eds., *Trails: Toward a New Western History* (Lawrence: University Press of Kansas, 1991), 161–81, at 173. See also Joan Swallow Reiter, *The Old West: The Women* (Alexandria, Va.: Time–Life Books, 1978), 47; White, *It's Your Misfortune*, 303.

**29.** Jeffrey, *Frontier Women*, 56.

### 23. "Who Do We Shoot?"

**1.** Paul Zweig, *The Adventurer: The Fate of Adventure in the Western World* (Princeton, N.J.: Princeton University Press, 1974), 229.

**2.** George W. Bush to reporters in the White House, Sept. 17, 2001.

**3.** In the shooting script, Clanton is not shot and wanders off alone; Robert Lyons, ed., *My Darling Clementine* (Brunswick, N.J.: Rutgers University Press, 1984), 131.

**4.** Ibid., 130.

**5.** Quoted in Richard Maxwell Brown, *No Duty to Retreat: Violence and Values in American History and Society* (Norman: University of Oklahoma Press, 1991), 37, 39.

**6.** Joseph McBride, ed., *Hawks on Hawks* (Berkeley: University of California Press, 1982), 130.

**7.** For discussion of how independent-labor ideals were central to the graphic art, oral poetry, and autobiographies by historical cowboys, see Blake Allmendinger, *The Cowboy: Representations of Labor in an American Work Culture* (New York: Oxford University Press, 1992).

**8.** From John Ford's Irish perspective, the Earp brothers also look like peasant laborers, condemned to wander without farmland – like those before the war in *Tobacco Road* and *The Grapes of Wrath* – as the Irish peasantry was evicted by the British. If there is an overall social pattern in the films of Ford – who grew up on the seacoast of Maine – it seems to reside less in the ideals of the Western than in his Irish-Americanism, in which the theme of land lost looms large. If his Westerns consistently convey a mournful sense of loss, it seems partly because the Westerns are one variety of the immigrant experience. Deborah Thomas has intelligently discussed *My Darling Clementine* in terms of the structure of "Eastern values like law and order" versus "Western violence"; *Reading Hollywood: Spaces and Meanings in American Film* (London: Wallflower Press, 2001), 10–25. However, Ford shows no evidence of thinking of the American experience as the West *versus* the East. Wyatt restores law and order, but not because he's brought it from some more lawful East. After all, the poster for *My Darling Clementine*'s unperformed play in Tombstone, *The Convict's Oath,* announces it as "A Blood Chilling Drama of New York's Lawless Tenderloin."

**9.** See Brown, *No Duty to Retreat,* 66–86.

**10.** Peter Wollen, *Signs and Meaning in the Cinema,* rev. ed. (Bloomington and London: Indiana University Press, 1972), 94, 96. Wollen's description influenced, or was accepted by, many commentators on Ford. See Tag Gallagher's comprehensive study *John Ford: The Man and His Films* (Berkeley: University of California Press, 1986), 226 (Wyatt "cloaks his wilderness moral code with the laws of civilization"), and Peter Stowell, *John Ford* (Boston: Twayne, 1986), 100 ("Wyatt is primarily concerned with becoming civilized"). Lindsay Anderson, a great film director himself, argued against Wollen's characterization in *About John Ford . . .* (New York: McGraw-Hill, 1981), 198.

**11.** Zanuck justified the addition of the kiss on the grounds that a preview audience had laughed at the handshake: "I like the ending of *My Darling Clementine* exactly as it is. Unfortunately 2,000 people who saw the picture at a preview do not agree"; Darryl Zanuck to Samuel Engel, Sept. 4, 1946, in Rudy Behlmer, ed., *Memo from Darryl F. Zanuck: The Golden Years at Twentieth Century–Fox* (New York: Grove Press, 1993), 106–7. Postwar audiences may have been expecting less formality from their Western heroes: Ford's original staging duplicates Henry Fonda's handshake-without-kiss farewell to Gene Tierney in the 1940 Zanuck production *The Return of Frank James;* Ford had also substituted a handshake for any kiss in the last scene of the Ringo–Dallas romance in *Stagecoach.* Zanuck, by Hollywood standards, was something of a foe of the happy ending – among his memorable rewritings were the final lines for *I Am a Fugitive from a Chain Gang;* Mosley, *Zanuck,* 112–13.

**12.** John Baxter, *The Cinema of John Ford* (New York: A. S. Barnes, 1971), 105; Wollen, *Signs and Meaning,* 96. See also Edward Gallafent, "Four Tombstones, 1946–1994," in Ian Cameron and Douglas Pye, eds., *The Book of Westerns* (New York: Continuum, 1996), 302–11, at 311; and John Saunders, *The Western Genre: From Lordsburg to Big Whiskey* (London: Wallflower Press, 2001), 45.

**13.** Gallagher, *John Ford,* 230; J. A. Place, *The Western Films of John Ford* (Secaucus, N.J.: Citadel Press, 1974), 65. See also William Darby, *John Ford's Westerns: A Thematic Analysis, with a Filmography* (Jefferson, N.C.: McFarland, 1996), 180: ". . . this final meeting will be the last one between these surviving characters."

**14.** James Fenimore Cooper, *The Pathfinder,* in *The Leatherstocking Tales,* vol. 2, Blake Nevius, ed. (New York: Library of America, 1985), 466: "Well, Mabel, if I talk wildly, I *am* half wild, you know; by natur', I fear, as well as by habits."

**15.** Owen Wister, *The Virginian: A Horseman of the Plains* [1902] (Boston: Houghton Mifflin, 1968), 296, 297.

**16.** For a discussion of this battle and of Frederic Remington's unpopular attempts to write fiction extending the Cooper pattern, see Christine Bold, *Selling the Wild West: Popular Western Fiction, 1860–1960* (Bloomington: Indiana University Press, 1987), 37–75.

**17.** Martha Wolfenstein and Nathan Leites, *Movies: A Psychological Study* (Glencoe, Ill.: Free Press, 1950), 47–59.

**18.** The complication with this reasoning is that Ford, much later, claimed he *had* wanted Earp to settle down in Tombstone with Clementine, and that the film's ending was forced upon him; Andrew Sinclair, *John Ford* (New York: Dial Press, 1979), 130. Although neither the shooting script nor the screenwriter's recollections bear Ford out – see "Interview with Winston Miller," in Robert Lyons, ed., *My Darling Clementine* (Brunswick, N.J.: Rutgers University Press, 1984), 141–50, at 148–9 – one of the early drafts does have Wyatt staying in Tombstone; Joseph McBride, *Searching for John Ford: A Life* (New York: St. Martin's Press, 2001), 430.

### 24. The Revenge of Film Noir

**1.** Paula Mitchell Marks, *And Die in the West: The Story of the O.K. Corral Gunfight* (New York: Simon & Schuster, 1989), 327–8.

**2.** *The Tempest,* I.ii.378. For discussion of *The Tempest* in relation to reports from the American colony, see Leo Marx, "Shakespeare's American Fable," *The Machine in the Garden: Technology and the Pastoral Ideal in America* (New York: Oxford University Press, 1964), 34–72.

**3.** Work Projects Administration, *Arizona: A Guide to the Sunset State* (New York: Hastings House, 1940), 244–5. Tombstone's population had fallen to nine hundred by the time of the WPA research in the mid-1930s and has grown to fifteen hundred by the year 2000 census. For an eloquent argument about the values in studying the collapse of Western towns, not just their growth, see Patricia Nelson Limerick, "Haunted by Rhyolite: Learning from the Landscape of Failure," in Leonard Engel, ed., *The Big Empty: Essays on Western Landscapes as Narrative* (Albuquerque: University of New Mexico Press, 1994), 27–47.

**4.** Cheyenne's yearning is comparable to a painful moment in *Buffalo Bill* (1944) when an Indian maiden sneaks into Maureen O'Hara's clothes: "I wanted to find out if I could be as beautiful as a white girl . . . in a white girl's way."

**5.** Since *Devil's Doorway* is not precise about the year of its climax (Lance has built up his ranch for at least five years after the Civil War), his lawyer *might* be a historically valid pioneer of her profession. The Wyoming territory granted voting rights to (non-Indian) women in 1869, more than half a century before the Nineteenth Amendment gave women voting rights nationally. A male writer for *Harper's Weekly* argued that this was because there were so few women in the state: "Wyoming gave women the right to vote in much the same spirit that New York or Pennsylvania might vote to enfranchise angels or Martians"; quoted in Richard White, *"It's Your Misfortune and None of My Own": A History of the American West* (Norman: University of Oklahoma Press, 1991), 356.

**6.** *Track of the Cat* is an ambitious failure, a color film with stylized black-and-white set design across its CinemaScope frame. The film uses film noir as a psychological metaphor rather than as the primarily social one in *Yellow Sky*. The black panther evoked in the title of *Track of the Cat* is a lethal projection, apparently, of the white man's repression of the wilderness. Promising issues about the darkness of Puritanism are set up only to be resolved by a kiss, and the self-destructive cat coiled within each of us becomes a soft pelt, a "good blanket for bed," as his Indian friend tells Harold Bridges (Tab Hunter), who will be "boss man now" in his marriage. So much for noir nightmares.

### 25. The Return of the Earps

**1.** Thomas Berger, *Little Big Man* (New York: Dell, 1964), 340.

**2.** Joseph McBride, *Searching for John Ford: A Life* (New York: St. Martin's Press, 2001), 435, 437; Phil Hardy, *The Film Encyclopedia: The Western*, rev. ed. (London: Aurum Press, 1991), 375.

**3.** Robert Warshow, "Movie Chronicle: The Westerner," *Partistan Review* 21.4 (Mar.–Apr. 1954): 190–203; rpt. in Jim Kitses and Gregg Rickman, eds., *The Western Reader: Selected Readings in the Western American Film* (New York: Limelight, 1998), 35–47, at 44.

**4.** The reappearance of these scenes in *Powder River* argues incidentally that they were cut from *Clementine* by Ford rather than Zanuck.

**5.** *Wichita*'s locations are identified in Chris Fujiwara, *The Cinema of Nightfall: Jacques Tourneur* (Baltimore: Johns Hopkins University Press, 1998), 308, which also argues for the film's "visual triumph," 226–8.

**6.** Pete Hamill, *Doc: The Original Screenplay* (New York: Paperback Library, 1971), 16–17.

**7.** Todd McCarthy, "*Wyatt Earp*," *Variety*, June 20, 1994.

**8.** Pat Dowell makes this point in "The Mythology of the Western: Hollywood Perspectives on Race and Gender in the Nineties," *Cinéaste* 21.1–2 (1995): 6–10.

**9.** There is no record that Wyatt Earp and Josephine Marcus were ever formally married, although Josephine later claimed they had been married in 1888, which would make for a forty-year marriage; Casey Tefertiller, *Wyatt Earp: The Life behind the Legend* (New York: John Wiley & Sons, 1997), 314.

### 26. Ford, Fonda, and the Death of the Classic Western

**1.** The phrase is Judge Learned Hand's, used in upholding convictions of American Communist Party leaders. In 1957, the Supreme Court shifted back to the "clear and present danger" doctrine; Geoffrey Perrett, *A Dream of Greatness: The American People, 1946–1963* (New York: Coward, McCann & Geoghegan, 1979), 180–4.

**2.** For an application of managerial theory to *My Darling Clementine* – alongside *Tombstone* and *Wyatt Earp* – see Ralph Lamar Turner and Robert J. Higgins, *The Cow-*

*boy Way: The Western Leader in Film, 1945–1995* (Westport, Conn.: Greenwood Press, 1999), 89–130.

**3.** This is, at least, one way to read the coda to *Fort Apache,* and it's the one encouraged by Ford in interviews: "We've had a lot of people who were supposed to be great heroes, and you know damn well they weren't. But it's good for the country to have heroes to look up to"; Peter Bogdanovich, *John Ford* (Berkeley: University of California Press, 1967), 86. For a reading along these lines, see Kenneth J. Nolley, "Printing the Legend in the Age of MX: Reconsidering Ford's Military Trilogy," *Literature/Film Quarterly* 14.2 (1986): 82–8. For an ingenious attempt to reconcile the coda with the rest of *Fort Apache* and read it in more liberal terms, see Leland Poague, "'All I Can See Is the Flags': *Fort Apache* and the Visibility of History," *Cinema Journal* 27.2 (1988): 8–26, and Robert Ray's commonsensical response in *Cinema Journal* 27.3 (1988): 45–59, as well as Ray's *A Certain Tendency of the Hollywood Cinema, 1930–1980* (Princeton, N.J.: Princeton University Press, 1985), 173. For more on the coda, see also Douglas Pye, "Genre and History: *Fort Apache* and *The Man Who Shot Liberty Valance,*" in Ian Cameron and Douglas Pye, eds., *The Book of Westerns* (New York: Continuum, 1996), 111–22; and Joseph McBride, *Searching for John Ford: A Life* (New York: St. Martin's Press, 2001), 456–8.

**4.** Bogdanovich, *John Ford,* 104.

**5.** The Irish had, after all, some experience with repression by a militarily stronger nation. The U.S.-published *Irish World* had an iconoclastic response to the massacre of Custer and his men: "But if SITTING BULL is a savage, JOHN BULL is a hundred times a greater savage. . . . SITTING BULL's unpardonable crime was in not letting himself get killed. Had he only granted us this small favor we could forgive him. SITTING BULL is said to be a savage; and the simple fact [is] that he stood between his people and extermination . . . ," July 29, 1876; quoted in Richard Slotkin, *The Fatal Environment: The Myth of the Frontier in the Age of Industrialization, 1800–1890* (Middletown, Conn.: Wesleyan University Press, 1985), 475–6. The U.S. correspondent to the Irish *Pilot* regularly attacked Indian Bureau policies: "We have too much and too old a sympathy with people badly governed, to join in this shameful cry for Modoc blood," John Boyle O'Reilly, 1873; quoted in Thomas Keneally, *The Great Shame, and the Triumph of Irish in the English-Speaking World* (New York: Nan A. Talese /Doubleday, 1998), 590. The consciously Puritan strain in Westerns was not Ford's version; the English Puritans also had an exterminationist policy against Celtic tribalism. In *Cheyenne Autumn,* Ford uses a Polish-American trooper (with his memories of the Cossacks) to evoke doubts about the U.S. Cavalry's actions. As Charles Ramírez Berg argues, Ford's Irish ethnicity is one key to his representation of minority groups; "The Margin as Center: The Multicultural Dynamics of John Ford's Westerns," in Gaylyn Studlar and Matthew Bernstein, eds., *John Ford Made Westerns: Filming the Legend in the Sound Era* (Bloomington: Indiana University Press, 2001), 75–101.

**6.** McBride, *Searching for John Ford,* 432. See also William Lehr's discussion of the "corrupt" Earp in "a bizarre and diegetically unnecessary intrusion into" *Cheyenne Autumn*; "Reception, Representation, and the O.K. Corral: Shifting Images of Wyatt Earp," in Bonnie Braendlin and Hans Braendlin, eds., *Authority and Transgression in Literature and Film* (Gainesville: University Press of Florida, 1996), 23–44.

**7.** Warner Bros. itself apparently also concluded that the Dodge City sequence was "pointless" (as Brian Garfield has called it; *Western Films: A Complete Guide* [New

York: Rawson Associates, 1982], 136). The industry trade paper *Variety* found "no valid reason" for the sequence "other than to drag in James Stewart for marquee and lure . . . ," Oct. 7, 1964; rpt. in *Variety Film Reviews* (New York: Garland, 1983), vol. 11, n.p. After *Cheyenne Autumn* opened, the twenty-minute Dodge City sequence was cut by eight minutes before the wide release. It is restored in currently available 159-minute videos.

**8.** In making Carl Schurz a sympathetic ally of the Cheyenne, once he is made aware of the facts of their treatment, Ford seems little more concerned with the facts of history than before. Schurz, a genuine hero among conservationists for his forestry policy, is remembered considerably less fondly by the Cheyennes. In 1879, Schurz agreed with General Sheridan that the Cheyennes should be marched back to their Oklahoma reservation from the Black Hills of Dakota in midwinter. To Native Americans he was "Big Eyes" Schurz, a marvel for having eyes so big and seeing so little; Dee Brown, *Bury My Heart at Wounded Knee: An Indian History of the American West* (New York: Bantam Books, 1972), 316–31; see also Mari Sandoz, *Cheyenne Autumn* (New York: Hastings House, 1953).

**9.** For this interpretation of Kennedy's relationship to the August 1963 "March on Washington," see Godfrey Hodgson, *America in Our Time* (New York: Vintage Books, 1976), 155–9, 179–80.

**10.** McBride, *Searching for John Ford*, 549–52.

**11.** *Dialogue on Film (American Film Institute)* 3.2 (Nov. 1973): 14–15. See also Christopher Frayling, *Sergio Leone: Something to Do with Death* (London: Faber & Faber, 2000), 270–1.

**12.** Pauline Kael, *Deeper into Movies* (Boston: Little, Brown, 1973), 229; Garfield, *Western Films*, 314.

**13.** Aristotle, *The Politics* [Book III, 4–5], in *"The Politics" and "The Constitution of Athens,"* Stephen Everson, ed. (Cambridge: Cambridge University Press, 1996), 65–9.

**14.** Among the "Hollywood Ten" Dmytryk had been the briefest adherent to the Communist Party. He "recanted" in his second appearance before the House Un-American Activities Committee in 1951 and named names of fellow party members – thus allowing his reemployment as a director in Hollywood – but he also chose to serve his jail sentence before he spoke out. For his side of things, see Edward Dmytryk, *Odd Man Out: A Memoir of the Hollywood Ten* (Carbondale: Southern Illinois University Press, 1996). Michael Coyne reads *Warlock* ("the finest psychological Western ever made") as something of a parable of Dmytryk's HUAC experience; *The Crowded Prairie: American National Identity in the Hollywood Western* (London: I. B. Tauris, 1997), 94–104. For an argument for the superiority of Oakley Hall's novel over Dmytryk's film, see Robert Murray Davis, "Time and Space in the Western: *Warlock* as Novel and Film," *South Dakota Review* 29.1 (Spring 1991): 68–75.

**15.** Tonino Valerii was a longtime assistant to Leone, whose direction of several sequences of *My Name Is Nobody* is discussed in Frayling, *Sergio Leone*, 348–63, and Christopher Frayling, *Spaghetti Westerns: Cowboys and Europeans from Karl May to Sergio Leone* (London: Routledge & Kegan Paul, 1981), 240.

**16.** Leo Braudy, *The Frenzy of Renown: Fame and Its History* (New York: Oxford University Press, 1986), vii.

# Select Bibliography

This bibliography selects the most helpful or historically essential works for this book. Pieces within the anthologies listed are not cited separately. For a full, intelligently annotated bibliography of writings on the Western film through 1987, see John G. Nachbar, *Western Films: An Annotated Critical Bibliography* (New York: Garland, 1975), and Jack Nachbar, Jackie R. Donath, and Chris Foran, *Western Films 2: An Annotated Critical Bibliography from 1974 to 1987* (New York: Garland, 1988).

Abel, Richard. *The Red Rooster Scare: Making Cinema American, 1900–1910.* Berkeley: University of California Press, 1999.

Ahlstrom, Sydney E. *A Religious History of the American People.* New Haven: Yale University Press, 1972.

Aleiss, Angela. "Hollywood Addresses Indian Reform: *The Vanishing American.*" *Studies in Visual Communication* 10.4 (Fall 1984): 53–60.

"Native Americans: The Surprising Silents." *Cinéaste* 21.3 (1995): 34–5.

Allmendinger, Blake. *The Cowboy: Representations of Labor in an American Work Culture.* New York: Oxford University Press, 1992.

Anderson, Lindsay. *About John Ford. . . .* New York: McGraw–Hill, 1981.

Anderson, Robert. "The Role of the Western Film Genre in Industry Competition, 1907–1911." *Journal of the University Film Association* 31.2 (1979): 19–26.

Aquila, Richard, ed. *Wanted Dead or Alive: The American West in Popular Culture.* Urbana: University of Illinois Press, 1996.

Arthur, Paul. "Murder's Tongue: Identity, Death, and the City in Film Noir." *Violence and American Cinema.* Ed. J. David Slocum, 153–75. New York: Routledge / American Film Institute, 2001.

Athearn, Robert G. *The Mythic West in Twentieth-Century America.* Lawrence: University Press of Kansas, 1986.

Baird, Robert. "Going Indian: Discovery, Adoption, and Renaming toward a 'True American,' from *Deerslayer* to *Dances with Wolves.*" *Dressing in Feathers: The Construction of the Indian in American Popular Culture.* Ed. S. Elizabeth Bird, 195–209. Boulder, Colo.: Westview Press, 1996.

Bakshy, Alexander. "The Romantic Western." *The Nation,* 12 Nov. 1930: 534–6.

Balshofer, Fred J., and Arthur C. Miller. *One Reel a Week.* Berkeley: University of California Press, 1967.

Barker, Martin, and Roger Sabin. *The Lasting of the Mohicans: History of an American Myth.* Jackson: University Press of Mississippi, 1995.

Barra, Allen. *Inventing Wyatt Earp: His Life and Many Legends.* New York: Carroll & Graf, 1998.

Barsness, John A. "Theodore Roosevelt as Cowboy: The Virginian as Jacksonian Man." *American Quarterly* 21.3 (1969): 609–19.

Bataille, Gretchen M., and Charles L. P. Silet, eds. *The Pretend Indian: Images of Native Americans in the Movies.* Ames: Iowa State University Press, 1980.

Bates, Craig D. "Dressing the Part: A Brief Look at the Development of Stereotypical Indian Clothing among Native Peoples of the Far West." *Journal of California and Great Basin Anthropology* 4.2 (1982): 55–66.

Batman, Richard Dale. "The Founding of the Hollywood Motion Picture Industry." *Journal of the West* 10.4 (Oct. 1971): 609–23.

Baxter, John. *The Cinema of John Ford.* New York: A. S. Barnes, 1971.

Bazin, André. "The Evolution of the Western." *What Is Cinema?* vol. 2. Ed. and trans. Hugh Gray, 149–57. Berkeley: University of California Press, 1971.

Bean, Robin. "Way Out West in Yugoslavia." *Films and Filming* 11.2 (Sept. 1965): 49–51.

Bederman, Gail. *Manliness and Civilization: A Cultural History of Gender and Race in the United States, 1880–1917.* Chicago: University of Chicago Press, 1995.

Behlmer, Rudy, ed. *Memo from Darryl F. Zanuck: The Golden Years at Twentieth Century–Fox.* New York: Grove Press, 1993.

Bercovitch, Sacvan. *The American Jeremiad.* Madison: University of Wisconsin Press, 1978.

*The Puritan Origins of the American Self.* New Haven: Yale University Press, 1975.

Berkhofer, Robert F., Jr. *The White Man's Indian: Images of the American Indian from Columbus to the Present.* New York: Vintage Books, 1979.

Bieder, Robert E. *Science Encounters the Indian, 1820–1880: The Early Years of American Ethnology.* Norman: University of Oklahoma Press, 1986.

"Bison Company Gets 101 Ranch." *Moving Picture World,* Dec. 9, 1910: 810.

"Bison-101 Feature Pictures." *Moving Picture World,* Jan. 27, 1912: 298.

Blackstone, Sarah J. *Buckskins, Bullets, and Business: A History of Buffalo Bill's Wild West.* New York: Greenwood Press, 1986.

Boatright, Mody C. "The Cowboy Enters the Movies." *The Sunny Slopes of Long Ago.* Ed. Wilson M. Hudson and Allen Maxwell, 51–69. Publications of the Texas Folklore Society, no. 33. Austin, Tex.: Southern Methodist University Press, 1966.

Bogdanovich, Peter. *Allan Dwan: The Last Pioneer.* New York: Praeger, 1971.

*John Ford.* Berkeley: University of California Press, 1967.

Boime, Albert. *The Magisterial Gaze: Manifest Destiny and American Landscape Painting, c. 1830–1865.* Washington, D.C.: Smithsonian Institution Press, 1991.

Bold, Christine. *Selling the Wild West: Popular Western Fiction, 1860–1960.* Bloomington: Indiana University Press, 1987.

Bowser, Eileen, *The Transformation of Cinema, 1907–1915.* New York: Charles Scribner's Sons, 1990.

ed. *Biograph Bulletins, 1908–1912.* New York: Farrar, Straus & Giroux, 1973.

Boym, Svetlana. *The Future of Nostalgia.* New York: Basic Books, 2001.

Braudy, Leo. *The Frenzy of Renown: Fame and Its History.* New York: Oxford University Press, 1986.

Brown, Bill, ed. *Reading the West: An Anthology of Dime Westerns.* Boston: Bedford Books, 1997.
Brown, Dee. *Bury My Heart at Wounded Knee: An Indian History of the American West.* New York: Bantam Books, 1972.
*The Westerners.* New York: Holt, Rinehart & Winston, 1974.
Brown, Richard Maxwell. *No Duty to Retreat: Violence and Values in American History and Society.* Norman: University of Oklahoma Press, 1991.
Brownlow, Kevin. *The War, the West, and the Wilderness.* New York: Alfred A. Knopf, 1979.
Burnett, W. R. *Saint Johnson.* New York: Dial Press, 1930.
Burns, Walter Noble. *Tombstone: An Iliad of the Southwest.* 1927. New York: Penguin Books, 1942.
Buscombe, Edward. *The BFI Companion to the Western.* New York: Atheneum, 1988.
"Inventing Monument Valley: Nineteenth-Century Landscape Photography and the Western Film." *Fugitive Images: From Photography to Video.* Ed. Patrice Petro, 87–108. Bloomington: Indiana University Press, 1995.
"Painting the Legend: Frederic Remington and the Western." *Cinema Journal* 23.4 (Summer 1984): 12–27.
*Stagecoach.* London: British Film Institute, 1992.
Buscombe, Edward, and Roberta E. Pearson, eds. *Back in the Saddle Again: New Essays on the Western.* London: British Film Institute, 1998.
Bush, W. Stephen. "The Overproduction of 'Western Pictures.'" *Moving Picture World,* Oct. 21, 1911: 189.
Calder, Jenni. *There Must Be a Lone Ranger: The American West in Film and Reality.* New York: McGraw–Hill, 1977.
Cameron, Ian, and Douglas Pye, eds. *The Book of Westerns.* New York: Continuum, 1996.
Cawelti, John G. *The Six-Gun Mystique.* Bowling Green, Ohio: Bowling Green University Popular Press, 1970.
Cherchi Usai, Paolo, ed. *The Griffith Project.* 6 vols. London: British Film Institute, 1999–2002.
Churchill, Ward. *Fantasies of the Master Race: Literature, Cinema, and the Colonization of American Indians.* Monroe, Maine: Common Courage Press, 1992.
Clark, David Anthony Tyeeme, and Joane Nagel. "White Men, Red Masks: Appropriations of 'Indian' Manhood in Imagined Wests." *Across the Great Divide: Cultures of Manhood in the American West.* Ed. Matthew Basso, Laura McCall, and Dee Garceau, 109–30. New York: Routledge, 2001.
Cole, Thomas. *The Collected Essays and Prose Sketches.* Ed. Marshall Tymn. St. Paul, Minn.: John Colet Press, 1980.
Cooper, James Fenimore. *The Leatherstocking Tales.* 2 vols. Ed. Blake Nevius. New York: Library of America, 1985.
Corkin, Stanley. "Cowboys and Free Markets: Post–World War II Westerns and U.S. Hegemony." *Cinema Journal* 39.3 (2000): 66–91.
Coyne, Michael. *The Crowded Prairie: American National Identity in the Hollywood Western.* London: I. B. Tauris, 1997.
Creekmur, Corey K. "Acting Like a Man: Masculine Performance in *My Darling Clementine.*" *Out in Culture: Gay, Lesbian, and Queer Essays on Popular Culture.* Ed. Corey K. Creekmur and Alexander Doty, 167–82. Durham, N.C.: Duke University Press, 1995.

Crèvecoeur, J. Hector St. John de. *Letters from an American Farmer.* 1782. New York: Oxford University Press, 1997.

Cronon, William, George Miles, and Jay Gitlin, eds. *Under an Open Sky: Rethinking America's Western Past.* New York: W. W. Norton, 1992.

Dary, David. *Cowboy Culture: A Saga of Five Centuries.* New York: Avon Books, 1981.

Davis, Robert Murray. "Time and Space in the Western: *Warlock* as Novel and Film." *South Dakota Review* 29.1 (Spring 1991): 68–75.

Deloria, Philip J. *Playing Indian.* New Haven: Yale University Press, 1998.

Deming, Barbara. *Running Away from Myself: A Dream Portrait of America Drawn from the Films of the 40's.* New York: Grossman, 1969.

Demos, John. *The Unredeemed Captive: A Family Story from Early America.* New York: Vintage Books, 1995.

Dench, Ernest A. *Making the Movies.* New York: Macmillan, 1915.

Dilworth, Leah. *Imagining Indians in the Southwest: Persistent Visions of a Primitive Past.* Washington, D.C.: Smithsonian Institution Press, 1996.

Dippie, Brian W. "The Moving Finger Writes: Western Art and the Dynamics of Change." *Discovered Lands, Invented Pasts: Transforming Visions of the American West.* Jules David Prown, Nancy K. Anderson, William Cronon, Brian W. Dippie, Martha A. Sandweiss, Susan P. Schoelwer, and Howard R. Lamar, 89–115. New Haven: Yale University Press, 1992.

*The Vanishing American: White Attitudes and U.S. Indian Policy.* Middletown, Conn.: Wesleyan University Press, 1982.

Dmytryk, Edward. *Odd Man Out: A Memoir of the Hollywood Ten.* Carbondale: Southern Illinois University Press, 1996.

Dowell, Pat. "The Mythology of the Western: Hollywood Perspectives on Race and Gender in the Nineties." *Cinéaste* 21.1–2 (1995): 6–10.

Drinnon, Richard. *Facing West: The Metaphysics of Indian Hating and Empire Building.* New York: Schocken Books, 1990.

Durgnat, Raymond, and Scott Simmon. *King Vidor, American.* Berkeley: University of California Press, 1988.

Dyer, Thomas G. *Theodore Roosevelt and the Idea of Race.* Baton Rouge: Louisiana State University Press, 1980.

Edgerton, Gary. "'A Breed Apart': Hollywood, Racial Stereotyping, and the Promise of Revisionism in *The Last of the Mohicans.*" *Journal of American Culture* 17.2 (Summer 1994): 1–17.

Egan, Timothy. "As Others Abandon Plains, Indians and Bison Come Back." *New York Times,* May 27, 2001: A1, A18.

Ellis, Joseph J. *American Sphinx: The Character of Thomas Jefferson.* New York: Vintage Books, 1998.

Engel, Leonard, ed. *The Big Empty: Essays on Western Landscapes as Narrative.* Albuquerque: University of New Mexico Press, 1994.

"Essanay Producers in Texas and Mexico." *Moving Picture World,* Dec. 4, 1909: 801.

Evans, Estwick. *A Pedestrious Tour of Four Thousand Miles, through the Western States and Territories, during the Winter and Spring of 1818.* Concord, N.H.: Joseph C. Spear, 1819.

Faragher, John Mack. *Daniel Boone: The Life and Legend of an American Pioneer.* New York: Henry Holt, 1992.

"The Tale of Wyatt Earp." *Past Imperfect: History According to the Movies.* Ed. Mark C. Carnes, 154–61. New York: Henry Holt, 1995.

*Women and Men on the Overland Trail.* New Haven: Yale University Press, 1979.

ed. *Rereading Frederick Jackson Turner.* New Haven: Yale University Press, 1994.

Fenin, George N., and William K. Everson. *The Western.* Rev. ed. New York: Grossman, 1973.

Fiedler, Leslie A. *Love and Death in the American Novel.* Rev. ed. New York: Dell, 1969.

*The Return of the Vanishing American.* Briarcliff Manor, N.Y.: Stein & Day, 1968.

Fisher, Philip. *Hard Facts: Setting and Form in the American Novel.* New York: Oxford University Press, 1987.

Flynn, Charles, and Todd McCarthy. "The Economic Imperative: Why Was the B Movie Necessary?" *King of the Bs: Working within the Hollywood System – An Anthology of Film History and Criticism.* Ed. Charles Flynn and Todd McCarthy, 13–43. New York: E. P. Dutton, 1975.

Frayling, Christopher. *Sergio Leone: Something to Do with Death.* London: Faber & Faber, 2000.

*Spaghetti Westerns: Cowboys and Europeans from Karl May to Sergio Leone.* London: Routledge & Kegan Paul, 1981.

French, Peter A. *Cowboy Metaphysics: Ethics and Death in Westerns.* Lanham, Md.: Rowman & Littlefield, 1997.

Fussell, Edwin. *Frontier: American Literature and the American West.* Princeton, N.J.: Princeton University Press, 1965.

Gallagher, Tag. "Brother Feeney." *Film Comment* 12.6 (Nov.–Dec. 1976): 12–18.

*John Ford: The Man and His Films.* Berkeley: University of California Press, 1986.

Garfield, Brian. *Western Films: A Complete Guide.* New York: Rawson Associates, 1982.

Gidley, Mick, and Robert Lawson-Peebles, eds. *Views of American Landscapes.* Cambridge: Cambridge University Press, 1989.

Goetzmann, William H. *New Lands, New Men: America and the Second Great Age of Discovery.* New York: Viking Books, 1986.

Goetzmann, William H., and William N. Goetzmann. *The West of the Imagination.* New York: W. W. Norton, 1986.

Gomery, Douglas. "Mise-en-scène in John Ford's *My Darling Clementine.*" *Wide Angle* 2.4 (1978): 14–19.

Goulden, Joseph C. *The Best Years: 1945–1950.* New York: Atheneum, 1976.

Green, Rayna. "The Pocahontas Perplex: The Image of Indian Women in American Culture." *Massachusetts Review* 16.4 (Autumn 1975): 698–714.

Greiner, Donald J. *Women Enter the Wilderness: Male Bonding and the American Novel of the 1980s.* Columbia: University of South Carolina Press, 1991.

Grey, Zane. *The Man of the Forest.* 1920. New York: Forge Books, 2000.

*The Vanishing American.* New York: Grosset & Dunlap, 1925.

"What the Desert Means to Me." *The American Magazine* 98 (Nov. 1924): 5–6.

Griffiths, Alison. "Playing at Being Indian: Spectatorship and the Early Western." *Journal of Popular Film and Television* 29.3 (Fall 2001): 100–11.

Grossman, James, ed. *The Frontier in American Culture.* Berkeley: University of California Press, 1994.

Guild, Thelma S., and Harvey L. Carter. *Kit Carson: A Pattern for Heroes.* Lincoln: University of Nebraska Press, 1984.

Gunning, Tom. *D. W. Griffith and the Origins of American Narrative Film: The Early Years at Biograph.* Urbana: University of Illinois Press, 1991.
Hahn, Steven. *The Roots of Southern Populism: Yeoman Farmers and the Transformation of the Georgia Upcountry.* New York: Oxford University Press, 1983.
Hamill, Pete. *Doc: The Original Screenplay.* New York: Paperback Library, 1971.
Handel, Leo A. *Hollywood Looks at Its Audience: A Report of Film Audience Research.* Urbana: University of Illinois Press, 1950.
Hansen, Miriam. *Babel and Babylon: Spectatorship in American Silent Film.* Cambridge, Mass.: Harvard University Press, 1991.
Hardy, Phil. *The Film Encyclopedia: The Western.* Rev. ed. London: Aurum Press, 1991.
Harrison, Louis Reeves. "The 'Bison-101' Headliners," *Moving Picture World,* Apr. 27, 1912: 322.
"*The Invaders.*" *Moving Picture World,* Nov. 9, 1912: 542.
"Wake Up! This Is 1912!" *Moving Picture World,* Jan. 6, 1912: 21.
Higgins, Steven. "I film di Thomas H. Ince." *Thomas H. Ince: Il profeta del western.* Ed. Paolo Cherchi Usai and Livio Jacob. *Griffithiana* nos. 18–21 (Oct. 1984) (special issue for Third Pordenone Silent Film Festival): 155–94.
"Thomas H. Ince: American Film Maker." *The First Film Makers: New Viewpoints on the Lives and Work of D. W. Griffith, Thomas Ince and Erich Von Stroheim.* Ed. Richard Dyer MacCann, 69–71. Metuchen, N.J.: Scarecrow Press, 1989.
Higham, John. "The Reorientation of American Culture in the 1890s." *The Origins of Modern Consciousness.* Ed. John Weiss, 25–48. Detriot: Wayne State University Press, 1965.
Hofstadter, Richard. *The Age of Reform.* New York: Vintage Books, 1955.
*The American Political Tradition.* New York: Vintage Books, 1948.
*Social Darwinism in American Thought.* 1945. Boston: Beacon Press, 1992.
Horak, Jan-Christopher. "Maurice Tourneur's Tragic Romance." *The Classic American Novel and the Movies.* Ed. Gerald Perry and Roger Shatzkin, 10–19. New York: Ungar, 1977.
Hutton, Paul Andrew. "Showdown at the Hollywood Corral: Wyatt Earp and the Movies." *Montana* 45.3 (Summer 1995): 2–31.
Hyde, Anne Farrar. *An American Vision: Far Western Landscape and National Culture, 1820–1920.* New York: New York University Press, 1990.
Ince, Thomas H. "The Early Days at Kay Bee." *Photoplay Magazine* (Mar. 1919). Rpt. in *Hollywood Directors, 1914–1940.* Ed. Richard Koszarski, 62–70. London: Oxford University Press, 1976.
Irving, Washington. *A Tour of the Prairies.* 1835. *Selected Writings of Washington Irving.* Ed. William P. Kelly. New York: Modern Library, 1984.
"James Young Deer." *Moving Picture World,* May 6, 1911: 999.
Jay, Gregory S. "'White Man's Book No Good': D. W. Griffith and the American Indian." *Cinema Journal* 34.4 (Summer 2000): 3–26.
Jefferson, Thomas. *Jefferson: Political Writings.* Ed. Joyce Appleby and Terence Ball. Cambridge: Cambridge University Press, 1999.
*Writings.* Ed. Merrill D. Peterson. New York: Library of America, 1984.
Jeffrey, Julie Roy. *Frontier Women: The Trans-Mississippi West, 1840–1880.* New York: Hill & Wang, 1979.
Jennings, Francis. "The Vanishing Indian: Francis Parkman versus His Sources." *Pennsylvania Magazine of History and Biography* 87 (1963): 306–23.

Jones, Daryl. *The Dime Novel Western.* Bowling Green, Ohio: Bowling Green University Popular Press, 1978.
Kammen, Michael. *Mystic Chords of Memory: The Transformation of Tradition in American Culture.* New York: Vintage Books, 1993.
Kasson, Joy S. *Buffalo Bill's Wild West: Celebrity, Memory, and Popular History.* New York: Hill & Wang, 2002.
Kazan, Elia. *A Life.* New York: Alfred A. Knopf, 1988.
Keil, Charlie. *Early American Cinema in Transition: Story, Style, and Filmmaking, 1907–1913.* Madison: University of Wisconsin Press, 2001.
Kennedy, David M. *Freedom from Fear: The American People in Depression and War, 1929–1945.* New York: Oxford University Press, 1999.
Kilborn, Peter. "Bit by Bit, Tiny Morland, Kan., Fades Away." *New York Times,* May 10, 2001: A1, A22.
King, Charles. *"The Deserter" and "From the Ranks."* Philadelphia: J. B. Lippincott, 1898.
Kinsey, Joni Louise. *Thomas Moran and the Surveying of the American West.* Washington, D.C.: Smithsonian Institution Press, 1992.
Kitses, Jim. *Horizons West: Anthony Mann, Budd Boetticher, Sam Peckinpah – Studies of Authorship within the Western.* Bloomington: Indiana University Press, 1969.
Kitses, Jim, and Gregg Rickman, eds. *The Western Reader: Selected Readings in the Western American Film.* New York: Limelight, 1998.
Klein, Kerwin Lee. *Frontiers of Historical Imagination: Narrating the European Conquest of Native America, 1890–1990.* Berkeley: University of California Press, 1999.
Klein, Marcus. *Easterns, Westerns, and Private Eyes: American Matters, 1870–1900.* Madison: University of Wisconsin Press, 1994.
Kolko, Gabriel. *Main Currents in Modern American History.* New York: Pantheon Books, 1984.
Kolodny, Annette. *The Land before Her: Fantasy and Experience of the American Frontier, 1630–1860.* Chapel Hill: University of North Carolina Press, 1984.
Kowalewski, Michael. *Deadly Musings: Violence and Verbal Form in American Fiction.* Princeton, N.J.: Princeton University Press, 1993.
ed. *Reading the West: New Essays on the Literature of the American West.* Cambridge: Cambridge University Press, 1996.
Kozloff, Sarah. *Overhearing Film Dialogue.* Berkeley: University of California Press, 2000.
Lake, Stuart N. *Wyatt Earp, Frontier Marshal.* 1931. New York: Pocket Books, 1994.
Lasch, Christopher. *The True and Only Heaven: Progress and Its Critics.* New York: W. W. Norton, 1991.
Lawrence, D. H. *Studies in Classic American Literature.* 1924. Harmondsworth, U.K.: Penguin Books, 1971.
Lears, T. J. Jackson. *No Place of Grace: Antimodernism and the Transformation of American Culture, 1880–1920.* New York: Pantheon, 1981.
Lehr, William. "Reception, Representation, and the O.K. Corral: Shifting Images of Wyatt Earp." *Authority and Transgression in Literature and Film.* Ed. Bonnie Braendlin and Hans Braendlin, 23–44. Gainesville: University Press of Florida, 1996.
Lenihan, John H. *Showdown: Confronting Modern America in the Western Film.* Urbana: University of Illinois Press, 1980.

Levine, Lawrence W. *Highbrow/Lowbrow: The Emergence of Cultural Hierarchy in America.* Cambridge, Mass: Harvard University Press, 1988.

Lewis, R. W. B. *The American Adam: Innocence, Tragedy and Tradition in the Nineteenth Century.* Chicago: University of Chicago Press, 1955.

Liandrat-Guigues, Suzanne. *Red River.* London: British Film Institute, 2000.

Limerick, Patricia Nelson. *Desert Passages: Encounters with the American Deserts.* Albuquerque: University of New Mexico Press, 1985.

*The Legacy of Conquest: The Unbroken Past of the American West.* New York: W. W. Norton, 1987.

Limerick, Patricia Nelson, Clyde A. Milner II, and Charles E. Rankin, eds. *Trails: Toward a New Western History.* Lawrence: University Press of Kansas, 1991.

Lingeman, Richard. *Small Town America: A Narrative History, 1620–The Present.* Boston: Houghton Mifflin, 1980.

Lovell, Alan. "The Western." *Movies and Methods: An Anthology* [vol. 1]. Ed. Bill Nichols, 164–75. Berkeley: University of California Press, 1976.

Lyons, Robert, ed. *My Darling Clementine.* Brunswick, N.J.: Rutgers University Press, 1984.

McBride, Joseph. *Searching for John Ford: A Life.* New York: St. Martin's Press, 2001.

ed. *Hawks on Hawks.* Berkeley: University of California Press, 1982.

McBride, Joseph, and Michael Wilmington. *John Ford.* New York: Da Capo Press, 1975.

McElvaine, Robert S. *The Great Depression: America, 1929–1941.* New York: Times Books, 1993.

McLaughlin, James. *My Friend the Indian.* 1910. Lincoln: University of Nebraska Press, 1989.

McMath, Robert C., Jr. *American Populism: A Social History, 1877–1898.* New York: Hill & Wang, 1993.

McNiven, Roger. "The Western Landscape of Raoul Walsh." *Velvet Light Trap* 15 (Fall 1975): 50–5.

Marks, Paula Mitchell. *And Die in the West: The Story of the O.K. Corral Gunfight.* New York: Simon & Schuster, 1989.

Marty, Martin E. *Righteous Empire: The Protestant Experience in America.* New York: Dial Press, 1970.

Marx, Leo. *The Machine in the Garden: Technology and the Pastoral Ideal in America.* New York: Oxford University Press, 1964.

"Pastoralism in America." *Ideology and Classic American Literature.* Ed. Sacvan Bercovitch and Myra Jehlen, 36–69. Cambridge: Cambridge University Press, 1987.

"Susan Sontag's 'New Left' Pastoral: Notes on Revolutionary Pastoralism in America." *TriQuarterly* 23–4 (Spring 1972): 552–75.

May, Dean L. *Three Frontiers: Family, Land, and Society in the American West, 1850–1900.* Cambridge: Cambridge University Press, 1994.

Michaels, Walter Benn. *Our America: Nativism, Modernism, and Pluralism.* Durham, N.C.: Duke University Press, 1995.

Milner, Clyde A., II, Carol A. O'Connor, and Martha A. Sandweiss, eds. *The Oxford History of the American West.* New York: Oxford University Press, 1994.

Mitchell, Alice Miller. *Children and Movies.* Chicago: University of Chicago Press, 1929.

Mitchell, Lee Clark. *Westerns: Making the Man in Fiction and Film*. Chicago: University of Chicago Press, 1996.

Mitry, Jean. "Thomas H. Ince: His Esthetic, His Films, His Legacy." 1965. Trans. and adapt. Martin Sopocy and Paul Attallah. *Cinema Journal* 22.2 (Winter 1983): 2–25.

Morgan, Arthur E. *The Small Community: The Foundation of Democratic Life – What It Is and How to Achieve It*. New York: Harper & Bros., 1942.

Morgan, David. "Frontier Myth and American Gothic." *Genre* 14 (Fall 1981): 329–46.

Morrill, George. "The West's Most Incredible Outlaw." *American History Illustrated* 18.8 (Dec. 1983): 40–4.

Morris, Edmund. *The Rise of Theodore Roosevelt*. New York: Ballantine Books, 1979.

*Theodore Rex*. New York: Random House, 2001.

Morse, David. "Under Western Eyes: Variations on a Genre." *Monogram* 6 (Oct. 1975): 34–9. Rpt. in *Passport to Hollywood: Film Immigrants Anthology*. Ed. Don Whittemore and Philip Alan Cecchettini, 202–15. New York: McGraw–Hill, 1976.

Moses, L. G. *Wild West Shows and the Images of American Indians, 1883–1933*. Albuquerque: University of New Mexico Press, 1996.

Murphy, Brenda. *American Realism and American Drama, 1880–1940*. Cambridge: Cambridge University Press, 1987.

Musser, Charles. *Before the Nickelodeon: Edwin S. Porter and the Edison Manufacturing Company*. Berkeley: University of California Press, 1991.

*Edison Motion Pictures, 1890–1900: An Annotated Filmography*. Pordenone, Italy: Le Giornate del Cinema Muto, and Washington, D.C.: Smithsonian Institution Press, 1997.

*The Emergence of Cinema: The American Screen to 1907*. Berkeley: University of California Press, 1994.

Myres, Sandra L. *Westering Women and the Frontier Experience, 1800–1915*. Albuquerque: University Press of New Mexico, 1982.

Nachbar, Jack, ed. *Focus on the Western*. Englewood Cliffs, N.J.: Prentice–Hall, 1974.

Naremore, James. *Acting in the Cinema*. Berkeley: University of California Press, 1988.

*More Than Night: Film Noir in Its Contexts*. Berkeley: University of California Press, 1998.

Nash, Roderick. "An Unprecedented Landscape: The Problem of Loving the Arid West." *American Renaissance and American West: Proceedings of the Second University of Wyoming American Studies Conference*. Ed. Christopher S. Durer, Herbert R. Dieterich, Henry J. Laskowsky, and James W. Welke, 69–77. Laramie: University of Wyoming, 1982.

*Wilderness and the American Mind*. New Haven: Yale University Press, 1973.

Nerlich, Michael. *Ideology of Adventure*. Trans. Ruth Crowley. Minneapolis: University of Minnesota Press, 1987.

Nevius, Blake. *Cooper's Landscapes: An Essay on the Picturesque Vision*. Berkeley: University of California Press, 1976.

"No Indians Wanted." *Moving Picture World*, Oct. 18, 1913: 258.

Nolley, Kenneth J. "Printing the Legend in the Age of MX: Reconsidering Ford's Military Trilogy." *Literature/Film Quarterly* 14.2 (1986): 82–8.

Noriega, Chon. "Birth of the Southwest: Social Protest, Tourism, and D. W. Griffith's *Ramona*." *The Birth of Whiteness: Race and the Emergence of U.S. Cinema.* Ed. Daniel Bernardi, 203–27. New Brunswick, N.J.: Rutgers University Press, 1996.

Novak, Barbara. *Nature and Culture: American Landscape and Painting, 1825–1875.* New York: Oxford University Press, 1980.

O'Neill, William L. *American High: The Years of Confidence, 1945–1960.* New York: Free Press, 1986.

Orvell, Miles. *The Real Thing: Imitation and Authenticity in American Culture.* Chapel Hill: University of North Carolina Press, 1989.

Owens, Louis. *Mixedblood Messages: Literature, Film, Family, Place.* Norman: University of Oklahoma Press, 1998.

Painter, Nell Irvin. *Standing at Armageddon: The United States, 1877–1919.* New York: W. W. Norton, 1987.

Parkman, Francis. *France and England in North America.* 1865–92. 2 vols. Ed. David Levin. New York: Library of America, 1983.

*"The Oregon Trail" and "The Conspiracy of Pontiac."* 1849, 1851. Ed. William R. Taylor. New York: Library of America, 1991.

"The Passing of the Western Subject." *The Nickelodeon,* Feb. 18, 1911: 181.

Patterson, James T. *Grand Expectations: The United States, 1945–1974.* New York: Oxford University Press, 1996.

Paul, Rodman W. *The Far West and the Great Plains in Transition: 1859–1900.* New York: Harper & Row, 1988.

Pearce, Roy Harvey. *Savagism and Civilization: A Study of the Indian and the American Mind.* Berkeley: University of California Press, 1988.

Pearson, Roberta E. "The Revenge of Rain-in-the-Face? or, Custers and Indians on the Silent Screen." *The Birth of Whiteness: Race and the Emergence of U.S. Cinema.* Ed. Daniel Bernardi, 273–99. New Brunswick, N.J.: Rutgers University Press, 1996.

Peck, H. Daniel. *A World by Itself: The Pastoral Moment in Cooper's Fiction.* New Haven: Yale University Press, 1977.

Perrett, Geoffrey. *A Dream of Greatness: The American People, 1946–1963.* New York: Coward, McCann & Geoghegan, 1979.

Peters, Arthur King. *Seven Trails West.* New York: Abbeville Press, 1996.

Pilkington, William T., ed. *Critical Essays on the Western American Novel.* Boston: G. K. Hall, 1980.

Place, J. A. *The Western Films of John Ford.* Secaucus, N.J.: Citadel Press, 1974.

Poague, Leland. "'All I Can See Is the Flags': *Fort Apache* and the Visibility of History." *Cinema Journal* 27.2 (1988): 8–26.

Podheiser, Linda. "Pep on the Range, or Douglas Fairbanks and the World War I Era Western." *Journal of Popular Film and Television* 11.3 (Fall 1983): 122–30.

Poirier, Richard. *The Renewal of Literature: Emersonian Reflections.* New Haven: Yale University Press, 1987.

Pratt, George C. "The Posse Is Ridin' Like Mad." *Image* 7.4 (Apr. 1958): 76–84.

*Spellbound in Darkness: A History of the Silent Film.* Greenwich, Conn.: New York Graphic Society, 1973.

Prucha, Francis Paul. *American Indian Treaties: The History of a Political Anomaly.* Berkeley: University of California Press, 1994.

Rabin, Jonathan. *Bad Land: An American Romance.* New York: Vintage Books, 1996.
Ray, Robert. *A Certain Tendency of the Hollywood Cinema, 1930–1980.* Princeton, N.J.: Princeton University Press, 1985.
Remini, Robert. *Andrew Jackson.* 3 vols. Baltimore: Johns Hopkins University Press, 1998.
Reynolds, David. *Beneath the American Renaissance: The Subversive Imagination in the Age of Emerson and Melville.* New York: Alfred A. Knopf, 1988.
Riesman, David, with Reuel Denny and Nathan Glazer. *The Lonely Crowd: A Study of the Changing American Character.* New Haven: Yale University Press, 1950.
Roberts, Randy, and James S. Olson. *John Wayne: American.* New York: Free Press, 1995.
Rogin, Michael Paul. *Fathers and Children: Andrew Jackson and the Subjugation of the American Indian.* New York: Alfred A. Knopf, 1975.
Rollins, Peter C., and John E. O'Connor, eds. *Hollywood's Indian: The Portrayal of the Native American in Film.* Lexington: University Press of Kentucky, 1998.
Roosevelt, Franklin D. "Campaign Address on Progressive Government at the Commonwealth Club, San Francisco, Calif. September 23, 1932." *The Public Papers and Addresses of Franklin D. Roosevelt,* vol. 1: *The Genesis of the New Deal.* Comp. Samuel I. Rosenman, 746–50. New York: Random House, 1938.
Roosevelt, Theodore. *An Autobiography.* 1913. New York: Da Capo Press, 1985.
*The Winning of the West.* 1889–96. 4 vols. Lincoln: University of Nebraska Press, 1995.
Rosenstone, Robert A. *Visions of the Past: The Challenge of Film to Our Idea of History.* Cambridge, Mass.: Harvard University Press, 1995.
Roush, Jon. "Square Places, Round Wholes." *Northern Lights: A Selection of New Writing from the American West.* Ed. Deborah Clow and Donald Snow, 22–5. New York: Vintage Books, 1994.
Sarf, Michael Wayne. *God Bless You, Buffalo Bill: A Layman's Guide to History and the Western Film.* Rutherford, N.J.: Fairleigh Dickinson University Press, 1983.
Saunders, John. *The Western Genre: From Lordsburg to Big Whiskey.* London: Wallflower Press, 2001.
Schatz, Thomas. *Boom and Bust: American Cinema in the 1940s.* Berkeley: University of California Press, 1999.
Scheckel, Susan. *The Insistence of the Indian: Race and Nationalism in Nineteenth-Century American Culture.* Princeton, N.J.: Princeton University Press, 1998.
Schlesinger, Arthur M., Jr. *The Age of Jackson.* New York: Mentor Books, 1949.
Schneider, Tassilo. "Finding a New *Heimat* in the Wild West: Karl May and the German Western of the 1960s." *Journal of Film and Video* 47.1–3 (Spring–Fall 1995): 50–66.
Schwartz, Joseph. "The Wild West Show: 'Everything Genuine.'" *Journal of Popular Culture* 3.4 (Spring 1970): 656–66.
Sears, Priscilla. "A Pillar of Fire to Follow: Myths of the American Indian Dramas, 1808–1859." *American Renaissance and American West: Proceedings of the Second University of Wyoming American Studies Conference.* Ed. Christopher S. Durer, Herbert R. Dieterich, Henry J. Laskowsky, and James W. Welke, 15–30. Laramie: University of Wyoming, 1982.
Seelye, John. "Some Green Thoughts on a Green Theme." *TriQuarterly* 23–4 (Winter–Spring 1972): 576–638.

Segal, Charles M., and David C. Stineback. *Puritans, Indians, and Manifest Destiny.* New York: G. P. Putnam's Sons, 1977.

Shively, JoEllen. "Cowboys and Indians: Perceptions of Western Films among American Indians and Anglos." *American Sociological Review* 57.6 (Dec. 1992): 725–33.

Short, John Rennie. *Imagined Country: Environment, Culture and Society.* London: Routledge, 1991.

Shulman, Robert. "Parkman's Indians and American Violence." *Massachusetts Review* 12 (1971): 221–39.

Simmon, Scott. *The Films of D. W. Griffith.* Cambridge: Cambridge University Press, 1993.

*Treasures from American Film Archives: 50 Preserved Films.* San Francisco: National Film Preservation Foundation, 2000.

Simon, William G., and Louise Spense. "Cowboy Wonderland, History, and Myth: 'It Ain't All That Different than Real Life.'" *Journal of Film and Video* 47.1–3 (Spring–Fall 1995): 67–81.

Sinclair, Andrew. *John Ford.* New York: Dial Press, 1979.

Singer, Ben. *Melodrama and Modernity: Early Sensational Cinema and Its Contexts.* New York: Columbia University Press, 2001.

Slotkin, Richard. *The Fatal Environment: The Myth of the Frontier in the Age of Industrialization, 1800–1890.* Middletown, Conn.: Wesleyan University Press, 1985.

*Gunfighter Nation: The Myth of the Frontier in Twentieth-Century America.* New York: Atheneum, 1992.

*Regeneration through Violence: The Mythology of the American Frontier, 1600–1860.* Middletown, Conn.: Wesleyan University Press, 1973.

Smith, Henry Nash. *Virgin Land: The American West as Symbol and Myth.* 1950. New York: Vintage Books, 1957.

Smith, Packy, and Ed Hulse, eds. *Don Miller's Hollywood Corral: A Comprehensive B-Western Roundup.* Burbank, Calif.: Riverwood Press, 1993.

Smith, Sherry L. *The View from Officers' Row: Army Perceptions of Western Indians.* Tucson: University of Arizona Press, 1990.

Sonnichsen, C. L. *From Hopalong to Hud: Thoughts on Western Fiction.* College Station: Texas A&M University Press, 1978.

Staiger, Janet. "Dividing Labor for Production Control: Thomas Ince and the Rise of the Studio System." *The American Movie Industry: The Business of Motion Pictures.* Ed. Gorham Kindem, 94–103. Carbondale: Southern Illinois University Press, 1982.

Standing Bear, Luther. *Land of the Spotted Eagle.* 1933. Lincoln: University of Nebraska Press, 1978.

*My Indian Boyhood.* 1931. Lincoln: University of Nebraska Press, 1988.

*My People the Sioux.* 1928. Lincoln: University of Nebraska Press, 1975.

Stanfield, Peter. *Hollywood, Westerns and the 1930s: The Lost Trail.* Exeter, U.K.: University of Exeter Press, 2001.

*Horse Opera: The Strange History of the 1930s Singing Cowboy.* Urbana: University of Illinois Press, 2002.

"The Western, 1909–1914: A Cast of Villains." *Film History* 1.2 (1987): 97–112.

Stephanson, Anders. *Manifest Destiny: American Expansionism and the Empire of Right.* New York: Hill & Wang, 1995.

Stowell, Peter. *John Ford.* Boston: Twayne, 1986.

Strickland, Rennard. *Tonto's Revenge: Reflections on American Indian Culture and Policy.* Albuquerque: University of New Mexico Press, 1997.
Studlar, Gaylyn, and Matthew Bernstein, eds. *John Ford Made Westerns: Filming the Legend in the Sound Era.* Bloomington: Indiana University Press, 2001.
Tanner, Tony. *Scenes of Nature, Signs of Men.* Cambridge: Cambridge University Press, 1987.
Tate, Michael L. *The Frontier Army in the Settlement of the West.* Norman: University of Oklahoma Press, 1999.
Taves, Brian. "The B Film: Hollywood's Other Half." *Grand Design: Hollywood as a Modern Business Enterprise, 1930–1939.* Ed. Tino Balio, 313–50. Berkeley: University of California Press, 1995.
Taylor, Alan. *William Cooper's Town: Power and Persuasion on the Frontier of the Early American Republic.* New York: Vintage Books, 1996.
Teague, David W. *The Southwest in American Literature and Art: The Rise of a Desert Aesthetic.* Tucson: University of Arizona Press, 1997.
Tefertiller, Casey. *Wyatt Earp: The Life behind the Legend.* New York: John Wiley & Sons, 1997.
Thomas, Deborah. *Reading Hollywood: Spaces and Meanings in American Film.* London: Wallflower Press, 2001.
Thompson, Frank. "The First Picture Show: Gaston Méliès's Star Film Ranch, San Antonio, Texas, 1910–1911." *Literature/Film Quarterly* 23.2 (1995): 110–13.
Thoreau, Henry David. *"A Week"; "Walden; or, Life in the Woods"; "The Maine Woods"; "Cape Cod."* Ed. Robert F. Sayre. New York: Library of America, 1985.
Tilton, Robert S. *Pocahontas: The Evolution of an American Narrative.* Cambridge: Cambridge University Press, 1994.
Tompkins, Jane. *Sensational Designs: The Cultural Work of American Fiction, 1790–1860.* New York: Oxford University Press, 1985.
*West of Everything: The Inner Life of Westerns.* New York: Oxford University Press, 1992.
"Topics of the Week: The Popularity of Western Films." *The Bioscope,* Aug. 18, 1910: 4–5.
Torgovnick, Marianna. *Gone Primitive: Savage Intellects, Modern Lives.* Chicago: University of Chicago Press, 1990.
*Primitive Passions: Men, Women, and the Quest for Ecstasy.* New York: Alfred A. Knopf, 1997.
Turner, Frederick Jackson. "The Significance of the Frontier in American History." 1893. Rpt. in *The Turner Thesis.* Ed. George Rogers Taylor, 3–28. Lexington, Mass.: D. C. Heath, 1972.
Tuska, Jon. *The American West in Film: Critical Approaches to the Western.* Lincoln: University of Nebraska Press, 1988.
*The Filming of the West.* Garden City, N.Y.: Doubleday, 1976.
Twain, Mark. *Roughing It.* 1872. *"The Innocents Abroad" & "Roughing It."* Ed. Guy Cardwell. New York: Library of America, 1984.
Unruh, John D., Jr. *The Plains Across: The Overland Emigrants and the Trans-Mississippi West, 1840–60.* Urbana: University of Illinois Press, 1982.
Utley, Robert M. *The Indian Frontier of the American West 1846–1890.* Albuquerque: University of New Mexico Press, 1984.
*The Last Days of the Sioux Nation.* New Haven: Yale University Press, 1963.

Van Dyke, John C. *The Desert: Further Studies in Natural Appearances.* 1901. New York: Charles Scribner's Sons, 1918.
Walker, Janet, ed. *Westerns: Films through History.* New York: Routledge/American Film Institute, 2001.
Wallace, Anthony F. C. "'The Obtaining Lands': Thomas Jefferson and the Native Americans." *Thomas Jefferson and the Changing West.* Ed. James P. Ronda, 25–41. Albuquerque: University of New Mexico Press, 1997.
Wallis, Michael. *The Real Wild West: The 101 Ranch and the Creation of the American West.* New York: St. Martin's Press, 1999.
Walsh, Raoul. *Each Man in His Time.* New York: Farrar, Straus & Giroux, 1974.
Ward, John William. *Andrew Jackson: Symbol for an Age.* New York: Oxford University Press, 1962.
Watson, Margaret G. *Silver Theater: Amusements of the Mining Frontier in Early Nevada, 1850–1864.* Glendale, Calif.: Arthur H. Clark, 1964.
Weatherford, Jack. *Indian Givers: How the Indians of the Americas Transformed the World.* New York: Fawcett Columbine, 1988.
"Western Operations of the New York Motion Picture Company." *Moving Picture World,* Aug. 12, 1912: 777.
Wexman, Virginia Wright. *Creating the Couple: Love, Marriage, and Hollywood Performance.* Princeton, N.J.: Princeton University Press, 1993.
"The Family on the Land: Race and Nationhood in Silent Westerns." *The Birth of Whiteness: Race and the Emergence of U.S. Cinema.* Ed. Daniel Bernardi, 129–69. New Brunswick, N.J.: Rutgers University Press, 1996.
"What Is an American Subject?" *Moving Picture World,* Jan. 22, 1910: 82.
"Where Do We Ride from Here?" *Photoplay* 15.3 (Feb. 1919): 37.
White, G. Edward. *The Eastern Establishment and the Western Experience: The West of Frederic Remington, Theodore Roosevelt, and Owen Wister.* 1967. Austin: University of Texas Press, 1989.
White, Richard. "Discovering Nature in North America." *Discovering America: Essays on the Search for an Identity.* Ed. David Thelen and Frederick E. Hoxie, 40–57. Urbana: University of Illinois Press, 1994.
*"It's Your Misfortune and None of My Own": A History of the American West.* Norman: University of Oklahoma Press, 1991.
Whitfield, Stephen J. *The Culture of the Cold War.* 2d ed. Baltimore: Johns Hopkins University Press, 1996.
Wickstrom, Gordon M. "Buffalo Bill the Actor." *Journal of the West* 34.1 (Jan. 1995): 62–9.
Wild, Peter. *The Opal Desert: Explorations of Fantasy and Reality in the American Southwest.* Austin: University of Texas Press, 1999.
Wills, Garry. *John Wayne's America: The Politics of Celebrity.* New York: Simon & Schuster, 1997.
Willson, Clair Eugene. *Mimes and Miners: A Historical Study of the Theater in Tombstone.* University of Arizona Bulletin 6.1. Tucson, 1935.
Wister, Owen. *The Virginian: A Horseman of the Plains.* 1902. Boston: Houghton Mifflin, 1968.
Woal, Linda Kowall. "Romaine Fielding: The West's Touring Auteur." *Film History* 7 (1995): 401–25.
Woal, Linda Kowall, and Michael Woal. "Romaine Fielding's Real Westerns." *Journal of Film and Video* 47.1–3 (Spring–Fall 1995): 7–25.

Wolfenstein, Martha, and Nathan Leites. *Movies: A Psychological Study*. Glencoe, Ill.: Free Press, 1950.
Wollen, Peter. *Signs and Meaning in the Cinema*. Rev. ed. Bloomington and London: Indiana University Press, 1972.
Wood, Robin. "Ideology, Genre, Auteur." *Film Comment* 13.1 (Jan.–Feb. 1977): 46–51.
"*Shall* We Gather at the River?: The Late Films of John Ford." *Film Comment* 7.3 (Fall 1971): 8–17.
Worcester, Donald E., ed. *Forked Tongues and Broken Treaties*. Caldwell, Idaho: Caxton Printers, 1975.
Work Projects Administration. *Arizona: A Guide to the Sunset State*. New York: Hastings House, 1940.
Wright, Will. *Six-Guns and Society: A Structural Study of the Western*. Berkeley: University of California Press, 1975.
Wrobel, David M. *The End of American Exceptionalism: Frontier Anxiety from the Old West to the New Deal*. Lawrence: University Press of Kansas, 1993.
Zweig, Paul. *The Adventurer: The Fate of Adventure in the Western World*. Princeton, N.J.: Princeton University Press, 1974.

# Films Cited

*Abilene Town* (1946, United Artists/Guild Prods.), dir. Edwin L. Marin
*Aborigine's Devotion, The* (1909, World Film Mfg. Co.)
*Ace in the Hole* (aka *The Big Carnival*) (1951, Paramount), dir. Billy Wilder
*Alamo, The* (1960, Batjac Prods./Alamo Co.), dir. John Wayne
*Along Came Jones* (1945, RKO/International Pictures/Cinema Artists), dir. Stuart Heisler
*Along the Great Divide* (1951, Warner Bros.), dir. Raoul Walsh
*Angel and the Badman* (aka *The Angel and the Outlaw*) (1947, Republic/Patnel Prods.), dir. James Edward Grant, prod. John Wayne
*Annie Oakley* (1894, Edison), prod. W. K. L. Dickson, cinematogr. William Heise
*Annie Oakley* (1935, RKO), dir. George Stevens
*Apartment for Peggy* (1948, Twentieth Century–Fox), dir. George Seaton
*Argonauts of California, The* (1916, Monrovia Feature Film Co.), dir. Henry Kabierske
*Arizona* (1940, Columbia), dir. Wesley Ruggles
*Arizonian, The* (1935, RKO), dir. Charles Vidor
*Arrival of Train, Cheyenne* (1903, American Mutoscope and Biograph), cinematogr. G. W. Bitzer
*As Seen through a Telescope* (1900, U.K.), dir. George Albert Smith
*Bad Day at Black Rock* (1955, MGM), dir. John Sturges
*Ballad of Cable Hogue, The* (1970, Warner Bros./Phil Feldman Prods.), dir. Sam Peckinpah
*Bandit's Waterloo, The* (1908, Biograph), dir. D. W. Griffith
*Bargain, The* (aka *The Two-Gun Man in the Bargain* [1920 reissue]) (1914, Paramount/New York Motion Picture Co.), dir. Reginald Barker, prod. Thomas H. Ince
*Bataan* (1943, MGM), dir. Tay Garnett
*Battle at Elderbush Gulch, The* (1913, Biograph), dir. D. W. Griffith
*Battleship Potemkin* (*Bronenosets Potemkin;* aka *Potemkin*), dir. Sergei Eisenstein (USSR, Goskino, 1925)
*Best Years of Our Lives, The* (1946, Goldwyn), dir. William Wyler
*Betrayed by a Handprint* (1908, Biograph), dir. D. W. Griffith
*Big Heat, The* (1953, Columbia), dir. Fritz Lang

*Big Trail, The* (1930, Fox), dir. Raoul Walsh
*Billy the Kid* (aka *The Highwayman Rides*) (1930, MGM), dir. King Vidor
*Birth of a Nation, The* (aka *The Clansman*) (1915, D. W. Griffith Corp./Epoch Producing Corp.), dir. D. W. Griffith
*Blazing the Trail* (1912, New York Motion Picture Co./101–Bison), dir. Thomas H. Ince
*Blood on the Moon* (1948, RKO), dir. Robert Wise
*Bluff from a Tenderfoot, A* (1899, American Mutoscope and Biograph), dir. Frederick S. Armitage
*Bonnie and Clyde* (1967, Warner Bros.–Seven Arts/Tatira–Hiller Prods.), dir. Arthur Penn
*Braveheart* (1925, Cinema Corp. of America), dir. Alan Hale
*Brigham Young – Frontiersman* (aka *Brigham Young*) (1940, Twentieth Century–Fox), dir. Henry Hathaway
*Broken Arrow* (1950, Twentieth Century–Fox), dir. Delmer Daves
*Broken Doll, The: A Tragedy of the Indian Reservation* (1910, Biograph), dir. D. W. Griffith
*Broken Lance* (1954, Twentieth Century–Fox), dir. Edward Dmytryk
*Buck's Romance* (1912, Selig Polyscope), dir. William Duncan
*Buffalo Bill* (1944, Twentieth Century–Fox), dir. William A. Wellman
*Buffalo Bill and the Indians; or, Sitting Bull's History Lesson* (1976, De Laurentiis / Talent Associates Ltd.), dir. Robert Altman
*Buffalo Bill's Wild West and Pawnee Bill's Far East* (1910, Buffalo Bill and Pawnee Bill Film Co.)
*Buffalo Dance* (1894, Edison), cinematogr. William Heise
*California* (1946, Paramount), dir. John Farrow
*Call of the Wild, The* (1908, Biograph), dir. D. W. Griffith
*Calling Wild Bill Elliott* (1943, Republic), dir. Spencer Gordon Bennet
*Canyon Passage* (1946, Universal/Walter Wanger Pictures), dir. Jacques Tourneur
*Captain Brand's Wife* (1911, Selig Polyscope)
*Carrying Out the Snakes* (1901, Edison), cinematogr. James H. White[?]
*Cat People* (1942, RKO), dir. Jacques Tourneur, prod. Val Lewton
*Cattle Fording Stream* (1898, Edison), cinematogr. Frederick Blechynden
*Chang* (1927, Paramount Famous Lasky), dir. Merian C. Cooper and Ernest B. Schoedsack
*Cheat, The* (1915, Paramount/Jesse L. Lasky Feature Play Co.), dir. Cecil B. De Mille
*Cheyenne Autumn* (1964, Warner Bros./Ford–Smith Prods.), dir. John Ford
*Chief's Daughter, The* (1911, Biograph), dir. D. W. Griffith
*Chingachgook, die große Schlange* [*Chingachgook: The Great Snake*] (1967, DEFA-Studio für Spielfilme, East Germany), dir. Richard Groschopp
*Chisum* (1970, Warner Bros./Batjac Prods.), dir. Andrew V. McLaglen
*Cimarron* (1931, RKO), dir. Wesley Ruggles
*Clash of the Wolves* (1925, Warner Bros.), dir. Noel M. Smith
*Coaching Party, Yosemite Valley* (1901, American Mutoscope and Biograph), cinematogr. Robert K. Bonine
*Code of the Cactus* (1939, Victory), dir. Sam Newfield
*Colorado Territory* (aka *North of the Rio Grande*) (1949, Warner Bros.), dir. Raoul Walsh
*Colt Comrades* (1943, United Artists/Harry Sherman Prods.), dir. Lesley Selander

*Comata, the Sioux* (1909, Biograph), dir. D. W. Griffith
*Come On, Tarzan* (1932, K-B-S), dir. Alan James
*Coroner Creek* (1948, Columbia/Producers–Actors Corp.), dir. Ray Enright
*Country Doctor, The* (1909, Biograph), dir. D. W. Griffith
*Covered Wagon, The* (1923, Paramount), dir. James Cruze
*Cowboy Commandos* (1943, Monogram), dir. S. Roy Luby
*Cowboy Justice* (1904), dir. G. W. Bitzer
*Cowboy Star, The* (1936, Columbia), dir. David Selman
*Crime of M. Lange, The* (*Le Crime de Monsieur Lange*) (1936, Obéron, France), dir. Jean Renoir
*Cripple Creek Bar-Room Scene* (1899, Edison), dir. James H. White
*Crooked River* (1951, Lippert), dir. Thomas Carr
*Cross Fire* (1933, RKO), dir. Otto Brower
*Crossfire* (1947, RKO), dir. Edward Dmytryk
*Custer's Last Fight* (1912, New York Motion Picture Co./Bison), dir. Francis Ford[?], prod. Thomas H. Ince
*Daisy Kenyon* (1947, Twentieth Century–Fox), dir. Otto Preminger
*Dakota* (1945, Republic), dir. Joseph Kane
*Dances with Wolves* (1990, Majestic Film/Tig Prods.), dir. Kevin Costner
*Daniel Boone* (1936, RKO/George A. Hirliman Prods.), dir. David Howard
*Daniel Boone; or, Pioneer Days in America* (1906, Edison), dir. Edwin S. Porter and Wallace McCutcheon
*Dark Command* (1940, Republic), dir. Raoul Walsh
*Dark Corner, The* (1946, Twentieth Century–Fox), dir. Henry Hathaway
*Dawn Rider, The* (1935, Monogram/Lone Star Prods.), dir. Robert N. Bradbury
*Dead Man's Claim, The* (1912, Essanay), dir. Gilbert M. Anderson
*Der letzte der Mohikaner* [*Lederstrumpf*, pt. 2] (aka *The Last of the Mohicans*) (1920, Luna Film, Germany), dir. Arthur Wellin
*Der Letzte Mohikaner* (aka *The Last Tomahawk; La valle delle ombre rosse; El Último mohicano*) (1965, International Germania Film/Cineproduzioni Associati/Balcázar Producciones Cinematográficas/Associate, West Germany– Italy–Spain), dir. Harald Reinl
*Der Wildtöter und Chingachgook* [*Lederstrumpf*, pt. 1] (aka *The Deerslayer and Chingachgook*) (1920, Luna Film, Germany), dir. Arthur Wellin
*Desert Gold* (1936, Paramount), dir. James P. Hogan
*Desert Justice* (aka *Crime's Highway* [U.K.]) (1936, Atlantic/Berke–Perrin Prods.), dir. William A. Berke
*Deserter, The* (aka *The Devil's Backbone; La spina dorsale del diavolo; Djavolja kicma*) (1971, Dino de Laurentiis Cinematografica/Heritage Enterprises/Jadran Film, Italy–USA–Yugoslavia), dir. Burt Kennedy and Niksa Fulgosi
*Destry Rides Again* (aka *Justice Rides Again*) (1939, Universal), dir. George Marshall
*Devil's Doorway* (1950, MGM), dir. Anthony Mann
*Directed by John Ford* (1971, American Film Institute/California Arts Commission), dir. Peter Bogdanovich
*Doc* (1971, Frank Perry Films), dir. Frank Perry, scr. Pete Hamill
*Dodge City* (1939, Warner Bros.), dir. Michael Curtiz
*Doorway to Hell, The* (aka *A Handful of Clouds* [U.K.]) (Warner Bros., 1930), dir. Archie Mayo

*Double Indemnity* (1944, Paramount), dir. Billy Wilder
*Dracula* (1931, Universal), dir. Tod Browning
*Drums along the Mohawk* (1939, Twentieth Century–Fox), dir. John Ford
*Duel in the Sun* (1946, Vanguard Films), dir. King Vidor, prod. David O. Selznick
*Empty Water Keg, The* (1912, New York Motion Picture Co./Bison), dir. Thomas H. Ince
*End of the Trail, The* (1932, Columbia), dir. D. Ross Lederman
*Enemy of the Law* (1945, Producers Releasing Corp.), dir. Harry L. Fraser
*Fatherhood of Buck McGee, The* (1912, Vitagraph)
*Female of the Species, The* (1912, Biograph), dir. D. W. Griffith
*Fighting Blood* (1911, Biograph), dir. D. W. Griffith
*For the Papoose* (1912, Pathé), dir. James Young Deer[?]
*Fort Apache* (1948, RKO/Argosy), dir. John Ford
*Forty Guns* (1957, Twentieth Century–Fox/Globe Enterprises), dir. Samuel Fuller
*Frankenstein* (1931, Universal), dir. James Whale
*From Broadway to Cheyenne* (aka *Broadway to Cheyenne*) (1932, Monogram), dir. Harry L. Fraser
*Frontier Marshal* (1934, Fox), dir. Lewis Seiler, prod. Sol Lesser
*Frontier Marshal* (1939, Twentieth Century–Fox), dir. Allan Dwan
*Furies, The* (1950, Paramount/Wallis–Hazen Inc.), dir. Anthony Mann
*Gabriel over the White House* (Cosmopolitan/MGM, 1933), dir. Gregory La Cava
*Gangsters of the Frontier* (aka *Raiders of the Frontier* [U.K.]) (1944, Producers Releasing Corp./Alexander-Stern Prods.), dir. Elmer Clifton
*Gentleman's Agreement* (1947, Twentieth Century–Fox), dir. Elia Kazan
*Ghost Patrol* (1936, Puritan/Excelsior Pictures Corp.), dir. Sam Newfield
*Girl and the Outlaw, The* (1908, Biograph), dir. D. W. Griffith
*Girl of the Golden West, The* (1915, Jesse L. Lasky Feature Play Co.), dir. Cecil B. De Mille
*Go West* (1925, MGM/Buster Keaton Prods.), dir. Buster Keaton
*Go West* (aka *Marx Brothers Go West* [U.K.]) (1940, MGM), dir. Edward Buzzell
*Gold Is Where You Find It* (1938, Warner Bros./Cosmopolitan Prods.), dir. Michael Curtiz
*Golden Stallion, The* (1949, Republic), dir. William Witney
*Good Sam* (1948, RKO/Rainbow Prods.), dir. Leo McCarey
*Grapes of Wrath, The* (1940, Twentieth Century–Fox), dir. John Ford
*Grass: A Nation's Battle for Life* (1925, Paramount/Famous Players–Lasky), dir. Merian C. Cooper and Ernest B. Schoedsack
*Great Northfield Minnesota Raid, The* (1972, Univeral), dir. Philip Kaufman
*Great Train Robbery, The* (1903, Edison), dir. Edwin S. Porter
*Greed* (1924, Metro–Goldwyn/Louis B. Mayer), dir. Erich von Stroheim
*Gunfight at the O.K. Corral* (1957, Paramount), dir. John Sturges
*Gunfighter, The* (1950, Twentieth Century–Fox), dir. Henry King
*Half-Breed, The* (1916, Fine Arts Film), dir. Allan Dwan
*Hamlet* (1948, J. Arthur Rank Films/Pilgrim Pictures/Rank Film Organization/Two Cities Films Ltd., U.K.), dir. Laurence Olivier
*Harvey Girls, The* (1946, MGM), dir. George Sidney
*Haunted Gold* (1932, Warner Bros.), dir. Mack V. Wright

*Heartland* (1980, Filmhaus/National Endowment for the Humanities/Wilderness Women), dir. Richard Pearce
*Hellfire* (1949, Republic/Elliott-McGowan Prods.), dir. R. G. Springsteen
*Hell's Heroes* (1929, Universal), dir. William Wyler
*Hell's Hinges* (1916, Triangle/New York Motion Picture Co.), dir. Charles Swickard [and William S. Hart, uncredited], prod. Thomas H. Ince
*Her Awakening* (1911, Biograph), dir. D. W. Griffith
*Her Indian Mother* (1910, Kalem), dir. Sidney Olcott
*Hiawatha: The Indian Passion Play* (1913, Gaumont/Fort Defiance Film Co.), prod. Frank E. Moore
*High Noon* (1952, United Artists/Stanley Kramer Prods.), dir. Fred Zinnemann
*High Plains Drifter* (1972, Universal/Malpaso), dir. Clint Eastwood
*High Sierra* (1941, Warner Bros.), dir. Raoul Walsh
*Hired Hand, The* (1971, Universal/Pando/Tartan Films, USA–U.K.), dir. Peter Fonda
*His Trust Fulfilled* (1911, Biograph), dir. D. W. Griffith
*Hondo* (1953, Warner Bros./Wayne–Fellows Prods.), dir. John Farrow
*Horizons West* (1952, Universal), dir. Budd Boetticher
*Hour of the Gun* (1967, United Artists/Mirisch), dir. John Sturges
*How Green Was My Valley* (1941, Twentieth Century–Fox), dir. John Ford
*How the West Was Won* (1962, MGM/Cinerama), dir. John Ford, Henry Hathaway, George Marshall [and Richard Thorpe, uncredited]
*Hudson's Bay* (1940, Twentieth Century–Fox), dir. Irving Pichel
*I Am a Fugitive from a Chain Gang* (1932, Warner Bros.), dir. Mervyn LeRoy
*I Wake Up Screaming* (1941, Twentieth Century–Fox), dir. H. Bruce Humberstone
*In Old California* (1910, Biograph), dir. D. W. Griffith
*In Search of the Oregon Trail* (1996, Nebraska ETV Network/Oregon Public Broadcasting/Oregon Historical Society), dir. and prod. Michael Farrell
*Indian Massacre, The* (aka *The Heart of an Indian*) (1912, New York Motion Picture Co./101–Bison), dir. Francis Ford[?], prod. Thomas H. Ince
*Indian Runner's Romance, The* (1909, Biograph), dir. D. W. Griffith
*Indian Wars, The* (aka *Wars of Civilization*) (1914, Essanay/Col. Wm. F. Cody Historical Picture Co.), dir. Vernon Day and Theodore Wharton
*Indiens et cow-boys* (1904, Pathé, France)
*Informer, The* (1935, RKO), dir. John Ford
*Intruder in the Dust* (1949, MGM), dir. Clarence Brown
*Invaders, The* (1912, New York Motion Picture Co./Kay-Bee), dir. Francis Ford[?], prod. Thomas H. Ince
*Iola's Promise* (1912, Biograph), dir. D. W. Griffith
*Iron Horse, The* (1924, Fox), dir. John Ford
*Italian, The* (1915, Paramount/New York Motion Picture Co.), dir. Reginald Barker, prod. Thomas H. Ince
*It's a Wonderful Life* (1946, RKO/Liberty Films), dir. Frank Capra
*Jesse James* (1939, Twentieth Century–Fox), dir. Henry King [and Irving Cummings, uncredited]
*Johnny Guitar* (1954, Republic), dir. Nicholas Ray
*Johnny Hamlet* (aka *Johnny Amleto; Quella sporca storia nel west; That Dirty Story of the West* [lit.]) (1968, Daiano Film/Leone Film, Italy), dir. Enzo G. Castellari

*Just Gold* (1913, Biograph), dir. D. W. Griffith
*Kit Carson* (1903, American Mutoscope and Biograph), dir. Wallace McCutcheon
*Kit Carson* (1940, United Artists/Edward Small Prods.), dir. George B. Seitz
*Lady of the Dugout, The* (1918, Al Jennings Prod. Co.), dir. W. S. Van Dyke
*Land beyond the Sunset, The* (1912, Edison), dir. Harold M. Shaw
*Lassoing Steer* (aka *Lassoing a Steer*) (1898, Edison)
*Last Drop of Water, The* (1911, Biograph), dir. D. W. Griffith
*Last Hunt, The* (1956, MGM), dir. Richard Brooks
*Last Hurrah, The* (1958, Columbia), dir. John Ford
*Last of the Dogmen, The* (1995, Carolco/Last of the Dogmen/Savoy), dir. Tab Murphy
*Last of the Line, The* (1914, New York Motion Picture Co./Kay-Bee), dir. Jay Hunt, prod. Thomas H. Ince
*Last of the Mohicans, The* (1920, Associated Producers/Maurice Tourneur Prods.), dir. Maurice Tourneur and Clarence Brown
*Last of the Mohicans, The* (1932, Mascot), dir. Ford Beebe and B. Reeves Eason, 12-episode serial
*Last of the Mohicans, The* (1936, Reliance Prods. of California), dir. George B. Seitz
*Last of the Mohicans, The* (1992, Twentieth Century–Fox/Morgan Creek Prods.), dir. Michael Mann
*Last of the Redmen* (aka *Last of the Redskins* [U.K.]) (1947, Columbia), dir. George Sherman
*Last Outlaw, The* (1936, RKO), dir. Christy Cabanne, story by John Ford
*Last Round-Up, The* (1947, Columbia/Gene Autry Prods.), dir. John English
*Law and Order* (aka *Guns A'Blazing*) (1932, Universal), dir. Edward L. Cahn, coscr. John Huston
*Law and Order* (aka *Lucky Ralston* [U.K.]) (1940, Universal), dir. Ray Taylor
*Law and Order* (1953, Universal–International), dir. Nathan Juran
*Law for Tombstone* (1937, Universal/Buck Jones Prods.), dir. B. Reeves Eason and Buck Jones
*Lawless Frontier* (1934, Monogram/Lone Star Prods.), dir. Robert N. Bradbury
*Lawless Nineties, The* (1936, Republic), dir. Joseph Kane
*Leather Stocking* (1909, Biograph), dir. D. W. Griffith
*Leave Her to Heaven* (1945, Twentieth Century–Fox), dir. John M. Stahl
*Left-Handed Gun, The* (1958, Warner Bros./Harroll Prods.), dir. Arthur Penn
*Lesser Evil, The* (1912, Biograph), dir. D. W. Griffith
*Life of a Cowboy* (1906, Edison), dir. Edwin S. Porter
*Life of Buffalo Bill, The* (1912, Buffalo Bill and Pawnee Bill Film Co.), dir. Paul Panzer[?]
*Life of General Villa, The* (1914, Mutual), dir. Christy Cabanne, cocinematogr. Raoul Walsh
*Lights of New York, The* (1928, Warner Bros.), dir. Bryan Foy
*Little Big Man* (1970, Cinema Center 100 Prods./Stockbridge–Hiller Prods.), dir. Arthur Penn
*Little Caesar* (1930, First National/Warner Bros.), dir. Mervyn LeRoy
*Little Dove's Romance* (1911, New York Motion Picture Co./Bison), dir. Fred Balshofer
*Lone Star* (1996, Columbia/Castle Rock/Rio Dulce), dir. John Sayles

*Long Voyage Home, The* (1940, United Artists/Argosy/Walter Wanger Prods.), dir. John Ford
*Lost Weekend, The* (1945, Paramount), dir. Billy Wilder
*Lucky Texan, The* (1934, Monogram/Lone Star Prods.), dir. Robert N. Bradbury
*Magic Town* (1947, RKO/Robert Riskin Prods.), dir. William A. Wellman, scr.-prod. Robert Riskin
*Man from Laramie, The* (1955, Columbia), dir. Anthony Mann
*Man from Music Mountain, The* (aka *Texas Legionnaires*) (1943, Republic), dir. Joseph Kane
*Man from Utah, The* (1934, Monogram/Lone Star Prods.), dir. Robert N. Bradbury
*Man of Conquest* (1939, Republic), dir. George Nicholls Jr.
*Man Who Shot Liberty Valance, The* (1962, Ford Prods./Paramount), dir. John Ford
*Marshal of Mesa City, The* (1939, RKO), dir. David Howard
*Massacre* (1934, First National/Warner Bros.), dir. Alan Crosland
*Massacre, The* (1912, Biograph), dir. D. W. Griffith
*Mended Lute, The* (1909, Biograph), dir. D. W. Griffith
*Miracle on 34th Street* (1947, Twentieth Century–Fox), dir. George Seaton
*Mister Roberts* (1955, Warner Bros./Orange), dir. John Ford, Mervyn LeRoy, [and Joshua Logan, uncredited]
*Moana: A Romance of the South Seas* (1926, Paramount/Famous Players–Lasky), dir. Robert J. Flaherty
*Mohawk's Way, A* (1910, Biograph), dir. D. W. Griffith
*Mollycoddle, The* (1920, United Artists/Douglas Fairbanks Pictures), dir. Victor Fleming
*Monte Walsh* (1970, Cinema Center 100 Prods./Palladian Pictures), dir. William A. Fraker
*Mr. Blandings Builds His Dream House* (1948, RKO), dir. H. C. Potter
*Mr. Smith Goes to Washington* (1939, Columbia), dir. Frank Capra
*Mussolini Speaks* (1933, Columbia), prod.-dir. Jack Cohn, codir. Edgar Ulmer, narr. Lowell Thomas
*My Darling Clementine* (1946, Twentieth Century–Fox), dir. John Ford
*My Friend, the Indian* (1909, Lubin)
*My Name Is Nobody* (*Il mio nome è nessuno*) (1973, Rafran Cinematografica/La Société Alcinter/La Société Imp. Ex. Ci./Les Productions Jacques Leitienne/Rialto Film, Italy–France–Germany), dir. Tonino Valerii [and Sergio Leone, uncredited]
*Mystery Ranch* (1932, Fox), dir. David Howard
*'Neath the Arizona Skies* (1934, Monogram/Lone Star Prods.), dir. Harry L. Fraser
*New Frontier* (1934, U.S. Resettlement Administration), dir. H. P. McClure
*New Frontier* (1935, Republic), dir. Carl Pierson
*New Frontier* (aka *Frontier Horizon*) (1939, Republic), dir. George Sherman
*New Land, The* (aka *Nybyggarna*) (1972, Sweden, Svensk Filmindustri AB)
*Night Riders, The* (1939, Republic), dir. George Sherman
*North of 36* (1924, Paramount), dir. Irvin Willat
*North West Mounted Police* (1940, Paramount), dir. Cecil B. De Mille
*Northern Lights* (1978, Nilsson–Hanson), dir. Rob Nilsson and John Hanson
*Northwest Passage* (1940, MGM), dir. King Vidor
*Objective, Burma!* (aka *Operation Burma*) (1945, Warner Bros.), dir. Raoul Walsh

*Oklahoma Kid, The* (1939, Warner Bros.), dir. Lloyd Bacon
*Old Indian Days* (1911, Pathé), dir. James Young Deer
*Old Shatterhand* (aka *Shatterhand; Les Cavaliers rouges; Battaglia di Fort Apache; Apaches' Last Battle* [U.K.]) (1963, CCC Filmkunst GmbH/Criterion Prod./Serena/Avala Film, West Germany–France–Italy–Yugoslavia), dir. Hugo Fregonese
*On the War Path* (1911, Kalem), dir. Kenean Buel
*Once upon a Time in the West* (aka *C'era una volta il West*) (1968, Rafran Cinematografica/San Marco/Paramount, Italy–USA), dir. Sergio Leone
*Only the Valiant* (1951, Warner Bros./Cagney Prods.), dir. Gordon Douglas
*Our Daily Bread* (1934, United Artists/Viking Prods.), dir. King Vidor
*Out of the Past* (aka *Build My Gallows High* [U.K.]) (1947, RKO), dir. Jacques Tourneur
*Outcasts of Poker Flat, The* (1937, RKO), dir. Christy Cabanne
*Outlaw, The* (1943 [and 1946], United Artists/Hughes Prods.), dir. Howard Hughes [and Howard Hawks, uncredited]
*Over Silent Paths* (1910, Biograph), dir. D. W. Griffith
*Overland Stage Raiders* (1938, Republic), dir. George Sherman
*Ox-Bow Incident, The* (aka *Strange Incident* [U.K.]) (1943, Twentieth Century–Fox), dir. William A. Wellman
*Pals of the Saddle* (1938, Republic), dir. George Sherman
*Panoramic View, Lower Kicking Horse Canyon* (1901, Edison)
*Parade of Buffalo Bill's Wild West Show [nos. 1 and 2]* (1898, Edison), cinematogr. William Heise
*Paradise Canyon* (aka *Paradise Ranch*) (1935, Monogram/Lone Star Prods.), dir. Carl Pierson
*Past Redemption* (1913, New York Motion Picture Co./Kay-Bee), dir. Burton L. King, prod. Thomas H. Ince
*Pat Garrett and Billy the Kid* (1973, MGM), dir. Sam Peckinpah
*Phantom Bullet, The* (1926, Universal), dir. Clifford Smith
*Phantom Empire, The* (1935, Mascot), dir. Otto Brower and B. Reeves Eason, 12-episode serial
*Pilgrim, The* (1916, Mutual/Mustang), dir. Frank Borzage
*Pinky* (1949, Twentieth Century–Fox), dir. Elia Kazan [and John Ford, uncredited]
*Pioneers, The* (1903, American Mutoscope and Biograph), dir. Wallace McCutcheon
*Pitch o' Chance, The* (1915, American Film Co./Mustang), dir. Frank Borzage
*Plainsman, The* (1936, Paramount), dir. Cecil B. De Mille
*Plymouth Adventure* (1952, MGM), dir. Clarence Brown
*Post Telegrapher, The* (1912, New York Motion Picture Co./101–Bison), dir. Francis Ford[?], prod. Thomas H. Ince
*Postman Always Rings Twice, The* (1946, MGM), dir. Tay Garnett
*Powder River* (1953, Twentieth Century–Fox), dir. Louis King
*Prisoner of Shark Island, The* (1936, Twentieth Century–Fox), dir. John Ford
*Public Cowboy No. 1* (1937, Republic), dir. Joseph Kane
*Pueblo Legend, A* (1913, Biograph), dir. D. W. Griffith
*Purgatory* (1999, Turner Network Television/Rosemont Prods. Ltd.), dir. Uli Edel
*Pursued* (1947, Warner Bros./United States Pictures), dir. Raoul Walsh, scr. Niven Busch

*Quantez* (1957, Universal–International), dir. Harry Keller
*Quiet Man, The* (1952, Republic /Argosy), dir. John Ford
*Rachel and the Stranger* (1948, RKO), dir. Norman Foster
*Rain* (1932, United Artists /Art Cinema Associates), dir. Lewis Milestone
*Rainbow Valley* (1935, Monogram /Lone Star Prods.), dir. Robert N. Bradbury
*Ramona: A Story of the White Man's Injustice to the Indian* (1910, Biograph), dir. D. W. Griffith
*Ramrod* (1947, United Artists /Enterprise Prods.), dir. André De Toth
*Ranchman's Rival, A* (1909, Essanay), dir. Gilbert M. Anderson
*Range Feud, The* (1931, Columbia), dir. D. Ross Lederman
*Rattlesnake, The: A Psychical Species* (1913, Lubin), dir. Romaine Fielding
*Rebel without a Cause* (1955, Warner Bros.), dir. Nicholas Ray
*Red Dawn* (1984, MGM /Valkyrie Films), dir. John Milius
*Red Deer's Devotion* (1911, Pathé), dir. James Young Deer
*Red Eagle's Love Affair* (aka *The Love of a Sioux*) (1910, Lubin), scr. Emmett Campbell Hall
*Red Girl, The* (1908, Biograph), dir. D. W. Griffith
*Red Girl and the Child* (1910, Pathé), dir. James Young Deer
*Red Raiders, The* (1927, First National /Charles R. Rogers Prods.), dir. Albert S. Rogell
*Red River* (1948, United Artists /Monterey), dir. Howard Hawks
*Redman and the Child, The* (1908, Biograph), dir. D. W. Griffith
*Redman's View, The* (1909, Biograph), dir. D. W. Griffith
*Redskin* (1929, Paramount Famous Lasky), dir. Victor Schertzinger
*Redskin's Bravery, A* (1911, New York Motion Picture Co. /Bison), dir. Fred Balshofer[?]
*Regeneration* (1915, Fox), dir. Raoul Walsh
*Renegade Ranger* (1938, RKO), dir. David Howard
*Return of Draw Egan, The* (1916, Triangle /New York Motion Picture Co. /Kay-Bee), dir. William S. Hart, prod. Thomas H. Ince
*Return of Frank James, The* (Twentieth Century–Fox, 1940), dir. Fritz Lang
*Return of the Bad Men* (aka *Return of the Badmen*) (1948, RKO), dir. Ray Enright
*Ride Him, Cowboy* (aka *The Hawk*) (1932, Warner Bros.), dir. Fred Allen
*Riders of Destiny* (1933, Monogram /Lone Star Prods.), dir. Robert N. Bradbury
*Rio Bravo* (1959, Warner Bros. /Armada), dir. Howard Hawks
*Rio Grande* (1950, Republic /Argosy), dir. John Ford
*River, The* (aka *Le Fleuve*) (1951, Oriental International Film, USA–France–India), dir. Jean Renoir
*Romance of the Western Hills, A* (1910, Biograph), dir. D. W. Griffith
*Rose o' Salem-Town* (1910, Biograph), dir. D. W. Griffith
*Ruggles of Red Gap* (1935, Paramount), dir. Leo McCarey
*Saddlemates* (1941, Republic), dir. Lester Orlebeck
*Sagebrush Hamlet, A* (aka *A Sage Brush Hamlet*) (1919, Jesse D. Hampton Prods.), dir. Joseph Franz
*San Antonio* (1945, Warner Bros.), dir. David Butler [and Robert Florey and Raoul Walsh, uncredited]
*Santa Fe Stampede* (1938, Republic), dir. George Sherman
*Santa Fe Trail* (1940, Warner Bros.), dir. Michael Curtiz

*Savage Innocents, The* (1959, Gray Film–Pathé/Joseph Janni–Appia Films/Magic Film, France–Italy–U.K.), dir. Nicholas Ray

*Scarlet River* (1933, RKO), dir. Otto Brower, prod. David O. Selznick

*Sea of Grass, The* (1947, MGM), dir. Elia Kazan

*Searchers, The* (1956, Warner Bros./C. V. Whitney Pictures), dir. John Ford

*Secrets* (1933, United Artists/Mary Pickford Co.), dir. Frank Borzage

*Serving Rations to the Indians [no. 1]* (1898, Edison), prod. James White, cinematogr. Fred Blechynden

*Shane* (1953, Paramount), dir. George Stevens

*Shanghai Gesture, The* (1941, United Artists/Arnold Pressburger Films), dir. Josef von Sternberg

*She Wore a Yellow Ribbon* (1949, RKO/Argosy), dir. John Ford

*Shootist, The* (1976, Dino de Laurentiis Cinematografica), dir. Don Siegel

*Silent Enemy, The* (aka *Silent Enemy: An Epic of the American Indian*) (1930, Paramount–Publix/Burden–Chanler Prods.), dir. H. P. Carver

*Silver River* (1948, Warner Bros.), dir. Raoul Walsh

*Sioux City Sue* (1946, Republic), dir. Frank McDonald

*Sioux Ghost Dance* (aka *Ghost Dance*) (1894, Edison), prod. W. K. L. Dickson, cinematogr. William Heise

*Sky Pilot, The* (1921, First National/Cathrine Curtis Corp.), dir. King Vidor

*Soldier Blue* (1970, AVCO Embassy/Katzka–Berne Prods.), dir. Ralph Nelson

*Somewhere in Sonora* (1933, Warner Bros.), dir. Mack V. Wright

*Song of the Wildwood Flute, The* (1910, Biograph), dir. D. W. Griffith

*South of Heaven, West of Hell* (2000, Delta Deuce/Goldmount/Movie Mongrel/Trimark), dir. Dwight Yoakam

*Spellbound* (1945, Selznick International), dir. Alfred Hitchcock

*Spirit Awakened, The* (1912, Biograph), dir. D. W. Griffith

*Squaw Man, The* (aka *The White Man* [U.K.]) (1914, Jesse L. Lasky Feature Play Co.), dir. Cecil B. De Mille and Oscar Apfel

*Squaw's Love, The* (1911, Biograph), dir. D. W. Griffith

*Stagecoach* (1939, United Artists/Walter Wanger Prods.), dir. John Ford

*Star Packer, The* (aka *He Wore a Star* [U.K.]) (1934, Monogram/Lone Star Prods.), dir. Robert N. Bradbury

*Stark Love* (1927, Paramount Famous Lasky), dir. Karl Brown

*Straight Shooting* (aka *Straight Shootin'; The Cattle War; Joan of the Cattle Country*) (1917, Universal/Butterfly Photoplays), dir. John Ford

*Strongheart* (1914, Biograph/Klaw & Erlanger), dir. James Kirkwood, "supervised" by D. W. Griffith

*Sun Shines Bright, The* (1953, Republic/Argosy), dir. John Ford

*Sunrise – A Song of Two Humans* (1927, Fox), dir. F. W. Murnau

*Sunset Range* (1935, First Division), dir. Ray McCarey

*Susannah of the Mounties* (1939, Twentieth Century–Fox), dir. William A. Seiter [and Walter Lang, uncredited]

*Sutter's Gold* (1936, Universal), dir. James Cruze

*Tangled Lives: A Strange Culmination of the Seminole War* (1911, Kalem), dir. Sidney Olcott

*Telegraph Trail, The* (1933, Warner Bros.), dir. Tenny Wright

*Temporary Truce, A* (1912, Biograph), dir. D. W. Griffith

*Terrible Ted* (1907, American Mutoscope and Biograph), dir. Joseph A. Golden, cinematogr. G. W. Bitzer
*Terrible Teddy, the Grizzly King* (1901, Edison), dir. Edwin S. Porter
*Texans, The* (1938, Paramount), dir. James P. Hogan
*Texas Rangers* (2001, Greisman Prod./Larry Levinson Prods./Price Entertainment), dir. Steve Miner
*That Chink at Golden Gulch* (1910, Biograph), dir. D. W. Griffith
*There Was a Crooked Man . . .* (1970, Warner Bros.), dir. Joseph Mankiewicz
*These Thousand Hills* (1959, Twentieth Century–Fox), dir. Richard Fleischer
*They Died with Their Boots On* (1941, Warner Bros.), dir. Raoul Walsh
*They Were Expendable* (1945, MGM), dir. John Ford, Captain USNR [and Robert Montgomery, uncredited]
*Third Man, The* (1949, Selznick International/British Lion), dir. Carol Reed
*Thirty Seconds over Tokyo* (1944, MGM), dir. Mervyn LeRoy
*3 Bad Men* (1926, Fox), dir. John Ford
*Three Faces West* (1940, Republic), dir. Bernard Vorhaus
*Three Godfathers* (aka *Miracle in the Sand*) (1936, MGM), dir. Richard Boleslawski
*3 Godfathers* (1948, MGM/Argosy), dir. John Ford
*Three Mesquiteers, The* (1936, Republic), dir. Ray Taylor
*Three Texas Steers* (aka *Danger Rides the Range*) (1939, Republic), dir. George Sherman
*3:10 to Yuma* (1957, Columbia), dir. Delmer Daves
*Tin Star, The* (1957, Paramount/Perlberg-Seaton Prods./Perlsea), dir. Anthony Mann
*Tobacco Road* (1941, Twentieth Century–Fox), dir. John Ford
*Tombstone* (1993, Cinergi Prods./Hollywood Pictures), dir. George P. Cosmatos
*Tombstone, the Town Too Tough to Die* (1942, Paramount), dir. William C. McGann
*TR, The Story of Theodore Roosevelt* (1996, PBS/WGBH; aired on *American Experience*), prod. David Grubin
*Track of the Cat* (1954, Warner Bros./Wayne–Fellows Prods.), dir. William A. Wellman
*Trail of the North Wind* (1923, Nell Shipman Prods.), dir. Nell Shipman and Bert Van Tuyle
*Travelin' On* (1922, William S. Hart Prods.), dir. Lambert Hillyer
*Treasure of the Sierra Madre, The* (1948, Warner Bros.), dir. John Huston
*Tumbleweeds* (1925, United Artists/William S. Hart Prods.), dir. King Baggot
*Twisted Trail, The* (1910, Biograph), dir. D. W. Griffith
*Ulzana's Raid* (1972, Universal/Carter de Haven/Robert Aldrich), dir. Robert Aldrich
*Unconquered* (1947, Paramount), dir. Cecil B. De Mille
*Union Pacific* (1939, Paramount), dir. Cecil B. DeMille
*Vanishing American, The* (aka *The Vanishing Race* [Australia]) (1925, Famous Players–Lasky), dir. George B. Seitz
*Vertigo* (1958, Paramount), dir. Alfred Hitchcock
*Virginia City* (1940, Warner Bros.), dir. Michael Curtiz
*Virginian, The* (1914, Jesse L. Lasky Feature Play Co.), dir. Cecil B. De Mille
*Virginian, The* (1923, B. P. Schulberg Prods.), dir. Tom Forman
*Virginian, The* (1929, Paramount Famous Lasky), dir. Victor Fleming

*Virginian, The* (1946, Paramount), dir. Stuart Gilmore
*Viva Villa!* (1934, MGM), dir. Jack Conway [and Howard Hawks and William A. Wellman, uncredited]
*Wagon Tracks* (1919, Famous Players–Lasky/Artcraft/William S. Hart Prods.), dir. Lambert Hillyer
*Walking Hills, The* (1949, Columbia), dir. John Sturges
*War on the Plains* (aka *Men of the Plains*) (1912, New York Motion Picture Co./101–Bison), dir. Thomas H. Ince
*Warlock* (1959, Twentieth Century–Fox), dir. Edward Dmytryk
*Way West, The* (1967, United Artists/Harold Hecht Prods.), dir. Andrew V. McLaglen
*Welcome to Hard Times* (aka *Killer on a Horse* [U.K.]) (1967, MGM), dir. Burt Kennedy
*Wells Fargo* (1937, Paramount), dir. Frank Lloyd
*West of the Divide* (1934, Monogram/Lone Star Prods.), dir. Robert N. Bradbury
*Western Heritage* (1948, RKO), dir. Wallace Grissell
*Western Hero, A* (1909, Pathé, France)
*Western Stage Coach Hold Up* (1904), cinematogr. Alfred C Abadie
*Westerner, The* (1940, Samuel Goldwyn Co.), dir. William Wyler
*Westward Ho* (1935, Republic), dir. Robert N. Bradbury
*Westward the Women* (1951, MGM/Loew's), dir. William A.Wellman, story by Frank Capra
*When the Tables Turned* (1911, Méliès Star Films), prod. Gaston Méliès
*White Fawn's Devotion* (1910, Pathé), dir. James Young Deer
*Wichita* (1955, Allied Artists), dir. Jacques Tourneur
*Wild and Woolly* (1917, Paramount–Artcraft/Douglas Fairbanks Pictures), dir. John Emerson, scr. Anita Loos
*Wild Bunch, The* (1969, Warner Bros./Seven Arts Prods.), dir. Sam Peckinpah
*Wild Horse Rustlers* (1943, Producers Releasing Corp./Sigmund Neufeld Prods.), dir. Sam Newfield
*Wild West Circus, The* (1912, New York Motion Picture Co./Bison), dir. Thomas H. Ince
*Wild West Days* (1937, Universal), dir. Ford Beebe and Clifford Smith, 13-episode serial
*Winchester '73* (1950, Universal International), dir. Anthony Mann
*Wind, The* (1928, MGM), dir. Victor Seastrom [i.e., Sjöström]
*Winners of the Wilderness* (1927, MGM), dir. W. S. Van Dyke
*Womanhandled* (1925, Famous Players–Lasky), dir. Gregory La Cava
*World Changes, The* (1933, Warner Bros./First National), dir. Mervyn LeRoy
*Wyatt Earp* (1994, Warner Bros./Paragon/Tig Prods.), dir. Lawrence Kasdan
*Wyoming Outlaw* (1939, Republic), dir. George Sherman
*Yellow Sky* (1948, Twentieth Century–Fox), dir. William A. Wellman
*Young Bill Hickok* (1940, Republic), dir. Joseph Kane
*Young Mr. Lincoln* (1939, Twentieth Century–Fox), dir. John Ford

# Index

Films are identified by release year, writings by author. Page numbers in bold italics indicate illustrations. Endnotes have been indexed only where they provide substantive information.

CPSIA information can be obtained
at www.ICGtesting.com
Printed in the USA
BVHW051641010922
646071BV00002B/14

9 780521 554732